Communities and Conflict in Early Modern Colmar: 1575–1730

STUDIES IN GERMAN HISTORIES
Series Editors: Roger Chickering and Thomas A. Brady, Jr.

PUBLISHED

Communal Reformation
Peter Blickle

Protestant Politics:
Jacob Sturm (1489–1553)
and the German Reformation
Thomas A. Brady, Jr.

Karl Lamprecht
A German Academic Life (1856–1915)
Roger Chickering

German Encounters with Modernity
Katherine Roper

Communities and Conflict in
Early Modern Colmar: 1575–1730
Peter G. Wallace

Communities and Conflict in Early Modern Colmar: 1575–1730

Peter G. Wallace

HUMANITIES PRESS
NEW JERSEY

First published in 1995 by Humanities Press International, Inc.,
Atlantic Highlands, New Jersey 07716.

© Peter G. Wallace, 1995

Library of Congress Cataloging-in-Publication Data
Wallace, Peter George, 1952–
    Communities and conflict in early modern Colmar, 1575–1730 /
Peter G. Wallace.
        p.   cm. — (Studies in German histories)
    Includes bibliographical references (p.   ) and index.
    ISBN 0-391-03822-2
    1. Colmar Region (France)—History. 2. Reformation—France—
Colmar Region. 3. Colmar (France)—Church history. 4. Middle
classes—France—Colmar—Registers. 5. Urbanization—Social
aspects—France—Colmar. I. Title. II. Series.
    DC801.C657W35   1994
    944′.3833–dc20   93–6916
                                                            CIP

A catalog record for this book is available from the British Library.

Printed in the United States of America

To
Mary E. (Baney) Wallace
and
Albert I. Wallace
for nurturing me and my love of history

Contents

List of Illustrations

Figure

Maps

Graphs

List of Tables

Sigla

AAEB	Archives de l'Ancien Evêché de Bâle, Porrentruy (Switzerland)
ADHR	Archives Départementales du Haut-Rhin, Colmar
AMC	Archives Municipales de Colmar
AMS/AST	Archives Municipales de Strasbourg/Archives du Chapitre de Saint-Thomas
Annales ESC	*Annales: Economies-Sociétés-Civilisations*
Annuaire de Colmar	*Annuaire de la Société d'Histoire et d'Archéologie de Colmar*
ARG	*Archiv für Reformationsgeschichte*
BMC	Bibliothèque Municipale de Colmar
JMH	*Journal of Modern History*
PAVC	Publications des Archives de la Ville de Colmar
PSSARE	Publications de la Société Savante de l'Alsace et Régions de l'Est
QFRG	Quellen und Forschungen zur Reformationsgeschichte
RA	*Revue d'Alsace*
RGST	Reformationsgeschichtliche Studien und Texte
SMRT	Studies in Medieval and Reformation Thought
SVENGEV	Schriftenreihe der Vereinigung zur Erforschung der Neueren Geschichte e. V.
SVRG	Schriften des Vereins für Reformationsgeschichte
VIEGM	Veröffentlichungen des Instituts für Europäische Geschichte Mainz

Acknowledgments

When I began to study Colmar's history for my dissertation, I naively hoped to write an *histoire totale* of the early modern city. Recent scholarship has questioned the "totality" of any history, while the volume of sources in Colmar's rich municipal archives made such a project impossible. Ultimately, my "compromise" decision to take the questions raised by Colmar's religious and political history and to assess their impact among the city's householders required a heavy investment of time and the support of many. The Society for Reformation Research introduced me to the challenge of paleography at their Summer Institute, and the Alliance Française of the Fulbright Program generously funded my dissertation research in 1980–81. In the ensuing years, the Trustees of Hartwick College have continuously supported my work, and a Summer Research Stipend from the National Endowment for the Humanities allowed me to transcribe the data in Colmar's *Gewerff* registers. I wish also to thank the staffs at the Archives Départmentales du Haut Rhin at Colmar, the Archives de l'Ancien d'Evêché de Bâle at Porrentruy, and the Archives Municipales de Strasbourg for their assistance. The Church of Jesus Christ of Latter Day Saints made available microfilm copies of Colmar's parish registers, and the staffs at their genealogical libraries at Eugene and La Grande, Oregon, and Vestal, New York, shared their expertise. I owe special gratitude to the staff at the Archives Municipales de Colmar who have supported this project every step of the way. In particular, I wish to thank Jean-Marie Schmitt, director of the archives, whose knowledge of regional history and critical judgment has sharpened my analysis, and Jean Bachschmidt, whose paleographic and research skills were extremely helpful. My fellow historians at Hartwick College, particularly Len Pudelka, and my students have served as a sometimes captive but always discriminating audience. I owe debts to numerous colleagues, who have commented on my ideas or offered insights from their own research. Many are recognized in the notes, but I would particularly like to acknowledge Christopher R. Friedrichs, Kaspar von Greyerz, James R. Farr, and William H. Beik, who have read and commented on all or part of this manuscript. My special thanks to Keith M. Ashfield of Humanities Press for his commitment to this series, to Kathy Delfosse for her editorial guidance and critical eye, and to the series' editors, Roger Chickering and Thomas A. Brady, Jr. Tom Brady has supported this study since its conception. He and Katherine G. Brady have read and commented on several versions of the text. Whatever insights this study offers owes much to their input, and its publication owes much to their sustained encouragement. Nevertheless, any errors in this text reflect my own limitations and not those of its editors. Finally, I would like to thank my sons, Erik and Evan, who have grown up with this book as a rival sibling, and to my wife, Shelley Burtner Wallace, who has worked in the archives and as an editor with patience and with strength. In so many ways we have shared this project.

Ehrenstetten, Germany

Introduction

Early modern towns in Central Europe were the focal points of tremendous religious, political, and economic changes. First, the confessional divisions produced throughout society by the Protestant Reformation proved particularly disruptive in the densely populated towns, where the struggle for peace and order took on harsh ideological tones. Secondly, the growth of modern territorial states deprived cities of their former political independence. Some cities were reduced to small settlements little more important than overgrown villages, while others flourished as princely administrative centers. Finally, the economic shifts brought on by the crisis of the seventeenth century and the birth of overseas empires disrupted the medieval interurban trading networks and the division of labor within city walls. In all, these diverse pressures forged the new patterns of modern urban life.

I. The Case of Colmar, 1575–1730

This work is an analysis of the religious, political, social, and economic changes in the Alsatian Imperial city of Colmar between 1575 and 1730. In 1575 the city's magistrates established a Protestant church which divided the citizenry into two confessional communities, one Protestant and one Catholic. In the 1630s the full horror of the Thirty Years' War descended on Alsace, severing the city's traditional trade routes and cutting its population in half. Full recovery took two generations, only to be undone during the wars of the late seventeenth century. In 1673 Louis XIV subjugated the city, and in the ensuing decades French rule disrupted Colmar's confessional balance and restructured its economy and society. Thus the early modern Colmarians contended with constant confessional pressure from both Catholic and Protestant powers, the gradual deterioration and eventual loss of their political autonomy, and the disruption of trade relations and local production due to chronic warfare. Colmar's outmoded walls could not prevent these external pressures from disrupting civic life. Within the urban landscape, guild rivalries, religious intolerance, personal arrogance, and social envy brought enmity between neighbors. The lines of division, however, crisscrossed civic society and never coincided to polarize factions. Nevertheless, various conflicts strained Colmar's communal institutions and values, as the Protestant and Catholic parishes, rival political groups, and competing economic interests struggled for control of civic life.

This study is divided into three parts which analyze three periods in Colmar's early modern history. The first, between 1575 and 1648, witnessed Colmar's Reformation, carried out by the conscious effort of municipal officials, and

1

the city's Counter-Reformation, enforced on it by the Imperial authorities. The second, between 1635 and 1680, was marked by the Colmarians' efforts to recover from the economic and demographic devastation of the Thirty Years' War while under the shadow of growing French power in Alsace. The third era, between 1680 and 1730, saw the full integration of the local oligarchy into the new French-dominated political order, while the traditional spine of the civic community, the guildsmen, became increasingly isolated due to their Germanic dialect, their Lutheranism, or their poverty. Throughout these eras the common thread in Colmar's social, political, and cultural life was the presence of two confessional communities.

In 1575 the city's leaders justified the introduction of Protestant worship under the constitutional guarantees of the Religious Peace of Augsburg, on the basis of which they claimed the *ius reformandi*, the right to reform.[1] The magistrates, however, could not compel all citizens to attend the new church, and the ensuing confessional division defined civic life. Colmar's Catholic clergy formed the backbone of resistance to the Protestant community, and they initially could rely on support from the bishop of Basel and the powerful duke of Austria, whose territories bordered Colmar. Colmar's Protestants were strong enough to sustain their parish until the emperor finally forced its dissolution in 1627 at the height of the Thirty Years' War. This Counter-Reformation was short-lived, however, as a Swedish army captured the city in late 1632 and reestablished Protestant services.

Colmar's Reformation and Counter-Reformation made it a microcosm for the political and religious tensions which plagued Imperial society in the late sixteenth and early seventeenth centuries. In recent years Reformation scholars have extended their research to the period after the Religious Peace of Augsburg in 1555 and, in so doing, have emphasized the close links between the institutionalization of the Reformation and Counter-Reformation and the emergence of the early modern territorial state through a process Heinz Schilling has called "confessionalization."[2] Since the 1520s confessions had gradually emerged as religiously self-conscious social groups which defined themselves by habits of daily behavior distinct from the broader community.[3] The Peace of Augsburg legitimized the construction of Lutheran or Catholic territorial churches and politicized both the discord between confessional groups and the pressure for conformity within them.[4] The rulers used their new authority to integrate the territorial church into the administrative machinery of state, by first demanding that local ministers adhere to confessional formula and then pressuring the lay subjects to follow sanctioned religious practices. Of course, men of faith and not the rulers had fashioned those practices in pursuit of truth and personal salvation. After 1555, however, the drive for confessional unity implied official churches and with them the agendas of the political leaders. Salvation remained a personal matter, but securing public peace through religious conformity was not a question of conscience but of submission to authority. This process, however, took generations to complete.

Unlike the princes, magistrates in the Imperial cities grounded their authority on contractual oaths with their subjects through a shared commitment to community norms (*Grundwerte*), which Hans-Christoph Rublack has called "principles legitimizing social action."[5] In early modern German cities, Rublack has identified three norms: peace, unity, and common weal, which acted as "integrators" to constrain individual interests, even those of the magistrates. Beginning in the 1520s the Reformation challenged these norms by dividing the community over questions of faith. The magistrates contended with the citizens and the Protestant preachers to control the city's churches, but everywhere compromises had to be made.[6]

Here the analysis of Colmar's bi-confessionalism proves fruitful, for compromise defined confessional relations in early seventeenth-century Colmar. Among the patchwork of estates in Upper Alsace, confessional groups encountered a degree of toleration from political authorities who lacked the power or incentive to force confessionalization.[7] Colmar had close economic ties to this confessionally mixed hinterland, and the city's Reformation succeeded because of a lack of political will among the neighboring Catholic authorities and the support of the Protestant lords. After 1575 political uncertainties and economic concerns discouraged the civic regime from enforcing confessional conformity on its citizens. Colmar was one of several Imperial cities which recognized two legal confessions, and in these bi-confessional towns public peace, unity, and common weal were desacralized in order to preserve them.[8] In Colmar confessionalization threatened political order rather than secured it.

Colmar's first Protestant parish had aligned with the Swiss Reformed church and initiated close ties with Basel. Under the rubrics of the Peace of Augsburg, Colmar's confessional choice was illegal, and, to legitimize the move, the civic regime relied on the tacit support of the guilds.[9] Prior to 1627 bi-confessionalism affirmed the communal foundation of Colmar's political order, and this relationship gave the confessional settlement its resiliency. In conquering the city, the Swedes recognized the rights of the local Catholic clergy and citizenry but insisted that Colmar's Protestants accept Lutheran ministers and confessional ties with Lutheran Strasbourg. When the Peace of Westphalia legitimized Colmar's bi-confessionalism, the two sanctioned confessional communities would henceforth be Lutheran and Catholic.[10] After 1648 Colmar's bi-confessionalism no longer depended on communal consent, and the new political context widened the distances between Catholics and Protestants, as confessional tensions shifted from the battlefield to the pulpit, classroom, marketplace, and town hall.[11]

The Thirty Years' War ushered in a second era in Colmar's early modern history which was marked by demographic decline, economic restructuring, and a prolonged legal struggle to maintain the city's Imperial status in the face of French pressure. Since the Middle Ages, Colmar had been a local market center, and in the sixteenth century it entered the Rhenish trading network through the export of wine and brandy.[12] The new markets enriched the city and diversified productive activity, but most Colmarians still functioned within economic horizons limited to the surrounding villages. A significant percentage of the city's guildsmen were peasants, and many others derived their livelihood indirectly from the land.[13] The Thirty Years' War disrupted the Rhenish trade, destroyed farms, and ruined vineyards. Peace brought little security to long-distance trade, and the Colmarians turned to the city's hinterland to rebuild their fortunes.

Colmar's economic health had always rested on the productivity of the fields and vineyards which surrounded it, and this dependence on its hinterland determined civic prosperity both as a central market and as a funnel for exports to distant Rhenish markets.[14] As a central "peasant" market, Colmar functioned as a locus for exchange, facilitated the division of labor, and improved the material well-being of its citizens and the neighboring villagers. Segments of Colmar's community replicated rural social and economic relations within the city walls, both in terms of lordship and peasant hierarchies. Many Colmarians worked in the fields and vineyards beyond the city walls, and they shared the worldview and values of other peasants.

Even in the city's workshops, the rhythms of agricultural production affected economic life. Colmar's size allowed it to support a broad range of craftsmen who serviced their fellow citizens and rural consumers. An important part of Colmar's sixteenth-century society was a broad middle class of master artisans and property holders, as well as the professional agents and merchants who served the great rural landlords, whether clerics or laymen. Rural social and economic relations left a clear imprint on civic life, and the city's leaders jealously preserved those ties, for Colmar's powerful neighbors, Strasbourg, Basel, and Freiburg-im-Breisgau, also sought to control production and distribution in the Upper Alsatian villages.[15]

Many early modern towns possessed much more polarized social structures derived from proto-industrial production organized for interurban commerce.[16] In the late sixteenth and early seventeenth centuries, Colmar's wine and brandy industry assumed a proto-industrial structure which enriched a cluster of powerful merchants and broadened the class of poor vineyard workers, coopers, and carters. Unlike rural cloth production, Colmar's proto-industry depended entirely on the quantity and quality of the grape harvest. The campaigns in Upper Alsace in the 1630s destroyed the vineyards and severed Colmar's ties to its traditional markets. The city had previously weathered cycles of expansion and contraction tied to the rhythms of agricultural production, but the crisis of the 1630s forced a restructuring of the regional economy. The Colmarians narrowed their investment horizons, purchased abandoned fields and vineyards, and pursued new markets for their products in Switzerland. The Thirty Years' War had broken Colmar's contacts with the Rhenish trading network, but it had also secured the city's economic dominance in Upper Alsace, which anticipated Colmar's role as a provincial administrative center under French rule.[17]

The Peace of Westphalia brought French political power into Alsace and threatened Colmar's survival as an Imperial city. For centuries Colmar had nurtured its customary legal rights within the medieval Imperial constitutional system of chartered liberties. The empire's constitutional fabric had unraveled during the Thirty Years' War, and after 1648 the estates had sought to reweave their constitutional guarantees into a system which recent literature has referred to as the "Old Reich."

The post-Westphalian Imperial institutions appear ossified to modern eyes, but they functioned as an effective framework for the Imperial estates. The empire served, according to James Allen Vann, as an "equation" whose "constitutional and institutional organization set the limits of maneuverability and created an arena in which competing interests bargained."[18] Mack Walker has depicted the Old Reich functioning as an "incubator" which protected the weak through a system of restraint and frustration of aggressive power.[19] In the empire "each little locality claimed to be not only a distinct geographical unit, but also a distinct constitutional unit, with its own laws and practices based on unique written and unwritten privileges, immunities and observances." The empire's hierarchical institutions "served as guarantors of the constitutional separateness of these layers of localities and regions."[20] In the decades after 1648, Colmar's magistrates quickly turned to the Imperial system to guard their liberties against the challenge of French claims to sovereignty.[21] They also had to familiarize themselves with royal institutions and practices in order to deal effectively with the king's agents in Alsace.

Post-Westphalian Alsace, according to Georges Livet, was the key to the French monarchy's relations with the empire. Until 1663 the Crown's Alsatian holdings were geographically separated from the kingdom's interior by the duchy of Lorraine. Louis XIV's Alsatian domains served as "a zone of contact" with the Imperial powers, and this, in Livet's eyes, shaped royal provincial administration in four ways. First, the French preserved the customary offices, destroying nothing a priori, in order to maintain the familiar facade. Secondly, the Crown adapted the existing administrative system by careful and controlled manipulation, in order to modernize the system secretly and in depth. Thirdly, the French substituted men rather than institutions and employed Alsatians, who were won over by a show of confidence, rather than newcomers from the kingdom's interior. Finally, the royal government never condoned scandal or abuse of office and encouraged access to the intendant, the king, and his council. These four principles combined with "a mood of compromise" to form the heterogeneous structural "appearance" of the king's Alsatian administration.[22]

Livet's model assumes a hidden coherency behind the confusing mix of traditional Alsatian institutions and practices and the new French provincial administrative networks. Such a coherency would require the long-term presence of the same personnel; but as we will see in chapters 3 and 4, Livet's analysis underestimates the pressure of fiscal expediency on French action and minimizes the tense and volatile relations among the king's men.[23] Furthermore, Livet overestimates French political strength in Alsace between 1648 and 1673. The "mood of compromise," which did exist between the royal agents and the Alsatian estates, was not part of a long-term royal plan. The French accepted compromise because they recognized their own weakness, and they adapted the Court's policies to Alsatian conditions in order to bridge the gap between bureaucratic schemes and practical politics. The political conflicts during these decades were carried out in a peculiar Imperial and French double-speak which juxtaposed gestures, institutions, and worldviews. At the same time, the initial tentative behavior of the royal agents gave the Colmarians a false sense of security which ended when the royal army arrived at the city's gates.

Beginning in 1680, the royal government "reunited" the Alsatian estates to the Crown, which led to the political restructuring of Colmar under the tutelage of French-speaking royal officials.[24] Reunion deprived the civic officials of many of their traditional responsibilities and altered the system of magisterial recruitment.[25] Strasbourg's regime faced a similar fate, which was made harsher by the Crown's insistence on confessional parity in the civic offices of the Lutheran town.[26] Colmar, however, already possessed a Catholic community, and within a generation, both Catholic and Lutheran elites had adapted to the new political order and had accepted their role as royal agents. The turning point came in the Crown's fiscal and political crisis of the 1690s, when a series of royal edicts introduced venal offices into municipal politics to be followed in 1698 with the establishment of the *Conseil souverain d'Alsace* at Colmar. This new cosmopolitan elite of lawyers and judges profoundly influenced the political ambitions and cultural tastes of Colmar's oligarchs.[27] By the early eighteenth century, Colmar, which had led the resistance to French sovereignty in the 1660s, was the most completely integrated of the Alsatian cities.

Not everyone in Colmar adjusted to the new order. The civic regime faced political opposition which in 1711 coalesced around the reform movement of an ambitious Lutheran councilor, Johann Jacob Sonntag.[28] Sonntag failed, however, to make the regime accountable to its citizens through regular elections, and his defeat completed the integration of civic officials into the royal government. As most of the elite adjusted to French rule, divisions among the residents of early eighteenth-century Colmar became much sharper. To be an official, to be Catholic, and to speak French brought privilege and access to power, but most Colmarians did not meet these criteria. Subjugation to Louis XIV brought wealth, influence, and immigrants to the city, but the fruits of French rule were distributed very unevenly.

II. THE SOURCES

In early modern Colmar the conflicts between the confessional communities, between political insiders and outsiders, and between rich and poor often intertwined. The contexts of these conflicts changed over time, as did the contestants. The foundation of my analysis is an effort to identify as many contestants as possible through a prosopographical study of Colmar's male taxpaying householders. Prosopography is the study of collective biography, that is, "the common background characteristics of a group of actors in history by means of a collective study of their lives."[29] My prosopographical profile emerges from three serial sources: the municipal tax (*Gewerff*) registers, the parish registers, and the registers of new citizens (*Bürgerbücher*).

Most early modern towns taxed their householders, and the surviving registers provide a rough image of the distribution of wealth among the residents.[30] Colmar's tax registers list assessments for all civic householders street by street, and I have analyzed the registers for every tenth year from 1600 to 1730.[31] From the sample, I have charted variations in taxable wealth for the householders plotted against their confessional affiliation, occupation, and neighborhood as these changed over time. Though tax registers list all householders, they provide only a rough barometer for social change, for due to poverty or privilege many residents do not appear in the registers. Nevertheless, major shifts that occurred in the number of taxable households in Colmar demarcated significant changes in Colmar's productive capacity and its demography.

Social historians have also worked extensively with early modern parish registers as a basis for demographic study, but they pose many problems.[32] Colmar's Protestant ministers began recording baptisms and marriages in 1575 with the foundation of the parish. Colmar's Catholic clergy first noted baptisms and marriages in 1603, and unfortunately their registers have many gaps into the 1650s. Colmar's parish registers also denote events which did not involve community members, or they list the same event twice. Marriage registers occasionally record the publication of banns rather than the actual marriage, or they inscribe marriages which took place elsewhere but were announced locally in the church. Military campaigns temporarily filled the city with refugees, who baptized their children, married, and died there, but who were never full community members. Furthermore, couples from the neighboring villages and towns also came to marry or to have their children baptized when their own parishes proved unsuitable because of religious choice or the absence of available clergy, particularly in the disordered decades of the mid-seventeenth century. For my analysis, I have chosen to use the tax registers as the basic source and to cross-reference them in the parish registers to determine, where possible, an individual's confessional allegiance. I have assumed that the decision to conduct major personal and familial events in a particular church reflected a householder's public confessional commitment.

The parish registers also provide other useful information. In the Catholic marriage registers, the priests regularly noted the places of origin for both bride and groom, though they seldom mention the groom's occupation. Colmar's Protestant ministers, both Reformed and Lutheran, conscientiously recorded the occupation of the groom, his father, and the bride's father or previous husband. They were less rigorous in noting place of origin, though the bulk of the persons recorded seem to have been native Colmarians. The parish registers have enabled me to identify the confessional affiliation of over 80% of Colmar's male householders, but neither parish registered funerals until the late seventeenth century, which frustrates full demographic reconstruction for the communities.[33]

Colmar's citizen registers form the final piece in reconstructing the community of male householders. The inscriptions of men purchasing citizenship at Colmar began in the fourteenth century.[34] I have included in my study all Colmarians who purchased citizenship between 1575 and 1730, even when they do not appear in the sampled tax registers. Their decision to purchase citizenship warrants their inclusion in the city's political community.

Beginning in 1580 these registers identify the guild affiliation for all new citizens. Each of Colmar's ten guilds (Zünfte) served as a social club and craft organization, and guild membership was the basis for political involvement. Occasionally the citizen registers note occupation and place of origin, and until 1673 they name the immediate neighbors of the new citizen. The guild lists and occupational data in the parish registers have allowed me to construct an occupational profile for the householders. For the Protestant community, the information in the parish registers has sharpened this image; for the Catholics, the citizenship registers help to establish the outlines of the relation between occupation and confession. The citizen registers, however, do not identify all citizens. I have discovered roughly 20% of the overall population who are identified as citizens in the parish registers but who are not included in the citizen registers. Though no specific guild, confessional, or familial pattern seems to have produced this discrepancy, these men were substantially poorer than their neighbors who were inscribed.[35] Based on this initial analysis, I would argue that until 1673, after which Colmar's citizen registers change in format, they record an act distinct from guild inscription and one apparently limited to the city's middling economic strata.

These three serial sources provide the foundation for this study, but I have also consulted a number of other archival and printed sources, such as the correspondence between the municipal regime and the neighboring powers, the protocols of the meeting of the municipal regime, and clusters of fiscal, religious, judicial, and guild documents, to make sense of the forces at work in the lives of Colmar's householders.

Since I began my research, I have tried to track down data for all the early-modern Colmarians, but this work will be limited to the most accessible, the male taxpaying householders. At Colmar women paid taxes and often headed households, though they were excluded from full participation in the political community. Furthermore the tendency of the documents to identify women only in terms of their relations to males, as daughter, wife, or widow, confuses efforts to reconstruct the lives of individual women or form a composite profile from the available sources.[36] Obviously, the city's women, children, and poor had an impact on the trajectories of its religious, political, and economic history, but the available evidence makes it extremely difficult to assess that impact.

Colmar's early modern history was marked by religious, political, social, economic, and cultural challenges, which the Colmarians shared with many residents of other towns. The Protestant Reformation divided Christians into conflicting confessional groups, which in some towns came to live side by side. At Colmar, bi-confessionalism survived under pressure from 1575, but the balance of power between the confessions shifted several times with dramatic effects on municipal life. After 1648 the Imperial city of Colmar faced a direct challenge to its liberties from the French monarchy. The magistrates resisted stubbornly, but ultimately they had to submit to force. The loss of autonomy was not disastrous for the civic elite, who adapted quickly to the new political culture, despite the difference in language and traditions. By 1730 Colmar had become an important royal administrative center. In many ways the city had prepared for this new role before the French conquest. In response to the demographic and economic disaster of the Thirty Years' War, the Colmarians increased their economic control over the city's hinterland. Under French rule most of the large property holders and seigneurial administrators for Upper Alsace settled in the city, which functioned as a hub for judicial proceedings and tax collection. The shift in political cultures was dynamic and rapid, yet it can be understood in an Imperial context. By the eighteenth century the prosperous urban centers in the empire were not the old Imperial cities but the newer princely capitals (*Residenzstädte*). By 1730 Colmar possessed much of the political culture, the social structure, the economic interests, and the confessional diversity of a small princely seat, which only lacked a resident prince. French conquest had prepared Colmar for a new role as a provincial administrative center in the emerging royal state. In time the French Revolution would complete the process, as Colmar became the administrative center of the department of Haut-Rhin.

Notes

1. For further study on Colmar's Reformation, see Kaspar von Greyerz, *The Late City Reformation in Germany: The Case of Colmar 1522–1628*, VIEGM, 98 (Wiesbaden, 1980); Erdmann Weyrauch, "Die politische Führungsgruppe in Colmar in der Zeit der Reformation," in Wolfgang J. Mommsen, with Peter Alter and Robert W. Scribner, eds., *Stadtbürgertum und Adel in der Reformation: Studien zur Sozialgeschichte der Reformation in England und Deutschland*, Veröffentlichungen des Deutschen Historischen Instituts London, 5 (Stuttgart, 1979), 215–34; Johann Adam, *Evangelische Kirchengeschichte der elsässischen Territorien bis zur französischen Revolution* (Strasbourg, 1928), 459–70; and the articles in a special edition of the *Annuaire de Colmar* (1975–76), esp. Gabriel Braeuner, "La préréforme à Colmar (1522–1575)," in ibid., 55–72.

2. This discussion is based on Ernst Walter Zeeden, *Die Entstehung der Konfessionen: Grundlagen und Formen der Konfessionsbildung im Zeitalter der Glaubenskämpfe* (Munich and Vienna, 1965). For further reading on confessionalization, see Wolfgang Reinhard, "Gegenreformation als Modernisierung? Prolegomena zu einer Theorie des konfessionellen Zeitalters," ARG 68 (1977): 226–52; idem, "Zwang zur Konfessionalisierung? Prolegomena zu einer Theorie des konfessionellen Zeitalters," *Zeitschrift für Historische Forschung* 10 (1983): 257–77; and idem, "Reformation, Counter-Reformation, and the Early Modern State: A Reassessment," *The Catholic Historical Review* 75 (1989): 383–404. See also Heinz Schilling, "Die 'Zweite Reformation' als Kategorie der Geschichtswissenschaft," in idem, ed., *Die reformierte Konfessionalisierung in Deutschland—Das Problem der "Zweiten Reformation,"* SVRG, 195 (Gütersloh, 1986), esp. 387–401; and idem, *Konfessionskonflikt und Staatsbildung: Eine Fallstudie über das Verhältnis von religiösem und sozialem Wandel in der Frühneuzeit am Beispiel der Grafschaft Lippe*, QFRG, 48 (Gütersloh, 1981). See also R. Po-chia Hsia, *Social Discipline in the Reformation: Central Europe 1550–1750* (London and New York, 1989).

3. Pierre Bourdieu has defined these daily practices as the *habitus*: "the durably installed generative principle of regulated improvisations." Pierre Bourdieu, *Outline of a Theory of Practice*, trans. Richard Nice, Cambridge Studies in Social Anthropology, 16 (Cambridge, 1977), 78. Cf. Thomas A. Brady, Jr., "In Search of the Godly City: The Domestication of Religion in the German Urban Reformation," in R. Po-chia Hsia, ed., *The German People and the Reformation* (Ithaca, 1988), 14–31; Robert W. Scribner, "Ritual and Reformation," in ibid., 122–44; Natalie Z. Davis, "The Sacred and the Body Social in Sixteenth-Century Lyons," *Past and Present* 90 (1981): 40–70.

4. Reinhard, "Zwang zur Konfessionalisierung?," 257–77.

5. Hans-Christoph Rublack, "Grundwerte in der Reichsstadt im Spätmittelalter und in der frühen Neuzeit," in Horst Brunner, ed., *Literatur in der Stadt: Bedingungen und Beispiele städtischer Literatur des 15. bis 17. Jahrhunderts*, Göppinger Arbeiten zur Germanistik, 343 (Göppingen, 1982), 9–36. For the following discussion, I will refer to the English translation, see "Political and Social Norms in Urban Communities in the Holy Roman Empire," in Kaspar von Greyerz, ed., Peter Blickle, Winfried Schulze, and Hans-Christoph Rublack, *Religion, Politics, and Social Protest: Three Studies on Early Modern Germany* (London, 1984), 24–60, here at 25, 27–28.

6. For a review of the literature, see Kaspar von Greyerz, "Stadt und Reformation: Stand und Aufgaben der Forschung," ARG 76 (1985): 6–63. Conditions in Strasbourg provide a rich case study; see Thomas A. Brady, Jr., *Ruling Class, Regime, and Reformation at Strasbourg, 1520–1555*, SMRT, 22 (Leiden, 1978);

Lorna Jane Abray, *The People's Reformation: Magistrates, Clergy, and Commons in Strasbourg, 1500–1598* (Ithaca, 1985); Erdmann Weyrauch, *Konfessionelle Krise und sozial Stabilität: Das Interim in Strassburg (1548–1562)*, Spätmittelalter und Frühe Neuzeit, Tübinger Beiträge zur Geschichtsforschung, 7 (Stuttgart, 1978). On political conditions after 1555, see Gerhard Pfeiffer, "Der Augsburger Religionsfrieden und die Reichsstädte," *Zeitschrift des Historischen Vereins für Schwaben* 61 (1955): 213–321.

7. Conditions in the nearby lordship of the counts von Rappolstein made it impossible to enforce confessional conformity, as Catholics, Lutherans, and Calvinists shared churches in the Leberthal. Adam, *Evangelische Kirchengeschichte*, 348–70.

8. Paul Warmbrunn, *Zwei Konfessionen in einer Stadt: Das Zusammenleben von Katholiken und Protestanten in den paritätischen Reichsstädten Augsburg, Biberach, Ravensburg, und Dinkelsbühl von 1548 bis 1648*, VIEGM, 111 (Wiesbaden, 1983); Heinz Schilling, "Between the Territorial State and Urban Liberty: Lutheranism and Calvinism in the County of Lippe," in Hsia, ed., *The German People*, 263–83.

9. On the spread of the Reformed church in the empire, see Martin Heckel, "Reichsrecht und 'Zweite Reformation': Theologisch-juristische Probleme der reformierten Konfessionalisierung," in Schilling, ed., *Die reformierte Konfessionalisierung*, 11–43.

10. Fritz Dickmann, *Der Westfälische Frieden* (Münster, 1959), 343–72.

11. Etienne François, "De l'uniformité à la tolérance: Confession et société urbaine en Allemagne, 1650–1800," *Annales: ESC* 37 (1982): 783–800; Joachim Whaley, *Religious Toleration and Social Change in Hamburg, 1529–1819* (Cambridge, 1985); Peter Zschunke, *Konfession und Alltag in Oppenheim: Beiträge zur Geschichte von Bevölkerung und Gesellschaft einer gemischtkonfessionellen Kleinstadt in der frühen Neuzeit*, VIEGM, 115 (Wiesbaden, 1984), 73–139.

12. Lucien Sittler, "La vie économique de Colmar (jusqu'à 1800)," *Annuaire de Colmar* (Numéro spécial, 1970): 25–40; idem, "Commerce et commerçants dans le Vieux-Colmar," *Annuaire de Colmar* (1966): 14–48.

13. Lucien Sittler, "Landwirtschaft und Gartenbau im alten Colmar," *Elsass-Lothringisches Jahrbuch* 20 (1942): 71–94; idem, *La viticulture et le vin de Colmar à travers les siècles* (Colmar, 1956).

14. For this and the following paragraphs, see John Langton and Göran Hoppe, *Town and Country in the Development of Early Modern Western Europe*, Historical Geography Research Series, 11 (Norwich, 1983); Paul M. Hohenberg and Lynn Hollen Lees, *The Making of Urban Europe 1000–1950* (Cambridge, Mass., 1985), 47–69; Richard Hodges, *Primitive and Peasant Markets* (Oxford, 1988).

15. On Strasbourg, see Brady, *Ruling Class*, 76–91; on Freiburg, see Tom Scott, *Freiburg and the Breisgau: Town-Country Relations in the Age of Reformation and Peasants' War* (Oxford, 1986); on Basel, see Robert Strittmatter, *Die Stadt Basel während des Dreissigjährigen Kriegs: Politik, Wirtschaft, Finanzen*, Europäische Hochschulschriften, Reihe III, 84 (Bern, 1977).

16. Hohenberg and Lees, *The Making of Urban Europe*, 59–69; Jan de Vries, *European Urbanization 1500–1800* (Cambridge, Mass., 1984).

17. The mid-seventeenth-century crisis had a profound effect on nearly all European cities. Hohenberg and Lees, *The Making of Urban Europe*, 99–171. On French cities, see Philip Benedict, "French Cities from the Sixteenth Century to the Revolution: An Overview," in idem, ed., *Cities and Social Change in Early Modern France* (London, 1989), 7–68. On German cities, see Christopher R. Friedrichs, "The Swiss and German City-States," in Robert Griffeth and Carol G. Thomas, eds., *The City-State in Five Cultures* (Santa Barbara, Calif., 1981), 109–42; Etienne François, "Des républiques marchandes aux capitales

politiques: Remarques sur la hiérarchie urbaine du Saint-Empire à l'époque moderne," *Revue d'Histoire Moderne et Contemporaine* 25 (1978): 587–603.

18. James A. Vann, "New Directions for the Study of the Old *Reich*," *JMH* 58 Supplement (1986): S3–S22, here at S9–S10. See also Hanns Gross, "The Holy Roman Empire in Modern Times: Constitutional Reality and Legal Theory," in James A. Vann and Steven W. Rowan, eds., *The Old Reich: Essays on German Political Institutions*, Studies presented to the International Commission for the History of Representative and Parliamentary Institutions, 47 (Brussels, 1974), 1–29.

19. Mack Walker, *German Home Towns: Community, State, and General Estate 1648–1871*, (Ithaca, 1971), 11–26, here at 11.

20. Carol M. Rose, "Empire and Territories at the End of the Old Reich," in Vann and Rowan, eds., *The Old Reich*, 59–76, here at 63.

21. On the place of the cities in the Imperial constitutional order, see Günter Buchstab, *Reichsstädte, Städtekurie, und Westfälischer Friedenskongress: Zusammenhänge von Sozialstruktur, Rechtsstatus, und Wirtschaftskraft*, SVENG, 7 (Münster, 1976), 34–49; Thomas A. Brady, Jr., *Turning Swiss: Cities and Empire, 1450–1550* (Cambridge, 1985); Rudolf Vierhaus, *Germany in the Age of Absolutism*, trans. by Jonathan B. Knudsen (Cambridge, 1988), 87–108, esp. 105–6.

22. Georges Livet, *L'intendance d'Alsace sous Louis XIV 1648–1715*, Publications de la Faculté des Lettres de l'Université de Strasbourg, fasc. 128 (Paris, 1956), 905. For a brief English introduction to the main points of his argument, see idem, "Royal Administration in a Frontier Province: The Intendancy of Alsace under Louis XIV," in Ragnhild Hatton, ed., *Louis XIV and Absolutism* (Columbus, Ohio, 1976), 177–96, see esp. 177, 186–87.

23. Julian Dent, *Crisis in Finance: Crown Financiers and Society in Seventeenth-Century France* (New York, 1973); Richard Bonney, *The King's Debts: Finance and Politics in France, 1589–1661* (Oxford, 1981). On administrative factions, see Roger Mettam, *Power and Faction in Louis XIV's France* (Oxford, 1988); Sharon Kettering, *Patrons, Brokers, and Clients in Seventeenth-Century France* (New York, 1986).

24. Gaston Zeller, *Comment s'est faite la réunion de l'Alsace à la France* (Paris, 1948).

25. Lucien Sittler, "La transformation du gouvernement de Colmar par le roi de France à la fin du XVIIe siècle," in *Deux siècles d'Alsace française, 1648–1848* PSSARE, 2 (Strasbourg and Paris, 1948), 133–58.

26. Franklin Ford, *Strasbourg in Transition 1648–1789* (Cambridge, Mass., 1958); Ingeborg Streitberger, *Der königliche Prätor von Strassburg 1685–1789: Freie Stadt im absoluten Staat*, VIEGM, 23 (Wiesbaden, 1961); Peter Hertner, *Stadtwirtschaft zwischen Reich und Frankreich: Wirtschaft und Gesellschaft Strassburgs 1650–1714*, Neue Wirtschaftsgeschichte, 8 (Cologne and Vienna, 1973); Paul Greissler, *La classe politique dirigéante à Strasbourg, 1650–1750*, PSSARE, 33 (Strasbourg, 1987).

27. The 1690s saw the coming of a cosmopolïtian culture in place of traditional municipal culture in Toulouse. Robert A. Schneider, *Public Life in Toulouse, 1463–1789: From Municipal Republic to Cosmopolitan City* (Ithaca, 1989), 255–75.

28. Georges Livet, "L'esprit d'opposition sous la monarchie absolue: L'affaire Sonntag à Colmar en 1711," *Annuaire de Colmar* (1953): 69–84.

29. Lawrence Stone, "Prosopography," *Daedelus* 100 (Winter 1971): 46–79, here at 46.

30. On the value of tax records, see Erdmann Weyrauch, "Zur Auswertung von Steuerbüchern mit quantifizierenden Methoden," in Horst Rabe, Hausgeorg Molitor, and Hans Christoph Rublack, eds., *Festgabe für Ernst Walter Zeeden: Zum 60. Geburtstag am 14. Mai 1976*, RGST, suppl. 2 (Münster, 1976), 97–127.

31. Colmar's archives possess two serial tax registers. The *Schatzung* registers run from 1542 to 1667 with several lacunae in the seventeenth century and provide a relatively accurate assessment of all taxpayers. See AMC, CC 153. Erdmann Weyrauch employed these in his study of Colmar's sixteenth-century political elite. Weyrauch, "Die politische Führungsgruppe," 215–34. The *Gewerff* registers cover the entire period, 1537–1789, with fewer lacunae. See AMC, CC 152. These registers form the basis of all civic tax assessments based on real and moveable property, but they factor in tax exemptions, which limit their full effectiveness as a measure of differences in wealth.

32. On the limitations of parish registers as demographic sources, see Jean-Pierre Kintz, *La société strasbourgeoise du milieu du XVIe siècle à la fin de la guerre de Trente Ans, 1560–1650: Essai d'histoire démographique, économique et sociale* (Paris, 1982), 11–39.

33. The Catholic registers begin for baptisms in 1603 and marriages in 1599, but there are many lacunae before 1620 and again in the 1650s. Death registers begin 1664. AMC, GG 188. The Reformed registers begin for baptisms and marriages in 1575. There is a break between 1628 and 1632, then the new Lutheran registers begin. Lutheran death registers begin in 1688. AMC, GG 189.

34. Lucien Sittler, ed., *Les listes d'admission à la bourgeoisie de Colmar, 1361–1494*, PAVC, 1 (Colmar, 1958); Roland Wertz, ed., *Les livres de bourgeois de Colmar: 1512–1609*, PAVC, 2 (Colmar, 1961); idem, ed., *Membres du magistrat, conseillers, et maîtres des corporations de Colmar, 1601–1700: Livre des bourgeois de Colmar 1610–1673*, PVAC, 4 (Colmar, 1967); Jean Bachschmidt, ed., *Le livre des bourgeois de Colmar: 1660–1789* (Colmar, 1985).

35. For example, in the tax registers of 1610, 58.7% of the householders (620 out of 1,057) were inscribed in the citizen registers. A further 18.4% (194) claimed to be citizens in the parish registers. In 1660 the percentage of inscribed citizens among Colmar's householders had fallen to 49.3% (433 out of 878) and the percentage claiming citizenship without inscription had risen to 22.5% (198 out of 878). Who were these men? They came from all ten guilds. For the period between 1580 and 1630, the guilds included anywhere from 11 to 31% of these "non-inscribed" citizens. Among these men native Colmarians (21.7%) and immigrants (22.3%) were equally represented, and at least one in four of the immigrant citizens did not use marriage to a widow or daughter of a Colmarian as an avenue for citizenship. The one factor that most of these men shared was poverty. The average assessed wealth for the male householders as a whole in 1620 was 470 florins, for the inscribed citizens 664 florins, and for the men claiming citizenship without inscription only 180 florins.

36. I recognize the need to find gender-sensitive models to study early modern society, but my efforts to trace the lives of specific women as taxpayers, workers, and churchgoers has provided limited data. For a survey of the issue, see Merry E. Wiesner, "Beyond Women and the Family: Towards a Gender Analysis of the Reformation," *The Sixteenth Century Journal* 18 (1987): 311–22.

Part I

Reformation, Counter-Reformation, and Confessionalization at Colmar, 1575–1648

1

Civic Politics in the Age of Confessionalization, 1575–1648

On Saturday, 14 May 1575, Colmar's regime members voted unanimously that the city possessed the *ius reformandi*, the right to initiate religious reform. In the predawn hours of 15 May, they visited each of the ten guildhalls. The city clerk, Beat Henslin, announced that at midmorning the pastor from the neighboring village of Jebsheim would preach in the vacant Franciscan chapel attached to the city's hospital. The regime's overnight reformation "from above" culminated a long and carefully orchestrated Protestant movement. Colmar's "late Reformation" confirmed the regime's authority within the walls and touted its independence before the neighboring powers. The Protestant leaders justified their act within the constitutional guarantees of the Religious Peace of Augsburg but recognized that their decision was not secure. Confessional division could trigger civic unrest which would undermine their power. Thus, to preserve civic peace, Henslin presented the assembled guildsmen with the choice of attending either the Protestant service or Catholic mass.[1] The morning passed without incident, and Colmar became a confessionally mixed community.

Not all Colmarians welcomed the new church. The Catholic clergy at St. Martin's, along with the city's Augustinian and Dominican communities, formed the backbone of resistance to the evangelical movement in defense of both the old religion and of their corporate rights. They could rely on support from the bishop of Basel and, more importantly, the Austrian territorial officials in nearby Ensisheim. Although the city's Protestant leadership lived under the constant threat of Catholic intervention, their confessional settlement held until the collapse of Imperial authority during the Thirty Years' War. In December 1627, an Imperial commission dismantled Colmar's Protestant parish, and all Protestants had to either abjure their faith or to sell their property and emigrate. In the first months of 1628, the ministers and civic leaders scattered to neighboring Protestant havens in Alsace and Switzerland, while a Jesuit mission from Ensisheim, supported by a garrison, implemented a Counter-Reformation.[2]

Shifting power politics had ended bi-confessionalism, and further shifts would undo Colmar's Counter-Reformation. In December 1632, the Swedes besieged the city and forced the Imperial garrison to capitulate. They signed an accord with the city which guaranteed Catholic rights and reestablished a Protestant church, though the Swedes insisted that the Colmarians adhere to Lutheran forms of worship.[3] Colmar's first Protestant parish had maintained close relations with the neighboring Swiss Reformed communities, and the Lutheran ministers, who arrived in the city after 1632, had to wage a prolonged campaign against "crypto-Calvinists." Nevertheless, when the Peace of Westphalia established 1624 as the normative year for confessional relations, the Reformed ministers did not return to Colmar. Henceforth Colmar's confessional mix would reflect the settlement of 1632, and the city's Lutheran leaders gradually strengthened links with the neighboring Lutheran powers of Strasbourg and Württemberg.[4]

By 1650 the Peace of Westphalia seemed to ensure Colmar's sovereignty, its bi-confessionalism, and the regime's authority. Confessional division had characterized public life for three quarters of a century, during which the separation of the religious communities from the political community constantly threatened civic peace. Yet the compromise of 1575 continued long after the disappearance of the Reformed Protestant community which had created it, and in time confessional diversity became a civic norm. Colmar's Protestant leaders combined an Erastian view of church governance with an irenic approach to interconfessional relations. Under this program the regime discouraged theological disputes among the clergy while recognizing that the Protestant pulpit could not fully serve as a means of social discipline for the civic community or as the moral arm of the regime's authority. Instead the Protestant leaders defined their authority in strictly political terms as a pragmatic course in a dangerous confessional environment. What factors had led to the compromise of 1575?

I. ANTECEDENTS TO COLMAR'S BI-CONFESSIONALISM

There were two attempts to bring the Reformation to Colmar. The first in the 1520s had the support of the agricultural work force: the peasants, gardeners, and vineyard workers. The reformers combined a call for a housecleaning among the city's lax clergy, improvement of the spiritual environment, and an agenda of social and political reforms. This Reformation "from below," which coincided with and drew strength from the great German Peasants' War, failed to achieve its ends.[5] Through the following decades anticlericalism sustained its pressure on the city's religious and lay leaders, and it would be the church officials' failure to respond effectively to the pressure that eventually produced Colmar's Reformation.

Colmar's religious communities were privileged corporations under the jurisdiction and protection of foreign ecclesiastical and lay lords and often at odds with the civic community and each other.[6] Early sixteenth-century Colmar belonged to the diocese of Basel and recognized the spiritual authority of its bishop, who resided in exile at Porrentruy. The medieval city had possessed three parish churches, but by the late sixteenth century they had consolidated into one, the collegiate chapter of St. Martin, located in the very center of the city.[7] By 1575 the parish community and the civic community were identical. St. Martin's tithes and patronage belonged to the Benedictine abbey near Münster in the Vosgian valley of St. Gregory.[8] A provost, elected by the canons and invested by the abbot, headed the collegiate chapter but was seldom in residence, while the number of canons declined from a fourteenth-century peak of sixteen to seven in 1583 and to only three in the early seventeenth century. The canons stood at the summit of a pyramid of canons-elect, vicars, and chaplains, who serviced the Colmarians' spiritual needs. The parish church was more like an ecclesiastical conglomerate with a main altar, over thirty side altars and devotional niches inside, while on the outside the civic cemetery and several chapels butted up against its walls.[9]

In the thirteenth century the city had also attracted several mendicant communities, which possessed their own corporate rights within the city and rendered obedience to superiors within their own orders rather than to episcopal or civic authorities. Early on the Franciscans had tended the larger of two civic hospitals, but by the sixteenth century the community was in full decline. In 1543 the order abandoned its precincts and sold them to the city. In the late thirteenth and early fourteenth centuries, the Dominicans had erected a monastery and Colmar's only two convents, St. Catherine's and Unterlinden, in the northern neighborhoods. The richly endowed Dominican communities were significant property owners, within the city walls and beyond, who recruited their members from the city's elite families and employed dozens of inhabitants to maintain the buildings, barns, vineyards, and fields. The only other religious house to survive the Middle Ages was the small Augustinian monastery, erected in 1316 near the city's center, which claimed only eight friars in 1495.[10]

Colmar's religious houses provided various social and educational services and functioned as integrators for various groups in the community. The Franciscans had administered the city's main hospital and a leprosarium (*Gutleuthaus*) beyond the city wall.[11] St. Martin's canons and the Dominican friars staffed schools for young boys, and the convents probably provided informal education for the daughters of the elite.[12] Many sixteenth-century Colmarians joined confraternities of the Rosary, St. Anne, and St. Francis, for whom the city's mendicants served as spiritual directors.[13] The religious houses also provided secluded cemeteries and commemorative masses for their lay patrons as well as their members.[14] As Colmar's parish church, St. Martin's cemetery occupied the largest open space in the city, which served as the site for the *Schwörtag*, the annual exchange of oaths between the regime and the citizenry.[15]

The consolidation of parish functions at St. Martin's and the closure of the Franciscan house focused clerical leadership on the collegiate chapter, the small Augustinian community, and the Dominican enclave. In the 1540s the municipal government assumed control over the civic hospital and the leprosarium, while the canons of St. Martin's and the Dominicans resisted pleas from civic officials to upgrade the curriculum at the schools and to assume civic responsibilities.[16] In the late 1540s the regime finally took charge of the schools. After 1555 relations between the city's lay and clerical elites further weakened, as outsiders assumed leading roles among the clergy and drew on external support for leverage in disputes with civic leaders.[17] The disputes, stirred up by the Protestant reformers over the proper relation between people and their God in daily rituals, openly challenged the sense of the sacred in every aspect of urban life.[18] The citizens, who felt pride in the construction and maintenance of ecclesiastical buildings which they supported through tithes and pious donations, could be quick to anger when the clergy flaunted privileges, shunned public service, or behaved as aliens in civic space. Colmar's Catholic clergy did all three.[19]

In 1535 the introduction of Lutheran worship in the nearby Württemberg lordship of Horbourg-Riquewihr encouraged a growing number of Colmarians to attend Sunday services outside the city walls. The canons of St. Martin's complained, but the regime would not interfere. Decades of investment and generations of intermarriage connected Colmar's elite and the leading families in the Württemberg lordship.[20] The civic regime tolerated this second wave of "popular" evangelical support, while its public adherence to Catholicism spared it the constitutional restructuring that fell on the Protestant Imperial cities that rebelled against Charles V in 1546.[21] Following the Religious Peace of Augsburg, a new generation of leaders with Protestant sympathies entered Colmar's regime. In 1565 magistrates in the Alsatian city of Hagenau established a Protestant parish without incurring the emperor's wrath. Even then Colmar's Protestant leaders carefully maneuvered toward sanctioning evangelical worship.[22] In the end bi-confessionalism in 1575 resulted from deep disillusionment with the recalcitrant civic clergy and the magistrate's secure political base and cautious policies.

Sixteenth-century Colmar was an Imperial city (*Reichsstadt*) which made it self-governing and answerable only to the emperor and the empire. Colmar's citizens formed a legal corporate body held together by the sinews of mutually sworn oaths and recognized in the Imperial assemblies and courts.[23] In medieval physiology, the corporal metaphor implied hierarchy, and in Colmar, as in many other Imperial cities, the citizens formed the foundation of civic authority in theory, while in practice the members of the civic regime (*Regiment*) exercised extensive power in their own right.[24]

Colmar's sixteenth-century political institutions were the product of Imperial and civic struggles in the thirteenth and fourteenth centuries. Conflicting candidates for the Imperial throne had granted the community the initial charters and liberties which made it a self-governing town.[25] Factional tension among the city's noble families later forced a constitutional reform in 1360 which shifted power to Colmar's guilds.[26] The reform, however, did not democratize the government, for, by and large, the new municipal leaders belonged to wealthy landed families who were buoyed by the region's agricultural richness and who dominated civic politics throughout the fifteenth century.[27] The constitution of 1360 served the city until 1521, when the civic leaders drew up a new document that would remain in effect until the 1680s.

The constitution of 1521 established a two-tier governmental structure consisting of a magistrate (*Meisterschaft*) and a council (*Rat*) (see figure 1.1). The council, which served as the outer circle of civic governance, included thirty members who were designated to three committees. The constitution also reduced the number of guilds from twenty to ten by consolidating many of the smaller guilds. After 1521 each guild was to supply the council with a guildmaster (*Zunftmeister*), a senator (*Ratherr*), and a XIIIer (*Dreizehner*). The magistrate was a small executive panel, which comprised the *Obristmeister*, three *Stettmeister*, and the *Schultheiss*.[28]

Civic administration lay in the hands of the magistrate. The Obristmeister served as Colmar's political and military leader and ruled the city during his year in office, and the three Stettmeisters each served four-month terms as city treasurer (*Ausrichtermeister*) and as advocates for cases that came before the council in its capacity as superior court. The Schultheiss acted as Colmar's chief justice, who presided over the lower court of jurors (*Schöffengericht*) and the council as superior court, with the assistance of the court clerk (*Gerichtsschreiber*), who was a hired professional.[29] A second critical professional was the city clerk (*Stadtschreiber*), who kept the minutes for all meetings of the magistrate and council, maintained the municipal archives, and directed the city's chancery. During the sixteenth century the city clerk and the court clerk became increasingly important figures as governing grew in complexity.[30]

The council did not initiate legislation but primarily advised the magistrate and broadened its base of authority.[31] Of the three committees, only the council of XIII played an active role in policymaking. The three Stettmeisters served as XIIIers, and the committee's foreign relations agenda gave it added prestige. Men who proved discrete and effective XIIIers sat on the committee year in and year out. The guildmasters and senators handled administrative functions for the regime, such as tax assessment, guild supervision, and jury duty, which brought them into daily contact with the common citizens. They acted as liaison between the magistrates and the community at large.

The new constitution also prescribed a complex electoral process that sharply curtailed direct participation by guild members in the annual elections, which took place on the weekend after the feast of St. Lawrence

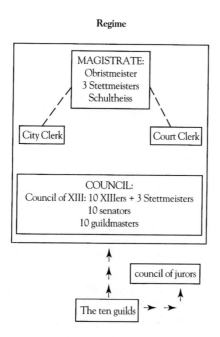

Regime

FIGURE 1.1   COLMAR'S POLITICAL STRUCTURE, 1521–1673

(10 August). On Friday the incumbent senators, guildmasters, and Obristmeister selected the new Obristmeister and presented him to the full council, which then appointed the new Schultheiss. On the following Sunday, each guild met separately to elect their guildmaster. The incumbent senators then met with the retiring and newly elected guildmasters to select the three new Stettmeisters. Afterward the retiring senators and guildmasters drew up the list of new XIIIers. Finally the new Obristmeister and Schultheiss announced their candidates for the new senate. If the electors disagreed on a particular candidate, the city clerk would break the deadlock, except in the case of the Obristmeister, when the Imperial Bailiff of Hagenau, the emperor's representative, carried the decisive vote. The carefully orchestrated process ensured continuity among the leaders. The only popularly elected officials, the guildmasters, were chosen early enough to allow the leaders to sort out the remaining posts within the magistrand and council. Traditionally, most officials rotated through offices during long careers which ended in death or retirement. On the Monday after the elections, the male citizens gathered

in the cemetery to swear their obedience to the new authorities.

Although Colmar's citizens had little direct access to their government and the magistrate and council never consulted the citizenry as a whole, outbursts of popular protest against the regime were rare in early modern Colmar. When faced with potentially divisive political decisions, the regime convened the council of jurors (*Schöffenrat*), an assembly of eight to twenty jurors (*Schöffen*) elected from each of the ten guilds, who in all comprised less than 20% of Colmar's citizenry.[32] In extremely sensitive situations, the magistrate presented its case to the citizens gathered in their separate guilds. Decision-making was always hierarchical, with the agenda determined by the magistrate in closed session then presented for consultation and approval to the council, followed by the council of jurors when necessary, and finally the assembled guilds.

In early modern Colmar, the political foundation of the community both in structure and function were the guildsmen. They formed the civic militia, and their taxes supported the municipal administration. Guild admission was expensive enough to restrict access to moderately wealthy individuals, perhaps 10–15% of the total population. Most but not all guildsmen were citizens.[33] Colmar's citizens had to belong to a guild, to own or rent a house in town, and to prove a five-year residency in the community. In the late sixteenth century, Colmar had approximately 1,000 citizens out of a population of around 7,000.[34] On *Schwörtag* the citizens repeated the oath of obedience which recalled for them and the regime their mutual obligation to civic traditions and laws. The citizens swore "obedience" to the magistrate "in all good and just things" and promised "to protect the city from all harm."[35] Daily reminders of shared goals, while serving the watch on the city ramparts, answering the fire bell, or walking on the streets and bridges maintained by their taxes, echoed softly the message of obligation and shared ownership.

Colmar's status as an Imperial city depended on its relations with the emperor and the empire. Since 1354 the city participated in Imperial politics as a member of the league of ten Alsatian cities known as the *Decapolis*.[36] Since the league's foundation, the Imperial Bailiff at Hagenau assumed the role of intermediary between the *Decapolis* and the empire. Hagenau became the league's unofficial capital, but Colmar, by far the largest of the ten cities, often quarreled with Hagenau over policy and precedence. Inevitably both towns dispatched representatives for the league to the Imperial Diets. In the sixteenth century, Colmar's officials also attended sessions of the Upper Rhenish Circle and the assemblies of the Upper Alsatian estates (*Ländestag*).

As an Imperial city, Colmar claimed direct obedience only to the emperor, but the Imperial Bailiff at Hagenau maintained specific rights over civic political life. He served as tax collector for Imperial levies, and he had helped bring about the constitutional reforms of 1360 and 1521. In fact the city could not alter its political structure without his approval. The Imperial Bailiff or his proxy attended all municipal elections and witnessed the oaths of office. In a deadlocked election for Obristmeister, the Imperial Bailiff held the deciding ballot.[37] He was an outsider, however, who had little influence on the normal business of governing the town. Colmar claimed privileges which freed it from the jurisdictional influence of the bailiff's court in Hagenau. Colmar's regime held the right of high justice in criminal matters, and parties could appeal municipal civil verdicts only in cases exceeding 100 florins. Following the Imperial reforms of 1495, all legal appeals went first to the Chamber of the Upper Rhenish Circle and then to the Imperial Aulic Council in Vienna. Colmar refused to allow the Imperial Bailiff to meddle in its military affairs, and the regime supervised its own garrison and arsenal.[38]

Colmar also had separate ties with the empire distinct from league membership. The city paid the emperor one-half of the revenues from the *Umgeld*, a tax on retail wine sales within the city, and the regime was responsible for meeting Imperial troop levies and for payment of Imperial taxes, such as the *Reichsmonate*, the *Gemein pfennig*, and the *Türkenhilfe*.[39] The blend of obligation and liberties created the context for the municipal regime's external relations with neighboring Imperial estates. In establishing a Protestant parish in Colmar, the magistrates navigated the narrow channels open to them within the Imperial system and anticipated that the same rules applied to their powerful neighbors.

II. BI-CONFESSIONALISM IN COLMAR, 1575–1627

Colmar's reformation undermined the two pillars of civic political culture, for it placed the city at odds with the emperor, whose authority legitimized power from above, and it soon divided the citizenry into separate communities of worship which fractured the communal contract.[40] The unsettling effect of bi-confessionalism drove the regime to justify its policies through appeals to Colmar's chartered liberties and to civic unity and peace. The appeals, so often repeated, revealed the regime's anxiety, for which there was indeed much cause. Anticlericalism had fueled the reform movement, and the Catholic clergy responded to the direct challenge. Clerical legal appeals finally produced an Imperial commission in 1579, which ordered the dissolution of the illegal Protestant parish. The civic regime assembled the council of jurors, who reaffirmed communal support for the confessional decision of 1575.[41] From 1579 onward Colmar's bi-confessionalism held a secure legal footing only within the community.

Confessional relations within Colmar were never fully peaceful. After 1575 Colmar's Catholic religious houses retained their corporate rights, which the Protestant political leaders reluctantly acknowledged as a logical corollary to the city's own liberties.[42] The regime retaliated with sniping gestures against the association of Catholic ritual with public life. The Protestant authorities restricted bell ringing in the Catholic churches and refused to honor the new "popish" Gregorian calendar. They curtailed public celebration of feast days and banned processions. Furthermore, they scoured away the Catholic symbolic association with public space. The regime demolished, secularized, or visibly neglected many chapels, such as St. Michael's and St. Eloi's, which became a powder magazine and a brickyard respectively, and the regime turned the vacant parish church of St. Peter's into an immense woodshed. Crosses and shrines disappeared from their niches on the streets and above the city gates. Perhaps the most dramatic gesture was the civic cemetery's transfer from St. Martin's churchyard to a new site beyond the walls. The authorities paved over the old cemetery.[43] Ritual reverence to the dead had been part of the old religious order. In the new order, the old graveyard became a parade ground for the civic militia.

The regime not only sought to separate political life from its Catholic past, but also recruited the new ministers and developed the confessional tenets for its Protestant parish. Throughout, the Colmarians worked to maintain cordial ties with their three principal Protestant neighbors: Strasbourg, Horbourg-Riquewihr, and Basel, all of whom by 1575 were Lutheran.[44] In the ensuing decades, confessional relations among the city's Protestant neighbors soured, and Colmar's Protestant community adapted to the changing conditions. From 1575 to 1589, the regime balanced ministerial recruitment from among its neighbors and attempted to maintain an open confessional stance. After 1577, however, the Duke of Württemberg began to press the city to sign the Lutheran Formula of Concord, and after 1585 Basel, under Johann Jacob Grynaeus, became confessionally aligned with Rhenish Calvinism.[45] By 1589 a peaceful balance was no longer possible.

From 1589 to 1600, Colmar's Protestant community became increasingly alienated from its Lutheran neighbors and deeply divided within itself. Trouble began with a bitter public dispute over the Lord's Supper between the pastor, Christian Serinus, who favored confessional alignment with Basel, and the first deacon, Johann Georg Magnus (Gross), an outspoken Lutheran with close ties to the Württemberg church, who railed from the pulpit against Serinus and his supporters in the regime.[46] His attacks produced a "Magnist" party among the Protestants and threatened the fragile confessional peace.[47]

In their oath of office, Colmar's Protestant preachers had sworn to avoid public dispute with civic Catholics and discord among themselves.[48] Magnus clearly broke the oath, but initially the regime did not censure him. Instead the city clerk, Andreas Sandherr, drafted a doctrinal statement, which sought to retain a connection with the original Confession of Augsburg.[49] This *Deklarationsschrift* served as the confessional formula for Colmar's Protestant church, but it failed either to placate the Lutheran neighbors or the quarrelsome Magnus, who refused to subscribe and was relieved of his office.[50] Throughout the 1590s, the regime's public confessional stance combined the *Deklarationsschrift*, the Württemberg catechism and church ordinance of 1559, and the obstinate desire to find suitable deacons with ties to Strasbourg.[51] The effort to please everyone pleased no one, and by 1594 the Lutheran pastor in Horbourg mocked Colmar's ministers and their "three different religions."[52] The confessional isolation of Colmar's Protestants increased.

As late as 1600, a Lutheran faction survived among the Protestant leadership. The city's deacon, Johann Ernst Fritsch, met regularly with the Latin schoolmaster, Christoph Kirchner, and three prominent citizens, Martin Stromeyer, Johann Barth, and Egenolph Wetzel. Kirchner was an immigrant, and Barth was from a prominent family of local merchants. Wetzel and Stromeyer had family members in the regime. All three citizens were assessed at over 2,000 florins in the *Gewerff* register of 1600, which placed them among the wealthiest citizens.[53] Yet this prominent group would fail to influence the magistrates' confessional policies, as they soon made the final shift toward confessional affiliation with Rhenish Calvinism. Beginning in 1603, Ambrosius Socinus, Serinus' successor, began to limit ministerial recruitment to candidates with Reformed pedigrees, and he convinced the regime to adopt a Reformed catechism and a modified church ordinance along Calvinist lines.[54] By the outbreak of the Thirty Years' War, Colmar's confessional break with Strasbourg and Württemberg was complete. In 1627 when the Imperial commission dissolved Colmar's Reformed church, the entire ministry fled to Switzerland.[55]

Reformed confessionalism developed among Colmar's Protestants slowly and probably incompletely. Despite the regime's control over the Protestant church, only the city's ministerial employees swore an oath to honor the *Deklarationsschrift*. The municipal regime recruited Protestant teachers for the municipal Latin and German schools, but there was no curriculum reform until Socinus organized the gymnasium in 1604, and Catholic tutoring continued unmolested in the Dominican houses.[56] Colmar's Protestant leaders never passed a comprehensive morals ordinance such as existed in neighboring Munster, though in 1581 the regime did institute a marriage court, which superseded the bishop of Basel's jurisdictional rights, but only for the city's Protestants.[57] The court heard marital disputes but could not assign ecclesiastical punishments, such as excommunication. When necessary, cases were turned over to the regime itself which passed final judgment and punished the guilty.[58] Bi-confessionalism hindered full implementation of Protestant moral discipline, so the regime relied on its chartered legal authority and punished transgressors in civic rather than church courts.

The growth of self-conscious confessional groups within the civic community after 1575 was a gradual and sometimes troubled process. The Catholic clergy remonstrated against Protestant legal rights, though their appeals depended for force on outside powers. Colmar's Catholic laity remained passive. Confessional tensions were sharpest among the Protestants. The growing rift between Lutherans and Calvinists beyond the city walls soured relations among their adherents at Colmar. Until 1600 the regime suffered Protestant confessional discord in the vain hope of preserving cordial ties with the neighboring Protestant powers. Ultimately, the Calvinist party came to dominate, but without a wholesale exodus of civic Lutherans. Who were the political leaders who carried through this complex policy? What were the confessional divisions within the regime?

III. CONFESSIONALISM AND THE CIVIC REGIME

> Wär' Bueb geblieben Knecht
> Und Link geblieben recht
> Und Goll geblieben stumm
> Wär' Colmar nit im Luthertum.[59]

This short poem highlights the critical role of the civic leadership in bringing about Colmar's Reformation. According to recent studies, selective recruitment of regime members allowed the Protestant party to lay the groundwork for the reform and afterwards to consolidate the ties between the Protestant parish and the civic government.[60] Let us briefly examine the regime and its recruitment before and after Colmar's Reformation.[61]

After 1521 Colmar's magistrates became the effective leaders in civic politics. Between 1521 and 1575, twenty-two men from twenty-two families served as magistrates, of whom more than half (twelve) served at least sixteen years (see table 1.1). The careers of Conrad Wickram and Hieronymous Boner spanned a quarter century, while Matthis Be(e)r, who succeeded Wickram in 1544, served for thirty-two years. After 1560 Michel Buob (twenty-nine years) and Hans Goll (twenty-eight years) joined Be(e)r to provide stable leadership in the decades prior to 1575. Despite the impression of ensconced oligarchical power, the sixteenth-century magistrate lacked dynasties, such as occurred in the fifteenth and seventeenth centuries. These men came from nine of Colmar's ten guilds with only the bakers and millers of *zum Kränzchen* unrepresented. Just the same, Colmar's agricultural guilds, which comprised one-half of the citizenry, produced few magistrates. Hans Fulweiss, from the gardeners' guild, *zum Haspel*, served only in 1521; and Lorentz Obrecht of the peasants' guild, *Ackerleute*, had a brief career in mid-century. Heironymous Boner belonged to the vineyard workers' guild, *Rebleute*, but he was a humanist who shared little in common with his fellow guildsmen.

Kaspar von Greyerz has argued that "the constitution of 1521 gave a fairly accurate rendition of the new social structure and of the resulting distribution of power within Colmar's urban community," which he feels favored the growing wine and brandy trade.[62] The merchants' guild, *zur Treue*, and the wine sellers' guild, *zum Riesen*, produced many magistrates, but other guilds were also represented. Greyerz's assessment holds, however, for the magistrates were men who shared commercial interests, professional background, and membership in the patrician society *zum Waagkeller*.[63] Colmar's constitution supported oligarchical government, but relatively open recruitment served the ambitions of the upwardly mobile, who normally developed their political skills while representing their guilds in the council.

TABLE 1.1
Magisterial Recruitment, 1521–1575

Name	Regime	Rec.	Mag.	Ten.	Ob.	Guild
REGIME IN 1521						
Ludwig Hutsch	1488	S	1501	10	4	Riesen
Conrad Wickram	1502	S	1517	26	11	Treue
Hans Mathissel	1497	G	1517	8	1	Holderbaum
Hans v. Rust	1521	M	1521	4	—	zur Krone
Hans Fulweis	1480	G	1521	1	—	Haspel
RECRUITS						
Hans Ruch	1517	S	1522	17	1	NA
Peter Ölftz	1522	G	1525	2	1	Adler
Hieronymus Boner	1527	O	1527	25	11	Rebleute
Diebolt Mentzer	1501	S (G)	1527	3	—	Löwen
Hans Stromeyer	1528	M	1528	16	—	NA
Peter Nuwgart	1521	G	1530	11	—	Treue
Lorentz Obrecht	1528	S (G)	1539	3	—	Ackerleute
Ruprecht Kriegelstein	1538	G	1541	19	3	Adler
Mathis Güntzer	1531	S (G)	1543	22	7	Riesen
Mathis Be(e)r	1544	M	1544	32	5	Treue
Jörg Vogel	1543	S (G)	1546	19	4	Riesen
Joseph Hecker	1532	G	1552	6	1	Wolleben
Michel Buob	1539	S (G)	1559	30	8	Löwen
Hans Goll	1551	S (G)	1560	28	8	Treue
Batholomäus v. Kirn	1540	XIII	1565	3	—	Holderbaum
Hans Henckel	1558	G	1565	17	—	Holderbaum
Gregorius Berger	1553	S (G)	1568	20	—	Treue

Key:
Regime   Year recruited into regime
Rec.   First post held in regime
    O   Obristmeister
    M   Magistrate
    XIII   XIIIer
    G   Guildmaster
    S   Senator
    (G)   Served as guildmaster during career
Mag.   Year recruited into magistrate
Ten.   Tenure of magisterial service
Ob.   Number of years served as Obristmeister
Guild   Guild in which inscribed
    NA   Does not appear in guild or citizen registers

Of the sixteen magistrates recruited between 1522 and 1575, five first entered government through guild election, but in all three out of four were elected guildmasters sometime during their careers. Only four men stepped directly into the magistrate, and only one, Mathis Be(e)r, after the turbulent 1520s. One other, Bartholomäus von Kirn, had served as a XIIIer for a quarter of a century before joining the magistrate in 1565.[64] Thus most magistrates had contact with the guilds and some sense of the political needs of their co-citizens.

In what ways did magisterial recruitment facilitate Colmar's reformation and how did confessionalism influence magisterial recruitment? In 1575 three of the five magistrates joined the Protestant community: Gregorius Berger, Michel Buob, and Hans Goll (see table 1.2). Matthis Be(e)r had close family ties to the regional monastic houses, and Hans Henckel remained a devout Catholic.[65] Nevertheless, Be(e)r and Henckel conceded to the will of their Protestant colleagues, who drew further support from Colmar's chief municipal employees, the city clerk, Beat Henslin, the court clerk, Andreas Sandherr, and the city physician, Thomas Schöpf.[66] In 1575 the Protestants dominated but did not monopolize the magistrate, but from 1575 down to 1627, all magisterial recruits would be Protestants. In 1576 the death of Matthis Be(e)r led to the unusual co-optation of the city clerk, Beat Henslin, who had never held elected office, and to the promotion of Andreas Sandherr to Henslin's vacant post. Henckel's death in 1582 allowed the co-optation of Sebastian Wilhelm Linck, a nobleman and prominent Protestant leader since the 1560s.[67] Both Henslin and Linck lacked guild roots, and the magistrate's pursuit of confessional unity within its chambers initially broke traditional recruiting patterns. In 1588 the deaths of Buob, Goll, and Berger swept away the last of the regime's prereform leaders. Unlike Linck and Henslin, the new magistrates, Dürninger, Espach, and Kriegelstein, had long careers in the council and deep guild roots.[68] The confessional crisis of 1589–90 soon followed, but it was the city clerk, Sandherr, and the pastor, Serinus, and not the magistrates, who delineated the new confessional stance. A decade later, Socinus, the new pastor, completed the break with neighboring Lutheran powers.

While the magistrate took a less direct hand in confessional policy, it assumed a more exclusive and oligarchical complexion. Of the fifteen magistrates recruited after the Reformation, only two began their careers as guildmasters, and ambitious men in the three agricultural guilds along with those in zum Kränzchen failed to rise to the city's highest political offices, while the merchants from zur Treue controlled the magistrate and in particular the post of Obristmeister. From 1587 until 1626, three men, the nobleman Linck and the merchants Kriegelstein and Wetzel, functioned as Obristmeister in all but five years. Furthermore, for the first time in nearly a century, sons, such as Heinrich Goll, Jacob Buob, Hans Espach, and Daniel Birr, succeeded their fathers in office.

TABLE 1.2
Magisterial Recruitment, 1575–1627

NAME	REGIME	REC.	MAG.	TEN.	OB.	GUILD	REL.
REGIME IN 1575							
Mathis Be(e)r	1544	M	1544	32	5	Treue	Cath
Michel Buob	1539	S (G)	1559	30	8	Löwen	Ref
Hans Goll	1551	S (G)	1560	28	8	Treue	Ref
Hans Henckel	1558	G	1565	17	—	Holderbaum	Cath
Gregorius Berger	1553	S (G)	1568	20	—	Treue	Ref
RECRUITS							
Beat Henslin	1576	M	1576	19	4	NA	Ref
Seb. Wilhelm Linck	1571	XIII	1582	30	12	NA	Ref
Philip Dürninger	1552	S (G)	1588	6	—	Riesen	Ref
Mattern Espach	1565	XIII (G)	1588	12	2	Löwen	Ref
Ludwig Kriegelstein	1573	G	1588	38	15	Treue	Ref
Martin Birr	1569	S (G)	1594	6	—	Löwen	Ref
Heinrich Goll	1582	S (G)	1596	11	—	Holderbaum	Ref
Elias Wetzel	1596	S	1600	26*	9	Treue	Ref
Jacob Buob	1597	G	1602	18	3	Holderbaum	Ref
Hans Espach	1607	S	1610	17	—	Riesen	Ref
Niclaus Schultheiss	1605	S (G)	1617	7	—	Wohlleben	Ref
Daniel Birr	1612	S (G)	1620	8*	1	Treue	Ref
Joseph Glaser	1614	S (G)	1624	4*	—	Treue	Ref
Anton Burger	1612	S	1626	2*	—	Treue	Ref
Conrad Ortlieb	1612	S (G)	1627	1*	—	Adler	Ref

Key:
Regime   Year recruited into regime
Rec.   First post held in regime
    O   Obristmeister
    M   Magistrate
    XIII   XIIIer
    G   Guildmaster
    S   Senator
    (G)   Served as guildmaster during career
Mag.   Year recruited into magistrate
Ten.   Tenure of magisterial service
Ob.   Number of years served as Obristmeister
Guild   Guild in which inscribed
    NA   Does not appear in guild or citizen registers
Rel.   Confessional affiliation
*   Went into exile in 1627

Beginning in 1617 a new generation of men entered the magistrate. All but Anton Burger joined the regime through co-optation, and only Daniel Birr was a descendent of a significant sixteenth-century political family. Niclaus Schultheiss and Joseph Glaser were the first in their families to serve in any civic office, and Conrad Ortlieb had immigrated from Riquewihr. This new magisterial cohort gradually developed the marital connections which would have secured their place in civic politics until mid-century had not the Counter-Reformation ended their government.[69] Only Ortlieb returned to the city in 1633 to head the new Protestant regime. As at Hagenau, the dissolution of Colmar's Reformed parish brought down the magistrates who had supported it.

Conditions within the sixteenth-century council also reflected shifts in political balance between the magistrates and the guildsmen as well as confessional divisions. Erdmann Weyrauch has identified an outer circle of 100 families recruited into the regime between 1540 and 1600, which suggests widespread political participation in a population containing around 400 patronymics in 1600.[70] Between 1521 and 1627, slightly more than one-third (34.5%) of the regime's recruits entered as guildmasters (see tables 1.3, 1.4). During the elections the guilds chose their masters first and could have filled nearly all vacancies, but by voting for men already in office the guildsmen permitted the regime to co-opt the majority of its successors. Over the decades the percentage of men entering the regime through guild election varied, with a steady decline from 37.8% in the 1520s to 15% in the 1570s. Furthermore, of the twelve men who joined the regime between 1565 and 1575, only one, Ludwig Kriegelstein, the future Stettmeister, was selected by his guild. Apparently following Hagenau's Reformation, the Protestant party in Colmar's regime, with the tacit support of the guilds, secured its political base; and co-optation remained the norm down to 1585. In the first post-Reformation election in 1576, nine recruits entered the government, a turnover matched only in severe plague years (1562, 1610) and during the Counter-Reformation. Only one, Hans Reech, was chosen by his fellow gardeners in *zum Haspel*. In all, between 1566 and 1585, the guilds elected only four of thirty-six new regime members. After 1590, however, thirty-three of the next eighty-one political careers began with a guild election. By the eve of the Thirty Years' War, the guilds had reclaimed their voice, at least in the council. Could the voices of the city's Catholics also be heard in council chambers?

In 1585 contemporary reports depicted an entirely Protestant regime, both magistrate and council, and this confessional monopoly apparently continued until 1623.[71] Research in the parish registers paints a different picture (see table 1.5). Of the thirty council members in office in 1575, at least seventeen joined the new parish while only one appears in later Catholic registers. Of the 106 men recruited between 1576 and 1627, only ten were Catholics, though this figure is probably low, for the Catholic parish registers

TABLE 1.3
Recruitment of Regime Members, 1521–1627

DECADE	GUILDMASTER (no.)	(%)	SEN.	XIIIer	MAG.	TOTAL
1521–29	14	37.8	17	3	3	37
1530–39	9	37.5	12	3	—	24
1540–49	7	30.4	13	2	1	23
1550–59	5	27.8	12	1	—	18
1560–69	8	26.7	17	5	—	30
1570–79	3	15.0	13	3	1	20
1580–89	6	30.0	10	4	—	20
1590–99	6	42.9	7	2	—	14
1600–09	12	57.1	8	1	—	21
1610–19	10	37.0	17	—	—	27
1620–27	5	41.7	6	1	—	12
Totals	85	34.5	132	24	5	246

TABLE 1.4
Recruitment of Regime Members, 1566–1585

YEARS	GUILDMASTER (no.)	(%)	SEN.	XIIIer	MAG.	TOTAL
1566–69	—		4	1	—	5
1570–75	1		5	1	—	7
1576–79	2		7	2	1	12
1580–85	1		9	2	—	12
Totals	4	11.1	25	6	1	36

Key:
Guildmaster	Joined regime as guildmaster
	No. number first elected as guildmasters
	% percentage of recruits entering as guildmasters
Sen.	Joined regime as senator
XIIIer	Joined regime as XIIIer
Mag.	Joined regime as magistrate

TABLE 1.5

Regime Recruitment and Confession, 1575–1627

YEARS	REFORMED	CATHOLIC	MIXED	NA	TOTAL
1575	17	1	—	12	30
1576–79	7	—	—	5	12
1580–89	17	—	—	3	20
1590–99	10	1	—	3	14
1600–09	15	4	—	2	21
1610–19	24	3	—	—	27
1620–27	9	2	1	—	12
Total	99	11	1	25	136

Key:
Mixed   Regime member married in both churches
NA   Confessional affiliation unknown

Catholic Regime Members, 1590–1627

NAME	GUILD	FIRST POST	YEAR
Hans Hüttenheim the Elder	Haspel	Senator	1594
Lorentz Obrecht	Ackerleute	Guildmaster	1602
Hans Pimperlin	Haspel	Guildmaster	1603
Martin Heimburger	Löwen	Guildmaster	1604
Georg Niemandtsfug	Haspel	Guildmaster	1606
Veltin Hanser	Ackerleute	Guildmaster	1610
Claus Buchinger	Rebleute	Guildmaster	1612
Hans Hüttenheim the Younger	Haspel	Senator	1615
Georg Sutor	Ackerleute	Guildmaster	1620
Johannes Obrecht	Ackerleute	Guildmaster	1625

only began in 1603 and are riddled with lacunae. Nevertheless, Catholics had a voice in the civic regime before 1625, and after 1590 the openness in council recruitment extended confessionally.

The Catholic councilors represented a distinct guild constituency with eight of them inscribed in the peasants' or gardeners' guilds and one each in the vineyard workers' and butchers' guilds. All, except Hans Hüttenheim and his son Hans the younger, entered the regime through election. Once in office, however, these men rotated posts with their Protestant colleagues, though only Martin Heimburger served as a XIIIer. The Protestants clearly dominated civic government, though they allowed Catholics access to office and normal political careers. The Counter-Reformation ultimately would disrupt the city's political and confessional relations and force a new cohort of officials to work out an acceptable compromise.

IV. COLMAR'S COUNTER-REFORMATION AND ITS AFTERMATH

Colmar's confessional crisis of 1627–33 was a direct result of the breakdown of the Imperial political order during the Thirty Years' War. Since the fifteenth century, the Habsburg dukes of Austria had been the major power in Alsace by virtue of their extensive domains in Upper Alsace and, after 1558, control of the Imperial Bailiwick of Hagenau. In 1607 the Habsburgs added a third power base with the elevation of Archduke Leopold to the See of Strasbourg.[72] Since 1575 Colmar's Protestant leaders had kept a close eye on the Austrian officials in nearby Ensisheim; but down to the accession of Ferdinand II as archduke and later Holy Roman Emperor, Austrian pressure on Colmar's Protestants had been sporadic and ineffectual. Unlike his predecessors, Ferdinand was committed to Counter-Reformation, and his policies did much to trigger hostilities in Bohemia in 1618 and then to expand the scope of the conflict.[73]

The Alsatian Protestants had not supported the Bohemian rebels and had avoided any gestures of opposition to the emperor. Strasbourg quickly abandoned the Evangelical Union, and most Alsatian territories followed suit.[74] In November 1621, however, the battered remnants of the count of Mansfeld's rebel army retired into Lower Alsace for winter quarters. Mansfeld captured the Imperial cities of Wissembourg and Hagenau, pillaged undefended villages, and unsuccessfully besieged the bishop of Strasbourg's capital at Saverne.[75] By spring Mansfeld had left, but his campaign brought home to the emperor the need to secure Alsace for his own interests.[76]

After 1622 a string of Imperial military successes allowed Ferdinand to implement a confessional offensive against the Alsatian Protestants, beginning in 1624 with confessionally divided Hagenau, where the emperor supported the Catholic citizenry against its Lutheran regime, which had collaborated with Mansfeld. An Imperial commission drew up a new constitution which placed the regime under closer supervision from the Imperial Bailiff and disbanded Hagenau's Lutheran parish, whose members had been limited to the civic elite. The Lutherans fled.[77]

Hagenau's Reformation had opened the door for evangelical worship in Colmar, its expulsion promised similar repercussions. Colmar's Protestant community had barely survived the censure of two previous Imperial commissions, and the Catholic clergy remained privileged and outspoken opponents to the city's Reformation. The regime's confessional alignment with Basel also deprived it of support from its Lutheran neighbors and of constitutional protection under the Religious Peace of Augsburg. Unlike Hagenau, however, tensions between Catholics and Protestants at Colmar had not exploded into open conflict. Up until 1627, the regime's irenic confessional policies had preserved civic peace, while the emperors had lacked the will or the opportunity to expel the Protestants. By 1627 Ferdinand II's military might and the need to secure Alsace brought the Counter-Reformation to Colmar.

In July 1627 the emperor called for a commission under Archduke Leopold, who governed the Austrian domains in Alsace, to study the complaints of Colmar's Catholic clergy. On 21 November 1627, the commissioners arrived at Colmar. The magistrates, who had drafted detailed responses to the Catholic grievances, convened the council of jurors for support on 27 November. The show of communal solidarity failed to dissuade the commissioners, who on 9 December forbade Protestant worship and expelled the Reformed ministers. The magistrates pleaded for time until their appeals could be heard in the Imperial courts, but on 19 December Imperial troops occupied the Reformed church.[78]

In a letter dated 26 January 1628, Ferdinand II dictated the community's new confessional order. Only Catholic services would be sanctioned within the city, and the Colmarians could not travel to neighboring villages to attend Protestant worship. Protestant citizens had six months to convert or to sell their property and emigrate. Catholics would assume all municipal offices, while the Catholic clergy resumed direct administration of all ecclesiastical properties, including the former Franciscan and Benedictine compounds. Finally, the city had to adopt the new Gregorian calendar.[79] On 26 February the edict was read to the guildsmen. On 11 March the commissioners witnessed the abjurations or resignations of the Protestant regime members. Twenty-seven resigned, and a new regime was "set up."[80] Two days later the citizens gathered in St. Martin's square to swear allegiance to the new officials. The Imperial commission had restored Colmar to its legal confessional relationship with the empire, as the earlier commission had restored Hagenau's. In January 1630 Ferdinand II reconfirmed Colmar's rights and privileges as an Imperial city.[81]

The emperor garrisoned the city to enforce the confessional settlement, while the Austrian regime in nearby Ensisheim, acting as an Imperial agent, supervised Colmar's Counter-Reformation. The Austrian officials asked the Jesuits at Ensisheim to spearhead the drive for conversions. On Christmas

Day 1628, they concelebrated a solemn high mass at St. Martin's church, whose bells chimed for the first time in decades. The following March they reconsecrated the long vacant Benedictine church, St. Peter's, and the former Franciscan church, which had housed the Protestant community. Soon after the Jesuits instituted a catechism program for all local children in order to begin the slow process of strengthening Catholic faith.[82]

Colmar's new Catholic regime quickly tried to distance itself from the emperor and to defend the rights of its citizenry whether Catholic or Protestant. The regime allowed Anton Schott, the city clerk, and Niclaus Sandherr, the court clerk, to retain their posts without abjuring, and these critical professionals stayed on to assist both the new regime and their exiled Protestant colleagues.[83] The civic officials also withheld punishment for Protestant youths who refused to attend the Jesuits' catechetical instruction. In early April 1629, the regime promised to support before the Imperial courts a petition from the city's Protestants seeking an extension of the grace period prior to forced expulsion.[84] Beginning in 1630 Sweden's stunning victories halted the political and religious momentum of the Catholic alliance within the empire and at Colmar.[85] The civic regime soon allowed the traditional Sunday "outings" to nearby Horbourg, for country air and Protestant preaching.[86] In their policies, the Catholic leaders were not opponents to their own religion; rather, they protested directives from the emperor which would either disrupt civic peace or drive away the bulk of the citizenry.

The difficulties civic officials faced peaked over the question of the Imperial garrison, and Austrian officials at Ensisheim created tensions when they sought to confiscate the homes vacated by the Protestant exiles as barracks for the garrison. Faced with a severe fiscal crisis, which was exacerbated by the garrison's demands, the Catholic regime turned to the Protestant exiles for help.[87] In November 1629 it proposed a special tax on the exiles' property and sent an embassy to Basel which negotiated a partial payment from them.[88] In November 1631 the arrival of a new garrison triggered a complaint from the guilds that the regime had overstepped its authority by not summoning the council of jurors before accepting the garrison. On 3 January 1632, the magistrate and council, in joint session, agreed to meet with the individual guilds the following day. During the regime's progress through the city, Peter Dietrich and Gall Gilg confronted the Obristmeister, Hans Obrecht, in the street. Dietrich and Gilg claimed to represent a citizen party, whose members included Valentin Barth, Simon Günther, Matthis Goll, Friedrich Einsiedel, and Daniel Espach.[89]

These men belonged to the two guilds most closely associated with Colmar's exchange economy, *zur Treue* and *zum Riesen*. Espach and Goll were merchants, Günther a cellarer, Einsiedel a barber, and Gilg the proprietor of one of Colmar's largest guest houses, *zum Schlüssel*. All except Dietrich were Protestants and well-to-do.[90] In 1630 Barth, at 6,400 florins, and Günther, at 4,100, had the city's second and fourth highest tax assessments respectively.

Gilg, Goll, and Espach came from important sixteenth-century political families. Matthias Goll had served in the regime before the Counter-Reform, and Espach and Günther would join him in the Protestant regime after 1633.[91] Their protest reflected continued confessional tensions between the community and Catholic officials, who pleaded for patience and promised to consult the guilds in the future.

In the fall of 1632 a new Imperial garrison, comprised of French-speaking recruits from the Franche-Comté, arrived at Colmar. In November Swedish forces crossed the Rhine bridge at Strasbourg, and the Imperial troops abandoned Ensisheim and surrendered without a fight at Sélestat. Only the garrison at Colmar remained.[92] The civic regime questioned the garrison's ability to defend the city and called a municipal council of war, which resulted in the unprecedented decision to arm both citizens and noncitizens.[93] On 19 November a Swedish advance guard demanded Colmar's surrender, which triggered a bitter argument between the Imperial commandant, Vernier, and the magistrates. Vernier demanded the arrest of all secret Protestants within the city, but the regime refused to arrest or disarm anyone. The following day the Catholic leaders consulted the guilds, which favored surrender over the risks of a long siege, but the regime pleaded for time.[94]

When the bulk of the Swedish army set up camp before the city walls on 17 December, the Colmarians soon saw the Imperial garrison as the only obstacle to a hopefully bloodless capitulation. On the morning of 20 December, rumors of Vernier's arrest touched off riots which left twenty garrison troops dead. That afternoon Vernier agreed to leave Colmar, and the following day the city submitted to the Swedes.[95] The articles of capitulation guaranteed the rights of both Catholics and Protestants in Colmar.[96] Only the Jesuits suffered atrocities at the hands of the Swedes, who cut off the priests' ears and noses and forced them to attend the first Lutheran service in the old Franciscan chapel.[97] Colmar's first Counter–Reformation had ended and so had the Catholic regime that supported it.

The Swedish officials restored Protestant worship to the city, and they invited Johannes Schmitt of Strasbourg to supervise the recruitment of new ministers, who would be staunch Lutherans drawn from Strasbourg and from among the chaplains in the Swedish army.[98] Colmar's Protestant leaders, who returned to public affairs, reluctantly accepted the new confessional order, though peace among the Protestants was far from secure. As late as 1638, Johannes Schmitt would publicly complain of Colmar's "crypto-Calvinists"; and for a time the regime tacitly supported Augustin Güntzer, an armorer, who held clandestine prayer meetings for Reformed citizens. In 1644 the magistrates even demanded the resignation of Samuel Gsell, a Lutheran councilor, for having verbally abused Güntzer at a wedding feast.[99] Once again Colmarians seemed to honor three religions; but without official support or ministers, Colmar's Reformed community gradually withered. Many of the Reformed exiles chose to remain at Basel and Mulhouse rather than return to their native city.[100] Following the Peace of Westphalia in 1648, Colmar would remain Lutheran, even though Reformed worship was now legalized in the empire. In 1650 Augustin Güntzer abjured his citizen's oath and left for Schaffhausen.[101]

V. Politics and Society in Colmar, 1627–1650

Between 1627 and 1650 the confessional balance of power had shifted twice, which led to the forced resignation of dozens of regime members and, according to traditional historiography, ushered in a revolution in civic politics.[102] The survivors and the new officials had to negotiate with conflicting powers, to administer the shifting confessional order, and to keep peace among the confessionally divided citizenry. Despite these traumas, the civic regime preserved order and managed civic life effectively. The continuity of the regime's authority can be explained in part by the surprising continuity in its personnel.

Conditions within the last Reformed regime in 1627 reflected the mixture of oligarchical continuity and upward mobility which had characterized sixteenth-century political life (see table 1.6). Some elite families, such as the Kriegelsteins, Fischers, and Lincks, had died out or abandoned civic politics. Others, such as the Dürningers, Wetzels, and Birrs, had come to predominate, each having two members in the regime. Among the magistrates, Conrad Ortlieb, Joseph Glaser, and Anton Burger were the first in their families to serve in the regime, and ten councilors also represented new political families.[103] Furthermore, the regime members were relatively inexperienced. Among the magistrates, only Elias Wetzel had served in the chamber for more than seven years, and fourteen of the twenty-seven councilors had less than ten years' experience. When the regime faced banishment, its magistrates and more established councilors chose to leave for Basel, Mulhouse, or the fortified villages of Horbourg-Riquewihr. The choice of refuge may have reflected confessional commitment, but it more likely reflected commercial and familial ties.[104]

As many Protestant leaders fled Colmar, some forever, the Catholics began to recruit a new regime filled with "converted" Protestant officials. In 1630, at the height of Catholic influence in Colmar, eight out of the thirty-two regime members had served before the Counter-Reform, and only two of these, Hans Obrecht and Georg Sutor, were Catholics. The six veterans, who had abjured, were joined by five other recent converts; however, after 1632 all but two of these eleven men, Hans Peter Kraus and Andreas Sybert, would join the Lutheran parish.[105] The difficulty in finding Catholic guildsmen, in particular in the cloth (*zum Adler*) and leather (*zum Wohlleben*) trades, forced the Catholic leaders to recruit Protestants into the Counter-Reformation regime. Through their official duties, these nominal converts maintained the lines of communication between the regime and the Protestant community.

TABLE 1.6
Civic Regime, 1627

NAME	OFFICE	GUILD	REL.	EXP.
MAGISTRATE				
Daniel Birr	Obrist.	Treue	Ref	15 (7)
Anton Burger	Stett.	Treue	Ref	15 (1)
Joseph Glaser	Stett.	Treue	Ref	13 (3)
Conrad Ortlieb	Stett.	Adler	Ref	15 (—)
Elias Wetzel	Schult.	Treue	Ref	31 (27)
XIII				
Joseph Glaser*	Treue	Treue	Ref	*
Hans Dürninger	Riesen	Riesen	Ref	—
Georg Gsell	Ackerleute	Ackerleute	Ref	16
Hans Jacob Schlachter	Haspel	Treue	Ref	21
Mathis Hoetzelbach	Rebleute	Rebleute	Ref	16
Matthaus Ryss	Löwen	Löwen	Ref	8
Anton Burger*	Kränzchen	Treue	Ref	*
Lorentz Froschesser	Holderbaum	Holderbaum	Ref	29
Conrad Ortlieb*	Adler	Adler	Ref	*
Rudolph Graff	Wohlleben	Wohlleben	Ref	7
SENATE				
H. Christoph Froschesser	Treue	Treue	Ref	22
Johann Caspar Sandherr	Riesen	Riesen	Ref	2
Andreas Sitter	Ackerleute	Ackerleute	Ref	12
Georg Sutor	Haspel	Haspel	Cath	7
Andreas Sybert	Rebleute	Rebleute	Ref	5
Claus Hurst	Löwen	Löwen	Ref	7
Matthaus Ritzenthaler	Kränzchen	Kränzchen	Ref	7
Hans Jacob Graff	Holderbaum	Holderbaum	Ref	16
Jacob Blanck	Adler	Adler	Ref	34
Hans Ulmer	Wohlleben	Wohlleben	Ref	3
GUILDMASTER				
Mathis Goll	Treue	Treue	Ref	3
Daniel Wetzel	Riesen	Riesen	Ref	1
Hans Obrecht	Ackerleute	Ackerleute	Cath	2
Thomann Göcklin	Haspel	Haspel	Ref	33
Hans Leiterer	Rebleute	Rebleute	Ref	9
Martin Birr	Löwen	Löwen	Ref	12
Hans Schindolph	Kränzchen	Kränzchen	Ref	1
Hans Jacob Lamprecht	Holderbaum	Holderbaum	Ref	12
—?—	Adler			
Jacob Hecker	Wohlleben	Wohlleben	Ref	13

Key:
Rel.   Religious affiliation
Exp.   Number of years served in the regime
       (n)   number of years served in magistrate
*   Magistrates serving jointly on council of XIII
?   No guildmaster listed for *zum Adler* in 1627

The political response to external pressure for confessional conformity in the civic regime becomes even more apparent when one examines the Lutheran regime of 1633, which included a hodgepodge of former officials and new men (see table 1.7). Eleven of the thirty-three members of the new govern-ment had served in the regime that had disbanded in 1627. Niclaus Sandherr, who had been court clerk continuously since 1627, the Catholic Georg Sutor, and the elderly Lorentz Froschesser had held office under three confessional banners. Six other regime members had begun their political careers during the Counter-Reformation, though only four of them were Catholics. In all, more than half (seventeen of thirty-three) of the "Lutheran" officials had held office in "Reformed" or "Catholic" regimes. The percentage of multiconfessional officials might have been higher had not several councilors died between 1627 and 1632.[106] Furthermore, every Protestant politician in the Lutheran parish had grown up listening to Reformed preachers. No wonder the Lutheran ministers were concerned about the political clout of the city's "crypto-Calvinists," and no wonder Augustin Güntzer could depend on official sanction for his prayer meetings. In the entire regime, only Johann Heinrich Mogg, the city clerk, who had previously served the counts von Rappoltstein and the Swedes, had purely Lutheran roots. A new coalition of leaders— Reformed, Catholic, and Lutheran—took up office and guided the city through the difficult final years of the war.[107] Out of thirty-two regime members in 1650, three were Catholics, seventeen had married in the Reformed church, and twelve had married in a Lutheran service. From 1627 to 1650, Colmar's political leaders sought to preserve their authority in the face of external confessional pressure. As a result, all three confessional groups participated in civic governance.

In an essay marking the 400th anniversary of Colmar's Reformation in 1975, Gabriel Braeuner argued that further research was necessary to clarify the religious, political, and economic factors which forced the event and molded its aftermath.[108] Jürgen Bücking had already begun the process in 1970 as part of his analysis of the career of the Alsatian Catholic reformer, Johann Rasser, who in the late 1570s bemoaned the poor quality of Colmar's Catholic clergy and the anticlericalism that fueled Colmar's evangelical move-ment.[109] Research continued after 1975, and by 1980 a critical essay by Erdmann Weyrauch had drawn attention to the central role of Colmar's political leaders, both in orchestrating the Reformation "from above" and in realizing the political necessity of bi-confessionalism. Weyrauch discounted the religious character of Colmar's Reformation, which lacked a popular call for reform, open theological discussion, preachers, and a direct assault on Catholic worship.[110] Finally, in the same year the book on Colmar's "late city Reformation" by Kaspar von Greyerz integrated the religious and political interpretations.[111]

Greyerz agrees with Bücking that a central motive for the reformers was

TABLE 1.7
Civic Regime, 1633

NAME	OFFICE	GUILD	REL.	R.	C.	B.
MAGISTRATE						
Conrad Ortlieb	Obrist.	Adler	R/L	x		
Mathis Goll	Stett.	Treue	R/L	x		
Andreas Meder	Stett.	Treue	R/L		x	
Niclaus Sandherr	Stett.	Treue	R/L			x
Emmanuel Röttlin	Schult.	Treue	R/L			
XIII						
Mathis Goll*	Treue	Treue	R/L	x		
Hans Dürninger	Riesen	Riesen	R/L	x		
Andreas Sitter	Ackerleute	Ackerleute	R/L	x		
Georg Sutor	Haspel	Haspel	Cath			x
Hans Leiterer	Rebleute	Rebleute	R/L	x		
Claus Hurst	Löwen	Löwen	R/L	x		
Andreas Meder*	Kränzchen	Treue	R/L		x	
Lorentz Froschesser	Holderbaum	Holderbaum	R/L			x
Elias Meyer	Adler	Adler	R/L			
Rudolph Graff	Wohlleben	Wohlleben	R/L	x		
SENATE						
Georg Willig	Treue	Treue	R/L		x	
Lorentz Espach	Riesen	Riesen	Cath		x	
Hans Bentz	Ackerleute	Ackerleute	R/L			
Claus Birgäntzlin	Haspel	Haspel	Cath		x	
Michel Hötzelbach	Rebleute	Rebleute	Cath		x	
Jacob Riefflin	Löwen	Löwen	R/L			
Christian Hügelin	Kränzchen	Kränzchen	Cath		x	
Michel Seebach	Holderbaum	Holderbaum	R/L			
Christian Scherb	Adler	Adler	R/L			
Hans Volck	Wohlleben	Wohlleben	R/L			
GUILDMASTER						
Jonas Walch	Treue	Treue	R/L			
Simon Günther	Riesen	Riesen	R/L			
Georg Gsell	Ackerleute	Ackerleute	R/L	x		
Jacob Seebach	Haspel	Haspel	Cath			
Mathis Weinsticher	Rebleute	Rebleute	R/L			
Elias Gerhardt	Löwen	Löwen	R/L			
Hans Georg Armbruster	Kränzchen	Riesen	R/L			
Martin Knetzpar	Holderbaum	Holderbaum	R/L			
Bartel Dürninger	Adler	Adler	R/L			
Jacob Hecker	Wohlleben	Wohlleben	R/L	x		

Key:
Rel. Religious affiliation
R. Regime member in 1627 who resigned rather than abjure
C. Regime member recruited during the Counter-Reformation
B. Regime member in 1627 who served during the Counter-Reformation
R/L Protestants who lived in Colmar before 1627
* Magistrates serving jointly on council of XIII

anticlericalism, but for Greyerz it was not a sufficient cause. In the decades before 1575, simple anticlericalism gave way to personal evangelical conviction for Colmarians of various social strata. Religious conditions within the city walls were ripe for reform; however, he notes that Colmar's reformation was not only a religious act but also a constitutional act, which reflected changes in the external political context. The Peace of Augsburg broke the mental connection between loyalty to the emperor and Catholicism, and fear of Austrian interference lessened following the successful establishment of an evangelical community in 1565 in Hagenau. With this in mind Greyerz confirms the political character of Colmar's Reformation. The civic regime was the chief agent, and the political leaders defended their action on constitutional grounds, yet after 1575 bi-confessionalism evolved from the defense of the rights of the subjects, whether the individual citizens, the Catholic religious houses, or the fledgling Protestant parish, rather than in the interest of Colmar's rulers. Protestant leaders pursued irenic policies in confessional issues in hopes of harmonizing these conflicting rights and sustaining civic peace and their own power. Colmar's Counter-Reformation was not a break with but a continuation of civic bi-confessionalism. Pressure from Ferdinand II, as emperor and as powerful overlord of the neighboring Austrian domains, ended Colmar's illegal Reformed parish. The emperor could outlaw Protestant worship, but only time would reduce Protestant sentiment in the community. Colmar's Counter-Reformation did not have enough time.

In 1649 the suffragan bishop of Basel visited Colmar to confirm the city's young Catholics. During his stay he delivered a letter to the Obristmeister, Johann Heinrich Mogg, the political leader of the Lutheran community. The prelate praised Mogg for preserving amiable relations between the confessions and asked him to watch over Colmar's religious peace.[112] The bishop's praise was not hollow. In truth the regime honored the praxis of confessional peace which Mogg's predecessors both Reformed and Catholic had fostered as a community norm.

By 1650 bi-confessionalism had become a normal condition in civic life as shared day-to-day experiences in the workplace and civic landscape counteracted the separateness of distinct religious rituals. Confessional tolerance in Colmar depended on the personal face-to-face nature of civic life. The corporate civic community was not comprised of individual members but smaller, sometimes interconnected, corporate groups: guilds, neighborhoods, households. Confessional groups became one more corporate subset within the body politic. In the next chapter we will analyze the final piece of Braeuner's research agenda, the economic factors, in order to complete the reassessment of Colmar's bi-confessionalism.

Notes

1. Andreas Waltz, ed., *Sigmund Billings Kleine Chronik der Stadt Colmar* (Colmar, 1891), 85. See also Jean Lebeau and Jean-Marie Valentin, eds., *L'Alsace au siècle de la Réforme (1482–1621): Textes et documents* (Nancy, 1985), 176–79. For an account from Colmar's leading Catholic official, Matthias Be(e)r, to the Habsburg regime in Ensisheim, see Jürgen Bücking, *Johann Rasser (ca. 1535–1594) und die Gegenreformation im Oberelsass*, RGST, 101 (Münster, 1970), 25.

2. Greyerz, *Late City Reformation*, 152ff; Georges Livet, ed., *Histoire de Colmar* (Toulouse, 1983), 105–6. On Colmar's Counter-Reformation, see Adam, *Evangelische Kirchengeschichte*, 476–83.

3. Adam, *Evangelische Kirchengeschichte*, 484–85. For the text of the Swedish accord with Colmar, see Paul Wilhelm Finsterwalder, ed., *Colmarer Stadtrechte* 1, Oberrheinische Stadtrechte, Abteilung 3, vol. 3 (Heidelberg, 1938), no. 210, 265–66.

4. Adam, *Evangelische Kirchengeschichte*, 485–89. On the city's Reformed community after 1632, see Philippe Mieg, "Les tribulations d'Augustin Guntzer, bourgeois de Colmar, durant la Guerre de Trente Ans," *Annuaire de Colmar* (1958): 48–65. As late as 1663, the Lutheran pastor, Niclaus Klein, complained of "Crypto-calvinism" among civic officials. Quoted in Henri Strohl, "Les expériences d'une église au cours de quatre siècles (Colmar)," in *Vom Wesen und Wandel der Kirche: Festschrift für Eberhard Vischer* (Basel, 1935), 116–61, here at 118.

5. Georges Bischoff, "Colmar et la crise révolutionnaire de 1524–1525," *Annuaire de Colmar* (1975/76): 43–54; and Greyerz, *Late City Reformation*, 44–64. On the ties between Colmar's movement and rural protest, see Franziska Conrad, *Reformation in der bäuerlichen Gesellschaft: Zur Rezeption reformatorischer Theologie im Elsass*, VIEGM, 116 (Wiesbaden, 1984), 49–76.

6. Dieter Demandt, "Konflikte um die geistlichen Standesprivilegien im spätmittelalterlichen Colmar," in Ingrid Bátori, ed., *Städtische Gesellschaft und Reformation*, Spätmittelalter und Frühe Neuzeit, 12, Kleine Schriften, 2 (Stuttgart, 1980), 136–55.

7. Greyerz, *Late City Reformation*, 25–34; Medard Barth, *Handbuch der elsässischen Kirchen im Mittelalter* (Brussels, 1980), col. 222–40.

8. François Auguste Goehlinger, *Histoire du Chapître de l'Eglise collégiale Saint-Martin de Colmar* (Colmar, 1951).

9. On St. Martin's clerical personnel, see ibid., 15–24; Greyerz, *Late City Reformation*, 27–31. On the altars and chapels, see Barth, *Handbuch der elsässischen Kirchen*, col. 224–27.

10. On the mendicant houses, see Greyerz, *Late City Reformation*, 32–33. On the Augustinians, see ibid., 77–79, 82–83.

11. On the leprosarium, see Auguste Scherlen, *Topographie von Alt-Colmar* (Colmar, 1922), 401–9; on the hospitals see ibid., 301–19.

12. Lucien Sittler, "Colmar au XVIe siècle," *Annuaire de Colmar*, (1975/76): 27.

13. Livet, ed., *Histoire de Colmar*, 90–91.

14. Jean-Marie Schmitt, "Les sepultures du XVIIIe siècle dans l'ancienne église des Dominicains de Colmar," *Annuaire de Colmar* (1990): 55–66.

15. Livet, ed., *Histoire de Colmar*, 61.

16. For example, there was a long dispute over the payment of civic taxes. AMC, GG 29, a–c.

17. Greyerz, *Late City Reformation*, 27–31.

18. Bernd Moeller has defined the late medieval city as a "sacral corporation." Bernd Moeller, "Imperial Cities and the Reformation," in idem, *Imperial Cities and the Reformation: Three Essays*, ed., and trans. H. C. Erik Middelfort and Mark U. Edwards (Philadelphia, 1972), 41–114, here at 44. Cf. Thomas A. Brady, Jr., "Rites of Autonomy, Rites of Dependence: South German Civic Culture in the Age of Renaissance and Reformation," in Steven Ozment, ed., *Religion and Culture in the Renaissance and Reformation*, Sixteenth Century Essays & Studies, 11 (Kirksville, Mo., 1989), 9–23.

19. Greyerz, *Late City Reformation*, 64–67, 74–90.

20. Ibid., 71–73. On the Reformation in the Württemberg domains in Alsace, see Adam, *Evangelische Kirchengeschichte*, 292–348, esp. 295–303.

21. On Strasbourg, see Weyrauch, *Konfessionelle Krise*. On Colmar, see Greyerz, *Late City Reformation*, 72–73.

22. Greyerz, *Late City Reformation*, 72–73, 94–99, 111–23, 193–96.

23. On medieval citizenship, see Susan Reynolds, *Kingdoms and Communities in Western Europe: 900–1300* (Oxford, 1984), 168–200. For the Imperial cities, see Brady, *Turning Swiss*, 9–15.

24. Antony Black, *Guilds and Civil Society in European Society and Thought from the Twelfth Century to the Present* (Ithaca, 1984), 68–75. See also Rublack, "Political and Social Norms," 24–60.

25. Livet, ed., *Histoire de Colmar*, 36–39; Finsterwalder, ed., *Colmarer Stadtrechte*, no. 34, 36–42.

26. Livet, ed., *Histoire de Colmar*, 54–58; Finsterwalder, ed., *Colmarer Stadtrechte*, no. 116, 141–44.

27. Lucien Sittler characterizes this regime as "democratic." Sittler, "Il y a six siècles: A Colmar en 1358," *Annuaire de Colmar* (1958): 18–27. Recent analyses have challenged his view. Greyerz, *Late City Reformation*, 17–18, esp. n. 31; Weyrauch, "Die politische Führungsgruppe," 220–21.

28. Greyerz, *Late City Reformation*, 21–22. Weyrauch equates the guilds' consolidation with a decline in their influence. Weyrauch, "Die politische Führungsgruppe," 221. The constitution permitted four noble senators and one noble Stettmeister in the regime, but within a decade the nobles ceased to serve. Sittler, "Colmar au XVIe siècle," 20.

29. Greyerz, *Late City Reformation*, 21.

30. The magistrate appointed the city clerk and the court clerk. Ibid., 21; Auguste Scherlen, *Perles d'Alsace* (Colmar, 1933), 3: 30–36.

31. The following paragraphs condense the description in Greyerz, *Late City Reformation*, 20–22.

32. In 1515 there were 122 *Schöffen* in Colmar, 138 in 1546, and 122 in 1622. Ibid., 22 n. 48. These numbers compare with figures of 984 guild members in 1554 and 1,012 guild members in 1619. See Lucien Sittler, "Les corporations et l'organization du travail à Colmar jusqu'au début de XVIIe siècle," in *Artisans et ouvriers d'Alsace*, PSSARE, 9 (Strasbourg, 1965), 47–78, here at 51.

33. Lucien Sittler, "Les bourgeois de Colmar," In *La bourgeoisie alsacienne: Etudes d'histoire sociale*, PSSARE, 5 (Strasbourg, 1967), 21–34, here at 30.

34. Sittler, "Les corporations à Colmar," 51; Henri Fleurent, "Essai sur la démographie et l'épidémiologie de la ville de Colmar," *Bulletin de la Société d'Histoire Naturelle de Colmar* 15 (1920/21): 45–111; Sittler, "Colmar au XVIe siècle," 19.

35. "Ir sollent schweren unnsrem aller genedigisten herren herren N. dem Romischen etc. etc. unserem herren dem Landtvogt, dem Schultheissenn, denn vier meistern, dem Rhat unnd zunfftmeistern und sunderlich dem oberstenmeister gehorsam zesinde, gutter und gerechter dinge unnd die Statt zewarnnen vor allem schaden

sower Ir wussendt oder entpfindent unnd by demselben eydte niemandt inn keyn Veyse zedienen, weder zu Ross noch ze fusse, one verlopnussen unnd willen meyster und Rhats zu Colmar." Quoted in Wertz, ed., *Le livre des bourgeois 1512–1609*, 2.

36. The league originally included Hagenau, Wissembourg, Colmar, Sélestat, Obernai, Rosheim, Kaysersberg, Turckheim, Munster in the valley of St. Gregory, and Mulhouse. When Mulhouse joined the Swiss Confederation in 1515, Landau replaced it in the Decapolis. Lucien Sittler, *La Décapole alsacienne, des origines à la fin du Moyen-Age* (Paris-Strasbourg, 1955).

37. German sources refer to the office as the *Reichslandvogt*, which I have translated as the Imperial Bailiff, cf. Greyerz, *Late City Reformation*, 23; Joseph Becker, *Geschichte der Reichslandvogtei im Elsass: Von ihrer Einrichtung bis zu ihrem Übergang an Frankreich, 1293–1648* (Strasbourg, 1905). When the French assumed authority in Alsace after 1648, they initially maintained the title. In the period after 1680, under the policy of "reunion," they dropped the term "Imperial" and referred to the official as the *Grand Bailli*. I will follow their lead and refer to the official as the Grand Bailiff.

38. Sittler, "Colmar au XVIe siècle," 16–19.

39. Ibid., 13–14.

40. Brady, *Turning Swiss*, 15–34.

41. Bücking, *Johann Rasser*, 25–26; Adam, *Evangelische Kirchengeschichte*, 473–74; Waltz, ed., *Sigmund Billings Kleine Chronik*, 86–88 and 100–101.

42. The Lutheran regimes in Ulm and Strasbourg faced similar problems. For Ulm, see Peter Lang, "Die katholische Minderheit in der protestantischen Reichsstadt Ulm," in Jürgen Sydow, ed., *Bürgerschaft und Kirche* (Sigmaringen, 1980), 89–96. For Strasbourg, see François-Joseph Fuchs, "Les catholiques strasbourgeois de 1529 à 1681," *Archives de l'Eglise d'Alsace* 38 (1975): 141–69.

43. Adam, *Evangelische Kirchengeschichte*, 474.

44. On Colmar's ministerial recruitment, see Greyerz, *Late City Reformation*, 124ff; Bernard Vogler, "Le corps pastoral de Colmar et des environs avant la Guerre de Trente Ans," *Annuaire de Colmar* (1975/76): 121–28. Individual biographies of the Alsatian Protestant ministers and teachers have been compiled in Marie-Joseph Bopp, *Die evangelischen Geistlichen und Theologen in Elsass und Lothringen von der Reformation bis zur Gegenwart*, Genealogie und Landesgeschichte, 1 (Neustadt a. d. Aisch, 1959). Bopp also compiled a list of Colmar's parish ministry and a brief parish history, see idem, *Die evangelischen Gemeinden und Hohen Schulen in Elsass und Lothringen von der Reformation bis zur Gegenwart*, Genealogie und Landesgeschichte, 3 (Neustadt a. d. Aisch, 1963), 270–73. A manuscript list of Colmar's Protestant ministers and teachers exists which includes individuals who do not appear in Bopp's study. BMC, Fonds Chauffour, I CH 79, 2 & 7.

45. On the pressure from Württemberg, see Greyerz, *Late City Reformation*, 133. On conditions in Basel, see idem, "Basels kirchliche und konfessionelle Beziehungen zum Oberrhein im späten 16. und frühen 17. Jahrhundert," in Martin Bircher, Walter Sparen, and Erdmann Weyrauch, eds., *Schweizerisch-deutsche Beziehungen im konfessionellen Zeitalter: Beiträge zur Kulturgeschichte 1580–1650*, Wolfenbütteler Arbeiten zur Barockforschung, 12 (Wiesbaden, 1984), 227–52.

46. On Serinus, see Greyerz, *Late City Reformation*, 127–28; Bopp, *Evangelischen Geistlichen*, 509, no. 4870. On Magnus, see Bopp, *Evangelischen Geistlichen*, 199, no. 1823.

47. Greyerz, *Late City Reformation*, 131ff.

48. Ibid., 134 n. 47.

49. Greyerz has determined that the document's tenets were "compatible with the basic stance of concurrent Lutheran eucharistic theology" but "none was genuinely Lutheran." Ibid., 135–40, here at 140.

50. In a provocative gesture, the Württemberg officials installed Magnus at Horbourg, where he remained through 1590. Bopp, *Evangelischen Geistlichen*, 199, no. 1823.

51. David Hiemeyer, Magnus's successor, initially subscribed to the *Deklarationsschrift* and then spoke out against civic Calvinists. He formed his own private Lutheran assembly and had verbally abused Serinus while drunk. Soon the regime had to release him. Greyerz, *Late City Reformation*, 146–47; Bopp, *Evangelischen Geistlichen*, 241, no. 2243. Two later recruits, Samuel Radspinner and Johann Ernst Fritsch, came to the city with Lutheran pedigrees but were willing to subscribe to the *Deklarationsschrift*. On Radspinner's career, see ibid., 423, no. 4066. On Fritsch's career, see ibid., 168, no. 1505.

52. Cited in Greyerz, *Late City Reformation*, 149 n. 114.

53. On Fritsch's faction, see Greyerz, *Late City Reformation*, 148 n. 109. Hans Strohmeyer had been a magistrate from 1528 to 1543, while at least five Wetzels had served in the sixteenth-century regime. See Lucien Sittler, ed., *Membres du magistrat, conseillers, et maîtres des corporations de Colmar: Listes de 1408–1600*, PAVC, 3 (Colmar: AMC, 1964), 49 and 53. On Barth, see Wertz, ed., *Le livre des bourgeois 1512–1609*, 153, no 1526.

54. On Socinus, see Bopp, *Evangelischen Geistlichen*, 516, no. 4935; Greyerz, *Late City Reformation*, 141–51, 155–56.

55. In 1628 the pastor, Matthias Könen, fled to Basel and assumed a post as pastor in the Swiss town of Biel. Bopp, *Evangelischen Geistlichen*, 302, no. 2851. Colmar's three deacons, Elias Pellitarius, Goerg Hopf, and Jacob Stephani, all settled in posts in the Bernese countryside. See ibid., 403, no. 3887; 254, no. 2379; and 529, no. 5052.

56. Greyerz, *Late City Reformation*, 35–36, 80–81; Adam, *Evangelische Kirchengeschichte*, 475.

57. Greyerz, *Late City Reformation*, 157. On Munster's ordinance, see Adam, *Evangelische Kirchengeschichte*, 245.

58. The court included the Obristmeister, two Stettmeisters, two ministers, two councilors, and two citizens. Greyerz, *Late City Reformation*, 157–59. On the marriage courts in nearby Basel, see Thomas Max Safley, "To Preserve the Marital State: The Basler Ehegericht, 1550–1592," *Journal of Family History* 7 (Summer 1982): 162–79.

59. Cited in Jacques Betz, *L'Eglise protestante de Saint-Mathieu de Colmar et sa paroisse* (Strasbourg, 1971), 43.

60. Weyrauch, "Die politische Führungsgruppe," 218–24; Greyerz, *Late City Reformation*, 114–17.

61. The following analysis is drawn from published lists of Colmar's regime members. Sittler, ed., *Membres du magistrat, 1408–1600*, 19–56; Wertz, ed., *Membres du magistrat, 1601–1700*, 3–32.

62. Greyerz, *Late City Reformation*, 20.

63. For example, a list of members in the society *zum Waagkeller*, compiled in 1579, included all the members of the current magistrate and seven future colleagues: Linck, Dürninger, Mattern Espach, Kriegelstein, Martin Birr, Buob, and Niclaus Schultheiss. AMC, HH 2, 7. See also Greyerz, *Late City Reformation*, 14–16; Eugène Waldner, "La distillation et le commerce de l'eau-de-vie à Colmar au seizième et au dix-septième siècle," *Bulletin du Musée Historique de Mulhouse* (1891): 3–12.

64. Sittler, ed., *Membres du magistrat, 1408–1600*, 37.
65. Bücking, *Johann Rasser*, 25–26.
66. Greyerz, *Late City Reformation*, 115–16.
67. Linck was a nobleman who served in many critical diplomatic posts for Colmar and had married into the noble and Protestant Kesselring family. See ibid., 115.
68. Dürninger came from a family of coopers which had already supplied the regime with three members. Mattern Espach's ancestors had served in the fifteenth-century government, while Kriegelstein came from a powerful sixteenth-century merchant family. See Sittler, ed., *Membres de magistrat 1408–1600*, 25, 26, and 37.
69. On 15 January 1602 Ortlieb married Gertrud, the daughter of Martin Schilling, the *Obristschreiber* of Hagenau. Ortlieb's sister, Anna, married Anton Burger on 17 August of the same year. Joseph Glaser's first wife had been the daughter of a guildsman, Veltin Brunner (29 October 1599). His second wife was Esther, the daughter of Anton Burger (22 January 1627). Elias Wetzel, who clearly dominated this cohort, married one son, Samuel, to the daughter of Anton Schott, the city clerk (1 September 1617) and another, Christoph, to the daughter of Martin Birr (5 November 1627).
70. Weyrauch, "Die politische Führungsgruppe," 223. For a full list of householders, see AMC, CC 152, 1600.
71. Greyerz bases the confessional assessment of the 1585 regime on a report in the ADHR, 4 G, 11 (n. d. [December 1585]). Cited in Greyerz, *Late City Reformation*, 155 n. 141.
72. On the Alsatian territories, see Paul Stinzi, "Die Habsburger im Elsaß," in Friedrich Metz, ed., *Vorderösterreich: Eine geschichtliche Landeskunde* (Freiburg, 1976 [1959]), 505–64; Georges Bischoff, *Gouvernés et gouvernants en Haute-Alsace à l'époque autrichienne*, PSSARE, 20 (Strasbourg, 1982).
73. Geoffrey Parker, *The Thirty Years' War* (London, 1987 [1984]), 38–61; R. J. W. Evans, *The Making of the Habsburg Monarchy, 1550–1700: An Interpretation* (Oxford, 1979), 62–77.
74. Jean-Pierre Kintz, "XVIIe siècle: Du Saint Empire au royaume de France," in *Histoire de Strasbourg des origines à nos jours* (Strasbourg, 1980), 3: 54–57; Rodolphe Reuss, *L'Alsace au dix-septième siècle: Tableau géographique, historique, politique et économique* (Paris: 1897–98), 1: 52–56.
75. Reuss, *L'Alsace*, 1: 59–62.
76. The Austrian branch of the Habsburg family signed the treaty of Oñate on 20 March 1617 with their Spanish cousins, which would have transferred the Austrian holdings in Alsace to Spain. See Reuss, *L'Alsace*, 1: 50; Livet, *L'intendance*, 24–25; Wolfgang Hans Stein, 'Protection Royale': Eine Untersuchung zu den Protektionsverhältnissen im Elsass zur Zeit Richelieus, 1622–1643, SVENGEV, 9 (Münster, 1978), 33–43.
77. Parker, *The Thirty Years' War*, 94–102. On Hagenau, see André Marcel Burg, "Patrizier und andere städtische Führungsschichten in Hagenau," in Hellmuth Rössler, ed., *Deutsches Patriziat, 1430–1740*, Schriften zur Problematik der deutschen Führungsschichten in der Neuzeit, 3 (Limburg/Lahn, 1968), 353–75, here at 362–64. Hagenau's Reformation "from above" had never taken root in the commons. Greyerz, *Late City Reformation*, 195–96.
78. Adam, *Evangelische Kirchengeschichte*, 477–78.
79. Ibid., 478.
80. Lorentz Espach in his chronicle describes it thus: "Mittwoch de 22 Mertz Nauen Kalender Anno 1628 Jar ist der allten rot allhie in der stat Collmar abgestanten worten beis auf 8 rot herren aus den alten rot ... und hat der

alte rot abgeschworen und ist der nauen Rot in dem dag eingesetz worten."
ADHR, 4 G, 12, fol. 2r.

81. Finsterwalder, ed., *Colmarer Stadtrechte*, no. 209, 264–65.

82. "Colmar," in Pierre Delattre, ed., *Les établissements de Jesuites en France depuis quatre siècles* (Wetterin, 1950), 1: cols. 1503–4.

83. Philippe Mieg, "Les réfugiés colmariens à Mulhouse au temps de la Contre-Réforme (1628–1632)," *Annuaire de Colmar* (1950): 45–56.

84. AMC, BB 45, 1623–31, pp. 547–50. See also Adam, *Evangelische Kirchengeschichte*, 483.

85. Parker, *The Thirty Years' War*, 121–31.

86. Adam, *Evangelische Kirchengeschichte*, 483.

87. X(avier) Mossmann, "Matériaux pour servir à l'histoire de la Guerre de Trente Ans tirés des archives de Colmar," *RA* 26 (1876): 313–18.

88. Mieg, "Les réfugiés colmariens," 48–52.

89. Mossmann, "Matériaux," 554–59.

90. Hans Peter Dietrich's background remains obscure, for he does not appear in the citizen register, though he is listed among the members of *zur Treue* in 1619. See AMC, HH 27, 21, 1v. He did not marry in Colmar, but he brought a daughter to be baptized at St. Martin's in 1617. See AMC, GG 188, Registres des baptêmes catholiques 1603–1650, February 1617. In 1630 he was taxed on wealth assessed at 300 florins, which placed him among the city's poorer householders. By 1640 his assessment had jumped to the substantial sum of 1,200 florins.

91. Wertz, ed., *Membres du magistrat, 1601–1700*, 15–33.

92. Reuss, *L'Alsace*, 1: 76–77.

93. Mossmann's chief source for these critical days is an anonymous journal. "Matériaux," 556–58.

94. Mossmann, "Matériaux," 571–72. See also AMC, BB 45, 1632–1636, pp. 51–57.

95. The figures on the number of dead are questionable. Goehlinger offers the figures without a footnote. Goehlinger, *Chapitre*, 319–20. Mossmann describes the riots but does not list any deaths. Mossmann, "Matériaux," 574–76.

96. Finsterwalder, ed., *Colmarer Stadtrechte*, no. 210, 265–66.

97. The Swedes believed that the Jesuits had mined the church. "Colmar," *Les établissements*, 1: col. 1504.

98. The new ministers included the pastor Jodocus Haas, a Strasbourg native, who had served in several parishes around Strasbourg and as a deacon at the cathedral at Strasbourg prior to his appointment at Colmar. The first deacon, Joachim Klein, was a native of Leipzig, who had earned his master's degree at Strasbourg. Klein's had previously served as chaplain with the Swedish army that besieged Colmar. The second deacon, Matthias Bardellar, had also studied at Strasbourg and served as a Swedish chaplain. Bopp, *Evangelischen Geistlichen*, 206, no. 1877; 292, no. 2758; and 38, no. 180.

99. On Schmitt's complaint, see Greyerz, "Basels kirchliche und konfessionelle Beziehungen," 227. On Güntzer's activities, see Mieg, "Les tribulations d'Augustin Guntzer," 48–65, here at 63.

100. Mieg, "Les réfugiés colmariens," 53.

101. Mieg, "Les tribulations d'Augustin Guntzer," 63–64.

102. Xavier Mossmann first described the "revolution of 1627" more than a century ago. Mossmann, "Matériaux" (1877): 446. The disruptive political image of Colmar's Counter-Reformation has informed the literature ever since. Livet, ed., *Histoire de Colmar*, 103.

103. Andreas Sitter was born in Horbourg. George Gsell, Matthis Hötzelbach, Andreas Sybert, Matthaus Ritzenthaler, Jacob Blanck, Hans Ulmer, Hans Leiterer, Hans Schindolph, and the Catholic Georg Sutor were native Colmarians. Wertz, ed., *Membres du magistrat, 1601–1700*, 15–31. See also Greyerz, *Late City Reformation*, 15, 116–17.

104. On the destinations of the refugees, see Raymond Oberlé, *La république de Mulhouse pendant la Guerre de Trente Ans*, Collection de l'Institut des Hautes Etudes Alsaciennes, 20 (Paris, 1965), 254–63; Mieg, "Les réfugiés colmariens," 51–52; Strittmatter, *Die Stadt Basel*, 61–78; and Scherlen, *Perles d'Alsace*, 3: 307. See also Edouard Metzenthin, "Anciennes familles colmariennes: Les Roettlin et leur origine," *Annuaire de Colmar* (1953): 58–68. See also Christian Wolff, "Les débuts de la famille Schneider à Colmar," *Annuaire de Colmar* (1957): 53–59. Claude Sysson moved to Mulhouse and continued his business enterprises in his new city. Mieg, "Les réfugiés colmariens," 51–52.

105. The Protestant officials in the regime of 1630 included Andreas Meder and Jacob Blanck in the senate and the guildmasters Georg Willig, Joseph Hecker, Andreas Sitter, Matthis Ryss, Hans Schindolph, Lorentz Froschesser, and Daniel Brunner. Wertz, ed., *Membres du magistrat, 1601–1700*, 15–31.

106. Matthis Göcklin, Thomann Göcklin, Hans Jacob Graff, Mathias Güntzer, Matthis Hötzelbach, Hans Jacob Lamprecht, Matthias Ritzenthaler, Matthaeus Ryss, and Hans Jacob Schlachter. Ibid.

107. Four of the five magistrates in 1648 had been elected members of the new regime of 1633. Wertz, ed., *Membres du magistrat, 1601–1700*, 7. The fifth, Johann Heinrich Mogg, had served as the city clerk in 1633. Scherlen, *Perles d'Alsace*, 3: 34.

108. Braeuner, "La préréforme à Colmar (1522–1575)," 55–70. For an overview of the historiography of Colmar's Reformation, see Greyerz, *Late City Reformation*, 8–10.

109. Bücking, *Johann Rasser*, 18–35.

110. Weyrauch, "Die politische Führungsgruppe," 215–34.

111. Greyerz, *Late City Reformation*, 163–69.

112. AMC, GG 173, 13.

2

Confessionalization and the Community, 1575–1648

On Sunday morning, 15 May 1575, the bells of two churches beckoned the Colmarians to worship. Neighbors, friends, relatives, and coworkers passed each other in the streets headed for different church doors and different sacral communities less than fifty yards apart. The morning passed without incident; and except for the brief interim of the Imperial Counter-Reformation, Colmar would be a bi-confessional city, that is, a city which officially recognized two faiths. The settlement rested on the regime's irenic policies, plotted out in the effort to preserve civic peace and their own authority despite political pressure from neighboring powers. Whether the leaders realized it or not, bi-confessionalism severed for good the medieval connections between the city's spiritual and political order.[1]

The Protestant leaders, who had introduced the movement, defended their action on the basis of the city's Imperial liberties, and their toleration of Colmar's Catholics was also political. The city formed the central market-place for a confessionally divided region, and those divisions naturally penetrated into Colmar's guildhalls and workshops. In 1575 the neighboring Austrian villages had barely felt the first stirring of Catholic Reformation, while in the Württemberg lordship of Horbourg-Riquewihr, a grey blanket of Protestantism covered over shadings of belief and practice.[2] In the 1580s Colmar's leaders had room to maneuver, and its citizens had time to listen to the Protestant preachers or to rediscover a changing Catholic piety. By 1600 the Catholic revival within the Austrian domains, a more dogmatic Lutheranism in Horbourg-Riquewihr, and the growth of Rhenish Calvinism had hardened the lines in the region's confessional topography and within Colmar, where the Protestants moved first. In the decade after 1600, they openly aligned with the Reformed confession. In the 1620s civic Catholics began an internal revival, which culminated in the arrival of the Imperial commission. Just the same, the confessional and political agendas for both movements came from the outside and only loosely fitted the needs of the city's confessional parties. Throughout, civic leaders resisted confessional

49

conformity because they recognized popular resentment against it. Confessional choices divided neighbors and guildsmen, and sometimes families. Once the confessional groups had formed, they would be resistant to any pressure which might undermine their place in the city. Bi-confessionalism did not exacerbate social and economic differences in Colmar; it reflected differences that were well established before 1575.

I. THE CITY AND ITS HINTERLAND

In the mid-sixteenth century, the humanist topographer Sebastian Münster described Colmar as what modern historians call an *Ackerbürgerstadt*, a city shaped by its agricultural wealth:

> The city rests upon very fruitful soil, for it grows grapes and grain on all sides and possesses especially good grain resources. It lies almost in the middle of Alsace, one league from Kaysersberg, Ammerschwihr, Riquewihr, and Ribeauvillé, where the best wine in Alsace is produced. It is watered by several nearby streams, the Lauch, Thur, Fecht, Ill and more, some of which flow through the city and some nearby, which makes the soil extremely fruitful.[3]

Later observers joined Münster in emphasizing the city's agricultural base and rural setting,[4] and when Colmarians "put their world in order," they included the countryside.[5] In 1700 the city's Lutheran pastor, Niclaus Klein, began his chronicle by claiming that Colmar ought to be referred to as the "fertile paradise of Upper Alsace," a peculiar boast for a town of 10,000.[6] Early modern Colmarians saw the land as an integral part of the town, and they invested heavily in vineyards, fields, and pastures within civic territory and in the domains of neighboring villages.[7]

Colmar was a substantial urban center with significant fortifications, numerous ecclesiastical complexes, guildhalls, and open markets. As a chief market for a relatively extensive region with rich agricultural and viticultural resources, its early modern economy had been shaped by its setting. Located close to the western slope of the broad U-shaped valley of the Upper Rhine (see map 2.1), Colmar sat on a shelf of land laced by small streams which descended from the south and west and emptied into the Ill River just north of the city. From this confluence, called the Ladhof, Colmar's merchants shipped their products in shallow boats northward to Strasbourg, where the Ill joined the Rhine and connected Colmar's merchants with the Rhenish urban network.[8] One overland route to the south carried commerce to Basel, and another, to the southwest through the Burgundian Gate, reached the French-speaking towns of the Rhône Valley. The Austrian domains in Upper Alsace straddled all three thoroughfares, which made civic merchants extremely sensitive to Austrian political pressure.

West of the city, rolling foothills gave way to a spine of heavily wooded ridges, known as the Vosges, which paralleled the Rhine's north-south axis, rising more than 3,000 feet. Though cut by several narrow valleys, the Vosges

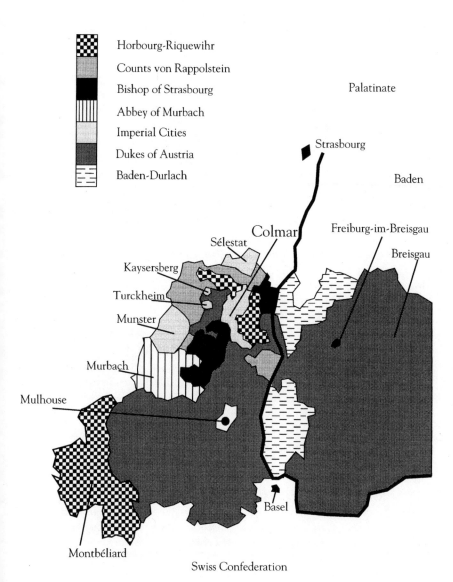

Horbourg-Riquewihr
Counts von Rappolstein
Bishop of Strasbourg
Abbey of Murbach
Imperial Cities
Dukes of Austria
Baden-Durlach

Palatinate

Strasbourg

Baden

Colmar

Sélestat

Freiburg-im-Breisgau

Breisgau

Kaysersberg

Turckheim

Munster

Murbach

Mulhouse

Basel

Montbéliard

Swiss Confederation

MAP 2.1   TERRITORIES IN THE UPPER RHINE VALLEY

limited contact with Lorraine and France. Late sixteenth-century Colmar was a Rhenish town, and the bulk of its economic and cultural ties followed the trade routes of the Rhine corridor, northward to the Low Countries and southward to Switzerland and on through the Alpine passes to Italy.[9] The light, stony soils in the foothills of the Vosges were ideal for grape cultivation, which was further enhanced by the region's dry climate. The best vineyards lay in the neighboring lordships or the tiny imperial cities of Turckheim and Kaysersberg. Only the western fringe of civic territory, an area known as the Harth, produced quality wines, though Colmarians cultivated grapes in less favorable soils.[10]

Colmar's civic territory, its *Bann*, covered more than 16,000 acres, mostly north of the city.[11] In its northwest corner, the soils were too light and stony for agriculture but were ideal for grazing cattle and horses in the pastures, while pigs rooted about in the hardwood forest called the Niederwald.[12] To the northeast, heavier soils of the Rieds supported the three-field rotation, though the best farmland lay to the west and southwest towards Wintzenheim and Eguisheim. Immediately south and east of the city walls, an alluvial pan, called the Au, formed by the numerous streams feeding the Ill, supported vegetable gardens.[13]

During the sixteenth century, Colmar expanded its territory and acquired the rights over several ecclesiastical properties scattered in and outside the *Bann*. In 1536 the city purchased the lordship of Heiligkreuz (Sainte-Croix), which included the villages of Nambsheim and Logelheim and the small fortified town of Sainte-Croix-en-Plaine. During the ensuing decades, as many of the religious orders consolidated their houses because of declining membership, the civic regime acquired several ecclesiastical properties.[14] The regime, however, did not appear to have engaged in the systematic territorial expansion pursued by nearby Freiburg-im-Breisgau, perhaps because the consolidated Austrian and Württemberg lordships restricted expansion.[15]

A majority of Colmar's sixteenth-century citizens and a declining but significant minority of its seventeenth-century citizens were members of one of the three agricultural guilds: *Rebleute*, *Ackerleute*, or *zum Haspel* (see table 2.1). Many others fabricated barrels for production of wine and its byproducts, vinegar and brandy, or supplied handicrafts for neighboring villagers. The city was not a prominent cloth town, and the weavers' guild, *zum Adler*, was among the smallest.[16] Colmar was essentially a central market for regional agricultural production, but it was not an overgrown village. Its craftsmen produced for urban as well as rural needs, worked in small shops run by masters, and experienced the tensions common in early modern guild life.[17] Colmar's merchants exchanged goods in distant Rhenish markets and welcomed buyers from all over the German-speaking world at the city's quarterly fairs. In early modern Colmar economic interests were diverse and entangled, as Colmarians confronted each other both as

TABLE 2.1
Guild Membership by Trade, Sixteenth and Seventeenth Centuries

ZUR TREUE
merchants, tailors, pursers, rope makers, drapers, glaziers, apothecaries, retailers, spice merchants

ZUM RIESEN
innkeepers, coopers, barbers, surgeons, writers, beer brewers, vat makers, musicians

ACKERLEUTE
peasants, carters

ZUM HASPEL
gardeners, foresters

REBLEUTE
vineyard workers

ZUM LÖWEN
butchers, fishermen, boatmen, bathhouse keepers

ZUM KRÄNZCHEN
bakers, millers, second-hand retailers

ZUM ADLER
weavers, furriers, hat makers

ZUM HOLDERBAUM
wheelwrights, carpenters, armorers, locksmiths, brick makers, moneyers, goldsmiths, clock makers, joiners, masons, potters

ZUM WOHLLEBEN
tanners, shoemakers, saddlers

Guildmembers, 16th and 17th Centuries

GUILD	EARLY 16th C. (no.)	(%)	1554 (no.)	(%)	1619 (no.)	(%)	1580–1630 (no.)	(%)
Treue	78	8.2	96	9.8	117	11.6	153	14.7
Riesen	62	6.5	65	6.6	105	10.4	119	11.4
Ackerleute	167	17.4	162	16.5	143	14.1	117	11.2
Haspel	126	13.1	152	15.5	66	6.5	47	4.5
Rebleute	203	21.2	222	22.6	190	18.8	157	15.0
Löwen	54	5.7	50	5.1	49	4.8	55	5.3
Kränzchen	54	5.7	51	5.2	91	9.0	101	9.7
Adler	58	6.1	50	5.1	64	6.3	72	6.9
Holderbaum	100	10.5	98	10.0	131	13.0	146	14.0
Wohlleben	53	5.6	55	5.6	56	5.5	77	7.4
Total	955	100.0	1,001	100.0	1,012	100.0	1,044	100.0

Note: The lists are drawn from the known occupations identified in the data base for these guilds and from Sittler, "Les corporations à Colmar," 50–51.

producers and as consumers. Moreover, the tensions between peasants and landlords, between artisans and merchants, and between the economic needs of the town and the countryside were often fought out within the city walls.

Most of Colmar's guilds represented several crafts, which were not always related in terms of production. For example, *zum Riesen* incorporated artisans associated with the processing and distribution of wine, but it also welcomed writers, musicians, and barbers. The crafts zealously guarded their autonomy within the guilds. Craftsmen elected separate governing councils, controlled access to membership, formed distinct confraternities, and supervised their own journeymen and apprentices.[18] Within Colmar's agricultural guilds, *Ackerleute*, *zum Haspel*, and *Rebleute*, the division of labor and status differed sharply from those in the city's craft guilds. Over the centuries the land in Upper Alsace had fragmented into tiny fields or vineyards, most of which were owned by large ecclesiastical houses, or noble or patrician families. In grain production, the tenant farmers (*Meyer*) held long-term lease rights to the land and only those who owned or leased enough land to meet the entry fee of one florin could join the guild. Resident and nonresident laborers, who met the intense seasonal demand for casual labor, did not belong to the guild, and the civic regime, rather than the guild, regulated their work and wages.[19] Meanwhile, the profitability of smaller vineyards and garden plots tended to allow access to guild membership in *zum Haspel* and *Rebleute* for middling tenants.

In the sixteenth and early seventeenth centuries, rising prices and shifting trade patterns altered the structure and size of Colmar's guilds. The data for guild membership in table 2.1 span a century, from the peasants' war to the Counter-Reformation.[20] The data for the first three pairs of columns are compiled from lists of all guildsmen, while the data for the fourth pair of columns note only those who are inscribed in the citizen registers between 1580 and 1630. The smaller guilds, *zum Löwen*, *zum Wohlleben*, and *zum Adler*, experienced little change in size throughout the era, though a higher percentage of *zum Wohlleben*'s members purchased citizenship. *Zum Holderbaum* grew slightly between 1554 and 1619, but it is unclear whether this reflected the extensive work on Colmar's fortifications or an expansion in the metal trades in relation to the mining industry in the nearby Leberthal.[21]

Among the other guilds, however, the century saw significant shifts as the agricultural guilds experienced a sharp decline in membership. In 1554 they accounted for over 53.5% (536 of 1,001) of Colmar's guildsmen, but by 1619 their share had fallen to 39.4% (399 of 1,012). The decline in agricultural guildsmen was even more dramatic in the citizen registers, where after 1580 they account for only 30.1% (321 out of 1,044). The price revolution, which affected the entire region, pinched the resources of the rural smallholder and tenant, and in Colmar land tenancy or ownership were the means of access to guild membership.[22] Though civic territory had grown through the purchase of ecclesiastical properties and the lordship of Sainte-Croix-en-Plaine, by the early seventeenth century, there were fewer tenant farmers in the city. Based on lists for 1597 and 1616, the leaseholds were controlled by thirty men, but there are no comparable lists for the early sixteenth century.[23] Furthermore, even among the vineyard workers and gardeners there were fewer guildmembers. The changes within these guilds apparently reflected a decline in the living conditions among the agricultural work force.[24]

While Colmar's late sixteenth-century agricultural guilds grew smaller, several other guilds dramatically increased their membership. *Zum Riesen*, whose tradesmen produced and distributed wine, brandy, and vinegar, swelled by over 60% between 1554 and 1619; and its growth carried over to the citizen registers. The millers and bakers in *zum Kränzchen* expanded by over 78% between 1554 and 1619, and many of its new members purchased citizenship. A fuller analysis of the forces behind these shifts awaits a detailed study of the regional economy. Nevertheless, two points are clear. In the decades between Colmar's late Reformation and the Thirty Years' War, the city expanded its role as a processing center for the products of its agricultural hinterland. At the same time, the city's own agricultural guilds shrank, as fewer men could afford the entry fee.

Finally, *zur Treue*, which included the city's merchants and several crafts, also experienced a sharp growth between 1554 and 1619. Colmar's merchants exported brandy and wine, and in the early seventeenth century a cluster of immigrant merchants, men such as Clade Sysson, Gideon Sarazin, and Frantz Wibert, settled in Colmar to direct a burgeoning trade in French cloth and Mediterranean spices for regional distribution. Their presence generated disputes over market privileges and forestalling; but as we will see, the new merchant elite connected Colmar to a much broader urban network and brought prosperity and demographic growth to the city.[25] What were the conditions in Colmar on the eve of the Thirty Years' War, and what was the demographic impact of the war and Counter-Reformation?

II. COLMAR'S DEMOGRAPHY

In the early modern period, Colmar's walls sheltered between 5,000 and 10,000 people. Civic officials attempted their first censuses only in the late seventeenth century, and, unfortunately, neither parish systematically recorded deaths before the 1680s. Thus the civic tax (*Gewerff*) registers form the one serial source which provides a rough measure of demographic change. First compiled in 1495, and annually since the late sixteenth century, they identified all taxable householders.[26] Depending on multipliers used per household, scholars have estimated Colmar's late fifteenth-century population at anywhere from 3,489 to 7,639. Most favor a figure closer to but less than 7,000.[27] Nevertheless, estimating overall population from householders is problematical, for the civic population included hundreds of apprentices, journeymen, and casual laborers, who do not appear in the tax rolls. Their numbers fluctuated seasonally based on shifting demands for labor and could change dramatically under the strains of economic and political crisis. Refugees from the neighboring villages and garrisoned troops swelled the town's population, and their marriages seasoned the parish registers with unusual names from exotic places. Thus any population estimate drawn solely from the tax or parish registers must be tentative. Nevertheless, the records suggest that Colmar's population grew slowly in the sixteenth century but never exceeded 7,000 residents, which placed it among the middling towns of the empire.[28]

In the late seventeenth century, French administrators conducted several population surveys. In 1683 Colmar possessed 930 families.[29] The population apparently grew in the following decades, for in 1697 the number of households had increased to 1,078 and contained 7,142 souls.[30] By July of 1709, the city's population had mushroomed to 9,023.[31] Another survey, apparently for 1718 but perhaps for later in the century, identified 1,877 households.[32] These censuses cannot be treated comparatively because the royal officials sought different information and measured the population differently. The census of 1697 suggests a multiplier of 6.625 to calculate total population from the number of households, and using this multiplier, the population derived from the household census for 1683 would number 6,161, which implies that at the outset of Bourbon rule Colmar was less populous than a century before. From 1683 the city's population grew to perhaps 12,435 by 1718.[33] Based on these estimates, under French lordship Colmar's population probably doubled within two generations!

How do these official figures compare with data drawn from the *Gewerff* registers? If the late seventeenth-century and early eighteenth-century data is comparable, what if any changes do the tax registers demarcate for the period before 1683 (see graphs 2.1 and 2.2)? The registers distinguish male and female householders, and I have tabulated the totals for both groups. The tax assessors identified 938 householders in 1680, which is very close to the census total of 930 for 1683. The census of 1697 counted 1,078 households, which is lower than the 1,132 taxable householders recorded in 1690, but the difference could be explained by depopulation produced by the war of the League of Augsburg and the famines of 1693 and 1695. In 1702 the tax assessors noted 1,232 households. Here the massive influx of refugees from the French-controlled Breisgau following the Peace of Ryswick may explain the sudden rise within five years. The unusually high census estimate of 1718 noted 1,223 citizen and 516 *habitans* households. The combined total of 1,739 far exceeds the 1,407 taxpayers recorded in 1720, but the census figure of 1,223 citizen households is very close to the 1,258 male householders taxed in 1720. As in Strasbourg, French rule brought a growing population of privileged wealthy residents and poor laborers, who

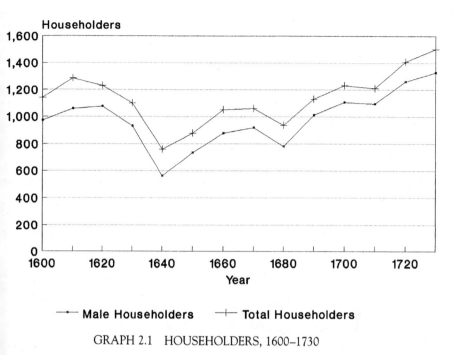

GRAPH 2.1   HOUSEHOLDERS, 1600–1730

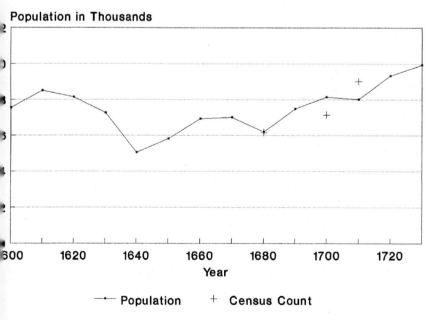

GRAPH 2.2   POPULATION ESTIMATES, 1600–1730

do not appear in the tax registers.[34] Furthermore, the tax registers did not record the *habitans* householders, and because of this they provide a less reliable measurement of overall demographic change.

Official census figures closely matched the tax rolls in the 1680s, and it is likely that the official multiplier used in 1697 can be applied to the tax rolls for the early seventeenth century. From the registers, we can distinguish three eras of demographic change in early modern Colmar: first, a slow then dramatic decline in population from a peak of more than 8,000 in 1610 down to just over 5,000 in 1640; second, a gradual recovery from the dramatic depopulation of the late 1630s; and finally, a boom under French lordship, which pushed the city's limits beyond its old walls. For the moment we will focus on conditions in the early seventeenth century.

If we employ the multiplier of 1697, the city contained 7,552 people in 1600, which is slightly higher than the 7,000 favored by most historical demographers. Colmar grew rapidly in the first decade of the seventeenth century to over 8,500 inhabitants, despite the fact that civic chroniclers claimed that the plague, which had swept through Alsace, had struck Colmar severely between 1609 and 1611.[35] The city's parish registers recorded a tremendous rise in marriages in these years as widows and widowers sought to rebuild broken families. Between 1600 and 1610, the Protestant community celebrated an average of 44 weddings each year, but in 1611, 146 Protestant couples exchanged marital vows. Parish records for the Catholic community are incomplete; but for the years prior to 1611, the highest number of inscribed marriages at St. Martin's was 32. In 1611 the canons recorded 94 unions.[36] The tax assessors in 1610 identified 229 households, nearly one in five, headed by widows. Just the same, there were more male householders in 1610 than in 1600 (1,057 to 972), and by 1620 the number of male householders had reached its seventeenth-century peak of 1,074, while the number of female householders (155) had fallen back to a more normal 12%.[37] Despite the plague, economic opportunity apparently attracted immigrants to Colmar and encouraged local sons and daughters to stay. In 1620 the Thirty Years' War had yet to reach Alsace, and Colmar's population stood at more than 8,000, which was close to its demographic limit within the old walls. Colmar had sixty-five empty houses in 1590, but only twenty-three in 1620.[38]

Within a decade, the war and the Counter-Reformation had reduced total householders by over 10% and males by over 13% to below the levels of 1600. The confessional shifts of 1627–33, however, were not nearly as devastating as the prolonged siege of nearby Breisach between 1637 and 1639. Pillaging troops requisitioned grain and livestock, and severe famine followed. By 1640 Colmar was a half-empty town whose population had probably fallen to around 5,000, or slightly more than 60% of the prewar peak, with widows heading one in four households.[39]

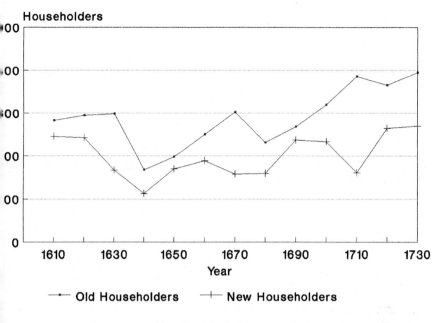

GRAPH 2.3   OLD/NEW HOUSEHOLDERS, 1600–1730

Between 1620 and 1640 the number of male householders declined by nearly half, (1,074 to 561), but the city was not empty. The tax registers do not record the hundreds of refugees from the city's hinterland, whose baptisms and marriages sustain the parish registers but who returned to the their villages as soon as the fighting ended.[40] The decline of taxable household-ers marked the long-term demographic impact of the war much more clearly than the parish registers. In 1640 the tax assessors identified 132 empty houses, many of which were uninhabitable (*eingefallen*).[41]

Immigration, emigration, death, and maturation all affect population es-timates based on adult householders, and graph 2.3 plots the rate of sur-vival among male householders from decade to decade and the degree to which newcomers, either sons of established householders or immigrants, affected population shifts. On the average only 60% of the male house-holders survived from decade to decade, which indicates a relatively rapid turnover. Only a minority of Colmar's householders survived for more than a generation, and newcomers stepped in quickly to pursue career opportuni-ies. On average, more than 40% of the male householders had paid taxes less than ten years. Aggregate population rose and fell, but households were constantly turning over.

The plague of 1609–11 reduced the percentage of surviving householders for both 1610 (58.1%) and 1620 (55.7%) to below the overall average, but for both those years the number of newcomers, 492 in 1610 and 485 in 1620, was the highest for the century. In 1620 the war was still far away at the gates of Prague. By 1630, though the war had not yet come to Upper Alsace, the Counter-Reformation had left its mark. The Imperial commissioners' demand that Protestants emigrate does not appear to have affected long-time householders, but it dramatically reduced the influx of new householders, which fell to 344, a decline of 31%. The Counter-Reformation discouraged Protestant immigrants, and perhaps the younger Protestant Colmarians, who had established households after 1620, were more likely to become confessional refugees than their elders. The murderous decade of the 1630s deepened the demographic crisis, with surviving householders falling 30% from 597 to 418 and newcomers falling 57% from 334 to 144. The late 1630s produced a true demographic crisis, which both depopulated the city and discouraged immigrants, and by 1650 of the 1,074 male householders in 1620 less than 10% (106) remained.[42] It would take Colmar several decades to recover.

Even in the best of times, Colmar's demographic survival depended on a steady influx of new householders, men such as the leader of Colmar's Reformed community after 1633, Augustin Güntzer, who was born in the Lower Alsatian town of Obernai. Güntzer travelled all over Europe to learn his trade as a tinsmith and settled at Colmar in 1623 because, in his own words, he could practice his faith freely there. Although he doesn't appear in the citizen registers, he claimed to have purchased citizenship for 8 florins and entered the guild *zum Holderbaum*. He married Marie Glöcklin, the widow of Martin Schick, and she introduced him to a circle of important Protestant families: the Buobs, Sandherrs, Glöcklins, and Birrs.[43] Güntzer was one of hundreds of young men who immigrated into Colmar in the late sixteenth and early seventeenth centuries. For the latter sixteenth century, Lucien Sittler has tabulated their geographic origins. Of the 922 identifiable cases, 385 (41.8%) were born in Colmar, 207 (22.5%) migrated from the villages of Alsace, and 330 (35.4%) came to the city from other regions. Late sixteenth-century Colmar, like most early modern cities, relied heavily on immigration to replenish its population.[44]

Based on the data available in Colmar's parish registers, I have analyzed the geographic origins for Colmar's early-seventeenth-century male householders and their wives (see table 2.2). In all I have identified origins for just over 41% of the male householders, of whom nearly 56% originated in Colmar. Among the immigrants 15.7% came from the towns and villages of Alsace, primarily the villages immediately surrounding Colmar, and another 15.8% came from the towns and villages of southwestern Germany. A handful of more distant immigrants settled in the city. The Swiss Confederation provided roughly as many new householders as Lower Alsace, while very few men were willing to cross the linguistic barrier formed by the Vosges to seek their fortune in Colmar. Most of Colmar's taxpayers came from estab-

TABLE 2.2
Origins of Men and Women, 1575–1630

PLACE OF ORIGIN	MALES (no.)	(%)	FEMALES (no.)	(%)
Colmar	590	55.8	427	54.8
Upper Alsace	136	12.9	185	23.7
Lower Alsace	29	2.8	22	2.8
Southwest Germany				
Breisgau	37		26	
Baden	8		3	
Württemberg	37	15.8	7	10.4
Swabia/Bodensee	67		38	
Bavaria	18		7	
Rhineland/Palatinate	19	1.8	2	0.3
Central Germany				
Hesse	5		—	
Hohenlohe	2	2.5	—	0.1
Thuringia	5		1	
Franconia	14		—	
Northern Germany				
Brandenburg-Prussia	2		—	
Saxony	2	0.5	1	0.1
Schleswig	1		—	
Eastern Regions				
Silesia, Moravia,				
Hungary, Poland,	5	0.5	3	0.4
Bohemia				
Switzerland	28	2.6	23	3.0
Italy	1	0.1	—	—
Western Francophone				
France/Lorraine	4		11	
Montbéliard	—	0.4	2	1.7
Region Unknown	47	4.5	21	2.7
Total Known	1,057		779	
Total Cases	2,535	41.7	1,962	39.7

lished civic families and the surrounding villages, and the early seventeenth-century immigration followed the sixteenth-century pattern discerned by Sittler.

Among the brides who appear in the parish registers, the fragmentary data suggest that the rate of immigration was roughly the same for women as for men, and by far the bulk of Colmar's female immigrants came from the immediate hinterland. More than three-quarters of the housewives whose origins are known were either native born or from Upper Alsace. The Breisgau, Lower Alsace, and Switzerland provided a further 10%, though a few women migrated from as far away as Swabia or Lorraine to marry at Colmar.

After 1575 Colmar was a bi-confessional town. What if any differences existed between the two confessional communities in their ability to recruit newcomers (see tables 2.3 and 2.4)? Colmar's Catholics formed a minority among the early seventeenth-century male householders (542 to 1,383). Among the Protestants, we can pinpoint the origin for 752 (54%) of the males. Less than 48% of them were native born. The Catholic community was much more ingrown, with nearly 78% (211) of the new householders drawn from local families. If we include the surrounding villages, over 86% of Colmar's Catholic male householders whose origins are known were born within the city and its hinterland, as opposed to just under 61% of the Protestants. The Protestant community attracted numerous outsiders from all over the empire and beyond, while the early seventeenth-century Catholics were more insular, drawing mainly from the neighboring villages.

Among the women, the contrast is much less dramatic, for they normally migrated to the city only from short distances. Catholic women (64%) were more likely to be native born than Protestants (50.2%), but if we add in women from Upper Alsace, the percentages become strikingly similar: 77.1% for Protestants and 79.8% for Catholics. Among the few women migrating from other regions, both parishes seem to have drawn equally from all regions except for Switzerland, from which the Protestants comprised over 90% of the immigrants (19 of 21). In all, the Catholics attracted only a few outsiders, primarily from the neighboring villages. What part of civic community belonged to this insular minority?

III. Citizens and Bi-Confessionalism

Colmar's citizens had to belong to a guild, to own or rent a house in town, and to prove a five-year residency in the community. The civic law code of 1593 set an admission fee of five pounds *Rappen*, a regional money of account, to purchase the rights of citizenship, though sons of citizens could claim exemption from this tax. For others this fee was steep enough to restrict access to moderately wealthy individuals. Though guild membership and citizenship were fundamentally interconnected, not all guildsmen

TABLE 2.3

Origins of Male Householders by Confession, 1575–1630

PLACE OF ORIGIN	PROTESTANT (no.)	(%)	CATHOLIC (no.)	(%)
Colmar	356	47.3	211	77.6
Upper Alsace	108	14.4	24	8.8
Lower Alsace	28	3.7	1	0.4
Southwest Germany				
Breisgau	30		6	
Baden	8		—	
Württemberg	34	19.0	2	7.7
Swabia/Bodensee	56		10	
Bavaria	15		3	
Rhineland/Palatinate	17	2.3	1	0.4
Central Germany				
Hesse	5		—	
Hohenlohe	2	3.3	—	0.4
Thuringia	5		—	
Franconia	13		1	
Northern Germany				
Brandenburg-Prussia	2		—	
Saxony	2	0.7	—	—
Schleswig	1		—	
Eastern Regions				
Silesia, Moravia,				
Hungary, Poland,	5	0.7	—	—
Bohemia				
Switzerland	27	3.6	1	0.4
Italy	—	—	1	0.4
Western Francophone				
France/Lorraine	2		2	
Montbéliard	—	0.3	—	0.7
Region Unknown	36	4.8	9	3.3
Total Known	752		272	
Total Cases	1,383	54.3	579	47.0

TABLE 2.4
Origins of Wives by Confession, 1575–1630

PLACE OF ORIGIN	PROTESTANT (no.)	(%)	CATHOLIC (no.)	(%)
Colmar	232	50.2	172	64.4
Upper Alsace	124	26.9	41	15.4
Lower Alsace	17	3.7	5	1.9
Southwest Germany				
Breisgau	16		10	
Baden	2		1	
Württemberg	6	9.7	1	12.4
Swabia/Bodensee	18		17	
Bavaria	3		4	
Rhineland/Palatinate	2	0.4	—	—
Central Germany				
Hesse	—		—	
Hohenlohe	—	0.2	—	—
Thuringia	1		—	
Franconia	—		—	
Northern Germany				
Brandenburg-Prussia	—		—	
Saxony	—	—	1	0.4
Schleswig	—		—	
Eastern Regions				
Silesia, Moravia,				
Hungary, Poland,	2	0.4	1	0.4
Bohemia				
Switzerland	19	4.1	2	0.7
Italy	—	—	—	—
Western Francophone				
France/Lorraine	8		3	
Montbéliard	2	2.2	—	1.1
Region Unknown	10	2.2	9	3.4
Total Known	462		267	
Total Cases	1,383	33.4	579	46.1

were inscribed in Colmar's citizen registers. Colmar's ten guilds listed 1,012 members in 1619, of whom nearly all were identified among the 1,074 taxable householders in 1620.[45] Only 602 (56.1%) of the male householders in 1620, however, either were already or would soon be inscribed in the citizen registers.[46]

What impact did Colmar's bi-confessionalism have on the decision to purchase citizenship, and did the dominance of the Protestants within the regime reflect a Protestant majority among the citizens? A guildsman chose to become a citizen, and his age, income, and sense of prestige, as well as the overall civic political climate, affected that choice. The number of men willing to purchase the status fluctuated widely from year to year, so I have compiled the figures in five-year segments from the Peace of Augsburg in 1555 in order to flatten out the annual variation while still highlighting overall trends (see graph 2.4).[47] On average around 100 guildsmen inscribed in the citizen registers every five years, with two peaks in inscriptions in the years immediately following the outbreak of plague in the 1560s and again in 1609–11. Colmar's Reformation did not discourage guildsmen from purchasing citizenship, for the inscriptions were well above average, at 129, between 1575 and 1579, though they dropped slowly down to 1589 then plummeted to 75 between 1590 and 1594 following the confessional crisis

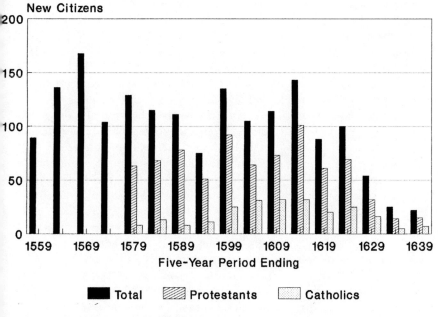

GRAPH 2.4   CITIZENSHIP AND CONFESSION, 1555–1639

within the Protestant community. After 1595 inscriptions rebounded and remained above average until 1614, with 143 in the years following the plague of 1609–11. The number of inscriptions then fell to 88 just prior to the war and never really recovered. The forced Counter-Reformation and the uncertainties of warfare deflated confidence in the future. In the 1630s Colmar's political status was questionable and its economy in shambles. Under these conditions, few householders were willing to pay for citizenship.

Did the regime's initial connection of confessional choice with the rights of citizenship produce a bi-confessional citizenry? Yes. By 1584 the majority (59.1%) of Colmar's newly inscribed citizens were Protestants, though Catholics also continued to inscribe. Over the next five years, the percentage of new Protestant citizens rose to 70.3%. The confessional crisis of 1589 had no apparent impact on Protestant inscriptions, and until 1624 Protestants comprised between 60 and 70% of all new citizens. The city was growing prior to the Thirty Years' War, and the Protestant dominance in the regime extended into the citizenry. Nevertheless, the Catholics remained a viable and stable minority, comprising at least 20% of the new citizens and perhaps 30%, for the gaps in Catholic parish records suggest that many citizens of unknown confessional affiliation may have been Catholics. Under the compromise of 1575, confessional choice did not hinder a guildsman from becoming a citizen.

Colmar's Counter-Reformation dramatically reduced the number of men seeking to purchase citizenship, but it had almost no impact on the confessional balance. The Protestants remained the majority between 1627 and 1633, when fifty-one Colmarians purchased citizenship: nineteen (37%) Catholics and twenty-five (49%) Protestants. The civic regime's initial recognition of bi-confessionalism held throughout the period. As had occurred in confessionally mixed towns in Swabia, the town had become predominantly Protestant, but a stable Catholic minority survived.[48] Colmar's Counter-Reform might have eventually reversed the balance, but initially young men in both communities felt comfortable enough to purchase citizenship no matter what official confessional banner the regime honored.

Colmar's citizens were guildsmen, and guild membership brought with it brotherhood in a smaller corporate community within the body politic. Colmar's citizen registers recorded guild affiliation beginning in 1580, and by 1630 over 1,000 Colmarians had purchased citizenship. Several hundred others appear in guild lists compiled in the 1590s and in 1619 (see graph 2.5). Among Colmar's late sixteenth-century and early seventeenth-century male taxpaying householders whose guild affiliation is known, over 65% (1,196 out of 1,820) belonged to the Reformed parish, while only slightly more than 20% (377) attended Catholic services. This echoes almost exactly the confessional distribution of newly inscribed citizens, but there are sharp differences from guild

Guilds

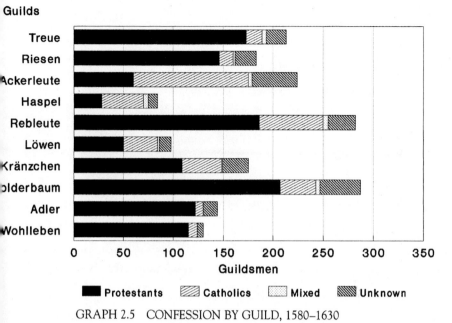

GRAPH 2.5   CONFESSION BY GUILD, 1580–1630

:o guild. Colmar's artisans in *zum Adler*, *zum Riesen*, and *zum Wohlleben* heavily favored the new Protestant worship and welcomed few Catholics.[49] Colmar's merchants' guild, *zur Treue*, was also predominantly Protestant [81.2%). The Protestants formed a minority only in *Ackerleute* and *zum Haspel*, while the Catholic parish drew the bulk of its worshippers from the agricultural work force and from Colmar's fishermen, butchers, millers, bakers, and the craftsmen in *zum Holderbaum*.

The confessional variations within the guilds reflected distinct worldviews among the various sectors of Colmar's economy. Colmar's merchants and artisans, who were involved in trade with other cities, had contacts with Protestant Strasbourg and Basel, and by 1600 their guilds had become predominantly Protestant. Colmar's agricultural guilds sheltered more Catholics, because Colmar's hinterland included the Catholic villages in the Austrian territories to the south and east. Colmar's vineyard workers came in contact with Protestants in the neighboring Württemberg villages and dealt more directly with the city's Protestant-dominated commercial sector, and in *Rebleute* confessional divisions within the guild (65.9% Protestant and 2.7% Catholic) matched divisions within the population as a whole. Finally the victualers, who bridged the rural and urban economies, were split almost evenly into two confessional groups. Despite the close connection between occupation and confessional choice, no guild was confessionally exclusive, which meant that guildsmen of both faiths shared the rituals of guild life.

The city's confessional split reinforced divisions within the city's economy, which could have produced outbursts of confessional violence exacerbated by economic and social tensions, yet there were few cases of violence and no organized protests. The Protestant authorities must be credited for the preservation of civic peace. On occasion the regime had to condemn individuals and guilds for disrupting the peace, but without official sanction, confessional animosity was limited to personal rather than political behavior.[50] The position of civic Catholics posed the greatest threat. The Catholics were a minority, and their visible leaders were privileged clerical corporations with politically dangerous allies beyond Colmar's walls. The election of Catholic councilors, drawn from the agricultural guilds, gave a voice to this confessional group in council chambers. Conflicts that did emerge could be resolved through normal channels.

Throughout the city, production centered in small workshops attached to the family residence, with many trades clustered in neighborhoods; for example, the fishermen, tanners, and butchers lived and worked together.[51] Most other trades were scattered about the town, and neighborliness did not reinforce occupational fellowship. Millers and metalsmiths required access to water to power their mills and cool their equipment. Their shops lined the Mühlbach, which passed through the city from the northwest to the southeast. Weavers, hat makers, and tailors lived in nearly every district. The agricultural workers settled in the outlying districts near the city gates, but coopers also inhabited these neighborhoods close to the wine cellars which needed their products. In the city's center the wealthier merchants set up their shops and warehouses within sight of the custom house. There were richer and poorer neighborhoods, but none were socially exclusive. Lay administrators for the cloistered communities and civic hospitals lived near them by the city walls. Tavern keepers and important rural property holders often resided near the city gates. Electoral practices, special craft needs, aristocratic factionalism, and an unwillingness to change family residence stamped Colmar as it did other cities with a mottled social topography. Rich and poor lived cheek by jowl.

In the thirteenth century, the Colmarians had enclosed the city within two walls. The second ring encompassed the inner city and suburbs to the north, east, and south, doubling the town's size to nearly 168 acres (see map 2.2).[52] This wall contained the city until the end of the seventeenth century. Within Colmar's walls, the narrow streets, alleys, and public squares formed the open spaces for commerce and conversation. The streets, though paved, were often choked with refuse and waste.[53] The topographer von Ichtersheim found Colmar's streets "beautiful and well-paved," but he was an Alsatian.[54] The French visitor L'Hermine complained that "the streets there [Colmar] appear to me to be narrow and tortuous, which is why I lost my way the first time I passed through [the town]."[55] Colmarians named

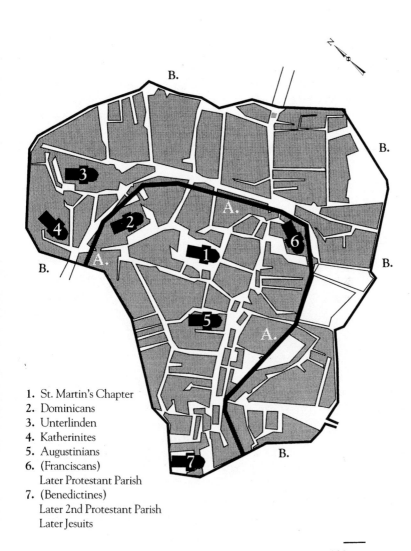

1. St. Martin's Chapter
2. Dominicans
3. Unterlinden
4. Katherinites
5. Augustinians
6. (Franciscans)
   Later Protestant Parish
7. (Benedictines)
   Later 2nd Protestant Parish
   Later Jesuits

100 meters

A. Original Wall
B. Outer Wall

MAP 2.2   WALLS, RELIGIOUS HOUSES, AND THOROUGHFARES

their streets and alleys after the trades practiced on them, such as the *Schlosserstrasse* or *Fischergasse*, or after significant landmarks, such as the *Kanzleigasse*. Street names changed over time, and some routes carried multiple names. For example, Colmar's main commercial thoroughfare, which led up to the custom house from the *Kerkertor*, was known as *Unter den Krämern*, *Krämer-*, *Käs-*, *Schädel-*, or *Kaufmannsgasse*.[56] Street names could persist long after their referents were gone; for example, the *Judengasse* retained its name for centuries after the Jews had been expelled from the city.[57] Colmar's "narrow and tortuous" streets widened occasionally into open markets, where producers sold livestock, grain, vegetables, wine, and finished products.[58] These squares provided assembly points for the civic musters and for fire-fighting brigades.

The city's tax collectors divided Colmar into twenty-three tax districts of varying size, from *Salzkasten* (XI), which never possessed more than four households, to *Kürsnersthürlein* (XXIII) and *Anfang* (I) with more than 100 (see map 2.3). Initially plotted in 1495 for the tax called the "common penny," most of these districts were not true neighborhoods because they lacked political or religious significance. One exception was *Anfang* (district I), known as the *Krautenau*, and located south of the old city and separated from it by the Lauch. The *Krautenau* was originally a suburb which sprung up along the road from Basel. Local fishermen and boatmen used the Lauch, and in 1620, for example, twelve of the fourteen fishermen householders resided here. Beyond the *Steinbruckertor*, Colmar's gardeners had access to the Au, where most of the vegetables grew. The *Krautenau* had been part of a separate medieval parish, and of all the neighborhoods, it retained a distinct personality.[59]

Of the twenty-three districts, thirteen, districts I, IX, and XIII through XXIII, were located between the original and outer wall. Districts XIII through XXIII covered the neighborhoods north and east of the city's core. *Zum Schlüssel* (XIII) enveloped the original wall in a tight band and included the *Kerkertor*, which was the traditional passage to the vineyards and the valleys of the Vosges.[60] Districts XIV through XXII were laid out in small blocks, while *Kürsnerthürlein* (XXIII), much like the *Krautenau*, was a sprawling, relatively poor neighborhood in the city's eastern corner, known locally as *Deinheimer Ort*. Here the last of Colmar's three gates, the *Deinheimertor*, opened to the pastures, fields, and woodlots of civic territory, and beyond to the Rhine, the Breisgau, and the Black Forest on the eastern horizon.[61] For the most part these outer districts lacked major landmarks.[62] *Sankt Katherinen-Nöhelin* (XVI) contained both Dominican convents, Unterlinden and St. Catherine. In Districts XIV through XXIII, the landscape resembled a walled village with the barns and granaries of the lay and ecclesiastical property holders mixed in with peasant and artisan dwellings. Colmar's two major agricultural guilds, *Ackerleute* and *Rebleute*, gathered in their *Trinkstuben* here.

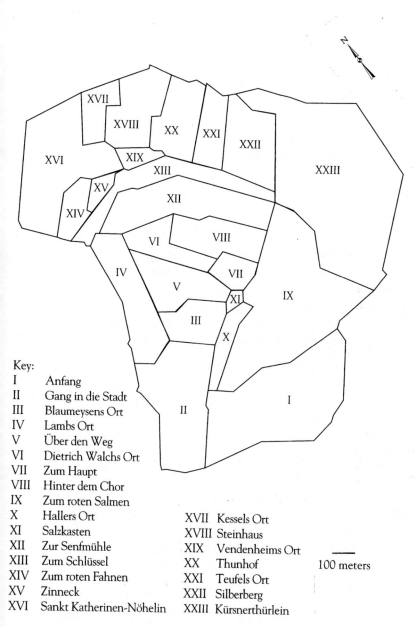

Key:

I   Anfang
II   Gang in die Stadt
III   Blaumeysens Ort
IV   Lambs Ort
V   Über den Weg
VI   Dietrich Walchs Ort
VII   Zum Haupt
VIII Hinter dem Chor
IX   Zum roten Salmen
X   Hallers Ort
XI   Salzkasten
XII   Zur Senfmühle
XIII Zum Schlüssel
XIV Zum roten Fahnen
XV   Zinneck
XVI Sankt Katherinen-Nöhelin

XVII   Kessels Ort
XVIII Steinhaus
XIX   Vendenheims Ort
XX   Thunhof
XXI   Teufels Ort
XXII   Silberberg
XXIII   Kürsnerthürlein

100 meters

MAP 2.3   COLMAR'S TAX DISTRICTS, 1495–1789

Though the Colmarians never distinguished between the inner and outer city, the original wall enclosed the hub of Colmar's economic, religious, and political life. Here even the poorer districts, such as *Gang in der Stadt* (II) and *Lambsort* (IV), included patrician family enclaves.[63] These neighborhoods formed the central core of civic life and included most of the ecclesiastical houses, the *Rathaus*, the major marketplaces, and the municipal custom house (*Koifhus*). In *Blaumeysens Ort* (III) the patrician society *zum Waagkeller* assembled in the cellar of the *Rathaus* from 1459 to 1698. The building later became the meeting hall for the *Conseil souverain d'Alsace*.[64] In the neighboring districts, the city scales, the cloth market, the chancellery, the *Wachtstube*, the great wine cellar (the *Weinhof*), and the grain market lay within a few hundred feet of each other to form the core of Colmar's political and economic life.

Did confessional distribution within occupations produce distinct religious neighborhoods? The richest data for both confessions prior to the Counter-Reformation pertain to 1620,[65] and the registers do suggest some neighborhood segregation (see maps 2.4 and 2.5). In that year over 62% (672 out of 1,074) of Colmar's taxpaying householders were Protestants. In the heart of the city, in the streets and alleys surrounding St. Martin's church, the *Rathaus*, and the marketplace, Protestants represented more than 70% of the population, and they formed a majority in every district, except for the extreme northern neighborhoods surrounding the Dominican convents, where Protestants comprised less than 40% of the householders. In 1620 the Catholics represented only 26% (282 out of 1,074) of all taxpayers and were outnumbered by Protestants in every district except around the Dominican houses (districts XIV, XVI, XVII). In general Catholics favored the outlying neighborhoods, particularly near the city gates, (districts I, XXIII, XIV). Confessional solidarity within occupational groups led to some natural neighborhood segregation, but in 1620 the city contained only two exclusively Protestant neighborhoods, the tiny districts X (*Hallers Ort*) and XI (*Salzkasten*). Prior to the Thirty Years' War, most Colmarians knew a neighbor who attended the other church.

Colmar's outlying neighborhoods were poorer. Did the presence of more Catholics in these neighborhoods reflect a socioeconomic division between the religious communities (see tables 2.5–7)? In the decades prior to the Thirty Years' War Colmar's economy was growing in terms of its taxable households, which rose by 10.5% between 1600 and 1620 (from 972 to 1,074), and aggregate taxable wealth, which swelled by over 28% between 1600 and 1610 and grew a further 16% in the next decade.[66] Wealth was never distributed evenly in Colmar, but much of the city's early seventeenth-century prosperity reflected the changing fortunes of a few householders at the top of civic society. In 1600 twenty-eight householders, less than 3% of the population, controlled more than one-fifth of the aggregate wealth. In the next decade the number of wealthy householders rose to

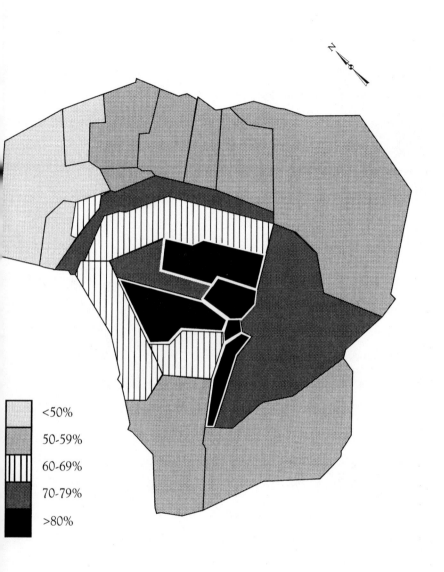

<50%

50-59%

60-69%

70-79%

>80%

100 meters

MAP 2.4   PROTESTANTS, 1620

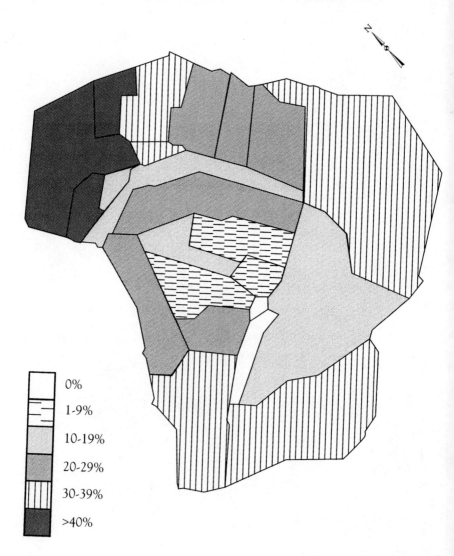

MAP 2.5   CATHOLICS, 1620

TABLE 2.5

Taxable Householders by Strata, 1600–1640

	1600 (no.)	(%)	1610 (no.)	(%)	1620 (no.)	(%)	1630 (no.)	(%)	1640 (no.)	(%)
>2,000 fl.	28	2.9	47	4.4	54	5.0	25	2.7	27	4.8
>1,000 fl.	64	6.6	64	6.1	76	7.1	57	6.1	70	12.5
230–990 fl.	233	24.0	275	26.0	273	25.4	287	30.8	194	34.5
80–200 fl.	605	62.2	633	59.9	636	59.2	531	57.1	248	44.1
Exempt	42	4.3	38	3.6	35	3.3	31	3.3	23	4.1
Total	972		1,057		1,074		931		562	

TABLE 2.6

Percentage of Overall Wealth by Strata, 1600–1640

	1600 (%)	1610 (%)	1620 (%)	1630 (%)	1640 (%)
>2,000 fl.	21.8	33.8	33.3	21.7	26.5
>1,000 fl.	25.0	19.5	20.3	20.2	30.1
230–990 fl.	32.5	28.8	26.1	37.2	30.5
80–200 fl.	20.7	17.9	16.3	20.9	12.9
Exempt	—	—	—	—	—
Total fl.	327,010	419,610	487,320	355,690	299,320

TABLE 2.7

Percentage of Change in Wealth by Strata, 1610–1640

	1610 (%)	1620 (%)	1630 (%)	1640 (%)
>2,000 fl.	+99.5	+28.2	−57.5	+ 2.7
>1,000 fl.	+ 0.1	+20.9	−27.4	+25.2
230–990 fl.	+13.5	+ 5.1	+ 4.2	−29.6
80–200 fl.	+10.9	+ 5.9	− 6.7	−47.8
Exempt	—	—	—	—
Community	+28.3	+16.1	−27.0	−15.9

forty-seven, and these men, who together comprised only 4.4% of the population, controlled more than one-third of Colmar's wealth. In this decade the combined taxable income of Colmar's wealthiest citizens had doubled, and it accounted for more than three-fourths of the overall growth. At the same time, both the numbers and the share of civic wealth among Colmar's moderately wealthy citizens, those assessed between 1,000 and 2,000 florins, remained unchanged. The bulk of the householders (86%) experienced a slight increase in wealth, but much of this was due to the raising of the base assessment from 80 to 100 florins.

Between 1610 and 1620, the number of wealthy householders increased to fifty-four, and their share of the community's wealth rose to over 37%. At the same time the number of householders listed in the lower tax strata increased by one to 909, while their share of the civic wealth fell from 46.7% to 42.4%. The city's continued prosperity had further stratified Colmar's society, though the gap was due to the expansion of a well-to-do elite rather than increased misery among the poorer citizens. Throughout the period, wealth in Colmar was distributed unevenly, and there were clear discrepancies between rich and poor householders. Between 1600 and 1620 average taxable wealth per household rose from 352 to 470 florins. In 1600, 77% of Colmar's householders fell below that average, and by 1620 more than 80% claimed less than average estates (865 out of 1,074). Furthermore, in 1620, 62.4% of the householders had taxable estates of 200 florins or less. Escalating prices combined with traditional wage rates to weaken the economic standing of many Colmarians, and the tax registers do not record the propertyless day laborers, domestic servants, and journeymen.

Disparity in wealth also had a confessional dimension. In 1600 the average Protestant householder had a taxable estate of 442 florins, while his Catholic neighbor claimed only 264 florins. Over the next twenty years, Protestant estates rose 26.7% to 560 florins. Catholic estates increased too, but only 20% to 318 florins. Catholics were poorer, and they shared less in the growing prosperity. Nevertheless, Colmar's society was not stratified into confessional classes (see table 2.8). A small percentage of Colmarians were tax exempt, often as part of their wages as civic officials. Some, such as the city clerk, were very wealthy, while city guards and policemen probably commanded economic resources comparable to the common artisans. For the population as a whole, the Protestants comprised slightly more than 62% and the Catholics slightly more than 26%. Protestants were overrepresented among householders assessed at more than 230 florins, and the wealthier the householder the more likely he was to be a Protestant. Colmar's Catholics were more likely to be poor, though both confessional communities included a large segment of Colmar's humbler citizens.

The confessional split was sharpest at the top of the city's economic hierarchy. Of the fifty-four richest Colmarians, forty-seven (87%) were Protestants, and their predominance seems to have been the norm throughout

TABLE 2.8

Tax Rates by Confession, 1620

ESTATE	PROTESTANTS (no.)	(%)	CATHOLICS (no.)	(%)	UNKNOWN (no.)	(%)	MIXED (no.)	(%)	Total (no.)
>2,000 fl.	46	85.1	5	9.3	2	3.7	1	1.9	54
>1,000 fl.	53	69.7	17	22.4	6	7.9	—	—	76
230–990 fl.	185	67.8	65	23.8	17	6.2	6	2.2	273
80–200 fl.	369	58.0	190	29.9	64	10.1	13	2.0	636
Exempt	19	54.3	5	14.3	10	28.6	1	2.8	35
Total	672	62.6	282	26.3	99	9.2	21	1.9	1,074

the early seventeenth century (see table 2.9). In 1600 only one identifiable Catholic belonged to Colmar's economic elite, though by 1620 five Catholics were counted among Colmar's richest citizens. Georges Bischoff has suggested that, in the period before the Thirty Years' War, Colmar was a "blocked society" whose richest citizens possessed excessive power in an environment which restricted social mobility and persecuted marginal individuals.[67] Colmar may have had a blocked society in the early seventeenth century, but the elite was not a closed circle of intermarried families. The most remarkable development of the era was the growing economic power of the Protestant merchants of the guild *zur Treue*, whose numbers more than doubled between 1600 and 1610. This growing merchant elite was predominantly Protestant, and many members were immigrants. Three men, Clade Sysson, Gideon Sarazin, and Frantz Wibert, were the *welsche Krämer* whose presence shifted the nature of commercial relations within the city.[68] Eight other immigrants, all Protestant merchants or officials from neighboring villages in Upper Alsace, paid taxes on property valued at over 2,000 florins.[69] In 1610 these eleven men were taxed on property valued at 38,300 florins, which was slightly less than the combined income of the city's 500 poorest householders. This was the same decade that Colmar's Protestant leaders formally aligned their church to Rhenish Calvinism. The "Latin merchants" (*welsche Krämer*) may have come to Colmar because of the confessional shift; or perhaps their presence helped force the issue for the civic regime.[70] Whatever the case, by 1620 conditions which could encourage social and confessional animosity existed within Colmar. At Hagenau in 1624 social, political, and religious animosities merged in support of the emperor's dissolution of the elite Lutheran parish.[71] Hagenau's Lutherans never returned. Would similar conditions produce similar results at Colmar?

TABLE 2.9
Colmar's Early-Seventeenth-Century Elite, 1600–1640

	Guild Membership and Wealth				
GUILD	1600	1610	1620	1630	1640
Treue	9	23 (2)	25 (3)	5 (2)	9 (1)
Riesen	5	4	6	5 (1)	7 (1)
Ackerleute	4	4 (1)	6 (1)	4 (1)	4 (4)
Haspel	—	1 (1)	2 (1)	—	—
Rebleute	—	1	1	1	1
Löwen	—	—	1	—	—
Kränzchen	1	2	2	2	3 (1)
Adler	2	3	—	1	—
Holderbaum	3	2	5	2 (1)	1
Wohlleben	1	3	3	1	—
NA <1580	2	2	1	—	—
NA	1 (1)	2	2	4	2
Total	28 (1)	47 (4)	54 (5)	25 (5)	27 (7)

Key:
(n)   Number of Catholics
NA <1580   Citizens inscribed before 1580 with guild unknown
NA   Does not appear in guild or citizen registers

	Confession and Wealth								
	1600		1610		1620		1630		1640	
CONFESSION	(no.)	(%)	(no.)	(%)	(no.)	(%)	(no.)	(%)	(no.)	(%)
Catholic	1	3.6	4	8.5	5	9.4	5	20.0	7	25.9
Reformed	25	88.1	41	87.2	47	87.1	16	64.0	—	—
Ref/Luth									13	48.2
Lutheran									5	18.5
Unknown	1	3.6	2	4.3	2	3.7	2	8.0	—	—
Mixed	1*	3.6	—	—	—	—	2**	8.0	2	7.4
Totals	28		47		54		25		27	

*On 5 May 1603, Martin Kriegelstein, brother of the Stettmeister, Ludwig, and a leader of the Reformed community, married the heiress of the Lordship of Oberberckheim in a Catholic ceremony.

**Gall Gilg, who came from an important family in the Reformed parish, was married in the Catholic church on 2 February 1629 and later became an important leader in Colmar's Lutheran parish. Andreas Sybert, who had abjured the Reform faith and served in the Counter-Reformation regime, remained a Catholic after 1633.

IV. THE COUNTER-REFORMATION AND DEMOGRAPHIC CRISIS, 1627–1640

When the Imperial commission dissolved the Protestant regime, many political leaders chose exile rather than abjure, and from 1627 onward Colmar
was an occupied city in a war zone. In the late 1630s, the deadly combina-
tion of campaigning armies, famine, and disease probably reduced Colmar's
population by nearly half. Given the hardships and intense political and
confessional pressure, one would expect dramatic shifts in the confessional
relations among the survivors. This did not occur. In its social, occupational, and confessional composition, Colmar in 1640 in many ways resembled the prewar city.

The men who directed civic affairs after 1627 tempered confessional pressures
to avert wholesale emigration. Even before 1627 the regime had been bi-
confessional, although Catholics had a rather limited influence. Given the
large block of Protestants within the city's craft guilds, the Counter-Reform
regime could not immediately force confessional conformity without risking
economic chaos. The establishment of the Lutheran church in 1633 further
complicated confessional relations. Within the regime itself, most officials
had grown up in Reformed households, and "crypto-Calvinism" maintained
strong roots within the civic community. The Catholic minority was protected by treaty, and the divided Protestants had little incentive to drive
the Catholics out of the depopulated city. In any case, after 1635 the French
garrison protected Catholic interests until the Peace of Westphalia.

Both the Counter-Reformation and the famine and disease which swept
through the region in the late 1630s eliminated significant segments of the
civic community. By 1640 forced exile, famine, and disease had reduced
the number of male householders on the tax rolls from the peak of 1,074 in
1620 to 562. About a third (31.1%) of these householders were survivors
who had paid taxes in 1620, though more householders had survived through
these years than the normal average of 28%. Colmar's population shrank
not so much because of the loss of householders, which occurred inevitably, but because of its inability to attract newcomers. Between 1627 and
1640, only eighty-two men purchased citizenship. Although the number of
new citizens had dwindled to six per year, the prewar confessional balance
held, with 21 (25.6%) Catholics and 45 (54.9%) Protestants. In fact, in
1640 Colmar's civic community resembled its prewar counterpart in its confessional structure both among the citizenry as a whole and within the guilds
(see graphs 2.6–7). In 1620 the Reformed community comprised 62.6% of
the male householders. By 1640 the Lutheran parish had fallen by only
.7%, to 61.9%. Known Catholics rose in percentage between 1620 and 1640
from 26.3% to 31.0%.

Furthermore, stability also categorized the confessional groupings within
the guilds. The early seventeenth-century confessional division of Protestant

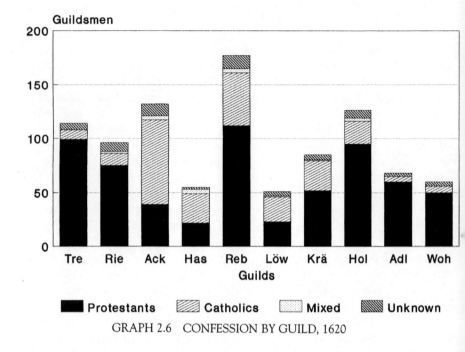

GRAPH 2.6   CONFESSION BY GUILD, 1620

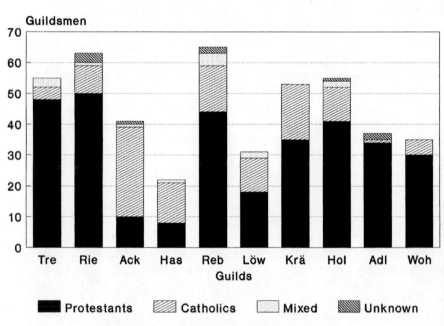

GRAPH 2.7   CONFESSION BY GUILD, 1640

merchants and artisans, Catholic peasants, and a confessionally mixed population among the vineyard workers and victualers remained into the 1640s. In 1620 the Protestant community held at least a three-fourths majority in *zur Treue, zum Riesen, zum Adler, zum Holderbaum,* and *zum Wohlleben.* By 1640 the percentage of men attending Protestant services in *zur Treue, zum Riesen,* and *zum Adler* had risen while in the other two artisan guilds they had fallen only slightly. In 1620 the Protestants formed a simple majority in *zum Kränzchen* and *Rebleute,* and that majority increased over the next two decades. In 1620 the Protestants were a minority in *zum Haspel, Ackerleute,* and *zum Löwen.* In 1640 their percentages in the agricultural guilds were down, while the Lutheran parish could claim a majority among Colmar's butchers and fishermen. Despite the demographic disruptions the Lutheran community in 1640 drew its members from the same guilds as had its Reformed predecessor.

The overall composition of Colmar's Catholic community likewise remained unchanged. In 1620 Catholics comprised less than 15% of the Protestant-dominated merchant and artisan guilds, except for *zum Holderbaum.* By 1640 there were even fewer Catholics in *zur Treue* and *zum Adler,* while the percentages of Catholics had risen slightly in *zum Riesen* and *zum Wohlleben* but was still not above 15%. In 1620 Catholics formed significant minorities in *zum Kränzchen, zum Holderbaum,* and *Rebleute.* By 1640 their presence in *zum Kränzchen* and *zum Holderbaum* had grown, while it had declined among the city's vineyard workers. In 1620 the Catholics formed a majority in *zum Haspel* and *Ackerleute,* and the two confessional communities were equally represented in *zum Löwen.* By 1640 the Catholics had become a minority in *zum Löwen,* but they had enlarged their majorities in the two agricultural guilds.

Despite the Counter-Reformation and population loss Colmar's guilds remained bi-confessional, and the balance between the two confessions had shifted only slightly, even with the dramatic decline among rural guildsmen. In 1620 the three agricultural guilds boasted 364 members, or 37.8% of the identifiable guildsmen; by 1640 they claimed only 129 members or 28.1%. All three had lost more than half of their members, and only the building trades in *zum Holderbaum* and the merchant trades in *zur Treue* had suffered similar declines. The armies had ravaged Colmar's hinterland and temporarily destroyed the livelihood of the city's agricultural workers. Yet the decline in agricultural guildsmen had preceded the war, which had only exacerbated the process. Furthermore, the guilds' decline marked a consolidation of tenant holdings and not a decline in agricultural wealth. The agricultural guilds accounted for 23.4% of the taxable wealth in 1620 and 19.8% in 1640, but the average assessment for the city's agricultural guildsmen in 1620 had been 315 florins and by 1640 it had risen to 478 florins despite the war. The small holders had suffered, but the middling and wealthy tenant farmers had weathered the storm.

Except for the changes in the rural guilds, the city's work force maintained its prewar diversity and occupational distribution, which reflected Colmar's continued role as a central market producing for its hinterland.[72] Based on evidence in the parish registers, in 1620 the Colmarians pursued at least ninety-one different occupations. Vineyard work formed the most common trade, employing eighty-five householders, and thirty-eight others worked in crafts associated with wine processing. Together these householders accounted for over 26% of those men with identifiable occupations. Next to the wine industry, statecraft formed the most frequent occupational category, with fifty-eight households headed by Protestant ministers, school teachers, members of the civic police force (*Weibel*), or gatekeepers. No other occupation could boast more than twenty practitioners. The profile downplays the agricultural householders because the Catholic parish registers do not list occupations.

In 1640 Colmar's householders pursued at least ninety-four different occupations. The absolute numbers may be deceptive, because we can identify the trade of almost 60% of the male householders as opposed to 43% in 1620. Nevertheless, the number of householders who worked in Colmar's vineyards had plummeted from eighty-five to thirty-six and the wine-processing householders had also fallen to twenty-three. Together they represented 17.9% of the householders with known occupations. Wine had been Colmar's great export commodity, and its commerce was sensitive to political and economic disruption. The war had produced a depression in the local industry, as fewer merchants came to the city's wine fairs.[73] Pillaged fields and granaries could rebound within one season provided the seed and labor were available, but a destroyed vineyard required several years to regain its productive capacity.

Outside of wine production and processing, the number of householders in the various trades remained the same despite the fact that the city's population had fallen by nearly half. Colmar's artisans serviced a local and regional economy which continued to require their products. The war had reduced the population throughout Upper Alsace, but the armies had replaced the destroyed villages as consumers. The city's tanners and shoemakers provided goods the garrisons needed, and its innkeepers prospered in slaking the soldiers' thirst. In the 1640s despite the war, Colmar remained the great central market for Upper Alsace, though the composition and tastes of its principal customers had changed.

By 1640 the swings in the confessional power and the demographic loss had made little impact on the balance between the two confessional communities. Was continuity also the norm in Colmar's confessional topography? Between 1620 and 1630, the male householders declined by 13% (1,074 to 931), partly because of Protestant emigration, but the Counter-Reformation was unable to produce a Catholic majority among civic householders (see graph 2.8). In 1630 the city had 497 male householders (53.4%) who

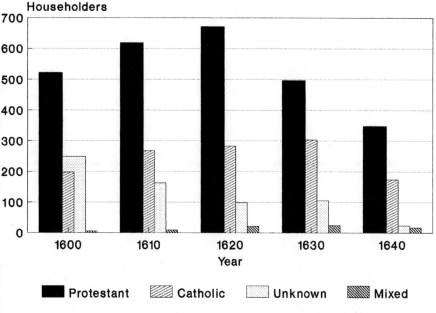

Householders

GRAPH 2.8 CONFESSIONAL DIVISION, 1600–1640

had married or baptized their children in the Protestant church. They had no church in 1630, and many may have truly converted. Nevertheless, I have only traced thirty-one householders who first married in the Reformed church and would later marry or baptize their children in the Catholic church after 1632. In 1630, 304 householders (32.7%) had or would appear in the Catholic parish registers, which was an increase of slightly less than 8% from 282 Catholic householders in 1620. At the same time, Protestant householders had fallen 26% from 672 to 497.

In 1620 the Protestants had formed a better than three-fourths majority in five neighborhoods (districts V, VII, VIII, X, XI) in the core of the city. In 1630 only district X (*Hallers Ort*), with fourteen out of eighteen Protestant households, had such a majority. Throughout the city there were fewer Protestants, but they were only a minority in districts XIV, XVI, XVII, and XIX. Despite Protestant emigration, Catholics had failed to penetrate into traditional Protestant neighborhoods in 1630. Districts X an XI still had no identifiable Catholics, while fewer Catholics resided in districts III and IV than a decade earlier. After the emigration of the Protestant political and merchant elite, the city's Catholic leaders sought to delay a public confessional reckoning for the Protestant tanners, shoemakers, weavers, and coopers, because Colmar needed these artisans no matter what their religious conviction. The regime also refused to confiscate émigré property, which limited Catholic movement into the central neighborhoods.

When the Swedes ended Colmar's Counter-Reformation, many Protestant refugees returned to their homes. Rich and poor of both confessions then faced the hardships of the late 1630s, and by 1640 the demographic loss was evident in Colmar's empty neighborhoods. Most lost nearly half of their male householders, but some, such as district XIX (*Vendenheims Ort*) with only four householders instead of twelve in 1620 and eleven in 1630, and district XV (*Zinneck*), also with four instead of twenty-one householders in 1620 and 1630, were practically deserted. Despite the devastating losses the city's confessional topography in 1640 resembled the patterns of the prewar era. By 1640 Catholics had made some inroads into the central neighborhoods, though they were still a minority which outnumbered the Protestants only in the Dominican enclave (districts XVI, XVII), and for the first time in the large and poor *Kürsnersthürlein* (district XXIII).[74] In districts VIII, XI, and XIX there were no Catholic householders. Catholics comprised less than 20% of the householders in nine districts in both 1620 and 1640. In 1620 the Protestant community comprised more than three-quarters of the householders in five districts, all at the city's core. Twenty years later, the number had risen to six, but the new neighborhood was the deserted *Vendenheims Ort*, where three of the four householders attended Lutheran services. Catholics continued to cluster in the city's northern districts and the neighborhoods near the city gates, while the Protestants predominated in the central commercial neighborhoods.

The Counter-Reformation and the famine of the late 1630s thus had not affected the confessional balance within the guilds, nor the distribution of the two confessional communities throughout the city, but they did alter Colmar's social structure (see above, tables 2.5–7). Between 1620 and 1630 the number of householders assessed at more than 1,000 florins fell by 36.9%, and among Colmar's wealthiest men, those assessed above 2,000 florins, the drop was 54%. Colmar's population, as a whole, only fell 13%, and the number of householders assessed between 230 and 900 florins actually increased. Among the city's wealthiest householders, the merchants' guild, *zur Treue*, was particularly hard hit with 80% fewer wealthy members during the Counter-Reform (see above, table 2.9). Even in 1630, however, sixteen of Colmar's twenty-five wealthiest men had married in the old Protestant church, but the impact of the Counter-Reform was permanent. In 1640 only eighteen of Colmar's twenty-seven richest men were Protestants, and among them only four, David and Hans Wetzel, Hans Georg Barth, and Andreas Sybert, had been among the city's wealthiest men in 1620.[75] The Protestant elite in 1640 came primarily from long-time local families. The *welsche Krämer* had left for good, and in their place only four immigrants were counted among the city's wealthiest men. Two men, David Andres and Johann Michael Faber, came from Strasbourg, while Diebolt Würth was originally from the lordship of Horbourg-Riquewihr. The fourth, Johannes

Lachner, was a Catholic from Swabia. In 1640 *zur Treue* had nine members among the city's wealthy, but the number was still well below the twenty-five merchants assessed at over 2,000 florins in 1620. Catholic merchants had not immigrated to Colmar during the Counter-Reformation to assume its commercial leadership, and in 1640 four of the seven wealthiest Catholic householders were tenant farmers in the peasants' guild with ties to the city's Catholic hinterland.

The Counter-Reformation and the military campaigns that followed reduced the size and altered the composition of Colmar's commercial elite. The Counter-Reformation had also reduced the assessed wealth of the civic community by 27% from 487,330 florins to 355,690 florins (see above, tables 2.6–7). Among the various social strata, the wealthiest householders were most deeply affected with a decline of 57.5%. In terms of householders, aggregate wealth, and share of communal wealth, the Counter-Reformation had wiped out the economic growth of the early seventeenth century for Colmar's elite. Just as in Hagenau, the Imperial commission had lopped off the top of Colmar's social structure. The Counter-Reform regime faced a revenue crisis, which must be factored into its policies of shielding the resident Protestants from pressure to emigrate and of protecting émigré properties.

The full impact of the emigration can be partially realized by examining the estates of the refugees who eventually returned. Forty-one householders married in the Reformed church, failed to appear on the tax rolls in 1630, but reappeared in 1640.[76] Thirty of these men had paid taxes in 1620, and they accounted for 2.8% of the householders and 6.4% of the city's overall assessment with 31,200 florins of taxable wealth. In 1620 their average assessed wealth was 1,040 florins, which put them in the upper-middle tax stratum. In 1640 the forty-one householders accounted for 7.3% of the taxpayers and 18% of the taxable wealth, in all 53,830 florins. Their average assessed wealth was 1,313 florins, which was more than twice the communal average (556 florins). The merchants from *zur Treue* accounted for more than half of the wealth of this group both in 1620 and 1640, and in 1640 the fourteen members of *zur Treue* were assessed at an average of 2,193 florins, which placed them as a group among the city's wealthiest taxpayers. The wealth brought back into the community by these returning refugees would have much to do with Colmar's mid-century recovery, but many of the richest merchants, in particular the *welsche Krämer*, Gideon Sazarin, Clade Sysson and Frantz Wibert, did not return.

The restoration of the Protestant community, even with its new Lutheran pedigree, convinced many of the confessional refugees to return to Colmar, and the city might have quickly recovered its commercial role had not the war come to the region and stalled the economic recovery. Between 1630 and 1640, the number of taxable householders fell by more than 39%, but in the same decade those assessed between 1,000 and 2,000 florins rose nearly 23%, from fifty-seven to seventy. In 1640 Colmar's wealthiest taxpayers still accounted for far less of the city's wealth (26.5%) than their predecessors had in 1620 (37.3%), while the share for all taxpayers assessed above 1,000 florins had rebounded to prewar levels (57.6% in 1620 and 56.6% in 1640). The demographic losses of the 1630s reduced Colmar's aggregate wealth by 15.9%, but, more significantly, the wealth controlled by those assessed over 1,000 florins rose by 12% during the crisis. Much of this growth came not from a new handful of very rich men, but rather a large block of relatively well-to-do guildsmen and merchants, with assessed values between 1,000 and 2,000 florins.

The Counter-Reformation had reduced Colmar's elite, but the demographic decline of the late 1630s took its toll among the city's lower-class households. The number of householders with an appraised estate between 230 and 1,000 florins fell by 32%, and the number assessed at less than 200 florins fell by more than 53%. During these difficult years, the poorer agricultural and artisan householders had died or abandoned the city, while the master artisans, tenant farmers, builders, victualers, and leading vintners survived with the support of consolidated resources acquired through inheritance. This swing upward in the social structure matched similar trends in Strasbourg and Mulhouse.[77]

Although the Counter-Reformation and the war had altered the city's social structure, the two confessional communities maintained their balance (see table 2.10). In 1640 the Protestants were slightly overrepresented among the householders assessed at 1,000 florins or more, while the Catholics were more likely to be poorer, but on the whole the confessional communities were better balanced. Between 1620 and 1640 the average assessed wealth per household had risen 86 florins from 470 to 556. For the Protestant community it had climbed only 58 florins from 562 to 620 florins. At the same time, the Catholics, though still poorer, had closed the gap, with assessed wealth climbing 172 florins from 318 to 490 florins. Colmar in 1640 was much smaller than it had been at the outbreak of the war, and the wealth within this tighter community was much more evenly distributed.

TABLE 2.10
Tax Rates by Confession, 1640

ESTATE	PROTESTANTS (no.)	(%)	CATHOLICS (no.)	(%)	UNKNOWN (no.)	(%)	MIXED (no.)	(%)	TOTAL (no.)
>2,000 fl.	18	66.7	7	25.9	—	—	2	7.4	27
>1,000 fl.	48	68.6	16	22.8	2	2.9	4	5.7	70
230–990 fl.	122	62.9	66	34.0	4	2.1	2	1.0	194
80–200 fl.	144	58.1	81	32.7	15	6.0	8	3.2	248
Exempt	16	69.6	4	17.4	2	8.7	1	4.3	23
Total	348	61.9	174	31.0	23	4.1	17	3.0	562

Between 1627 and 1640 two blows, one confessional and one demographic, struck Colmar. Each had its impact. The Counter-Reformation did not end civic bi-confessionalism; in fact it could not end Protestant dominance in civic governance or in the community at large. The Imperial commission succeeded in driving away an important segment of the Protestant political and commercial elite, and many did not return. In time a new Protestant elite would emerge, but its economic and political interests would be more provincial. The Counter-Reformation severed ties between Colmar and Rhenish Calvinism and the Swedish Reformation brought Colmar's Protestant community into closer contact with Alsatian Lutheranism, with its two centers in Strasbourg and Horbourg-Riquewihr. The war depopulated Colmar, but those who survived were better off than their parents or grandparents. Between 1627 and 1640 Colmarians weathered confessional turmoil, military occupation, famine, and disease. By 1648 the survivors found themselves in a position to substantially improve their lives in a bi-confessional town. The original division of the city into two confessional communities, no matter how undesirable to the political leaders who had authorized it in 1575, had proven remarkably resilient. When the bells summoned the Colmarians to celebrate the signing of the Peace and Westphalia in their respective churches, neighbors and co-workers passed each other on their way to separate communities of worship less than fifty yards apart.

Between 1575 and 1640, confessional division within Colmar's political community forced a reorientation of daily life in the city. Protestant leaders who wished to establish their own church in 1575 could do so only by continuing to tolerate Catholic worship. Their Reformation never received the emperor's sanction of the *ius reformandi*, but the citizens approved the arrangement and confirmed their support in the face of external opposition which posed a continual threat to this fragile internal settlement. When the Imperial commission arrived in 1627, it only sought to restore Colmar to its proper confessional relation with the empire, but even the city's Catholic leaders realized that such a restoration would take time. Colmar's Counter-Reformation never had the time to produce significant confessional change. The Swedish takeover restored Protestant worship to what had remained a bi-confessional and predominantly Protestant town. In 1624 Colmar's Protestant parish had been attached to the Swiss Reformed church in Basel, but after 1633 would become a Lutheran church with ties to Strasbourg. Despite the wording of the Peace of Westphalia, henceforth, the normative year for confessional relations in Colmar would be 1633, not 1624.

The confessional banners attached to the city were critical to the outside powers, but they may have meant less to the Colmarians than the existence of confessional choice. Members of the same church tended to work together, to live near one another, and to share common economic expectations and anxieties. Nevertheless, the communities did not live in isolation, for they shared civic responsibilities, guild halls, and neighborhoods. Perhaps most critically the communities never polarized between rich and poor. Shared day-to-day experiences in the workplace and civic landscape counteracted the separateness of distinct religious rituals. Confessional tolerance in Colmar depended on the personal face-to-face nature of civic life. The corporate civic community was not comprised of individual members but of smaller sometimes interconnected corporate groups: guilds, neighborhoods, households. Confessional groups became one more corporate subset within the body politic.

In Alsace there were two bi-confessional cities, Hagenau and Colmar, which had initiated evangelical worship after 1555. In Hagenau, the merchant elite led the civic reformation and constituted the Lutheran parish. The artisans and the officials who depended on ecclesiastical and Habsburg patronage preserved their Catholic faith. The failure to extend Lutheran practice beyond the small merchant community eventually isolated Hagenau's Protestants, who were driven out for good by the Habsburgs in 1624.[78] The Counter-Reformation in Hagenau reduced the city to a local market and administrative center. At Colmar tensions between the clergy and the citizenry had fueled the regime's drive to establish an evangelical church, and these tensions affected confessional relations after 1575. Colmar's productive and exchange economies were heavily controlled by the Protestant community. The power of the monasteries as landowners and employers and the existence of a primarily Catholic hinterland, however, prevented a complete swing to Protestantism. In Hagenau the Counter-Reformation scattered the Lutheran community, which was limited to the city's merchants. In Colmar the Counter-Reformation also cost the city its merchant elite, but the Protestant artisans stayed on and adapted to the changing confessional circumstances. In a sense, the Alsatian bi-confessional towns experienced similar Counter-Reformations.

Notes

1. On the diverse relations between civic politics and the Reformation, see R. Po-chia Hsia, "The Myth of the Commune: Recent Historiography on City and Reformation in Germany," *Central European History* 20 (September/December 1987): 203–15.
2. On the Austrian lands, see Bücking, *Johann Rasser*, 36–84. For Horbourg-Riquewihr, see Adam, *Evangelische Kirchengeschichte*, 292–347, esp. 306–14.
3. Sebastian Münster, *Von dem Elsaß und seiner großen Fruchtbarkeit dem kein Lande am Rheinstrom mag verglichen werden* (Freiburg-im-Briesgau, 1976 [1544]), 65. For a discussion of the place of the *Ackerbürgestädte* in premodern German history, see Karl Czok, "Zur Stellung der Stadt in der deutschen Geschichte," *Jahrbuch für Regionalgeschichte* 3 (1968): 15. See also Langton and Hoppe, *Town and Country*, 36–41.
4. In the mid-seventeenth century, Matthaeus Merian again referred to Colmar's

"beautiful and fruitful soil." Matthaeus Merian, *Topographia Alsatia* (Frankfurt a.m., 1663), 10, col. 1. Cf. Franz Ruprecht von Ichtersheim, *Gantz neue elsäßiche Topographia* (Regensburg, 1710), 21.

5. Robert Darnton, *The Great Cat Massacre and Other Episodes in French Cultural History* (New York, 1984), 107–43. On Colmar's chroniclers, see Fritz Kiener, "Aperçu sur l'historiographie de Colmar," *Annuaire de Colmar* (1935): 11–38.

6. Quoted in Livet, ed., *Histoire de Colmar*, 7.

7. In 1642 members of all ten guilds held properties in the neighboring villages. AMC, DD 22, 7, fol. 1r. A survey of civic territory in 1721 produced an equally diversified picture. Sittler *La viticulture*, 33.

8. On Alsatian geography, see Reuss, *L'Alsace*, 1: 10–18; and *Histoire de l'Alsace rurale*, eds. Jean-Michel Boehler Dominique Lerch, and Jean Vogt (Strasbourg and Paris, 1983), 13–19. On the economic role of the Ill river, see Lucien Sittler, "Etudes sur l'histoire économique du Vieux-Colmar: Le Ladhof et la navigation colmarienne," *Annuaire de Colmar* (1957): 13–23.

9. On the Vosges, see Reuss, *L'Alsace*, 1: 5–10. On the Rhenish trade routes, see Hertner, *Stadtwirtschaft*, 2–4. On the scope of Colmar's trade relations, see Sittler, "Commerce et commerçants," 14–48.

10. On the history of Alsatian wine production, see Medard Barth, *Der Rebbau des Elsass und die Absatzgebeite seiner Weine: Ein geschichtlicher Durchblick* (Strasbourg and Paris, 1958). On wine production in neighboring communes, see Christian Wolff, *Riquewihr, son vignoble et ses vins à travers les ages* (Ingersheim, 1967); Andre Billich, *Histoire d'une ancienne ville impériale: Turckheim* (Colmar, 1975), 144–53. On civic vineyards, see Sittler, *La viticulture*, 9–10, 35–38.

11. Henri Doubled, "La notion du ban en Alsace au Moyen Age," *Revue Historique de Droit Français et Etranger*, ser. 4, 39 (1961): 30–75.

12. Lucien Sittler, "L'élevage à Colmar au Moyen Age et au début des temps moderns," *Annuaire de Colmar* (1968): 47–55.

13. Sittler, "Landwirtschaft und Gartenbau," 71–94.

14. Sittler, "Colmar au XVIe siècle," 21.

15. Scott, *Freiburg and the Breisgau*, 15–46. There is no modern study of the Württemberg lordships, but the Austrian domains are well served by Bischoff, *Gouvernés et gouvernants*; Stinzi, "Die Habsburger im Elsaß," 505–64.

16. Colmar's weavers supplied markets at Freiburg-im-Breisgau and Mulhouse. Hector Ammann, "La place de l'Alsace dans l'industrie textile du Moyen Age," in *La bourgeoisie alsacienne*, 71–102, here at 90–91.

17. Colmar's regime often regulated relations between journeymen and masters; Lucien Sittler, "Les mouvements sociaux à Colmar du XIVe au XVIe siècle," *RA* 95 (1956): 129–45.

18. Sittler, "Les corporations à Colmar," 47–78. On the guilds in early modern cities, see Black, *Guilds and Civil Society*, esp. 123–28. On the craft confraternities and Colmar's journeymen, see Sittler, "Les mouvements sociaux," 138–40.

19. Auguste Scherlen, *Colmar, village et ville* (Colmar, 1931), 96–98; Sittler, *La viticulture*, 54–61; Sittler, "Landwirtschaft und Gartenbau," 71–93.

20. The figures in the first three pairs of columns are from Sittler, "Les corporations à Colmar," 51–52. The final pair of columns combines the annual data in Wertz, ed., *Le livre des bourgeois, 1512–1609*, 150–220; idem, ed., *Membres du magistrat, 1601–1700*, 43–75.

21. On the mining industry in the Leberthal, see A(uguste) Hanauer, *Etudes économiques sur l'Alsace ancienne et moderne* (Strasbourg and Paris, 1876–78) 1: 190–208; and Reuss, *L'Alsace*, 1: 612–14.

22. Wilhelm Abel, *Agricultural Fluctuations in Europe: From the Thirteenth to the Twentieth Centuries*, trans. by Olive Ordish (New York, 1980), 99–158.

23. Sittler, "Landwirtschaft und Gartenbau," 77–78. He works from lists available in AMC, HH 21, 3–4.
24. Kintz, La société strasbourgeoise, 280–339.
25. Sittler, "Commerce et commerçants," 28–32.
26. AMC, CC 152.
27. Auguste Scherlen favors the smaller figure. Scherlen, Colmar, 128–29. Henri Fleurent originally posited the higher figure. Fleurent, "Essai sur la démographie," 7. For the argument in favor of this higher figure, see Sittler, "Colmar au XVIe siècle," 19. Others favor a lower figure. Greyerz, Late City Reformation, 13–14; Livet, ed., Histoire de Colmar, 70. Here Georges Bischoff settles for a figure of 6,000–7,000 based on comparative population density figures (Colmar at 100–110 per hectare) with late medieval Sélestat (100 per hectare), Saverne (85), and Strasbourg (72). Colmar's first tax roles emerged in response to the Imperial Diet's call for a common penny tax. On the use of the common penny tax assessment for demographic and social history, see Steven Rowan, "The Common Penny (1495–1499) as a Source of German Demographic and Social History," Central European History 10 (1977): 148–64.
28. A. G. Dickens, The German Nation and Martin Luther (New York, 1974), 179.
29. AMC, AA 171, 1. The report recorded the numbers of guild members for each guild, along with widows and available wagons: zur Treue, 109 guildsmen, 18 widows, and 6 wagons; zum Riesen, 96, 13, and 6; Ackerleute, 92, 11, and 26; zum Haspel, 90, 19, and 13; Rebleute, 88, 15, and 3; zum Adler, 45, 4, and no wagons; zum Löwen, 48, 10, and no wagons; zum Kränzchen, 66, 9, and one wagon; zum Wohlleben, 93, 11, and no wagons; zum Holderbaum, 82, 11, and one wagon; for a total of 809 guildsmen, 121 widows, and 56 wagons. The document also noted 1,020 houses so that the city was apparently underpopulated.
30. AMC, AA 171, 2. This survey identified two parishes (one Catholic and one Lutheran), 1,078 feux, 7,142 ames (of which 3,109 were Catholic, 3,527 were Lutheran, and 506 were "Huguenots," and no Jews). A second document drawn from the same data noted that the adult male population of the 1,078 feux included 988 citizens and 192 "habitans qui n'ont possédes demeure fixe et la changement à leur volonté." The city also sheltered 103 "garçons non mariés au-dessus de dix-huit ans." The work force also included 43 laboureurs, 221 vignerons, and 14 meuniers, AMC, AA 171, 6. AMC, AA 171, 7 is a German draft of the same assessment.
31. The census listed 1,737 men, 1,945 women, 3,703 children, 6 secular priests, 62 male religious, 72 nuns, and 1,048 "valets et servantes," for a total of 9,023 persons. AMC, AA 171, 8.
32. The document itself lacks a date, but it is classified with a request for the information from Chateauvillard, a royal agent in Strasbourg, dated 1 October 1718. AMC, AA 171, 9. The assessment only notes feux, of which 1,223 belong to bourgeois, 516 to habitans, 22 to ecclesiastics, 36 to nobles associated with military and provincial administration, and 80 associated specifically with the Conseil souverain d'Alsace, for a total of 1,877. AMC, AA 171, 10.
33. All figures must be treated cautiously. Henri Fleurent estimates 8,579 inhabitants in 1730 and then steady growth to 13,214 in 1790. Fleurent, "Essai sur la démographie," 9–10. The estimates' veracity rests on the attitude of census takers to tax-exempt households and the floating population of poor.
34. Suzanne Dreyer-Roos, La population strasbourgeoise sous l'ancien régime, PSSARE, Collection "Recherches et Documents," 6 (Strasbourg, 1969), 51–67.
35. The plague arrived in Colmar in November of 1609 and continued through 1610. Waltz, ed., Sigmund Billings Kleine Chronik, 102.
36. The Protestants recorded the following marriages: 1600: 33; 1601: 42; 1602:

43; 1603: 34; 1604: 42; 1605: 49; 1606: 40; 1607: 54; 1608: 51; 1609: 49; 1610: 43; 1611: 146; 1612: 76; 1613: 42; 1614: 44; 1615: 56. For the Catholics data is available for 1603: 24; 1604: 28; 1606: 24; 1607: 19; 1608: 32; 1609: 30; 1610: 19; 1611: 94. The Catholic register records no marriages again until 1616: 10. AMC, GG 188 & 189.

37. For the entire era, the households headed by women ranged from 10% in 1690 to 26% in 1640. With 229 out of 1,286 households (17.8%) headed by women in 1610, there were more women householders than in any year sampled for the period; and they represented the second highest percentage of female householders, next to the crisis year of 1640.

38. The assessors noted 27 empty houses in 1564, 33 in 1580, and 65 in 1590. These figures lead Bischoff and others to assume that the city was not overpopulated. Livet, ed., *Histoire de Colmar*, 70. For my estimate for 1620, see AMC, CC 152, 1620.

39. These figures seems to coincide with recent estimates of population loss for Alsace during the war. Gerhard Benecke, ed., *Germany in the Thirty Years' War* (New York, 1979), xv.

40. Between 1615 and 1624 the Reformed parish recorded an average of 44.5 marriages per year. Between 1635 and 1644, the Lutheran parish inscribed 41 marriages per year. The Catholic registers are much more problematic because of irregular record keeping, but the pattern holds. Between 1617 and 1621, the registers note an average of 24.8 marriages per year. Between 1636 and 1640 the average dropped slightly to 23.2. AMC, GG 188, 189.

41. AMC, CC 152, 1620 and 1640.

42. This figure is well below the long-term retention for other decades. For example of the 972 male householders identified in 1600, 151 (15.5%) paid taxes in 1630 despite the Counter-Reform emigration. Among the 736 male householders identified in 1650, 126 (17.1%) paid taxes in 1680.

43. Mieg, "Les tribulations d'Augustin Guntzer," 50–52.

44. Wertz, ed., *Le livre des bourgeois, 1512–1609*, x. On migration in early modern Germany, see Steve Hochstadt, "Migration in Pre-Industrial Germany," *Central European History* 16 (September 1983): 195–221. On conditions in Alsace, see Jean-Pierre Kintz, "La mobilité humaine en Alsace: Essai de présentation statistique: XIVe–XVIIIe siècle," *Annales de Démographie Historique* (1970):157–83.

45. Extant guild lists exist for *zum Riesen* (1622–23), AMC, HH 38, 51; and in 1619 for *zur Treue*, AMC, HH 27, 21; *Ackerleute*, AMC, HH 20, 1; *zum Haspel*, AMC, HH 25, 5; *Rebleute*, AMC, HH 18, 3; *zum Kränzchen*, AMC, HH 55, 7; *zum Löwen*, AMC, HH 60, 45; *zum Holderbaum*, AMC, HH 74, 6; *zum Adler*, AMC, HH 63, 4b; and *zum Wohlleben*, AMC, HH 35, 2.

46. A pound *Rappen* was a regional money of account. See Hanauer, *Etudes économiques*, 1: 19–21. The oath book of 1570 set the requirement of 100 florins of property for all outsiders who wished to purchase citizenship. See AMC, BB 51, Livre des Serments III, p. 316. A full list of civic responsibilities appears in the law code of 1593; see AMC, JJ Divers 6, pp. 94–95; or AMC, FF 60, 1, fol. 85r–86r. On the changing requirements of citizenship in Colmar, see Sittler, "Les bourgeois de Colmar," 21–34.

47. The inscriptions varied from forty-two in 1610 to zero in 1638–39. Wertz, ed., *Membres du magistrat, 1601–1700*, 43–46 and 79.

48. Paul Warmbrunn, *Zwei Konfessionen in einer Stadt: Das Zusammenleben von Katholiken und Potestanten in den paritätischen Reichsstädten Augsburg, Biberach, Ravensburg, und Dinkelsbühl von 1548 bis 1648*, VIEGM, 111 (Wiesbaden, 1983), 188–89.

49. In *zum Wohlleben* only 9 Catholics appear (6.9%); in *zum Adler* 8 (5.5%); and in *zum Riesen* 14 (7.6%).

50. In 1603 and again in 1622, the regime had to admonish the guildsmen to live up to the religious peace or face a fine. Adam, *Evangelische Kirchengeschichte*, 475.
51. On neighborhood clustering by occupation, see Kintz, *La société strasbourgeoise*, 94–108. Colmar's fishermen, for example, lived in the Krautenau in what was called the *Fischerstadt*, Scherlen, *Topographie*, 117–27. In 1600 all 7 of the known fishermen lived here; in 1620, 12 of 14; in 1640 all 11. The butchers and tanners worked in *zum roten Salmen* (district IX). Scherlen, ibid., 291–321. Among the tanners, 6 of 8 (1600), 5 of 7 (1620), and 4 of 6 (1640) settled here; for the butchers, 9 of 11 (1600), 10 of 13 (1620), and 8 of 15 (1640). See also Dietrich Denecke, "Sozialtopographie und sozialräumliche Gliederung der spätmittelalterlichen Stadt: Problemstellungun, Methoden, und Betrachtungsweisen der historischen Wirtschafts- und Sozialgeographie," in Josef Fleckenstein and Karl Stackmann, eds., *Über Bürger, Stadt, und städtische Literatur im Spätmittelalter: Bericht über Kolloquien der Kommission zur Erforschung der Kultur des Spätmittelatlers, 1975–1977* (Göttingen, 1980), 161–202, esp. 172–73.
52. François J. Himly, *Atlas des villes medievales d'Alsace*, Publications de la Fédération des Sociétés d'Histoire et d'Archéologie d'Alsace, 6 (Colmar, 1970), 23; X(avier) Mossmann, *Recherches sur l'ancienne constitution de la commune à Colmar*, 2nd, rev. ed. (Colmar, 1978), 3–4; Sittler, "Colmar au XVIe siècle," 18–19.
53. In 1692 the civic regime imposed fines on citizens who left human and animal waste for more than a month in front of their houses. Scherlen, *Topographie*, 114.
54. Quoted in ibid., 115.
55. J. de L'Hermine, *Guerre et paix en Alsace au XVIIe siècle* (Toulouse, 1981), 48.
56. Scherlen, *Topographie*, passim, here at 186–87.
57. Ibid., 104–10.
58. For example, the grain market in the *Hallers Ort*, ibid., 322–25; the cattle market in *Kürsnerthürlein*, ibid., 386, 399–400; or the wine market in *zur Senfmühle*, ibid., 327–28.
59. Ibid., 116–27.
60. Ibid., 340–47.
61. Ibid., 386–400.
62. Scherlen, *Topographie*, devotes sixty-one pages (340–400) to describing the landmarks and famous personages of districts XIII through XXIII. Districts V and VI are allocated eighty-one pages (186–266).
63. For *Gang in der Stadt*, ibid., 128–56; for *Lambsort*, ibid., 170–86.
64. Ibid., 160–64.
65. AMC, CC 152, 1620.
66. The wealth assessments are drawn from Colmar's *Gewerff* registers, which formed the basis of all municipal tax assessments. AMC, CC 152, 1600, 1610, & 1620. The tax assessment reflected on average .05% of one's property and liquid assets, though those paying at higher rates were probably underassessed. Thus the overall image compresses the actual social structure. Weyrauch, "Die politische Führungsgruppe," 225. On the use of the *Steuerbücher* for analyzing the social structure in a community, see idem, "Über Soziale Schichtung," in Bátori, ed., *Städtische Gesellschaft und Reformation*, 5–57, esp. 44ff.
67. Livet, ed., *Histoire de Colmar*, 81–86.
68. Sittler, "Commerce et commerçants," 28–29. Wibert, Sarazin, and Sysson were all identified as Savoyard cloth merchants whose presence at Colmar initially triggered a call for expulsion from other merchants in *zur Treue*. AMC, HH 27, 33. Instead they joined the guild and submitted to its regulations. In 1610 together they were assessed at 9,000 florins, which was more than the com-

bined wealth of the 103 householders in the lowest stratum.
69. Hans Barth, originally from Riquewihr, was assessed at 2,400 florins in 1610.
Georg Würtzlein from Ensisheim was assessed at 4,800 florins; Andreas Meder
from Herlisheim was assessed at 2,500 florins; Anthon Burger from Hausen
was assessed at 5,600 florins. All were Protestant merchants in the guild *zur
Treue*, and Burger would serve in the Reformed magistrate. Lorentz Beck and
Balthasar Schneider were officials who administered local noble estates. Beck,
from Ammerschwihr, was assessed at 6,000 florins and was the second richest
man in Colmar. Schneider, also an outsider, was the founder of a dynasty of
civic officials and was assessed at 3,000 florins. Georg Kleindienst, a tenant
farmer from Sainte-Croix-en-Plaine, and Niclaus Güntzer, a draper, who had
joined the weavers' guild, *zum Adler*, had come from Sélestat. Güntzer was
assessed at 3,000 florins and Kleindienst at 2,000 florins. All of these immigrants were Protestant.
70. Livet, ed., *Histoire de Colmar*, 79–81.
71. On Hagenau's Reformation and Counter-Reformation, see Burg, "Patrizier,"
353–75, here at 362–64; Greyerz, *Late City Reformation*, 195–96.
72. Hohenberg and Lees, *The Making of Urban Europe*, 125–36.
73. Sittler, *La viticulture*, 74–76.
74. Forty-five out of eighty-nine householders (51.1%).
75. On the impact of Colmar's refugees for the economy in Mulhouse, see Oberlé,
La république de Mulhouse, 254–63. For conditions in Basel, see Stritmatter,
Die Stadt Basel, 61–78.
76. The forty-one householders break down as follows:

GUILD	(no.)	1620 (total wealth)	(no.)	1640 (total wealth)
Treue	9	15,570	14	30,700
Riesen	4	5,500	7	9,130
Ackerleute	—	—	—	—
Haspel	1	600	1	1,600
Rebleute	2	1,150	2	1,200
Löwen	1	150	1	300
Kränzchen	3	1,600	3	3,300
Holderbaum	4	2,250	4	1,700
Adler	4	1,950	6	4,650
Wohlleben	1	2,100	1	1,450
Unknown	1	150	2	100
Totals	30	31,020 6.4%	41	54,130 18.1%

77. Kintz, *La société strasbourgeoise*, 460–77; Oberlé, *La république de Mulhouse*,
402–12.
78. Greyerz, *Late City Reformation*, 193–96.

Part II

A Post-Westphalian "Home Town"
Caught between the Empire and
France, 1640–1679

3

From Protection to Subjugation: Colmar and the French Crown, 1634–1679

On 2 October 1649 the seventy-man French garrison paraded out of Colmar's gates. For over twenty years the Colmarians had housed and fed unwanted soldiers: first Imperial, then Swedish, and finally, since 1634, French. For Colmar the garrison's departure was the final act of the Thirty Years' War, which had ravaged the city and region. The treaties signed at Osnabrück and Münster in Westphalia called for the evacuation of the French garrison and the restoration of Colmar's Imperial status.[1]

The Peace of Westphalia ended French protection over Colmar, but it also established French rule for the first time in Alsace, where French power supplanted Austrian power and posed a threat to Colmar's sovereignty, more dangerous than the Austrian one had ever been. French power, though initially dampened by the political disorder within France generated by "the Fronde," grew within a generation to subjugate Colmar and end its status as an Imperial city. Colmar's regime had thwarted several earlier attempts to legally integrate the city into the kingdom, but on 30 August 1673, when Louis XIV entered Alsace at the head of an army prepared to besiege the city, the Colmarians could not resist. The king razed their fortifications and left the city open like "a village."[2] In 1679 the Treaty of Nijmegen confirmed Colmar's transfer from the empire to France.

In 1649 the loss of the city's Imperial status seemed unlikely, because the constitutional fabric of the empire was coming together once again in defense of the Imperial estates. Colmar's political leaders, however, did face two challenges. First, they had to quickly learn to use the refurbished Imperial system to fend off Bourbon claims to sovereignty, which grew increasingly stronger. Secondly, the Colmarians had to learn the royal system of governance in order to deal effectively with the king's agents. As the French garrison left the city, the magistrates had reason for optimism, for they had already had their first lesson in translating between French and Imperial political cultures during the years of French protection.

I. "Royal Protection" and the Search for Peace, 1634–1649

When the Swedes occupied Colmar in 1633, they took it under their "protection" (*Schutz*) on terms favorable to the city. The Colmarians paid an initial plunder tax and accepted a Swedish garrison, but the city retained its self-governance. The Swedes, however, were willing to pressure the civic regime in its external relations and coerced the Colmarians to join the Protestant League of Heilbronn.[3] In late 1633 the fighting began to turn against the Swedes, who pressured their allies to assume the burden of financing the field armies. Colmar's magistrates convinced the council of jurors to accept the added tax burden, but by April 1634 the city pleaded insolvency. The League of Heilbronn responded by awarding Colmar partial control over the revenues of the Abbey of Munster and stewardship over the neighboring villages of Herlisheim, Soultzbach, Holtzwihr, and Wickerswihr to help relieve civic financial problems until the peace.[4] The Swedish defeat at Nördlingen, however, threatened to shatter the League of Heilbronn and drove the Swedes to negotiate the transfer of their protectorates in Alsace to the French.[5] On 9 October 1634, the Swedish agent in Strasbourg, Mockel, delivered Colmar into French protection. The Franco-Swedish accord reaffirmed the inviolability of Colmar's chartered rights and promised to restore the city's prewar political status after the general peace. The French agreed to recognize the municipal constitution and legal code as well as the confessional rights of Colmar's Lutherans and Catholics. The Colmarians, however, were not consulted, which troubled them.[6]

As the Swedes withdrew to the north, French troops and administrators poured into Alsace, including a military governor dispatched to Colmar to handle the transfer of protection. Later, an intendant, a special army commissioner, headed the king's local officials.[7] For the civic regime, the first order of business was to substitute a direct accord with France for the Franco-Swedish pact. In August 1635 the city clerk, Johann Heinrich Mogg, negotiated a treaty at Rueil near Paris, which assured the Colmarians that the military protection would remain in effect only until the peace, when Colmar would regain the status it possessed "prior to the troubles in Germany and Bohemia in the year of 1618." The treaty safeguarded Colmar's chartered liberties and confirmed the regime's authority within the city, though, as with Sweden, the Colmarians accepted French tutelage in foreign policy. Finally, Mogg inserted clauses which guaranteed the freedom of worship for both confessional communities and provided the civic authorities with a degree of influence over the French garrison.[8] Though the rights granted by Louis XIII followed royal practice, they must have seemed miraculous to the civic leaders on Mogg's return.[9] This treaty laid the groundwork for nearly forty years of political relations between the city and the royal government.

The first years of French protection were filled with hardship. The Austrians clung to the crucial fortress at nearby Breisach, and the French, now fully engaged in the fighting, suffered a string of military setbacks. The morale among Colmar's French garrison was low, and three consecutive years of campaigning had devastated the countryside and caused acute grain shortages. During the hard winter of 1635–36, supplies had to be hauled by sled through the Vosges to prevent starvation in the city, while royal agents demanded forced loans and corvée labor on the fortifications.[10] By 1637 the worst had passed, and the new governor and new intendant eased the pressure on the city.[11]

In December 1638 Duke Bernard of Saxe-Weimar, the mercenary commander of French forces in Alsace, captured Breisach and drove the Austrian and Imperial forces from the Upper Rhine. Saxe-Weimar held ambitions of becoming lord of the region, and the Colmarians, recognizing his growing power and independence, negotiated reciprocal tariff privileges with him, while maintaining cordial relations with the royal agents in Alsace.[12] Breisach's capture had reduced Colmar's strategic significance for the French, and within months the regime managed to substitute a flat payment for its former obligation to quarter troops and to gain control over the reduced garrison.[13]

In 1639, just as the Colmarians were beginning to breathe more easily, Louis XIII appointed a new governor, Montausier, with sweeping authority over Colmar and the surrounding region. The magistrates bristled at the language of his commission and protested that traditional liberties forbade the Crown to treat the city "like a slave or a subject." Montausier promised the regime that "the intention of the king was never to choke liberty nor the treaty he had made with the Republic," but his commission stood without correction.[14] Shortly afterwards the royal government demanded an oath of obedience from the Alsatian estates under royal protection. The Colmarians resisted, while many others acquiesced. The royal officials did not force the issue; for the moment at least, they recognized the need "to treat the city well on all occasions."[15]

Throughout the 1640s Colmar's political leaders faced a dilemma. As a small Imperial city, Colmar could neither protect itself from marauding armies nor depend on the Imperial institutions for peacekeeping, and Mogg and his associates saw French protection as the only viable means of preserving their independence. Despite written guarantees, they soon realized that they had no certainty of French intentions, which led them to court Bernard of Saxe-Weimar and his successor, the count of Erlach, as alternative protectors. French military weakness and lack of leadership after the deaths of Richelieu and Louis XIII in 1643 threw conditions further into doubt. As peace negotiations began, the civic leaders found it crucial to preserve the distinction between French protection and French sovereignty.

The Peace of Westphalia established a new constitutional balance within the empire which favored the Imperial princes at the expense of the emperor and at the risk of the smaller estates.[16] In the core of the empire the smaller estates found security in the Imperial Circles and courts.[17] On the empire's periphery, where the Swedish, Austrian, and French rulers were the new Imperial territorial princes, the insulation of Imperial institutions was frayed.[18]

In Alsace the treaty provided the French monarchy with territorial "satisfactions" at the expense of Austria.[19] From the moment they raised the issue of "satisfaction" at the negotiations in January 1646, the French were divided over whether their Alsatian claims should remain in the empire or be annexed into the kingdom.[20] Cardinal Mazarin, who intended to find an entry into Imperial politics, and the emperor's negotiator, Count von Trauttmannsdorff, who sought to deny him, both inserted articles into the treaty which would obscure the exact nature of French power in Alsace.[21] The treaty's ambiguities, which spawned the legal disputes between Colmar and France from 1648 to 1673, deserves a brief examination.

In article 74 Austria ceded to France "all rights, properties and domains, possessions and jurisdictions" in "the city of Breisach, the landgraviate of Upper and Lower Alsace, Sundgau, and the provincial lordship [the Imperial Bailiwick] of the ten Imperial cities situated in Alsace." The next article then claimed that the cession was made "without any prejudice to the privileges and liberties . . . of the ten cities nominated and their dependencies."[22] The treaty thus defined French lordship by means of Imperial formulas. To further clarify the issue for all parties, the negotiators drafted article 92 to include a specific explanation of Imperial traditions. Louis XIV's agents promised to leave the cities:

> in the liberty and possession [of the rights] they have enjoyed hitherto, to arise as immediately dependent on the empire; so that he cannot depend on royal sovereignty over them, but shall be contented with the rights which appertained to the House of Austria. . . . In such manner, nevertheless, that by present declaration, nothing is intended that shall derogate from sovereign dominion already here above agreed to.[23]

In this short passage, the treaty drew a line between liberty and sovereign dominion, and then erased it. It guaranteed the chartered rights of the Alsatian estates to the extent that these rights did not interfere with the exercise of French power. The document allowed as many interpretations as there were interested parties. As the Imperial commissioner, Volmar, remarked: "The strongest will explain them to his advantage."[24]

The Austrians ceded to France certain clearly defined territories and certain rights over other territories. The ceded lands lay primarily in Upper Alsace to the south of Colmar, though the prize piece, the fortress at Breisach, gave the French a bridgehead on the Rhine's right bank. The French acquired outright sovereignty over these "hereditary lands."[25] The Austrians' second concession, the landgraviates of Upper and Lower Alsace, proved more difficult to define. Originally established in the ninth century, the two landgraviates were separate offices without territorial domains and with limited authority in Alsatian politics, since the landgraves claimed no rights over any Alsatian estate. The Habsburgs felt they had given nothing but titles. The French, on the other hand, viewed the landgraviates as territories and after 1648 claimed that the Habsburgs had ceded to them "all of Alsace," even though Alsace was a geographic region and not a political entity.[26]

For the Colmarians, French control of the Imperial Bailiwick of Hagenau was the most significant Habsburg concession. The bailiwick possessed two layers of power. First, the office administered forty villages and extensive forests in the plain surrounding Hagenau, and this cession gave France sovereignty over the villages and forest rights. Secondly, the Imperial Bailiff held various rights over the ten Alsatian Imperial cities, the Decapolis, but these rights derived from the bailiff's Imperial office and not from lordship.[27] Yet the treaty's ambiguities and Colmar's Protestant leaders' concerns over French confessional policies led Colmar's Westphalian negotiator and court clerk, Hans Balthasar Schneider, to propose language that would distinguish between the Imperial Bailiff's rights over the villages and his rights over the Decapolis. Schneider failed, however, because the French threatened to reopen the whole document if the change were approved.[28] The Peace of Westphalia therefore left the specific nature of French sovereignty in Alsace unresolved.

In 1650 Colmar's leaders must have felt some pride in the preservation of civic liberties, but the king was now a major power in Alsace with institutional leverage in municipal politics. During the quarter century after 1648, the civic regime jealously defended its place in the Imperial system, while the French, who had yet to work out their political objectives, pursued several, often conflicting, policies. The regime fought so tenaciously because, along with communal oaths, the Imperial system formed one of the two pillars of the regime's authority. As peace settled over war-torn Alsace, the royal officials and the Alsatian estates sought to find the balance which would allow them to live together.

II. ALL THE KING'S MEN IN SEARCH OF A POLICY

The Peace of Westphalia had made Louis XIV the major power in Alsace, but the royal government could not, at first, assert its leadership, because the crisis created in the kingdom by "the Fronde" left its central agencies divided and weakened. In particular, the frondeurs sought to eliminate the intendants, who were essential to provincial administration. In Alsace the office survived, but its agents received little direction from Paris. Furthermore, Spain, which was still at war with France, continued to occupy Frankenthal in the Palatinate, and royal officials in Alsace devoted their attention to provincial defense.[29] The Spanish invasion never materialized, but the threat of further bloodshed kept garrisons in the province and weighed down recovery efforts among the Alsatian communities.

Charles IV of Lorraine, whose domains separated Alsace from the main body of France, was also at war with the young king. In December 1651 his armies invaded Alsace, and the estates of Lower Alsace, which had earlier denied France a seat in their assembly, raised a modest defense force under Strasbourg's leadership.[30] This army deflected the marauding Lorrainers southward into Upper Alsace, where they campaigned unmolested, despite the large French garrison at Breisach. The duke's troops pillaged Ribeauvillé, Kaysersberg, Turckheim, Riquewihr, and Munster. Colmar, too large and too well fortified to provide an easy target, once again served as a haven for the region's refugees until May 1652, when the Lorrainers retired across the Vosges.[31] Finally, in August the French officials invited the Upper Alsatian estates to Colmar to draw up an ambitious defense plan, based on substantial French support. The project never materialized, and each community fell back on its own resources.[32] The protective umbrella of French power had failed its first test.

The royal administration suffered a further loss of prestige and influence when the Fronde spilled over into Alsace and neutralized the intendant. The principal royal representative in Alsace became the governor, Henry of Lorraine, count of Harcourt, who also held the post of Imperial Bailiff of Hagenau.[33] Within months of his appointment, the new governor joined the revolt against the Regency. Following in the footsteps of Bernard of Saxe-Weimar, Harcourt attempted to form a semi-independent state in the upper Rhine valley centered at Breisach, where the garrison had rallied to him.[34] In September 1652, as Mazarin began to recover his authority within the kingdom, Harcourt offered to transfer the province to Spain.[35] Despite his treason, he was strong enough that Mazarin could not arrest him; and finally, in 1654, the royal government signed what amounted to a peace treaty with the rebellious count. Harcourt kept his titles and revenues in Alsace, though he lost all power in the province. In the following years, Mazarin and, later, the royal minister Colbert carefully selected faithful clients for Alsatian administrative posts to prevent a second rebellion and to counteract the damage and division which was the legacy of Harcourt's governorship.[36] Thus, the royal administration failed to establish an effective political presence in its first years in Alsace, and the disorder allowed the Alsatian estates to rebuild their ties with the Imperial institutions.

During his revolt Harcourt attempted to bully the Decapolis into submission. In November 1649 he invited the cities to send representatives to Hagenau to swear an oath of allegiance. The Alsatians demanded that Imperial commissioners present the new bailiff in the traditional formula before they would comply, and they refused to pay the *Reichssteuer* to Harcourt until he would provide them with Imperial receipts. Harcourt countered that he held his office by the sovereign will of his king, but the Alsatians categorically denied French sovereignty and protested against Harcourt's oath before the Imperial cameral tribunal (*Reichskammergericht*) at Speyer.[37] The issue was sovereignty, and the Colmarians defended their resistance in letters to the Imperial Chancellor, the elector of Mainz, and to the emperor. To the elector the Colmarians noted that if they renounced reciprocal oaths, as Harcourt wished, then they would renounce "the protection of the empire," which would spell the end of "our independence and our security." In their letter to the emperor, they added their concerns about the possible reprisals in which "vengeance will be had on one [city] or the other, which will then pay for everyone."[38] Colmar, as the leader of the Alsatians' opposition, seemed the likely whipping boy.

The legal appeals shifted the debate to the Imperial courts. Harcourt, already at odds with the Regency, could not muster the legal proofs or the military might to enforce his will. In July 1653, with his revolt collapsing, Harcourt agreed to the customary procedures.[39] Shortly afterwards Colmar dispatched its first *Reichssteuer* payment to the bailiff.[40] The settlement was short lived, for Mazarin, who had regained the upper hand in Paris, ordered Harcourt to renege on his promise. The cardinal hoped that the cities would appeal to the Diet at Regensburg, so that he could counter with a claim to a seat in its sessions for the king. When the Decapolis raised the issue, the emperor quickly tabled the discussion.[41] Neither the Imperial courts nor the Diet gave the parties what they wanted, but the absence of resolution apparently favored the interests of the cities. Both the French and the Alsatians understood that the issue was sovereignty, which for the royal agents meant obedience to the king and for the cities independence as free estates. For the moment the French were not strong enough to break the deadlock.

By 1654 Harcourt's power in Alsace had ended, though he continued to hold his posts. The royal government possessed other administrative bureaus with interests in Alsace and a cadre of local agents engaged in fiscal or military matters. The king's men had yet to bring coherency to his rule in Alsace. That task fell to a new intendant, Charles Colbert de Croissy. Within a few years of his appointment, he effectively centralized administration in the territories directly controlled by the king. He failed, however, to extend royal authority over the other estates, in part because of rivalries among the king's local agents and in part due to disputes between factions at court over the role of Alsace in royal foreign policy.

Colbert de Croissy was the younger brother of Jean-Baptiste Colbert, and in September 1655, after a brief tour of duty in Toulon, the younger Colbert became intendant of Alsace.[42] He was a loyal "creature" of Mazarin's patronage system, and his presence reinforced Mazarin's influence in the region.[43] Croissy officially answered to the minister of foreign affairs, and diplomatic objectives would circumscribe his acts.[44] Intendants had served in Alsace for nearly twenty years, but Croissy took over an administration that lacked even a rudimentary structure.[45] He brought with him his trusted personal secretaries, his *commis*, and he inherited a handful of local agents, *subdélégués*, who owed him no special allegiance. Croissy proceeded to overhaul and rationalize the system to achieve two objectives: to consolidate royal power in the "territories of old dominion," that is the Austrian hereditary lands; and to centralize "provincial" judicial structures through the establishment of the *Conseil souverain d'Alsace*.[46]

The Austrian "territories of old dominion" in Upper Alsace comprised several distinct lordships administered from the town of Ensisheim. The medieval assembly of territorial estates (*Ländestag*) had not met since 1631, except for the emergency session of 1649, and Croissy chose to ignore them as he began his reform of the territorial fiscal system.[47] The Austrian system had encompassed dozens of special taxes, both direct and indirect, against which the estates claimed privileges. Croissy first standardized and centralized record keeping to gain a coherent picture of the system, and then in 1661 he consolidated the various direct taxes into one annual payment. The reform eliminated traditional privileges, but to sweeten the pill, he reduced the tax burden by two-thirds.[48] The estates acquiesced, and Croissy assumed control of the territorial fiscal system.

In 1663 Croissy rationalized indirect taxes by eliminating the customs barriers within the "territories of old dominion" and again offering a rate reduction. Shortly afterwards the intendant auctioned the right to collect the tariffs to a group of Parisian tax farmers.[49] Tax farming reduced administrative costs and provided steady revenue for the royal government, and the tax farmers favored standardized rates and opposed traditional exemptions, which complicated collection and restricted profits. They also supported Croissy's desire to foster trade for the same reasons. The marriage of fiscal administration and private enterprise spawned a new type of official in the Alsatian communities. Initially these entrepreneurs were "carpetbaggers" from the kingdom's interior, but soon the system would serve as a magnet for local capital.

In his reforms Croissy had ignored the local estates' privileges. He did not deny the legitimacy of exemption and privilege, only their source. In a letter to the foreign ministry in 1663, Croissy noted that despite the claims of the estates, "the king is no less their sovereign than for his subjects that he has in France and he can govern as it pleases him." Furthermore he felt that the Alsatian estates "ought to recognize the free exercise of the rights they claim as a particular gift His majesty has made to them and not as an obligation."[50] For Croissy royal authority was to be the unquestioned arbitrator of Alsatian political relations, and from the beginning he attempted to apply his definition of sovereignty beyond the old Austrian domains.

The fiscal reforms in the "territories of old dominion" directly affected Colmar, which was the chief commercial center of Upper Alsace. Croissy first stirred up civic opposition in 1656, when he taxed Colmarian property in the king's Alsatian villages.[51] The Colmarians had purchased extensive holdings in the neighboring territories during the crisis of the 1630s.[52] Traditionally the Austrian regime at Ensisheim had levied a military tax on rural property, and both the Swedes and Bernard of Saxe-Weimar had augmented the tax during the war.[53] Nevertheless, Colmarians claimed exemption from the tax, and in 1644 Mazarin had acknowledged the exemption.[54]

In 1656 Croissy saw no obligation to honor the Colmarians traditional rights, and he threatened to confiscate their harvest unless they paid the tax. His first warning went unheeded, and Croissy repeated the threat, which he apparently could not carry out.[55] In the early months of 1657, the civic regime attempted to gain leverage by appealing to Croissy's superiors. Civic officials recognized that Croissy was an agent for someone in the central government. Therefore they petitioned a half-dozen French officials, with the argument that Croissy, like Harcourt, was acting independently of his superiors.[56] The Colmarians held that their rights were grounded in customary reciprocity, dating back to contracts in 1331 between the Austrians and the Upper Alsatian estates which exempted Colmar's citizens from taxes on properties in the Austrian domains and granted reciprocal rights for Austrian subjects.[57] The Colmarians added that the duke of Württemberg and the bishop of Strasbourg, each of whom held substantial domains in Upper Alsace, had always respected the fourteenth-century pact.[58] Finally, the Colmarians held up Mazarin's concession of 1644, though Croissy, they noted, had argued the Peace of Westphalia superseded Mazarin's pact. The regime admitted that the king could exercise "supreme dominion" over his subjects; but the Colmarians, it stressed, were not royal subjects.[59] Finally, the civic regime reminded the French officials that the crown had sworn at Westphalia to observe Alsatian customs.[60]

Colmarians had purchased most of the contested properties during the Thirty Years' War, and the extent of the city's holdings in neighboring communes, not just the former Austrian villages, angered the villagers, who shouldered a larger share of the tax burden.[61] Colmar's neighbors complained that the Colmarians had gobbled up land at debased prices and taken advantage of them. The municipal regime did not deny the bargain prices but replied that the land had been on the open market and that the Colmarians had worked these holdings at great expense since the war.[62] As a compromise the Colmarians offered to resell the properties to the king's subjects at the original price plus expenses. Their offer was not accepted, and by the following harvest, the Regency ordered the Colmarians to pay the tax.[63] The intendant's success derived from effective use of royal power, but also from Alsatian animosity and pressure. The king's Alsatian subjects favored taxing the Colmarians because reciprocity had become so one-sided, and the Imperial city of Turckheim and the Württemberg regime in Riquewihr made similar demands.[64] Colmar's officials faced too many angry neighbors and ultimately were unable to resist royal will in royal territory.

Croissy had managed to force his direct tax reforms on the Colmarians. When he challenged the customs privileges of the local estates, however, the intendant encountered a deeply entrenched network of charters and

reciprocal liberties with Colmar at the nerve center and leading the opposition. During the Thirty Years' War, customs duties had risen to extortion-
ate levels, and the Peace of Westphalia stipulated their reinstatement to
prewar rates. Immediately following the peace, the intendant, Baussan, had
lowered the duties at the former Austrian customs stations.[65] Baussan, however, had limited influence with local agents who dealt face-to-face with
claims of privilege and exemption. For Colmar's merchants, the most significant royal customs barrier was just north of the city at Illhäusern on
the Ill river, the main artery for trade with Strasbourg and the Rhenish
markets beyond.[66]

As early as 1650, Colmar's merchants and the royal customs officials had
begun to bicker about the rates.[67] The royal agents insisted on their rights
as they understood them, though the tangle of exemptions and partial exemptions and the volume of charters applicable to individual customs stations hindered efforts to regulate effectively. Finally in 1652 the royal
government published a general ordinance based on the archducal ordinance of 1600, which reestablished all customs duties "in the same order
and state in which they had been paid and received before the ruinous
German and Imperial wars."[68] Under the royal ordinance a merchant paid
only once when transporting goods to market, which offered a substantial
savings in transport costs in a region as politically fragmented as Alsace.
The tariff exempted all goods transported for personal consumption and
discounted foodstuffs by one-half. The neighboring cities, which were "mixed
in with this government of Alsace," were eligible for certain exemptions.
Colmar was a "mixed in" city, whose regime could issue passports to merchants signifying that their wine and grain was for personal consumption.
If the merchants failed to produce a passport, they owed the full duty.[69] In
keeping with Austrian precedent, the royal ordinance recognized the exemptions for "mixed in" cities as contractual and reciprocal.[70] Harcourt's
revolt, however, delayed the tariff's implementation.

After 1652 Colmar's merchants periodically encountered difficulties with
the customs agents at Illhäusern, who seized merchandise and forced the
Colmarians to petition the intendant for redress. In October 1654 the civic
regime and the agents at Illhäusern contested the rate and the city's use of
the passport system.[71] Obristmeister Johann Heinrich Mogg penned a long
memorandum which catalogued Colmar's tariff rights and privileges under
traditional practice.[72] Baussan censured the tax collector and ordered resti-
tution, though the intendant warned Mogg that "the majority of the things
you claim by right you have only by the grace of the house of Austria."[73] In
early 1655, in the interim between Baussan's death and the arrival of Croissy,
the tax collector at Illhäusern confiscated goods carried by Johann Michael
Fridt, who was one of Colmar's wealthiest men and would later be a member of the society *zum Waagkeller*.[74] The *subdélégué* in Breisach reprimanded
the local official over the confiscations because they were "useless and would

only attract hatred." The *subdélégué* confirmed the reduced rate for wine and foodstuffs but classified brandy and vinegar as processed goods to be assessed at the full rate.[75]

Croissy's drive to rationalize indirect tax collection ran counter to the royal ordinance of 1652 and triggered confrontation at the customs station. In February 1656 the civic regime, citing a series of clashes at Illhäusern, presented Croissy with copies of its ancient charters, a record of previous decisions by royal officials, and a copy of the tariff of 1652.[76] Croissy agreed to maintain the status quo, yet he tolerated the further harassment of Colmar's shipping.[77] Civic merchants soon learned that they could not expect clear passage without a passport granted by the intendant.[78] Ultimately the issue revolved around two definitions of privilege, and the Colmarians were beginning to realize that only the French interpretation would secure civic commerce.[79]

In 1662 the intendant farmed the Alsatian indirect taxes to a consortium of private entrepreneurs under the direction of the *receveur général* in Metz.[80] Colmar's customs disputes now became the concern of the local agent for the Parisian investors, named Barbault, who endeavored to avoid confrontations and delays which cut the flow of revenue. Barbault moved in an environment of patronage and favor, where official and personal interest merged. For example he interceded for the regime with local agents and the intendant and then asked the magistrate to store a shipment of salt for him.[81] In 1666 Barbault contracted a one-year exemption on customs duties for Colmar's wine merchants for a flat payment of 300 florins.[82] Shortly afterwards Barbault and the civic regime signed a general accord which confirmed the wine exemptions, as well as blanket personal exemptions for Colmar's magistrates, and a general rate reduction for all Colmarians. In return the city exempted Barbault and his family from any fiscal obligation on their properties and goods in Colmar.[83]

Croissy and the royal government won this first fiscal struggle with Colmar's regime. Both sides had clearly articulated their views of the king's rights in Alsace. The regime produced medieval charters and argued for traditional privileges, while the royal officials viewed taxation as a sovereign right which could not be abrogated by legal contracts. Under the accord with Barbault, Colmar's tax privileges in the king's Alsatian domains rested once again on contractual reciprocity. More important, Barbault showed civic officials that royal privileges could be easily negotiated and treated as personal possessions and investments. Colmar's political leaders were learning to speak the language of the royal administration, and for them "personal privilege" would become a tantalizing new phrase in their vocabulary.

III. COLMAR AND THE *CONSEIL SOUVERAIN D'ALSACE*

During his tenure as intendant, Croissy wanted to unify the diverse local systems of juticial appeal under one royal institution, the *Conseil souverain d'Alsace*, which he established at the former Austrian capital at Ensisheim.

The *Conseil souverain* traced its pedigree from an earlier Austrian tribunal, whose jurisdiction extended only to the borders of Austrian territories, within which older local courts still functioned.[84] Croissy, however, envisioned the *Conseil souverain* as the provincial supreme court, which would insulate the local courts from Imperial justice and break the ties with the high courts at Speyer and Vienna.[85] In 1656 Croissy was able to carry out his plan as part of a new aggressive royal policy in Alsace in the wake of French failure to deny Leopold I the Imperial throne. The first two decrees registered by the *Conseil souverain* were its own royal commission and a declaration of the king's sovereignty over the lands ceded by the Peace of Westphalia, including the Decapolis.[86] Croissy also used the new court to strengthen his hand in Alsatian politics. He served as the first president of the seven-member chamber and handpicked the *conseillers* from his French and Alsatian clients. The new court neutralized the influence of the old governor, the count of Harcourt, who had no voice in its sessions.[87]

The Alsatian estates, in particular the Decapolis, gave the new court a cool reception. Colmar's regime hand delivered a complaint at the inaugural session of the *Conseil souverain*, which argued that "the creation of the judicial body did not dissipate the political tensions . . . it aggravated them since it assumes to give to the new council, successor to the Austrian regency, power, which despite [French] claims, the regency never held."[88] Croissy refused to receive the document, and in the ensuing weeks he dispatched a commission which requested that the ten cities formally register the new tribunal's edict of creation in their protocols. The six Lower Alsatian cities accepted the terms, while Munster, Kaysersberg, and Turckheim protested against the pressure but inscribed the decree. Colmar's magistrates flatly refused on the grounds that their attendance at the inauguration had fulfilled their obligation, and they repeated their protest against the tribunal's claims to authority which threatened their judicial rights and liberties.[89]

The key to membership in the post-Westphalian empire was participation in the judicial system, and Colmar's leaders correctly equated their own authority with their Imperial judicial prerogatives. Indeed, the regime held the right of high justice without appeal in all criminal cases, and in civil cases, appeals were limited only to judgments over fifty florins. Connected to the regime's judicial authority over its citizens was its right to defend its own interests before the *Reichskammergericht* at Speyer or the Aulic Council (*Reichshofrat*) at Vienna. Earlier, the archducal court at Ensisheim and the Imperial Bailiff's tribunal at Hagenau had unsuccessfully tried to insulate Colmar from access to Imperial justice. Down to 1656 provincial French officials had respected Colmar's judicial rights, and Mazarin himself had sanctioned the city's right to commission jurists to represent it at Speyer.[90]

Croissy could not force the Colmarians to acquiesce, but he also could not appear impotent before this direct challenge to his will. The intendant decided to bribe the key men in the civic regime to gain their compliance. In a letter to his brother, Jean-Baptiste Colbert, Croissy isolated two magistrates, Johann Heinrich Mogg and Daniel Birr, as the dominant men in Colmar's politics. Mogg, the intendant noted, was by far the more powerful, for his resistance against the Austrians during the Thirty Years' War and his negotiation of French protection in 1635 made him "the savior of his homeland." Croissy, however, had little respect for Mogg, whom he passed off as a "proud, vain, pushy, and conniving" man of "low extraction." Mogg, he added, ruled the city "with the rod and even tyrannically, without anyone daring to complain of it." Croissy believed that Daniel Birr, a university-trained lawyer, had a "more kindly" personality which served as a counterweight to Mogg's "excesses."[91] The intendant felt that he had to sway these two men to break the regime's defiance and proposed to tempt Mogg and Birr with offices and power. Croissy would move the *Conseil souverain* to Colmar and turn the royal government's most obstinate opponent into its provincial capital. To secure the magistrates' cooperation, he would offer them lucrative posts within the court itself. He sweetened the proposal with gifts of silver, but the real bribe was personal power and prestige. In Croissy's terms, "in place of the three months during which they personally govern their city each year, they will govern all the ten Imperial cities and generally all of Alsace."[92]

The intendant, with the Regency's approval, made the offer, but Birr's death in early 1659 left Mogg the central figure in the plan. The "savior of his homeland" seemed willing to accept Croissy's bribe, but two obstacles prevented the move. First, the royal government had to sanction the Lutheran Mogg as a *conseiller* at a time when no Protestant served on the court. Secondly, Mogg had to persuade the civic regime to accept a French garrison. The regime seemed willing to accept a garrison, provided the crown gave assurances of religious freedom. At the last moment, however, a shift in French relations with the Imperial estates tabled negotiations.[93]

By the summer of 1659, Leopold I's election as emperor triggered a shift in French policies in Alsace. Louis XIV's advisors pushed for the formation of the Rhenish League as a counterweight to revived Habsburg power. League membership forced the king's agents to dust off the image of Louis XIV as "the defender of German liberties," and a heavy-handed policy in Alsace could tarnish that image. Croissy was ordered to break off negotiations with the Colmarians and to soften the claims of the *Conseil souverain*. In 1661 Croissy became intendant of both Lorraine and Alsace, with his new headquarters in the great fortress at Metz, and the *parlement* at Metz assumed authority over the *Conseil souverain*, whose status diminished to a provincial chamber.[94]

In Alsace the administrative restructuring distanced royal governance. Local agents and the tax farmers remained, while the renamed *Conseil provincial* at Ensisheim asserted no authority outside the old Austrian hereditary lands. The Crown continued to claim judicial suzerainty over all of

Alsace but waived appeals to Metz because of the difficulty of the jour-
ney.[95] In 1663, when the intendancies of Alsace and Lorraine were again
divided, Croissy's Alsatian successors, his cousin Charles Colbert and then
Poncet de la Rivière, would prove less forceful.[96] From 1663 to 1673, the
intendants played only a minor role in Colmar's relations with the kingdom. The arena of conflict shifted once again to the powers of the Imperial Bailiff of Hagenau.

IV. COLMAR AND THE IMPERIAL BAILIWICK OF HAGENAU

As we have seen, since 1648 the rights of the Imperial Bailiff of Hagenau
formed the focus of much of Colmar's struggle with the royal government.
After 1648 the Crown viewed the king's control of the Imperial Bailiwick
as a sovereign possession, which the cities should recognize through a formal oath of obedience. The cities, on the other hand, insisted that the king
held the post in trust from the empire, as had the previous incumbents.
The Decapolis weathered pressure by the count of Harcourt to force an
oath on them, and then Harcourt's failed revolt neutralized his power in
Alsace until his dismissal in 1659. During this reprieve, the Alsatian cities
studiously observed traditional protocol with the bailiff to reinforce their
legal argument, while the crown relaxed pressure due to its diplomatic objectives in the empire.[97]

During the 1650s the French ambassadors to the Diet at Regensburg sought
to advance the king's influence without antagonizing the Imperial estates.
Though they lacked voice or vote in the deliberations, the French painted
the Habsburgs as aggressors and recruited a system of clients to compete
with the Habsburgs.[98] When French influence could not prevent Leopold's
election as emperor in 1658, the king's ambassadors arranged to have Louis
XIV invited to join the Rhenish League, a defensive alliance of the major
western Imperial estates. Soon afterward, the Peace of the Pyrenees ended a
quarter-century of war between France and Spain and finally lifted the threat
of Spanish invasion from Alsace.

In 1659 Louis XIV replaced the count of Harcourt as governor and Imperial Bailiff in Alsace with the aging Cardinal Mazarin. The old minister,
who died in 1661, never visited the region and his tenure had little impact
on provincial politics. Mazarin's successor was his heir, Charles-Armand de
la Porte de La Meilleraye, who had married the cardinal's favorite niece.
On the minister's death, La Meilleraye became the duke de Mazarin and
assumed numerous official posts in Paris, Normandy, and Alsace.[99] Between
December 1661 and March 1664, the duke visited Alsace three times, and
each tour stirred up heated controversy. His objective from the beginning
was to secure an oath of obedience from the Decapolis.[100] On his first visit
in 1661, only Landau and Colmar resisted him, but within weeks the ten
cities had filed formal protests with the Imperial courts and the emperor.[101]
Louis XIV's advisors, in particular Robert de Gravel, the royal ambassador

to the Imperial Diet, convinced the king that respect for Alsatian liberties furthered French influence at Regensburg and with the Rhenish League.[102] Under the sway of this strategy, the king restrained his impulse to crush the Alsatians' resistance.

Between September 1662 and January 1663, Mazarin returned to Alsace for a second tour. Prior to his arrival, Colmar's regime had enraged the duke when it declined to delay municipal elections, normally scheduled in August, so that he could attend.[103] The court cautioned the duke to maintain peace "by every means" in order to preserve the king's place in the Rhenish League.[104] The tour passed in icy calm while the royal government awaited the reopening of the Diet at Regensburg.[105] When it finally reconvened, negotiations over the oath of 1661 stalled, which left the Alsatians' liberties intact and once again frustrated royal officials.[106]

The impasse triggered storm warnings for the duke's third tour in March 1664.[107] When he arrived, La Meilleraye hand delivered an ultimatum to each city which claimed that the *Parlement* of Metz had full jurisdiction over the Decapolis, that the Bailiff could inspect municipal arsenals in case of war, that he also had the right to preside over the installation of the municipal regimes, and that the king reserved authority in "ecclesiastical matters."[108] Ensuing events suggest that the duke was acting without direct royal sanction in openly challenging the municipal regimes. The Catholic cities met the demands and registered the ultimatum in their protocols, but Colmar's leaders rallied the Protestant cities of Wissembourg, Landau, and Munster to form a common front.[109] At Colmar, while the duke and his entourage waited, the regime successfully argued its case before the council of jurors and refused to register the document.[110] The duke prepared to beseige the city, until the king ordered him to withdraw. Colmar's victory was stunning and apparently complete. The king's decision to await the Imperial Diet favored the status quo and the cities' rights.[111]

The bailiff's aborted siege of Colmar in 1664 was the last instance of open hostilities between Colmar and France until 1673. For the next decade, royal diplomatic objectives within the empire softened administrative aggression in Alsace. In 1666 the regime celebrated its sovereignty by minting the first civic coin since before 1618. On it was inscribed the phrase: *Moneta liberae Civitatis Imperialis Colmariensis.*[112] It would be the last coin minted by the "free Imperial" city. After 1648 power within the empire rested in princely territorial states, and many cities had suffered the loss of sovereign status.[113] For Colmar the years between 1648 and 1673 were an Indian summer during which its fragile liberties survived because of political tensions and agendas which lay well beyond its walls. The Imperial constitution preserved Colmar's sovereignty only because the French were willing for a time to be an intermediary power within the empire. When the king changed his mind, Colmar's liberties were only as strong as its outmoded walls.

V. The Conquest of the City, 1673–1679

On 30 August 1673 Louis XIV conquered Colmar. The conquest evolved out of the king's invasion of the Netherlands in 1672, which had provoked a defensive coalition among the emperor, the king of Spain, and the duke of Lorraine. In the 1670s Alsace remained an exposed French outpost held by conquest and only loosely integrated into the kingdom, and Louis's conflict with the Dutch and their allies once again turned Alsace into a battlefield.[114] In the early 1660s the royal government's Imperial diplomacy had tempered its Alsatian policies, but in 1667 Louis XIV allowed the Rhenish League to dissolve and shortly afterwards invaded the Spanish Netherlands.[115] As these strategic shifts occurred, the king's quarrel with the Decapolis remained in arbitration at the Diet at Regensburg, but French interest in negotiation was fading.[116] When war resumed in 1672, military necessity demanded a more aggressive policy in Alsace. In November Louis XIV had the bridge on the Rhine at Strasbourg destroyed and warned Strasbourg's regime to leave the bridge in disrepair, despite its importance to the city's commercial life.[117]

In January 1673 the prince of Condé made a personal tour of Alsace to assess the strategic situation, and his reports convinced the king to employ force against the Decapolis. Condé wrote that "[t]he king's authority is disappearing altogether in Alsace" and that "the ten Imperial cities are almost enemies." The prince encouraged Louis XIV "to straighten things out with Colmar and Hagenau."[118] That winter and spring other observers seconded Condé's opinions. The duke of Navailles remarked that the Colmarians "were affecting a great independence . . . and they appeared little disposed to receive orders from the king or to submit to them if they came." Louvois, the minister of war, also toured the province and bluntly informed the king that he must "force the ten cities to receive French garrisons."[119] Other royal agents had used such language in the past, but in 1673 Louis XIV was prepared to act.

Colmar's regime was ill-prepared to react. The city's fortifications had never been truly tested, and its army consisted of 100 mercenaries and the civil militia, which had last campaigned in 1669 when a boundary dispute on the Ill produced a confrontation with the militia from Horbourg-Riquewihr.[120] For several days the two forces menaced each other with insults, then they withdrew when a settlement was reached. The only casualties were hundreds of small wine casks, which gave their name to this "War of Little Casks" (*Logelnkrieg*).[121] The Colmarians held no illusions that they could withstand a prolonged siege by battle-seasoned French troops.

Nevertheless in early January 1673, the regime chose to renew its legal assault against French claims to sovereignty with an appeal to the Imperial courts at Speyer and Vienna against jurisdictional infringements by the provincial council at Ensisheim, the unwarranted demands of the royal tax farmers, and the damages inflicted on municipal property by French troops.[122] When Condé toured the province later that month, he delivered a thorough tongue-lashing to Colmar's envoys at Breisach. Later in the spring, the intendant, Poncet de la Rivière, disputed the appointment of a Stettmeister as bailiff of Sainte-Croix-en-Plaine and insisted that the new bailiff be a Catholic and swear an oath of obedience to the king.[123] Relations between the civic regime and the royal government were clearly worsening.

On 30 June 1673, the French army's unexpectedly brief campaign in the Netherlands culminated in the fall of the Dutch fortress at Maastricht. With much of the campaigning season still ahead, the king chose to march south-eastward into Alsace and the empire.[124] As the royal armies entered Lorraine, administrative supervision of both Lorraine and Alsace shifted from the Secretary of Foreign Affairs to the Secretary of War and diplomatic objectives would no longer determine royal policies in Alsace.[125] On 7 July 1673, Stettmeister Johann Heinrich Klein and the city clerk, Sammuel Röttlin, travelled to Breisach to meet with the Secretary of War, Louvois, who treated them harshly and commanded them to obey all royal orders.[126] The next day French troops began foraging in the villages around Colmar without protest from civic property holders. By mid-August the royal army had gathered in Nancy, and the Decapolis sent an embassy to the king to stave off a confrontation. The king denied them an audience.[127]

On 19 August, Colmar's regime submitted to a request from the provincial council at Ensisheim to transfer hay and grain to a royal storehouse near Turckheim. On the following day a cavalry regiment arrived to collect the supplies and set up camp among the ripening vineyards between Colmar and Turckheim. On 25 August, the day before municipal elections, the regiment's commander, Coulonges, opened negotiations with civic leaders in preparation for the king's arrival.[128] On 26 August, municipal elections proceeded normally; but the new regime's decision to remove the canon from the ramparts angered many citizens. The following day, concerned over the volatile atmosphere, the regime canceled *Schwörtag* and directed the citizens to swear their oaths in the guildhalls.[129] Ironically, the regime broke the traditional ritual of its renewal on the final day of its independence. On 28 August, Coulonges captured the city.

The municipal leaders capitulated unconditionally to Louis XIV, but they had little time to reflect on their difficult position. The royal *commissaires des guerres* badgered the Colmarians for supplies, and a steady stream of royal regiments demanded quartering. The expenses forced the regime to raise loans at Basel and Strasbourg and among the regional religious communities.[130] Civic officials helplessly watched as royal agents took control of municipal politics. The new intendant, Jacques de La Grange, appointed a Catholic member of the *Conseil provincial* as the new "royal" bailiff of Sainte-Croix-en-Plaine.[131] For a time Colmar maintained its representative at the Diet at Regensburg, but the dispute between Colmar and the royal government was no longer constitutional; it was now military.

Colmar's political future depended on the success or failure of Louis XIV's Imperial campaign, and by late autumn of 1674 the regime had reason to hope for a restoration of its Imperial status. In October Frederick William II, the elector of Brandenburg-Prussia, drove the French under Turenne out of Alsace, across the Vosges, and into Lorraine. The Imperial forces settled into winter quarters in Alsace with Frederick William headquartered at Colmar, where the city's leaders began to draw up plans for rebuilding its fortifications.[132] The plans were never realized, for in mid-December Turenne began a stunning campaign in the Sundgau. The Elector hurriedly assembled his scattered forces; and on 5 January 1675 the two armies fought to a draw in the frozen vineyards between Colmar and Turckheim. The Elector, fearing for his lines of communications, withdrew northward across the bridgehead at Strasbourg.[133] The Imperial interim had ended, and Colmar was once again at the mercy of the royal army.

Turenne's troops did not pillage Colmar as they had Turckheim. Nevertheless, the Colmarians faced a very hard winter, with hundreds of sick and wounded soldiers crammed into the municipal hospital and a regiment of healthy troops quartered in their houses.[134] The regime raised another loan of 20,000 *Reichsthaler* from Barbault, the tax farmer, with the revenues of Sainte-Croix-en-Plaine as collateral.[135] In 1677 Imperial troops made a brief foray into Upper Alsace, passing one night in the defenseless city. This "liberation" had no political significance, and the troops angered the citizenry by destroying many of the nearby vineyards.[136] From this point onward, throughout the numerous wars of Louis XIV's reign, Upper Alsace was no longer a battlefield but a staging area for the French troops. The Peace of Nijmegen in 1679, which ended the Dutch War, legitimized Bourbon power in Colmar and paved the way for royal reorganization of the civic regime.

"The rise of absolutism in Germany," wrote Hajo Holborn, "was the chief political consequence of the Thirty Years' War."[137] Years later Perry Anderson countered that "[t]he historical terrain presented by Western Germany as a whole . . . proved incompatible with the emergence of any major Absolutism."[138] These statements are not contradictory because political centralization in the post-Westphalian empire did not produce a German nation-state but rather regional territorial states and the encroachment of neighboring monarchies at the empire's periphery. The Old Reich survived with this power imbalance because it "was geared up to preserve the Public Peace," which did not require equality among the estates but respect for hierarchy and privileged liberties.[139] Under this system, the empire supplied "legal protection from territorial aggression and arbitrary action."[140] The empire's regional power systems "entailed a gradation of political authority, a stratification of what Montesquieu called the 'intermediary powers' between sovereign and subject."[141]

Between 1648 and 1673, royal officials in Alsace observed Imperial protocols because they sought a legitimate place for the king within the Imperial constitutional system. At the same time, the strategic significance of the province to the king and his enemies loaded each confrontation between the crown and the Alsatian estates with military consequences. In the 1650s the invasion by the duke of Lorraine, Harcourt's complicity in the Fronde, and the war between France and Spain maintained the military heat in provincial politics. The royal government, struggling through its own divisions, applied pressure on Colmar in fits and starts. The two critical officials were the Imperial Bailiff of Hagenau and the intendant. The French bailiffs, Harcourt and the duke de Mazarin, bristled under the Imperial cloak of charters and legal checks attached to their office. Both men were mavericks within a patronage system which did not honor independent action. Their efforts to break down resistance, led by Colmar, to a formal oath of obedience from the Decapolis foundered, in part because the king's other advisors favored Imperial protocols in the dealings between the bailiff and the cities. The intendants were freer to create new political relations. Unhindered by an Imperial legacy, an aggressive and innovative official like Colbert de Croissy ultimately forced the Colmarians to recognize the need to develop new traditions under new circumstances defined by royal privilege and patronage. When Louis XIV asserted his sovereignty over the city, its political leaders had already learned the rudiments of Bourbon political culture.

Colmar's relations with France floated on the bubble of peace between the kingdom and the empire. In this precarious position, civic officials and royal agents argued over the nature of sovereignty. The Colmarians viewed sovereignty as a hierarchical network of mutual constraints designed to preserve peace in the context of emperor and empire. The king's officials understood sovereignty to come from the grace of the king. In the atmosphere of peace, the Colmarians definition seemed to hold sway. Ultimately, the civic regime's pride in its successful resistance against Harcourt and the duke de Mazarin and its confidence that the crown would be willing to observe the drawn-out protocol of Imperial politics were misplaced. The city had not gained a victory, only a reprieve. When the context of French policies in the empire changed, Colmar's sovereignty came to an end at the hands of Louis XIV himself.

Notes

1. Waltz, ed., *Sigmund Billings Kleine Chronik*, 131–32.
2. Pierre Burger, "Il y a 300 ans ... L'annexion de Colmar par Louis XIV en 1673," *Annuaire de Colmar* (1973), 7–41; Gabriel Braeuner, "L'opinion publique et le rattachement de Colmar à la France en 1673," *Annuaire de Colmar*, (1973), 43–50. The quote comes from the diary of the Lutheran shoemaker, Mathias Tauberer; see Julien Rathgeber, ed., *Colmar und Ludwig XIV*

(1648–1715): Ein Beitrag zur elsässischen Städtegeschichte im siebzehnten Jahrhundert (Stuttgart, 1873), 66.

3. Stein, *Protection Royale*, 161–62.
4. Rathgeber, ed., *Colmar und Ludwig XIV*, 4–5.
5. Parker, *The Thirty Years' War*, 140–42. On Swedish negotiations with France in Alsace, see Reuss, *L'Alsace*, 1: 80–82; Stein, *Protection Royale*, 313–53.
6. A text of the Franco-Swedish accord appears in André Waltz, ed., '*A l'ombre de lys*': *Correspondance diplomatique échangée entre la couronne de France et la république de Colmar, 1634–1646* (Colmar, 1935), no. 255, 229–30. The French garrison arrived on 22 October; see Stein, *Protection Royale*, 295–99, 328–29.
7. Livet, *L'intendance*, 43, 101–2; Stein, *Protection Royale*, 406.
8. Livet, *L'intendance*, 30. Article 6 of the Treaty of Rueil stated that "[l]a Guarnison que le Roy mettra dans la Ville, sera maintenue aux depens de Sa Majesté." Article 8 granted the civic regime authority over quartering the troops, and in article 9 the officials maintained possession of the city's keys. Waltz, ed., *A l'ombre du lys*, no. 256, 231–34, here at 233.
9. On local reaction to Mogg's embassy, see Stein, *Protection Royale*, 621 n. 8; Livet, *L'intendance*, 45–46.
10. Reuss, *L'Alsace*, 1: 90–97; Stein, *Protection Royale*, 396–97.
11. The Colmarians listed d'Aigre as a citizen and invited him to sessions of the society *zum Waagkellar*. Livet, *L'intendance*, 66–67.
12. Parker, *The Thirty Years' War*, 148–52; Reuss, *L'Alsace*, 1: 90–97; Livet, *L'intendance*, 68–95, 113.
13. Stein, *Protection Royale*, 417–18, 510.
14. Quoted in Livet, *L'intendance*, 70.
15. Ibid., 71–75.
16. Parker, *The Thirty Years' War*, 170–79; Dickmann, *Der Westfälische Frieden*, 36ff; Evans, *The Habsburg Monarchy*, 274–308.
17. Rose, "Empire and Territories," 67–69; and Gross, "The Holy Roman Empire," 12–18; Dickmann, *Der Westfälische Frieden*, 124–48.
18. Stein employs this core-periphery dichotomy in *Protection Royale*, 10–21.
19. Georges Bardot, *La question des dix villes impériales d'Alsace: Depuis la Paix de Westphalie jusqu'aux arrêts de "réunions" du Conseil souverain de Brisach 1648–1680* (Paris, 1899), 13.
20. Philippe Dollinger, "Le Traité de Westphalie et l'Alsace," in *Deux siècles d'Alsace française*, 7.
21. On Mazarin's plans, see Bardot, *La question*, 50. On Trauttmannsdorf, see Dollinger, "Le Traité de Westphalie," 6; Dickmann, *Die Westfälische Frieden*, 265–300.
22. I have used an English translation of the text in Geoffrey Symcox, ed., *War, Diplomacy, and Imperialism, 1618–1763* (New York, 1974), 39–62, both quotes at 51.
23. Ibid., 54.
24. Quoted in Dollinger, "Le Traité de Westphalie," 11.
25. Reuss, *L'Alsace*, 1: 361–80. See also Stinzi, "Die Hasburger im Elsaß," 505–64; Bischoff, *Gouvernés et gouvernants*.
26. The French diplomats were confused over what they actually possessed. Livet, *L'intendance*, 119–20; Reuss, *L'Alsace*, 1: 167–69.
27. Livet, *L'intendance*, 120; Bardot, *La question*, 15–16, 54–57.
28. Livet, *L'intendance*, 121. See also Buchstab, *Reichsstädte*, 86.
29. On the political conditions within France and its impact on the border provinces such as Alsace, see Richard Bonney, *Political Change in France under Richelieu and Mazarin, 1624–1661* (Oxford, 1978), 53–67, 401–18. See also

Mettam, *Power and Faction*, 45–101; Livet, *L'intendance*, 127.

30. Reuss, *L'Alsace*, 1: 187–90. On the Lower Alsatian Estates, see F. W. Müller, *Die elsässischen Landstände: Ein Beitrag zur Geschichte des Elsasses* (Strasbourg, 1907), 142–45.

31. Auguste Scherlen, *Histoire de la ville de Turckheim* (Colmar, 1925), 87; idem, *Perles d'Alsace* 2: 241, 3: 311.

32. The last formal session of the Upper Alsatian Estates had been in 1631. Livet, *L'intendance*, 182. The estates which attended the meeting in Colmar included the French, as possessor of the former Austrian holdings, the abbot of Murbach, the abbot of Lure, representatives from the Württemberg lordship of Horbourg-Riquewihr, and the Imperial cities of Colmar, Kaysersberg, Munster, and Turckheim. X(avier) Mossmann, "La France en Alsace après la Paix de Westphalie," *Revue Historique* 101 (1893): 26–43, 225–49, here at 237. On the meeting's overall failure, see Reuss, *L'Alsace*, 1: 189.

33. Reuss, *L'Alsace*, 1: 177–79.

34. Harcourt revived the former Austrian administrative center at Ensisheim, as had Saxe-Weimar. See Reuss, *L'Alsace*, 1: 184–87; Livet, *L'intendance*, 141.

35. The negotiations were treasonous, for at the time France was at war with Spain. Livet, *L'intendance*, 143–44.

36. Ibid., 144–46.

37. Bardot, *La question*, 88; Mossmann, "La France en Alsace," 35.

38. Quoted in Mossmann, "La France en Alsace," 38–39.

39. Rathgeber, ed., *Colmar und Ludwig XIV*, 5.

40. In another sign of civic prosperity, the payments covered the years 1649 through 1653. AMC, CC 62, 1.

41. Bardot, *La question*, 92–100.

42. Jean-Baptiste Colbert would found a dynasty of royal officials. John C. Rule, "Louis XIV, Roi-Bureaucrate," in John C. Rule, ed., *Louis XIV and the Craft of Kingship* (Columbus, Oh., 1969), 30–35; Inès Murat, *Colbert* (Paris, 1980), 13–71, 346–50; Reuss, *L'Alsace*, 1: 215–16.

43. Reuss, *L'Alsace*, 1: 199–202.

44. Livet, *L'intendance*, 193.

45. According to Livet, the institutions up to the peace of Westphalia were still in an "empirical stage." Livet, "Royal Administration," 179. The Fronde had not improved the situation. What was true in 1648 was still true in 1655.

46. Livet, *L'intendance*, 200–209.

47. On the local estates, see Bischoff, *Gouvernés et gouvernants*, 213–23. On Croissy's program, see Livet, *L'intendance*, 182–83.

48. Livet, *L'intendance*, 215–20.

49. Ibid., 215–21, 343–44, 689–701.

50. Both previous quotes are in ibid., 220–21. See also Livet, "Les intendants d'Alsace et leur oeuvre 1649–1798," in *Deux siècles d'Alsace française*, 84–87.

51. AMC, AA 145, 44–70.

52. "Andere aber so zwar in dargleichen orthen alzeytt verburgert gewesen, von denen in diessen vergangenen Krieges wesen undt seithero erkhauffen ligendten güthern, einig onus real, als Magazin wein- oder frucht zuegeben nicht vermeinen schuldig zur sein." AMC, AA 145, 45, fol. 1r. For Colmar's acquisitions in Turckheim, see Andre Billich, "Colmar et Turckheim," 96–97. For Riquewihr, see Scherlen, *Perles d'Alsace*, 3: 312. Colmar was not the only fortified Alsatian town whose citizens acquired extensive properties in the countryside during the crisis of the 1630s. For Strasbourg, see François-Joseph Fuchs, "Bourgeois de Strasbourg, propriétaires ruraux au XVIIe siècle," in *Paysans d'Alsace* (Strasbourg, 1959): 99–119; for Mulhouse, see Oberlé, *La république de Mulhouse*, 402–12.

53. Livet, *L'intendance*, 182.
54. AMC, AA 145, 47 and 54. The Colmarians used the agreement of 1644 to support their claims directly to Mazarin: "Il y a treize ans passés que vre. Em[inence] ... trouva ... nos raisons, privileges, et coustomes si relevantes et si bien fondées ... qu'elle fit defenses de ne rien lever sur les nostres ny leurs biens qu'ils possederent dans d'autres territoires, ce qu'a esté observé sans y contrevenir jusques à l'année precedente." AMC, AA 145, 47, fol. 1r. For the original agreement of 1644, see Waltz, ed., *A l'ombre du lys*, no. 221, 202.
55. The first warning was dated 8 October 1656. AMC, AA 145, 44–45. The second followed ten days later. AMC, AA 145, 46.
56. The magistrate addressed appeals to Robert de Gravel, the French ambassador to the empire at Frankfurt (AMC, AA 145, 75–76), Mazarin's captain of the guard (ibid., 52), the count de Brienne, the Secretary of State Le Tellier (ibid., 53–57), the Swedish ambassador in Paris (ibid., 60), and to Mazarin himself (ibid., 47–48). In the letter to Mazarin's captain of the guard, they clearly voiced their belief in Croissy's insubordination. "Cette pretension nouvelle [the tax] nous est tant plus estrange puis qu'elle va directement contre nos droicts et privileges, ce que nous croyons fermement estre contre la volonté de son Eminence" (ibid., 52, 1r.).
57. AMC, AA 145, 56, fol. 1r–v.
58. "La maison d'Autriche ny est jamais contrevenu [et] a tousjours faict observer cette coustume reciproque d'Alsace comme aussy l'Evesque de Strasbourg et le Prince de Wurtembourg, la quelle aussy Sa Ma [jesté] très chrestienne a promis par le traicté de paix de faire maintenir et ne pretendre pas davantage, que ce qu'on possedé ces predecesseurs." AMC, AA 145, 56, fol. 1v.
59. "Cet cas pose que les ordres du Roy donné en temps de guerre ne puissant pas faire préjudice aux droicts qui luy ont estés cedés par un traicté de paix ... que la souveraineté permettait ces impositions vi. *supereminentes dominy*, qu'elles ne se peuvent faire aux subjects, et pas à d'autres exteri n. supereminenti dominio nullo modo subsunt." AMC, AA 145, 57 fol. 1r–v. On the original response of Croissy, see Livet, *L'intendance*, 333–34.
60. AMC, AA 145, 57, 1r.
61. Stein, *Protection Royale*, 498–99.
62. "Ce qui touche le prix, qu'on dit avoir esté très vil, il a esté tel comme le temps et la saison du pays l'avait fait, et qui depuis les a tellement en dommage pas les retraicts qu'on a faict sans leur rembourses les frais." AMC, AA 145, 57 fol. 2r.
63. On the resale offer, see AMC, AA 145, 57, 2r. In October 1657 the Secretary of State, Lionne, informed the magistrate that he had questioned Croissy and found "toutes les raisons qu'il m'a deduites pour resondre aux vostres et en faveur des droits du Roy si pertenantes et si fortes que je ne doute pas que si je pouvais par une simple lettre vous en informer ... [que] elle [the tax] n'est pas mesme contre les privileges que vous pretendez avoir autrefois obtenus des Empereurs qui ne peuvent s'estendre contre et au prejudice des droits du Souverain." AMC, AA 145, 70.
64. Billich, "Colmar et Turckheim," 96–97; Scherlen, *Perles d'Alsace*, 3: 312.
65. On the augmentation of the customs duties during the war, see François-Joseph Fuchs, "Aspects du commerce de Strasbourg avec Montbéliard et la Franche-Comté au XVIIe siècle," in *Trois provinces de l'Est* (Strasbourg, 1957), 109–17, here at 114. For the French reforms, see Livet, *L'intendance*, 341.
66. Sittler, "Le Ladhof et la navigation colmarienne," 18–19.
67. In June 1650 Charlevois, the royal lieutenant at Breisach, asked the magistrate of Colmar "d'avertir vos d. bourgeois d'aquitter aud. Ilhiser les droits du

Roy de la mesme sorte qu'ils le faisant durant la paix et du temps que led. peage se levoit pour la maison d'Austriche." AMC, CC 188, 11.

68. "Il a esté convenu entre autres que les peages, cy devant fixés et ordonnés par les Empereurs et la maison archiducale, soient remis et restablis dans le mesme ordre et estat qu'ils ont esté payes et reçeus devant les guerres ruineuses d'Allemagne et de l'Empire Romain." AMC, CC 187, 1, fol. 1r. See also Livet, *L'intendance*, 341.

69. "On observera le mesme vers les villes voisines . . . Mulhausen, Colmar, Selestatt, Kaysersperg, Thurckheim et Ammerschwir, qui sont meslées en ce Gouvernement d'Alsace. Et lesd. marchands presenteront toutefois de leurs Magistrats une attestation, contenant, que le vin et les fruicts soient de leur propre terre et biens, et point d'autres denrées et qu'ils appartiennent à leur propre usage et necessité dans les susd. villes et lieux, et ne songeant de les mener de ça ou de là pour le revendre . . . car à faute de ne pas presenter ces attestations, ils payeront tout le peage." AMC, CC 187, 1, fol. 2r–v.

70. "Sa Majesté pour fair le zele qu'Elle a pour le maintien de la paix conclue et jurée . . . a très gratieusement commandé, de regler la reduction des peages sur la pied des anciens droicts, toutefois avec la protestation expresse que la voisins et autres Estats observiroyent reciproque l'equité et le debvoir, autrement on n'y vouloit point y estre obligé." AMC, CC 187, 1, fol. 1v.

71. The civic regime complained that the rates exceeded the traditional levels. AMC, CC 187, 2 & 3. The customs agents complained that inflation necessitated higher payments and that Colmar's merchants abused the passport system. AMC, CC 187, 4, fol. 1v. See also Livet, *L'intendance*, 341.

72. AMC, CC 187, 4, fol. 1v.

73. "Je vous diray seulement que la plus part des choses que vous pretendez Icy par droict vous ne les avez jamais eu que gratification de la maison d'autriche." AMC, CC 187, 8.

74. Fridt had purchased citizenship through *zum Riesen* in 1655. Wertz, ed., *Membres du magistrat, 1601–1700*, 94, no. 584. He lived in district XXI (*Teuffels Ort*) and was assessed at 3,200 fl. in 1660, 5,200 fl. in 1670, and 6,400 fl. in 1680. He served in the municipal regime between 1670 and 1679. On his inscription in the society *zum Waagkeller*, see AMC, HH 8, 13.

75. "Je vous prie de ne luy rien arrester parce que ce seroit inutile et rien que vous attirer de la haine." AMC, CC 150, 11. The civic regime received a copy of the letter.

76. AMC, CC 187, 12.

77. For Croissy's promise to the regime, see AMC, CC 187, 13, 14. Ten days later, Mogg again complained that the customs collector had confiscated ships carrying merchandise belonging to several Colmar merchants, including Fridt again. The agent responded that Croissy's initial order "a esté aussi tost cassé par un autre ordre ensuivre." AMC, CC 187, 15.

78. AMC, CC 187, 16–18. In 1657 the newly appointed municipal architect had his furniture seized at Illhäusern, even though he carried an official passport as a civic employee. In their complaint the Colmarians argued for reciprocal exemptions for royal and civic officials. AMC, CC 187, 19. Croissy released the goods only after the regime petitioned him for a royal passport. AMC, CC 187, 20.

79. In 1662 when a Colmarian merchant, Stephen Geopp, was arrested with contraband firearms in Lorraine, the civic regime petitioned the crown for the release of Geopp and his goods, and Louis XIV agreed because the Colmarians recognized his right to seize the goods. AMC, BB 20, 6; AMC, CC 188, 10; Livet, *L'intendance*, 215.

80. For a general discussion of tax farming see Dent, *Crisis in Finance*, 7–109. On conditions in Alsace, see Livet, *L'intendance*, 689–700.

81. On Barbault's appointment, see AMC, CC 189, 1. For an example of Barbault's intercession and the regime's response, see AMC, CC 189, 9–12.

82. AMC, CC 189, 13.

83. The document is undated; but given its reference to other documents, I suspect it was drawn up in 1666. The city received three grants: "1) daß er die Statt Colmar deß trauben Zolls, so lange er oder die seinige die admodiation hette, befreyen sollte... 2) was des Statt, oder einem undt dem andern Lobl. Magistrats zustandig, gleicher gestalten Zoll frey zuhalten. 3) Were der Zoll zu Ilhäußern, soviel unsere handelsleuth undt burger betrifft, üf den alten fueß, neml. das halbe zustetzen." In return the city promised: "1) Will man sein alhie habende behausung solang die bey Ihn und seiner Familie bliebt, frey lassen, neml. soviel das Gewerff dess hauses der Jahrlichen Zwey pfundt oder Crönen belangend... vorstehender... puncten sollen solange gültig sein und observirt werden, alß die admodiation bey Ihme herren Barbault und seinen Family blieben wird." AMC, CC 189, 6, fol. 1r–v.

84. The Austrians had never successfully established the court's exclusive right of *Hofgericht*. A plaintiff could still appeal to the Imperial courts, and the local seignorial courts still played a significant role within the Austrian holdings. Bischoff, *Gouvernés et gouvernants*, 218–21. On Croissy's program, see Livet, *L'intendance*, 179, 235–42.

85. Bonney, *Political Change in France*, 411; Livet, *L'intendance*, 235.

86. For the role of the *Conseil souverain* in France's Imperial diplomacy, see Bardot, *La question*, 104–18. Colmar's custom-house chronicler joyfully noted Leopold's election. Rathgeber, ed., *Colmar und Ludwig XIV*, 7. Leopold was the last emperor to renew Colmar's medieval charters. Finsterwalder, ed., *Colmarer Stadtrechte*, no. 214, 268.

87. Livet, *L'intendance*, 235–50.

88. The Colmarians accepted Croissy's invitation to attend the session. AMC, AA 164, 26 and 27. The text of the protest is quoted in Georges Livet, "Colmar et l'établissement du Conseil souverain d'Alsace (1658–1698)," *Annuaire de Colmar* (1958): 72. The Colmarians saw the new council as a threat to their religious freedoms: "Der König ein Edict wegen Errichtung eines *Conseil Provincial* zu Ensisheim publiciren, die er Macht gab alle *Civil und Criminalsachen* in Elsass, sogar in dem 10 Reichsstädten zu entschieden, auch die Katholische Religion aufrecht zu erhalten." Rathgeber, ed., *Colmar und Ludwig XIV*, 7.

89. Quoted in Livet, *L'intendance*, 241–42.

90. Livet, "L'établissement," 70. On Colmar's legal system, see Sittler, "Crimes et châtiments dans le Vieux-Colmar," *Annuaire de Colmar* (1962): 7–17.

91. All quotes found in Livet, *L'intendance*, 335.

92. Ibid., 336.

93. Birr's death was untimely; he was only forty-seven. Rathgeber, ed., *Colmar und Ludwig XIV*, 6. On the negotiations, see Livet, *L'intendance*, 336–39. In the end the king's advisors thought the move would jeopardize France's entry into the Rhenish league. Bardot, *La question*, 77, 127–34.

94. Livet, *L'intendance*, 229–35.

95. Ibid., 247. For the grant of freedom from appeal to Metz, see Livet, "L'établissement," 73–74.

96. Livet, *L'intendance*, 331, 361–63; idem, "Les intendants et leur oeuvre," 88.

97. To honor traditional observance, Colmar's regime regularly paid the *Reichssteuer* to Harcourt. AMC, CC 62, 1–7.

98. Bardot, *La question*, 91–100.
99. On the Cardinal's tenure as provincial governor, see Reuss, *L'Alsace*, 1: 203. La Meilleraye had descended from a family of modest origins which had risen to power in the service of Richelieu and Mazarin. See Georges Livet, ed., *Le Duc Mazarin: Gouverneur d'Alsace (1661–1713): Lettres et documents inédits* (Strasbourg and Paris, 1954), 13–21.
100. See Livet, ed., *Le Duc Mazarin*, 120.
101. Bardot, *La question*, 151–58.
102. During Colmar's struggle with Croissy over taxes, Gravel seemed the most sympathetic of the French officials that the Colmarians petitioned. AMC, AA 145, 75–76. See also Bardot, *La question*, 104–18.
103. He expressed his anger in a letter to Lionne dated 20 September 1662. Livet, ed., *Le Duc Mazarin*, 132.
104. Ibid., 127.
105. The duke had earlier complained that the Colmarians "ne m'ont mesme envoye visiter et ne disposent en façon du monde à payer le droict de protection." Quoted in Livet, ed., *Le Duc Mazarin*, 127. The Colmar regime, however, was willing to pay the *Reichssteuer* in civic coin which had depreciated due to the inflationary practices of the French crown. The collector of the Imperial Bailiwick's revenues, a Sr. Zipper of Angelstein, insisted that Colmar pay in Strasbourg coin. The ensuing legal debate continued into the 1690s. See AMC, CC 62, 9–11 & 39–45. On the scene, the duke wanted a direct confrontation. Livet, ed., *Le Duc Mazarin*, 132–33. In his reply Lionne reaffirmed the king's desire for patience. Ibid., 135.
106. Bardot, *La question*, 161–65.
107. In July 1663 the marquis de Ruzé, the bailiff's immediate subordinate, ordered Colmar and the neighboring cities of Turckheim and Munster to resolve a dispute before the parlement in Metz and not the Imperial courts in Speyer. Rathgeber, ed., *Colmar und Ludwig XIV*, 10. A year earlier, to appease his allies in the Rhenish circle, Louis XIV had freed the Alsatian cities from having to appeal to Metz. Bardot, *La question*, 160.
108. The text of the ultimatum appears in Rathgeber, ed., *Colmar und Ludwig XIV*, 10–11; Livet, ed., *Le Duc Mazarin*, 150.
109. Bardot, *La question*, 164–67.
110. The participation of the council of jurors was significant. This was the community's response and not only the regime's. See AMC, BB 16. See also Livet, ed., *Le Duc Mazarin*, 150.
111. The arbiters met without resolution for the next nine years. See Bardot, *La question*, 171–83, 201–45.
112. Rathgeber, ed., *Colmar und Ludwig XIV*, 11.
113. Erfurt, Münster in Westphalia, Brunswick, Königsberg, and the towns of the duchy of Cleves submitted to greater princely control. Christopher R. Friedrichs, "German Town Revolts and the Seventeenth-Century Crisis," *Renaissance and Modern Studies* 26 (1982): 27–51.
114. Robert Mandrou, *Louis XIV en son temps 1661–1715* (Paris, 1973), 261–62, 524–47.
115. On the War of Devolution, see ibid., 224–43. On the collapse of the Rhenish league, see Bardot, *La question*, 206.
116. Bardot, *La question*, 216–17.
117. Carl J. Ekberg, *The Failure of Louis XIV's Dutch War* (Chapel Hill, 1979), 34; Mandrou, *Louis XIV en son temps*, 243–61. On the destruction of the Rhine bridge and French negotiations with Strasbourg, see Hertner, *Stadtwirtschaft*, 230–31.

118. Quoted in Ekberg, *The Dutch War*, 34–35.
119. Both quotes from ibid., 35.
120. On Colmar's fortifications, see Sittler, "Colmar au XVIe siècle," 18–19. On the civic militia and the citizens' responsibilities in public defense, see Reuss, *L'Alsace*, 1: 219; AMC, BB 11, 4.
121. René Victor Wehrlen, "Il y a 300 ans: La Guerre des Tonnelets de Colmar en 1669," *Annuaire de Colmar* (1969–1970): 49–58.
122. Burger, "L'annexion," 7–8.
123. Both incidents are described in ibid., 11–12.
124. Ekberg, *The Dutch War*, 22–23.
125. Livet, *L'intendance*, 363–64. The shift also brought a new intendant into the province, Jacques de la Grange, who would serve from 1673 to 1698. See Jean-Benoist d'Athenay, *Le premier administrateur de l'Alsace française: Jacques de La Grange, intendant d'Alsace de 1673 à 1698* (Paris and Strasbourg, 1930).
126. Burger, "L'annexion," 13–15.
127. Ibid., 15–20; Rathgeber, ed., *Colmar und Ludwig XIV*, 13.
128. Rathgeber, ed., *Colmar und Ludwig XIV*, 14; Ekberg, *The Dutch War*, 35.
129. Braeuner, "L'opinion publique," 45; Rathgeber, ed., *Colmar und Ludwig XIV*, 14.
130. The one house mentioned is the Abbey of Pairis located in the Vosges, which possessed extensive properties within the city. Pierre Burger, "Il y a 300 ans . . . Colmar entre le Maréchal-Vicomte de Turenne et Frédéric-Guillaume Prince-Elécteur de Brandenbourg," *Annuaire de Colmar* (1974–75): 82. See also Rathgeber, ed., *Colmar und Ludwig XIV*, 23–24. In 1688 the city sought a moratorium on debt payments. AMC, CC 35, A2 & A3.
131. The candidate, Duvaille, was already known to the regime as a *commissaire des guerres*. Burger, "L'annexion," 37.
132. For a general, if polemical, survey of the Great Elector's Alsatian campaign, see Heinrich Rocholl, *Der Grosse Kurfürst von Brandenburg im Elsass 1674–1675: Ein Geschichtsbild aus der Zeit, als das Elsass französisch werden musste* (Strasbourg, 1877). Cf. Burger, "Entre Turenne et Brandenbourg," 85, 87–89; Rathgeber, ed., *Colmar und Ludwig XIV*, 26–27.
133. Because of his long extracts from original local sources, the best account of the battle of Turckheim is Scherlen, *Histoire de Turckheim*, 106–50. Cf. the patriotic accounts of Rocholl, *Der Grosse Kurfürst*, 45–98; Burger, "Colmar entre Turenne et Brandenbourg," 90–91.
134. Burger suggests that Turenne, who was a convert from Calvinism, felt some sympathy for Colmar, where he had spent time convalescing from wounds during the Thirty Years' War. See Burger, "Colmar entre Turenne et Brandenbourg," 81–82, 91–95. It seems just as likely that Turenne did not wish to destroy the community he needed for quartering his troops after the battle. On the sack of Turckheim, see Scherlen, *Histoire de Turckheim*, 146–50. For the demographic impact of the campaign on the countryside around Colmar, see Livet, *L'intendance*, 612–15.
135. The city later pawned six church bells to financiers in Strasbourg to raise additional money. Rathgeber, ed., *Colmar und Ludwig XIV*, 29; Sittler, "La transformation du gouvernement," 138.
136. Sittler, "La transformation du gouvernement," 139.
137. Hajo Holborn, *A History of Modern Germany, 1648–1840* (New York, 1964), 21.
138. Perry Anderson, *Lineages of the Absolutist State*, 2nd. ed. (London, 1979), 252.
139. Gross, "The Holy Roman Empire," 17.
140. Ibid., 15.
141. Rose, "Empire and Territories," 69.

4

Civic Politics in a Post-Westphalian Home Town, 1640–1679

The French officials believed that Colmar's political leaders were a narrow oligarchy which lacked heartfelt support from their citizenry. In 1664 during the tense confrontation between the Imperial Bailiff and the civic regime, one of the duke's agents noted "the oligarchy has lasted since the war. It is time to cut its roots and save the citizens from magisterial slavery."[1] Several years earlier, when Croissy planned to break down Colmar's resistance to the *Conseil souverain*, he had tried to bribe Johann Heinrich Mogg and Daniel Birr, whom he assumed controlled the city.[2] Johann Frischmann, the royal agent at Strasbourg, had also seen the power of the civic oligarchies as the root cause of Alsatian resistance to the Crown: "They [the municipal elite] would not wish to change places with the great lords, for once they have taken control into their own hands and they are seated at the helm, everything passes through their hands."[3] The French agents' image of the narrow and oppressive ruling circles in the Alsatian cities informed royal policy toward the municipal regimes, and the image remains a part of French historiography for the period.[4]

The truth is that in the years after 1648 the Alsatian civic regimes continued to govern within the context of communal norms, even if the foundation for those norms had changed. True, the civic officials possessed authority (*Obrigkeit*), but that authority ultimately rested on communal grants which were ritually and publicly renewed under oath, even at Strasbourg.[5] Colmar possessed a much smaller and more intimate political community than its mighty neighbor, and the Thirty Years' War had tightened Colmar's communal bonds by reducing population, restricting immigration, and disrupting trade networks. In the last decade of the war, civic leaders had become more sensitive to the political community within the walls, to the economic potential in the immediate hinterland, and to the role of Imperial institutions in nurturing stability. It was under pressure that the rhetoric of "shared ownership" and the appeal to "communal norms" took on full meaning.[6]

After 1650 the commune remained the official foundation for civic institutions, and Colmar's citizens and officials honored the traditions of civic history as embodied in Imperial charters and dramatized in communal rituals, such as the annual oaths.[7] Colmar's political ethos remained both contractual and public, which was critical in the regime's defense against the innovations proposed by the royal government. When threatened with siege by the duke de Mazarin, the regime called on the council of jurors, as representatives of the community, to both indentify and strengthen the base of its resistance.

In its struggle against French sovereignty between 1648 and 1673, the Colmarians had also relied on the institutional checks and balances of traditional Imperial politics. As in other post-Westphalian Imperial cities, Colmar's leaders relied on the Imperial system, where governance took place in a customary framework of reciprocal rights and privileges which protected the status of the weak. The strategy appeared to work, for the intendants and the French bailiffs failed to force the civic officials to swear new oaths that ran counter to Imperial formulas. Appeals to Imperial tradition and reciprocal rights also framed the political relations between the regime and its own subjects, the citizens. In their exercise of *Obrigkeit* within the city, the Lutheran civic elite had to act gently or risk civic unrest. Such unrest could separate Colmar's regime from its Imperial constitutional moorings or offer easy access for French interference in civic politics. Thus internal and external conditions encouraged caution and sober judgment in day-to-day politics.

I. Oligarchy and Conflicting Political Cultures

Urban oligarchies were not unique to Alsace, nor to the seventeenth century, yet the devastation wrought by marauding armies during the Thirty Years' War closed many communities in on themselves and tightened oligarchical rule. Within the Holy Roman Empire, endemic internal political tensions between the citizenry and the regimes deteriorated under the corrosive external influence of the emerging territorial states. The civic regimes responded with traditional calls for "order," which they sought to achieve through rigid social stratification, economic regulation, and ever-tightening oligarchical control over governance.[8] The economic and political pressure affected the entire empire, but within each city conflicts occurred at unique friction points within their peculiar constitutional structures. In the new political order, the Imperial cities labored to preserve the vestiges of their once proud heritage, but inevitably it was the new princely *Residenzstädte* which became the vibrant centers of urban life.[9]

In the post-Westphalian empire, civic regimes were caught between the constitutional commitment to the commonweal, which remained the pronounced source of their political ethos, and the dominant new political order embodied in the princely territorial states, which emphasized their

Obrigkeit.[10] Christopher Friedrichs has argued that the civic regimes were caught in a constant "tug-of-war" with their citizens, who were animated by a "conception of communal self-government and mutual obligation."[11] But elsewhere Friedrichs has noted that even oligarchical power rested on the consensus of the citizenry as a whole and that it often collapsed "when the moral basis of the magistracy's authority was felt to have broken down."[12] The visible key to preserving the moral basis of authority was the allocation of power, which extended beyond the question of regime recruitment to common tensions in day-to-day governance: magisterial secrecy, financial mismanagement, excessive privilege, and the mishandling of foreign relations.[13] These tensions produced a constant static in civic political discourse, and internal bickering and external meddling often unleashed deepseated animosities between the regime and the citizenry.

In the years after 1648, fiscal pressures and gradual silencing of the political voice of the common citizens triggered numerous constitutional crises.[14] In each case, the meddling of an external prince, often as head of an Imperial commission, had much to do with the course of events.[15] In the early eighteenth century, two of the empire's largest cities, Frankfurt am Main and Hamburg, underwent protracted constitutional overhauls.[16] Yet even if the regimes could avoid open conflict, alienation widened the gap between the governors and governed. In Nördlingen, a community which in many ways fit the "home town" model, the regime distanced itself from the artisan citizens, as merchants and professionals came to dominate public office after 1648, though they never formed a closed elite. Furthermore Nördlingen's officials functioned with paternal care, particularly in regards to economic regulations which favored civic guildsmen.[17] As in many other towns, Nördlingen's officials granted the citizens economic protection, confessional purity, and political privileges against outsiders, while denying them access to office. In general, recent scholarship has suggested that political tensions continued within the urban environment after 1648. At issue was access to political decision-making in an era when governance had become increasingly professionalized. Even the most careful regime could face a dangerous political crisis if confronted by internal factionalism or external forces beyond its control.[18]

The French brought their own political traditions to Alsace, which, though they reflected the interest of the nobility, were concentrated in royal hands. Early modern historiography has traditionally applied the model of absolutism to this political system, particularly under Louis XIV. Louis' absolutism formed at the conjuncture of his powerful personal monarchy, the emerging bureaucratic apparatus, which he inherited from Richelieu and Mazarin, and the growth of the French army. The centrality of the king in French politics reflected the feudal political heritage of the system.[19] Though royal governance still operated in the medieval environment of personal loyalty and privilege, the bureaucracy had already begun to depersonalize administration in order to break down the vestiges of feudalism that resisted central power. Historians often have viewed that process as an assault on noble privilege, but Perry Anderson, for one, has suggested that bureaucratic centralization did not reflect a struggle between the Crown and the nobility but rather the integration of the nobility into one coherent system for exploiting the surplus produced by the peasantry.[20] The driving force for political centralization was the fiscal appetite of the royal army, and the king's agents marshalled the realm's resources to support Louis's dynastic ambitions.

From the perspective of the various localities of the kingdom, the growing power of the center threatened traditional institutions, but local elites in provinces such as Languedoc adjusted and joined in with their "oppressors."[21] Involvement in royal administration did not modernize the nobility, because court life and royal governance were essentially large-scale extensions of seignorial practices marked by personal loyalty, patronage, and factionalism.[22]

Sharon Kettering has described the sinews of patron-client relations in the Bourbon body politic.[23] Patronage reflected the feudal tradition of personal political fidelity and respect for hierarchy. Patrons, from among the king's top advisors, exercised normal governance through the agency of personal clients at provincial and local levels. The key figures in the systems were regional brokers, who acted as the links between patrons at court and provincial clients.[24] The system possessed its own ethos of fidelity and guardianship, often grounded in familial ties. Royal governance was not one great system, however, with the king as the ultimate patron. Systems of patronage often worked at cross purposes and generated internal administrative conflict. Factionalism revealed the tensions that existed between systems of patronage and the fact that exercising power meant making choices between opposing political interests. With this in mind, the growth of Louis XIV's power did not reflect so much his subjugation of the unruly nobility as the integration of their contentions into the day-to-day operation of royal administration.[25] The integration was not a conscious act but a natural marriage of interests. The non-noble financiers and robe nobles emulated the values of their contentious social betters, as they too became faithful servants and brokers. The ongoing disputes within the administration marked the domestication of the mêlée.

In the provinces, Louis XIV's government did not present a monolithic front when it sought to exercise the king's will. In Alsace we have seen that conflict between the intendants and the Imperial Bailiffs provided leverage for the Alsatian estates against expanding royal power. The Colmarians learned that they might expect different answers from different agents. Furthermore, Colmar's magistrates had always distributed patronage, and they understood the fractious nature of politics. What was new and still confusing was determining who were the most effective brokers in dealing with the still distant royal power. For twenty-five years following the Peace of Westphalia, the kingdom remained a dangerous external threat to civic peace. Within the city walls, Colmar's political leaders still held the reigns of authority in their own hands.

II. THE INDIAN SUMMER OF INDEPENDENT CIVIC POLITICS

During the struggle between the duke de Mazarin and the Decapolis, the officials in Paris asked Johann Frischmann, their agent in Strasbourg, to explain the cities' stubbornness. He offered four reasons. First, the municipal regimes felt obliged to preserve their historical legacy of sovereignty. Secondly, they were deeply attached to the liberties which secured their power in municipal affairs, and, thirdly, they felt a personal loyalty to the empire, which they renewed through oaths on election day. Finally, Frischmann identified specific fears among member cities over garrisons or religious freedoms.[26] In Frischmann's eyes, the civic officials honored imperial political tradition because they recognized the connection between it and their power.

In the Alsatian cities, pride in a glorious historical legacy informed community self-consciousness. The urban ruling classes traced their ancestry back to the fourteenth century and considered themselves equal to the local nobles, who had long since lost their political power within the cities. At Strasbourg the noble families continued to hold the office of Stettmeister, but their political significance had declined.[27] Strasbourg, moreover, was the only city in mid-seventeenth-century Alsace with a substantial noble citizenry. Colmar possessed a patriciate of lesser nobles, university-trained lawyers, and wholesale merchants, but its civic nobility had shrunk to such an extent that the surviving von Reusts and Lincks had abandoned their private society *zur Krone* and joined the non-noble elite in the society *zum Waagkeller*. Furthermore, Colmar's nobles had lost their distinct constitutional place in civic politics in the mid-sixteenth century.[28]

After 1648 the civic elite had begun to fracture into two distinct layers. Some signs pointed to a democraticization of status and honor. For example, a growing number of Colmarians claimed the title of "Herr" in the parish registers. In 1620, 100 householders (9.3%) employed the title, but by 1650, 109 householders (14.8%) claimed the name. Almost half (53) of these honorable men belonged to either *zur Treue* or *zum Riesen*.[29] Over the next twenty years, the number of "Herren" rose to 121, but in the growing city they represented only 13.1% of the householders. Among these distinguished men were the magistrates, the councilors, the major civic employees, most merchants, and others whose trades entailed special education, such as the apothecaries.

Other signs pointed to a narrowing of special status. In the decades after the Thirty Years' War the private patrician society *zum Waagkeller* became more exclusive. In the late sixteenth century, the society had fifty-eight members, including nearly all civic regime members as well as ten leading men from the neighboring lordships.[30] Following the confessional turmoil of 1628–33, the society counted only twenty-five men, among them five Catholics from the Counter-Reform regime.[31] By 1637 the society had grown to thirty-one members, including several Catholics, two noblemen, Christian Linck and Friedrich von Reust, the magistrates, the leading civic employees, but only five of the twenty-seven council members.[32] By 1664 the society *zum Waagkeller* still had thirty-three members, who, when assembled for their annual feast, included two royal agents, three noblemen, the magistrates, the principle civic employees, and eight of the twenty-six councilors.[33] At this time the members came from only five of the ten guilds, with *zur Treue* and *zum Riesen* accounting for 63.6% (21) of the members.[34] Besides the king's agents, the only Catholic was the former Counter-Reform Stettmeister Matthias Johner. The members owed their place primarily to political office, public administration, or business interests. From 1665 to 1683, the society grew steadily smaller until it consisted of only thirteen members from the Lutheran oligarchy.[35]

In the years after 1640, university education and professionalization among the political elite also grew more common in Alsace. At Colmar, as at Strasbourg and Hagenau, many sons of prominent merchants and politicians attended neighboring universities as a means of social mobility.[36] Many Colmarians studied at Strasbourg, which strengthened political and confessional ties to the center of provincial Protestant culture. The students who returned to Colmar often served in the civic regime or as professional administrators for the nobility of Upper Alsace. For example, the future magistrates Friederich Binder, Daniel Birr, and Andreas Sandherr, the long-time councilor and city clerk Samuel Röttlin, and the two sons of Johann Heinrich Mogg, Matthias Ambrosius and Heinrich Friedrich, who resided in Colmar while serving as legal advisors for the regional nobility, all studied for a time at Strasbourg.[37] The development of professional esprit de corps among the Alsatian civic politicians had complex roots, but in a large part it reflected the risks to profitable trade and the growing social status attached to political office.

Many of these developments began in Colmar after 1648. The disruption caused by the Imperial Counter-Reformation and the military campaigns of the late 1630s had little immediate impact on the structure of Colmar's political life. As we have seen in chapter 1, a new generation of families had replaced the sixteenth-century ruling elite in the decade before the Counter-Reformation, which broke their power but did not endure long enough to fashion a Catholic elite to replace them. When the Swedes restored Protestant worship, the new Lutheran parish proved distasteful to some of the Protestant exiles, while others had established their businesses and their political interests in Mulhouse and Basel. Remnants of the old elite families remained in the city after 1632, but for a time the Lincks, Golls, Buobs, and Espachs did not participate in the new regime.

As in most Imperial cities, the post-Westphalian Colmarians did not practice electoral politics, despite the ritual of annual elections.[38] The constitution of 1521 was still in force, which called for the election of guildmasters by their respective guilds as the first step in renewing the municipal regime.

This formula granted the guilds the opportunity to fill all vacancies or simply to elect new men. Yet, even in the sixteenth century, Colmar's guildsmen often waived their rights by selecting an incumbant, and between 1521 and 1627 only one-third of the city's officials first joined the regime through guild election. Furthermore, the guilds seemed most reluctant to exercise their franchise during periods of political uncertainty, for example, the decades before and after the city's Reformation when guild election provided only 11% of the new regime members. The normal route of entry into civic office was co-optation.

The successive depositions of the Reformed and Catholic regimes between 1627 and 1632 created an opening for increased electoral involvement for Colmar's guilds. The rapid turnover of officials also permitted ambitious men to pursue political careers, an opportunity they might not have had during more stable times. Nevertheless, based on evidence from individual political careers, the guilds apparently lost or gave up their electoral leverage after 1633, though they remained political institutions which regulated membership, production, and prices, and effectively lobbied before the magistrate to protect their economic interests against neighboring competitors. At Colmar electoral disputes were not a source of political instability, and if the citizens needed saving from "magisterial slavery," they were unwilling to push the issue through elections. Co-optation into the regime remained the norm in post-Westphalian Colmar, and careful recruitment allowed the magistrates to stabilize civic politics.

The backgrounds and careers of the magistrates who held office between 1632 and 1673 were very similar to those of the early seventeenth-century political elite (see table 4.1). Twenty men served on the magistrate from the Swedish takeover until the Peace of Nijmegen in 1679. Twelve magistrates served as Obristmeister, but only five held the office more than three terms. The political dominance of these five men falls into three distinct eras. Conrad Ortlieb, the one magistrate to return from exile, dominated civic politics from 1633 to 1643, then his power weakened in the years before his death in 1649. Johann Heinrich Mogg replaced Ortlieb at the center of government from 1645 to 1660, when Mogg, in turn, gave way to Andreas Sandherr and Johann Jacob Riegger, who shared power until Riegger's death in 1673.

Ortlieb dominated civic politics in the wake of the Swedish takeover, but he did not function alone. Ortlieb worked closely with Jonas Walch and probably Mogg, and none of these men was a native Colmarian.[39] In fact, among the initial magistrates, Andreas Meder, a long-time city resident though a native of the nearby village of Herlisheim, and Emmanuel Röttlin were also outsiders. Röttlin came from a significant family of Württemberg officials from nearby Riquewihr and entered civic politics as a Swedish candidate, as he had travelled with the army and held the official title of councilor to the Swedish court. Two of his sons, Johann Matthaeus and Johann Michel,

TABLE 4.1
Magisterial Recruitment, 1632–1679

NAME	REGIME	REC.	MAG.	TEN.	OB.	GUILD	REL.
REGIME IN 1632							
Conrad Ortlieb	1612	S (G)	1627	16	7	Adler	R/L
Emmanuel Röttlin	1632	M	1632	2	—	Treue	R/L
Andreas Meder	1628	S (G)	1632	5	—	Treue	R/L
Matthias Goll	1624	S (G)	1632	11	—	Treue	R/L
Niclaus Sandherr	1632	M	1632	3	1	Treue	R/L
RECRUITS							
Jonas Walch	1633	G	1634	10	3	Treue	R/L
Johann Dürninger	1627	XIII	1635	21	2	Riesen	R/L
Johann Heinrich Mogg	1638	M	1638	31	8	Haspel	Luth
Christian Scherb	1633	S (G)	1645	11	—	Adler	R/L
Niclaus Birckinger	1643	XIII	1645	7	1	Treue	R/L
Johann Burger	1640	G	1650	14	1	Treue	R/L
Daniel Birr	1647	G	1652	7	3	Treue	Luth
Johann Jacob Riegger	1645	S (G)	1658	15	6	Riesen	R/L
Andreas Sandherr	1645	S (G)	1658	40	10	Treue	Luth
Daniel Schneider	1660	M	1660	25	—	NA	Luth
Philip Schultz	1666	M	1666	2	—	NA	Luth
Friedrich Binder	1654	S (G)	1668	11	—	Treue	Luth
Johann Heinrich Klein	1669	M	1669	9	2	NA	Luth
Ambrosius Riegger	1659	G	1675	23	11	Holderbaum	Luth
Jacob Oberlin	1649	G	1679	8	—	Riesen	Luth

Key:
Regime   Year recruited into regime
Rec.   First post held in regime
   O   Obristmeister
   M   Magistrate
   XIII   XIIIer
   G   Guildmaster
   S   Senator
   (G)   Served as guildmaster during career
Mag.   Year recruited into magistrate
Ten.   Tenure of magisterial service
Ob.   Number of years served as Obristmeister
Guild   Guild in which inscribed
   NA   Does not appear in guild or citizen registers
Rel.   Confessional affiliation
   R/L   Married or politically active before 1627
   Luth   Married or politically active after 1632

would later find careers as government officials in Sweden. Röttlin was Niclaus Sandherr's brother-in-law and first cousin to Andreas Meder, and all shared ties to officials in the lordship of Horbourg-Riquewihr. Sandherr had served as court clerk for both the Reformed and Counter-Reform regimes, and along with Röttlin he provided professional expertise for the Lutheran magistrate.[40] Sandherr was the son of Andreas Sandherr, who had drafted Colmar's Reformed *Deklarationsschrift*, and along with Matthias Goll, a descendant of a sixteenth-century patrician family who had studied law at Metz, Sandherr connected the Lutheran regime with the city's early seventeenth-century oligarchy. Goll also had connections with Horbourg-Riquewihr, for he spent his exile there during the Counter-Reformation.[41] Rounding out the new Protestant regime was the city clerk, Johann Heinrich Mogg, who along with Röttlin had served as an official with the Swedish army. Mogg had Alsatian roots, however, having earlier served as an official of the counts von Rappoltstein.[42]

In general, the new political elite came to the city as returning exiles or outsiders, but among them only Mogg seemed unwilling to form ties with the civic community. Unlike his colleagues, Mogg married outside the city and encouraged his children to follow his lead.[43] He delayed inscribing into a guild (*zum Haspel*) until after becoming Stettmeister in 1638. In 1635, with his successful negotiation of the treaty of Rueil, Mogg had established himself as a man who could handle the pressure in the new provincial political environment. His career was anomalous. For example, he retained his post as city clerk until 1640 even though he had become a Stettmeister in 1638. Mogg's rise probably occurred with Ortlieb's tacit approval, but the old Obristmeister would not relinquish his executive post until 1645. Once Mogg had assumed the reins "everything passed through his hands," and Ortlieb would not hold the chief office again.

From 1645 until 1660, Mogg dominated civic politics. With the assistance of the city clerk, Hans Balthasar Schneider, he negotiated Colmar's restoration as an Imperial city at the Peace of Westphalia. He handled the challenge of placating both Harcourt and the intendants during the Fronde, and he led the resistance of the Decapolis to Croissy's claims for the *Conseil souverain*. Mogg's forte was foreign policy, and to secure his place within Colmar he needed helpful allies with stronger ties within the civic community.

Christian Scherb and Niclaus Birckinger also joined the magistrate in 1645, Mogg's first year as Obristmeister, and their elevation may have secured Mogg's appointment. Mogg probably also orchestrated the selection of his successor as city clerk, Johann Jacob Saltzmann, who was, like Mogg, a native of Ribeauvillé.[44] As for his colleagues, Scherb, another nonnative, lacked the power, experience, and family contacts to have been much of a factor, but Birckinger, who had married Emmanuel Röttlin's sister and had succeeded Niclaus Sandherr as court clerk in 1635, had both expertise and contacts.[45] Birckinger, Johann Dürninger, a descendent of an important native family of sixteenth-century coopers and wine merchants, and Johann Burger, whose father, Anton, had served in the Reformed magistrate, alternated as Obristmeister with Mogg over the next several years and connected his leadership with the important members of the city's Protestant oligarchy. In 1652 Daniel Birr, who in Croissy's eyes softened Mogg's rashness, became Mogg's new associate. Birr, the son of a Reformed Stettmeister, had studied law at Strasbourg and had married into the powerful Wetzel family.[46] By 1658 Mogg was the only nonnative in the magistrate. The death of Birr in 1659 and the personal favor shown to Mogg by Croissy may have cost the old leader; for in 1661 two new men, Andreas Sandherr and Johann Jacob Riegger, rose to power.

Sandherr and Riegger were originally co-opted into the regime in the critical year of 1645, and they perhaps helped Mogg in his rise to power. Andreas Sandherr was the son the former Stettmeister, Niclaus, and he had studied philosophy at Strasbourg. In 1636 he married, Cleophe, the daughter of Egenolph Wetzel. Riegger was the son of one of the richest men in early seventeenth-century Colmar, and in 1620 he had married Catharina Schott, the daughter of the city clerk. Between 1655 and 1661 Sandherr and Riegger's children married into the Röttlin, Wetzel, Birr, and Andres families. Once the two men entered the magistrate in 1658, they probably would have challenged Mogg even if Birr had lived. From 1661 until Louis XIV's conquest, their control of civic government was unquestioned, and Sandherr and Riegger alternated as Obristmeister.

Between 1633 and 1679, Colmar's magistrates were all Protestants, but their commitments to the new Lutheran parish were not deep-seated. The city's earliest Lutheran magistrates had acquired their political education in the Reformed regime. They also traced their family roots to the city's early seventeenth-century elite. Counting the five new magistrates in 1632, of the eight men who joined the executive before 1640, four had served in the Reformed regime. Furthermore, Sandherr had held the appointive post of court clerk, Andreas Meder had been the *Umgelter* before 1628, and both had retained their offices during the Counter-Reformation. Nevertheless, those with a formal education had studied in Strasbourg and they married into important families from the Lutheran lordship of Horbourg-Riquewihr. Those civic leaders committed to Calvinism remained in exile after 1633, though the tolerance experienced in the 1640s by the leader of Colmar's Reformed community, Augustin Güntzer, made sense in light of the magistrates' own backgrounds. Under Mogg, however, the confessional atmosphere among Colmar's Protestants would change.

In the late 1630s, the military campaigns, disease, and political tensions of royal protection stretched the energies of the civic leadership. The pursuit of order in governance led to the co-optation of experienced professionals, such as Röttlin, Sandherr, Birckinger, and Mogg, into the magistrate. Sandherr, Mogg, and Birckinger maintained their posts as civic employees while holding "elective" magisterial office. If the constitution of 1521 governed electoral procedures after 1627, then of the magistrates co-opted between 1633 and 1648, only Jonas Walch had begun his career as a guildmaster, although Ortlieb, Meder, Goll, and Scherb had served as guildmasters at least once. In all, between 1633 and 1679, twelve magistrates had once been guildmasters, but the exceptions form a noteworthy pattern. Five of the eight magistrates who never received guild support entered civic office during the Thirty Years' War. Two men, Dürninger and Birckinger, were the only magistrates to enter the regime as XIIIers between 1632 and 1679; and both may have played critical roles in consolidating Mogg's power after 1645.

Once Mogg had secured his position, magisterial recruitment became less circumscribed. Burger, Birr, Riegger, and Sandherr had local roots and had all come through the ranks. As Mogg's power faded, Riegger and Sandherr apparently once again tightened magisterial recruitment, for three of the four new magistrates in the 1660s were directly co-opted into highest office from among the salaried civic officials. Daniel Schneider, son of Colmar's city clerk, Hans Balthasar Schneider, had previously served as the city's official representative to the French Court, while Philip Schultz and Johann Heinrich Klein had both held the post of city clerk before their appointment.[47] None of these men had been formally inscribed into Colmar's guilds, and of the four men co-opted between 1660 and 1673, Friederich Binder alone had served as guildmaster. He had also served in the pivotal post of *Umgelter* and been admitted to the society *zum Waagkeller* before his co-optation into the magistrate.[48] In his eleven years in magisterial office, he never held the post of Obristmeister. Whether Riegger and Sandherr sought to consolidate their authority or simply to professionalize the leadership, the result was that the magistrate had lost touch with the citizenry, and the civic leaders who exercised *Obrigkeit* had little contact with the guildsmen. Initially the French takeover did not end this oligarchical pattern in civic government. Riegger's death in 1673 brought Klein to the Obristmeister's post, and he would carry the burden of office for two years 1675–76. Then Ambrosius Riegger would assume his father's place next to Sandherr as the regime's Lutheran leaders until the French constitutional reform of 1680 and beyond.

Between 1633 and 1679, only five of Colmar's ten guilds produced magistrates, and the city's leaders were normally either educated professionals or merchants. Schneider, Klein, and Schultz were salaried officials, who may have joined a guild but never appeared in Colmar's guild registers. Of the five guilds represented, *zum Holderbaum* and *zum Haspel* produced one magistrate each; but one must question Mogg's affiliation with the political interests of Colmar's gardeners. *Zum Adler*, the weaver's guild, which also included cloth merchants, claimed two magistrates, and Christian Scherb, for one, had begun his career as a wool weaver. Two guilds, *zur Treue* and *zum Riesen*, produced thirteen of Colmar's magistrates, with the merchants of *zur Treue* by far the most significant with ten. With the exception of Scherb, Colmar's tenant farmers, victualers, and craftsmen could no longer aspire to be magistrates.

Access to civic office had risen beyond the reach of all but a few chosen men. Magisterial ties to the guilds had long since withered, and the core officials were thoroughly professionalized, which mirrored similar trends in other municipal governments in the empire.[49] At Colmar appointment to the magistrate signified one's arrival at the pinnacle of the political hierarchy, and the pattern of recruitment marked a shift in social values among the city's Lutheran oligarchs. As Frischmann had suggested to the royal government, Colmar's leaders felt themselves better than lords.[50] The civic nobles were insignificant as a distinct social group, and the Lutheran magistrates intermarried or married into the official families of nearby Horbourg-Riquewihr.[51]

In counterpoint to the magistrate, the council remained accessible to Colmar's leading guildsmen (see table 4.2). For the period between the first Lutheran regime and the last fully Lutheran regime in 1679, 113 new regime members were recruited, including six magistrates. Of these, forty-four (38.9%) entered office as guildmasters, which is slightly higher than for the sixteenth-century regime (34.5%). Moreover, if we consider the careers of all regime members for the period, then eighty-six (76.1%) received guild sanction at least once. The percentage would have been higher if the turbulent 1630s were not factored into the study. Of the sixty-eight new regime members recruited after 1640, fifty-seven (83.8%) served at least once as guildmasters, and if the co-opted magistrates are excluded, the percentage rises to 87.7. Nonetheless, other changes in civic politics discounted the guildsmen's apparent electoral voice.

By the mid-seventeenth century, the council of XIII was in full decline, though the process had begun earlier. From 1590 to 1627 only three men had entered the regime as XIIIers, and by 1600 and perhaps earlier, the council had already shrunk to ten members, with the three Stettmeisters assuming posts normally filled by councilors. Between 1633 and 1648, three more men entered the regime as XIIIers, and two of them, Niclaus Birckinger and Johann Dürninger, soon became magistrates. The third, Bartel Dürninger, had joined the Swedish-backed regime in 1632. Unlike Sebastian Wilhelm Linck and Batholomäus von Kirn in the sixteenth century, no regime member served on the council of XIII over extended terms. After 1633 a councilor normally rotated through the three chambers of the council once every three years. After 1648 the council of XIII ceased to serve as a vehicle for political recruitment, and no longer functioned as a liaison between the magistrate and the council. The council, which the guildsmen had forced on the magistrate in 1424, had gradually lost its place in civic politics, and its decline weakened the influence of councilors in day-to-day affairs. The magistrate held the reins, and though the council survived as an assembly of leading guildsmen, its members lacked access to higher office or much influence in decision-making. The shrinkage of the council of XIII highlighted the declining political influence of the guilds. With access to only twenty-seven council offices, not all of the ten guilds could expect an equal share of representatives.

As we have seen, between 1632 and 1679 nearly four out of ten regime members began their political careers as guildmasters, and over three out of four served as guildmasters at some point during their career. Not all guilds, however, provided an equal number of regime members (see table 4.3). Of the 113 men recruited into the regime during this era, thirty (26.5%) purchased citizenship in the merchants' guild. Most guilds provided between nine and thirteen regime members, but *Ackerleute*, *zum Löwen*, and *zum Kränzchen* provided far fewer, with six, five, and four members respectively. The apparently small role played by Colmar's peasants and victualers in civic politics may be explained by the longevity of their representatives. Most men who entered the regime served for life. The dominance of the merchants' guild, however, suggests that Colmar's merchants held posts in the name of other guilds besides their own. An examination of the regimes in 1640, 1650, 1660, and 1670 support this contention.[52]

In 1640 seven of the thirty-two regime members had purchased citizenship in the merchants' guild. Two of the seven were magistrates, Jonas Walch and Matthias Goll. Goll, serving as Stettmeister that year, doubled as a XIIIer for *Ackerleute*. *Zur Treue* had its proper representatives in all three chambers of the council: Hans Georg Barth as XIIIer, Samuel Wetzel as senator, and Matthis Brunner as guildmaster. Two other merchants, Hieronymous Lichteisen and Hans Burger, represented the gardeners' guild as senator and guildmaster respectively. Johann Heinrich Mogg was the only officeholder from *zum Haspel* in the regime, and he held the posts of Stettmeister and XIIIer. All the other officials served their own guilds except Bartel Dürninger, who, though inscribed in *zum Riesen*, held the post of guildmaster in *zum Adler*. In 1640 Colmar's gardeners, peasants, and cloth workers were underrepresented in government.

In 1650 one in four (eight of thirty-two) regime members were inscribed in *zur Treue*. More significantly, the connection between guild membership and political office had apparently ended. If we include the three Stettmeister on the council of XIII, thirteen of the thirty councilors were not representing the guilds of their origin, compared with six in 1640. In the council of XIII, *Ackerleute*, *zum Löwen*, and *zum Kränzchen* were represented by men from other guilds. The senate included four merchants and two men from *zum Haspel*, with *Ackerleute*, *Rebleute*, *zum Riesen*, and *zum Adler* represented by outsiders. Among the guildmasters, those in *zum Adler*, *zum Haspel*, *zum Riesen*, and, surprisingly, *zur Treue* had inscribed in other guilds. Except for *zum Adler*, these guilds had members representing other guilds in the regime. It seems very unlikely that the guildsmen had decided to choose their masters from the political community at large, so without a constitutional

TABLE 4.2
Regime Recruitment, 1632–1679

DECADE	G	C/G	XIII	M	TOTAL
1632–39	16	24/13	2	3	45
1640–49	7	9/8	1	—	17
1650–59	5	13/10	—	—	18
1660–69	7	8/7	—	3	18
1670–79	9	6/4	—	—	15
Total	44	60/42	3	6	113

Key:
G   Recruited as guildmaster
S/G   Recruited as senator/served as a guildmaster
XIII   Recruited as XIIIer
M   Recruited directly into magistrate

TABLE 4.3
Regime Recruitment by Guild, 1632–1679

GUILD	1630s	1640s	1650s	1660s	1670s	TOTAL
Treue	8	6	6	7	3	30
Riesen	4	2	3	—	1	10
Ackerleute	2	2	1	—	1	6
Haspel	6	1	2	—	—	9
Rebleute	6	1	1	2	2	12
Löwen	3	1	—	—	1	5
Kränzchen	—	—	2	1	1	4
Adler	8	1	1	1	2	13
Holderbaum	4	2	2	—	2	10
Wohlleben	4	1	—	4	1	10
Unknown	—	—	—	3	1	4
Totals	45	17	18	18	15	113

referendum, the connection between guild elections and office had clearly ceased by the end of the war.

The dominance of the merchants in council chambers and the separation between guild membership and political representation continued through the peaceful decades down to the French conquest. By 1660 the regime included two non-guildsmen: Daniel Schneider in the magistrate; and Zacharias Buob, the court clerk and guildmaster for the weavers. By 1660 the council of XIII included only six councilors, as the Schultheiss became the fourth magistrate to assume a post in the chamber. In addition to these four, seven of the remaining twenty-six council seats were held by men who did not represent their own guilds, and four of these were guildmasters. Seven members of *zur Treue* sat in the regime, but only one member each of *zum Kränzchen* and *zum Adler*. Ten years later, nine members of *zur Treue* served in the regime, and twelve out of thirty conciliar posts were held by men inscribed in different guilds. Although eight of ten guildmasters served from their own guilds, this did not reflect a recovery by the guilds but rather the particular distribution in the rotation of offices.

Since 1521 the guilds had elected their masters first, and, according to a description of the civic elections composed for the intendant in 1685, the guildsmen continued to elect their masters, who then presided over the guild meetings. Yet the same document claimed that the regime still included ten XIIIers from the ten guilds.[53] Based on a reconstruction of individual regimes from the general lists of regime members, however, Colmar's constitutional order had changed long before the coming of French power. Guild membership no longer played a central role in officeholding, which was probably due to the elimination of guild elections.

The merchants' guild, *zur Treue*, habitually provided more than its share of regime members, as did the wine processing guild, *zum Riesen*.[54] What guilds were underrepresented? We have noted above that the gardeners had only Mogg as their political voice in 1640. In the same year, the peasants' guild (*Ackerleute*) had only two representatives. If one includes the magistrates, all other guilds had at least three members in civic office. At the end of the crisis of the 1630s, the guilds still had a relatively equal voice in council deliberations. In 1650, despite the break with guild elections, the representative balance held, with only *Ackerleute* underrepresented, with one regime member. All the other guilds had at least two representatives. Under Mogg and then Sandherr and Riegger, balanced representation ended. In 1660 the weavers' guild counted only one member in the regime, as did *zum Kränzchen*, and in 1670 *zum Löwen*, *zum Haspel*, and *zum Kränzchen* each had but one representative. Perhaps these men were the elected guildmasters, who then were assigned a post in one of the chambers. Whatever the case, specific occupational groups lost their political voice as a gulf developed between the political and economic roles of the guilds. More and more, the regime reflected the interests of the merchants, who dealt in wine, cloth, or brandy, while the artisans' political role diminished. Perhaps, as was the case in Strasbourg, the artisans faced with difficult economic times focused their political interests on protectionist legislation and market relations.[55] So long as the merchant-dominated regime delivered favorable regulations, the artisans ignored electoral grievances.

The decline of the guilds in municipal politics had a long history. The reduction of the council of XIII to a council of X, which had occurred as early as 1600, had already broken the symmetry of three representatives per guild. The Counter-Reformation forced the city's Catholic leaders to construct a regime without regard to guild affiliation, because of the absence of Catholics among the artisans. During the troubled 1630s the Lutheran regime possibly sought to bring order to civic politics by restricting elections. However, such an action was never discussed in council chambers or protested by the guilds. By 1650 council members often represented more than one guild in the course of their political careers, and they often served as guildmasters of different guilds. We have no record of shifts in guild membership among the elite, and the simplest explanation is that the guilds gradually lost their political voice over the course of the seventeenth century.

The new pattern of co-optation paved the way for the Lutheran authorities to construct a confessionally uniform regime, and in fact the Lutherans monopolized the magistrate and dominated the council. In the 1630s the regime included several Catholics, such as Georg Gsell in *Ackerleute*, Christian Hügelin in *zum Kränzchen*, Lorentz Espach in *zum Riesen*, and Michel Hötzelbach in *Rebleute*, who had begun their careers before 1627 or during the Counter-Reformation. At least five Catholics were recruited after 1633 into the regime.[56] In 1633, Jacob Seebach was elected guildmaster for *zum Haspel* and served one year. In 1640 Claus Dorss was elected guildmaster for *Ackerleute*. Dorss, a tenant farmer and the wealthiest Catholic in the city, served in the council for thirty years.[57] Despite his wealth and political longevity, he never received an invitation to join the society *zum Waagkeller*. Traditionally the Catholic leadership had its roots in the agricultural guilds, but in 1659 Elias Hermann was chosen guildmaster for *zum Holderbaum*, which housed the smiths and building trades. If the guild elections still carried weight, these three men were initially popular candidates. The next two Catholics were co-opted: Hans Benedict as a senator for *Rebleute* in 1662, and Georg Hannser as a senator for *Ackerleute* in 1670. They replaced deceased Catholic councilors, Matthis Hötzelbach and Claus Dorss respectively. Given the changes in regime recruitment, Colmar's Lutheran leaders, perhaps consciously, sought to provide a voice, albeit a limited one, for the Catholics in the council. At any given time, at least three Catholics held seats in the regime, and they regularly served on the council of XIII. No Catholic, however, became a magistrate. Colmar's Lutheran leaders governed a confessionally mixed citizenry, and they allowed the Catholics a clearly circumscribed place in civic governance.

In the decades after the Thirty Years' War, the municipal government had become restrictive but not exclusive. The typical member of the regime was a merchant or an educated professional; he attended Lutheran services and lived in the core neighborhoods of the city. The more important officials also belonged to the society *zum Waagkeller*. The voice of Colmar's guildsmen, by contrast, had faded in the regime, as had the Catholic voice. Yet there was still room for a shoemaker or middling tenant farmer or vintner in the government. Nevertheless, Colmar's citizen guildsmen must have felt the distance between themselves and the powerful men who administered their public interest. When the regime, faced with French overlordship in 1673, turned to its citizens, they would not respond.

III. THE REGIME UNDER SIEGE, 1673–1680

Louis XIV's conquest of the imperial city had its deepest initial impact on Colmar's political leaders. The regime's policies had forced the crisis, and it now had to govern with questionable authority. Its members retained their posts but found themselves caught between the demands of the royal government and the citizenry. When the regime carried out the king's orders, they faced the citizens' wrath. The magistrate had to call in French troops to collect the subsidies to finance the demolition of civic fortifications.[58] Dissident citizens stoned the windows of the magistrates' homes. French troops dispersed an assault on Obristmeister Andreas Sandherr's house, and one angry townsman confronted the city clerk, Samuel Röttlin, in the street with a halberd. The rioters were butchers, bakers, millers, and inn keepers, men who were closely involved in the processing of the region's agricultural products, not the long-distance merchants, the artisans, or the often volatile agricultural work force.[59] With the destruction of the wall and the probable dissolution of civic economic privileges these men had much to lose economically and confessionally.[60] In the tax rolls these trades filled the middle rungs of civic wealth, and were predominantly Lutheran. The citizens' chief complaints concerned troop quartering, new taxes, and loss of civic pride, though they were also concerned about requisitions for the French troops and the possible destruction of their rural properties. Nevertheless, the bakers and millers of *zum Kränzchen* also could reflect on twenty-five years of near exclusion from civic office. The regime was packed with merchants and professional men under the leadership of Sandherr and Johann Jacob Riegger. The frustration of the commons against the regime reflected a collapse in faith in this leadership, which sent the magistrates to the royal government for support.

During the municipal elections of 1674, the underlying contradictions of the municipal regime's status came into focus. In early August, the magistrates petitioned the intendant, La Grange, and the *subdélégué* of the rechristened Grand (Imperial) Bailiff of Hagenau, the marquis de Ruzé, for permission to forgo the elections, because the citizens' traditional oath no longer applied. The magistrates feared an assembly in which their lost authority would be proclaimed, though they also wanted to ensure obedience. The oath referred to loyalty to the emperor, but more critically it emphasized the contractual nature of civic politics in binding the citizens to obey the magistrates "in all good and just things."[61]

The intendant responded to the regime's request by canceling the elections and commanding the citizens to obey their leaders.[62] La Grange's orders apparently had little effect, for within a month Obristmeister Sandherr had become so disenchanted by popular disobedience that he asked the intendant to discharge him from office.[63] La Grange refused to accept the resignation. Instead he issued a new directive commanding obedience to the municipal leaders "in all things" the magistrates demanded of the citizens "for his majesty's service and the public interest."[64] Thus as early as 1674, civic officials understood that the traditional foundation of their authority, the exchange of mutual oaths, no longer functioned. They turned to the French to support their rule, and La Grange responded by commanding obedience in the name of the king. The lines of authority and power had quickly changed in Colmar.

Fear within the tense community easily deteriorated into panic. On 30 September 1674, two agents seeking grain for the royal storehouse at Breisach mistakenly delivered the requisition to the civic granary rather than to the city hall. In the document, the intendant tersely ordered the collection of all available grain within forty-eight hours and threatened the full "rigors of war" for noncompliance.[65] The magistrates had to shout down the mob assembled before the city hall and to convince the worried citizens that the French did not wish them to starve. The regime's hastily dispatched embassy to Breisach returned with assurances from La Grange that he only wished to purchase whatever grain was for sale.[66] Before the embassy could return with this news, however, the municipal watch mistook a band of workers returning from Breisach for troops coming to carry out La Grange's orders. Someone sounded the alarm, and the frantic citizens, who had no firearms, gathered at their posts with whatever weapons they could find: hunting spears, pitchforks, hatchets. They overturned wagons in the narrow streets to form barricades. The magistrates finally restored order hours after dark.[67] Despite its comic moments, the day's events reflected the fragile public peace, the popular sentiment against the French, and the difficulty of maintaining order in an atmosphere charged with insecurity. It would become the formula for governance and public life in Colmar for the next several decades.

Colmar had escaped the worst ravages of the Thirty Years' War, and in 1648 the citizens had many reasons to be optimistic about their future. The city had made political and economic advances at the expense of its neighbors. The regime had weathered the crisis of the Counter-Reformation and had strengthened itself under the leadership of Conrad Ortlieb and Johann Heinrich Mogg. Though the Peace of Westphalia had made the French the central power in the region, the king's agents were in disarray, and their initial impact was slight.

The French officials confronted a civic regime which was gradually assuming a distinct oligarchic character, in which patronage and the collective self-interest of a group of Lutheran merchants and professional men played a critical role. The French understood such political behavior, even if they found it uppity in a simple mayor. The royal officials practiced patronage and guarded their collective aristocratic interests. The Colmarians soon learned that the king's government was large enough to harbor extensive and powerful aristocratic factions, and in dealing with the French, the civic officials had tried to play one group against another, until the king's personal interest led to Colmar's conquest in 1673.

At issue throughout the period was the question of authority. Colmar's regime had fought the royal provincial agents over the issue of the king's authority within the city. The regime wanted the debate carried out within the Imperial judicial system, where strong and weak powers coexisted under rules appreciated by the Colmarians. At the same time the Colmarians had learned the rules of royal governance and the significance of patronage, loyalty, and privilege. These mores of early modern political culture had already entered civic life before the French takeover. The office holders had become increasingly professionalized, civic officials often held multiple posts, and their offices sometimes provided tax exemptions. The magistrate in particular had come to dominate the regime as a close network of political allies jealously guarded access to office, in particular to the post of Obrist-meister. Patterns of officeholding depicted a growing break between political office and guild membership. Many officials did not join any guild, and many councilors represented guilds other than their own. No constitutional changes reflected these practices, which signalled a break between the regime and the guilds. How did the city leaders justify their political behavior?

The regime saw itself embodying authority (*Obrigkeit*). As recently as the early seventeenth century, that authority claimed to be grounded in the community and was confirmed in the annual oath. We have also seen that political practice often involved assembling the council of jurors or the individual guilds. By the end of the Thirty Years' War, the council of jurors seldom gathered, and the guilds were never consulted. The regime had come to see authority embodied in its own expertise and esprit de corps had replaced contractually based authority. What is striking is that the city's guildsmen did not rebel against this "magisterial tyranny." Perhaps the paternal nature of the regime's authority reflected their own authority in the workshop. Perhaps the pride of professional administrators mirrored their own pride as craftsmen. Most likely, the city's leaders avoided political confrontations by fostering the self-interest of the guildsmen. Low taxes, careful protection of civic market privileges, and defense of rural properties, all of which formed part of the regime's resistance to the royal provincial officials, were policies designed to protect the private interests of Colmar's citizens. Only when the city had fallen to the French, which threatened all of the gains of the previous decades, did Colmar's guildsmen vent their anger at the magistrates.

The city's conquest by Louis XIV deprived the regime of its traditional foundation for authority without providing a clear substitute. When the civic officials turned to the king's provincial agents for support, their move subtly shifted the foundation of their authority. They were no longer individual power brokers who could secure their place through marriage alliances and political patronage. They were local administrators of royal will, that is, a local extension of the provincial administrative hierarchy. The network of loyalty, familial ties, and professional pride remained, but it needed to be woven into the fabric of French provincial governance. This would occur in the final critical decades of the seventeenth century.

Notes

1. Quoted in Livet, ed., *Le Duc Mazarin*, 150.
2. Livet, *L'intendance*, 335–40.
3. Quoted in ibid., 333.
4. Bardot, *La question*, 24–25. On Colmar see Sittler, "La transformation du gouvernement," 135–36.
5. Greissler, *La classe politique*, 47–48.
6. Walker, *German Home Towns*, 2–5; Rublack, "Political and Social Norms," 24–60.
7. Wertz, ed., *Membres du Magistrat, 1601–1700*, 38ff.
8. Jan De Vries, *The Economy of Europe in the Age of Crisis* (Cambridge, 1976), 148–59; idem, *European Urbanization*, 3–84. Heinz Stoob has suggested that the inability of municipal leaders to become involved in the dynamic monarchical states led to the ossification of urban social and political structures. Heinz Stoob, "Frühneuzeitliche Städtetypen," in idem, ed., *Die Stadt: Gestalt und Wandel bis zum industriellen Zeitalter* (Cologne and Vienna, 1979), 159–97. This was not the case in Strasbourg, Hertner, *Stadtwirtschaft*, 15–36, 318–76; Greissler, *La classe politique*, 205–12. See also Ingrid Bátori, *Die Reichsstadt Augsburg im 18. Jahrhundert: Verfassung, Finanzen, und Reformversuche*, Veröffentlichungen des Max-Planck-Instituts für Geschichte, 22 (Göttingen, 1969), 17–28; Erwin Riedenauer, "Kaiserliche Ständeserhebungen für reichsstädtische Bürger 1519–1740: Ein statistischer Vorbericht zum Thema 'Kaiser und Patriziat,'" in Rössler, ed., *Deutsches Patriziat*, 27–98.
9. François, "Des républiques marchandes," 587–603.
10. Rudolf Vierhaus has also emphasized the commitment to the commonweal among the civic authorities along with the recognition that they carried a political charge from their citizens. Vierhaus, *Germany in the Age of Absolutism*, 105–6. Cf. Walker, *German Home Towns*, 59–72.
11. Christopher R. Friedrichs, "Citizens or Subjects? Urban Conflicts in Early Modern

Germany," in Miriam Usher Chrisman and Otto Gründler, eds., *Social Groups and Religious Ideas in the Sixteenth Century* (Kalamazoo, Mich., 1978), 46–58, here at 52.

12. See Christopher R. Friedrichs, "Urban Conflicts and the Imperial Constitution in Seventeenth-Century Germany," *JMH* 58, Supplement (1986): S98–S123, here at S100.

13. Ibid., S119.

14. Otto Brunner, "Souveränitätsproblem und Sozialstruktur in den deutschen Reichsstädten der frühen Neuzeit," in idem, *Neue Wege der Verfassungs- und Sozialgeschichte*, 3rd ed. (Göttingen, 1980), 294–321.

15. Friedrichs, "Urban Conflicts," S120–S123.

16. On the eighteenth-century constitutional crisis at Frankfurt, see Gerald Lyman Soliday, *A Community in Conflict: Frankfurt Society in the Seventeenth and Early Eighteenth Centuries* (Hanover, N.H., 1974), 13–32, 231–35. On Hamburg, see Whaley, *Religious Toleration*, 16–22.

17. Christopher R. Friedrichs, *Urban Society in an Age of War: Nördlingen, 1580–1720* (Princeton, 1979), 170–220.

18. See Brunner, "Souveränitätsproblem," 294–321; Adolph Laufs, *Die Verfassung und Verhaltung der Stadt Rottweil, 1650–1806* (Stuttgart, 1963), 31–34; Soliday, *A Community in Conflict: Frankfurt*, 231–35; Friedrichs, *Urban Society: Nördlingen*, 186–95.

19. Herbert H. Rowan, *The King's State: Proprietary Dynasticism in Early Modern France* (New Brunswick, 1980), esp. 75–123.

20. Anderson, *Lineages of the Absolutist State*, 17–42; David Parker, *The Making of French Absolutism* (London, 1983); Roger Mettam, *Power and Faction in Louis XIV's France* (Oxford, 1988).

21. William H. Beik, *Absolutism and Society in Seventeenth Century France: State Power and Provincial Aristocracy in Languedoc* (Cambridge, 1985); Maurice Gresset, *Gens de Justice à Besançon de la conquête par Louis XIV à la Revolution française (1674–1789)*, 2 vols. (Paris, 1978); Robert R. Harding, *The Anatomy of a Power Elite: The Provincial Governors of Early Modern France* (New Haven, 1978).

22. See, for example, the essays in Yves Durand, ed., *Homage à Roland Mousnier: Clientèles et fidélités en Europe à l'époque moderne* (Paris, 1981).

23. Kettering, *Patrons, Brokers, and Clients*, 12–39.

24. Ibid., 40–67.

25. Mettam, *Power and Faction*, 45–106.

26. Livet, *L'intendance*, 333. This sense of history was a key factor in community consciousness throughout Europe. J. H. Elliot, "Revolution and Continuity in Early Modern Europe," *Past and Present* no. 42 (1969): 35–56, here at 48.

27. For provincial conditions, see Livet, "Royal Administration," 190. For Strasbourg, see Kintz, "XVIIe siècle: Du Saint-Empire au royaume," 16–17; Hertner, *Stadtwirtschaft*, 20–22. On the relations between noble and patrician families at Strasbourg, see Alfred Graf von Kageneck, "Das Patriziat im Elsass unter Berücksichtigung der Schweizer Verhältnisse," in Rössler, ed., *Deutsches Patriziat*, 386–93; Greissler, *La classe politique*, 54–55, 66–67.

28. On Colmar's nobles and patricians, see Sittler, "Les bourgeois de Colmar," 24–27. In 1664 three of the thirty-three members of the society *zum Waagkeller* were identified with the status "Junker": Johann Friederich von Reust, Georg Wilhelm Kesselring, and Wolfgang Friederich Kesselring. AMC, HH 8, 13. On the changing role of the nobility in the civic constitution, see Greyerz, *Late City Reformation*, 16–21.

29. In 1650 the ten guilds could boast the following numbers of householders claiming the title "Herr" (of these, 10 were Catholics, and their guild affiliation is

marked in parentheses): *zur Treue*, 28; *zum Riesen*, 25 (2); *Ackerleute*, 5 (2); *zum Haspel*, 5; *Rebleute*, 6 (3); *zum Kränzchen*, 4 (2); *zum Löwen*, 4; *zum Holderbaum*, 7; *zum Adler*, 7; *zum Wohlleben*, 7; and 11 (1) of unknown guild origin.

30. For 1579 see AMC, HH 2, 7.
31. AMC, HH 8, 7.
32. AMC, HH 8, 8.
33. AMC, HH 8, 13.
34. The guilds represented included the following: *zur Treue*, 14; *zum Riesen*, 7; *Ackerleute*, 2; *zum Haspel*, 2; and *zum Adler*, 2. Six members, including the French agents and the three noblemen, had no guild affiliation.
35. AMC, HH 8, 14–30.
36. A manuscript list of the Colmarians contains the names of those who attended the University at Strasbourg between 1621 and 1789. It includes the sons of many mid-century political leaders, who in turn would become critical officials in the later decades. Among them were Johann Georg Barth (Philosophy) [13]; Valentin Barth (Law) [14]; Matthias Binder (Philosophy) [26]; Friederich Binder (Philosophy and Law) [27]; Daniel Birr (Law) [30]; Johannes Buob (Philosophy) [45]; Andreas Burger (Philosophy) [46]; Johann Georg Dörnberger (Theology) [83]; Bartholomaus Dürninger (Medicine) [89]; Johannes Hertenbrodt (Medicine) [137]; Elias Lichteyssen (Law) [193]; Johann Georg Metzger (Philosophy) [226]; Johann Heinrich Mogg (Law) [238]; Matthias Ambrosius Mogg (Law) [239]; Heinrich Friderich Mogg (Law) [240]; Anton Riegger (Philosophy) [291]; Johann Michael Röttlin (Philosophy) [295]; Samuel Röttlin (Philosophy) [296]; Andreas Sandherr (Philosophy) [307]; Michael Scherb (Law) [315]; Abraham Schmucker (Philosophy) [321]; Emmanuel Schneider (Philosophy) [322]; Johann Heinrich Schneider (Philosophy) [323]; Johann Heinrich Schott (Philosophy) [327]; and Anton Schott (Law) [328]; BMC, ms. 774, Die Colmarer Studenten an der Strassburger Universität in den Jahren 1621–1789.
37. This was certainly the case in the other leading Alsatian cities. Greissler, *La classe politique*, esp. 95–112; Reuss, *L'Alsace*, 1: 428–32. See also Hertner, *Stadtwirtschaft*, 20–22; Kintz, "XVIIe siècle: Du Saint-Empire au royaume," 16; Kagenack, "Das Patriziat im Elsass," 391–93. On Hagenau see Burg, "Patrizier und andere städtische Führungsschichten," 363–66.
38. On Imperial practices, see Christopher R. Friedrichs, "Urban Politics and Urban Social Structure in Seventeenth-Century Germany," *European History Quarterly* 22 (1992): 187–216, here at 191–92. On Colmar's mid-seventeenth century elections, see AMC, BB 18, 1.
39. Ortlieb had migrated to the city from nearby Riquewihr. Mogg had served the Counts von Rappoltstein and was a native of Ribeauvillé. Jonas Walch was probably from a Colmar family, but his origins were not listed for his marriage in 1608 to Margaretha Eck, the daughter of Hans Eck, who operated one of Colmar's largest guest houses, *zum Schlüssel*.
40. On Sandherr, see Sittler, "Notice sur la famille Sandherr," *Annuaire de Colmar* (1950), 59. On Röttlin, see Metzenthin, "Les Roettlin," 61. On the full list of Swedish regime members, see AMC, BB 13, 70.
41. Goll had found refuge in Sundhofen. Edouard Metzenthin, "Anciennes familles Colmariennes: Les Goll et leur origine," *Annuaire de Colmar* (1955), 60.
42. Scherlen, *Perles d'Alsace*, 3: 34.
43. Mogg married into administrative families outside of the civic elite and his children followed his lead. On 19 June 1637, the young Mogg married Anna Catherina Tieffenbach, daughter of Herr Ambrosius Tieffenbach a regime member

from Riquewihr. Of their three sons only Ambrosius appears in Colmar's marriage registers. In 1694 he married the daughter of a Protestant fermier general for the royal properties in Thann, Philippe Martin Anthes.

44. Saltzmann held this post until his death in 1656. Scherlen, *Perles d'Alsace*, 3: 34.

45. On Birckinger's marital ties, see Metzenthin, "Les Roettlin," 59. On his tenure as court clerk, see BMC, Fonds Chauffour, I CH 83, "Familia Colmariensis," fol. 2r. Scherb, on the other hand, was a wool weaver and perhaps later a wool merchant from Niedermorschwihr. In 1601 he married Agnes Martin from Colmar, and he lacked roots in the Protestant elite. His son Michel, who would later serve as administrator of the city's Leprosarium, married the daughter of Herr Niclaus Güntzer, in 1637.

46. On 10 August 1646, he married Margaretha Wetzel, the daughter of the deceased councilor David Wetzel.

47. AMC, HH 8, 13. On Schneider see Wolff, "La famille Schneider," 58. On Schultz and Klein, see Scherlen, *Perles d'Alsace*, 3: 34–35. Nicolaus Klein had first served as the city-archivist as early as 1654. AMC, CC 187, 12.

48. AMC, HH 8, 13.

49. Soliday, *A Community in Conflict: Frankfurt*, 98–115; Friedrichs, *Urban Society: Nördlingen*, 196; Bátori, *Augsburg*, 41–51.

50. Livet, *L'intendance*, 333; idem, "Royal Administration," 190–91.

51. The neighboring cities, except Munster, were Catholic. On circumscribed marital ties among Protestant patricians in the Swabian Protestant cities, see Albrecht Rieber, "Das Patriziat von Ulm, Augsburg, Ravensburg, Memmingen, Biberach," in Rössler, ed., *Deutsches Patriziat*, 327–29.

52. My reconstructions of these regimes derives from the data in Wertz, ed., *Membres du magistrat, 1601–1700*, 15–32. I have also analyzed contemporary lists found in AMC, BB 13.

53. AMC, BB 18, 1, fol. 2r.

54. *Zum Riesen* provided the regime with five members responsible for six posts in 1640; in 1650 five members in five posts; in 1660 four members in four posts; and in 1670 again five members in six posts.

55. Kintz, *La société strasbourgeoise*, 477–94.

56. Wertz, ed., *Membres du magistrat, 1601–1700*, 15–32.

57. In 1640 Dorss, who lived in the packed and poor suburb of *Kürsnerthürlein*, was assessed 3,400 florins. In 1650 his wealth had fallen to 2,600 florins and in 1660 to 2,000 florins.

58. Burger, "L'annexion de Colmar," 36–37.

59. The riot took place on 30 November. "Beschwerte sich der Magistrat vor gesessenem Rath über das üble Betragen der Bürger, indem eine grosse aufrührische Rotte dem Obristmeister Herrn Andreas Sandherr das Haus gestürmet, eine dem Herrn Syndicus Röttlin einem Partisan erstechen wollen, den übrigen die fenster eingeworfen und sie der Verrätheren beschuldiget worden. Insonderheit nimmer die Müller, Becker, Metzger und Wirthe ihre Schuldigkeit nimmer beobachten." Rathgeber, ed., *Colmar und Ludwig XIV*, 22.

60. Braeuner, "L'opinion publique," 45–46.

61. In a letter dated 11 August 1674, they informed de Ruzé that they sought the waiver because "le serment du temps passé est tant incompatible d'avec l'estat present où nous somes." AMC, BB 24, 3, fol. 2r. For the letter to La Grange, see AMC, BB 24, 1. The traditional oath featured reference to the emperor, see Wertz, ed., *Membres du magistrat*, 40. A version, edited sometime after 1680, dropped the reference to the emperor but did not replace it with a reference to the king. AMC, BB 11, 4.

62. "Nous ordonnons par la presente à tous et chacune de la dite bourgeois et habitants [of Colmar] de rendre à leur Magistrats et préposés des tribus tout le respect, fidelité et obeissance accoustomée et permittons à cette fin, que les bourgeois y soyent de nouveau obligé par serment qu'ils presterent entre les mains de leur préposés." AMC, BB 24, 3, fol. 1r. Dated 13 August 1674. The regime administered the oath in the separate guildhalls. Rathgeber, ed., *Colmar und Ludwig XIV*, 25. See also AMC, BB 24, 4.

63. AMC, BB 24, 5–7.

64. The intendant's orders, dated 13 September 1674, stated "très expressement à tous bourgeois et habitans . . . de les [the magistrates] recognoistre en general et en particulier . . . et de leur obeir pour touttes les choses qu'ils leur commandant pour la service de Sa Majesté et l'Interest du publique." AMC, BB 24, 6.

65. The Colmarians were "de faire voiturer incessement et en deux fois vingt et quatre heures touts les grains et farines qui se trouvent dans cette ville sur pein aux contrevants de n'estre severement chastie par les rigeurs de la guerre." AMC, BB 24, 8. Cf. Burger, "Colmar entre Turenne et Brandebourg," 82–85. The chroniclers attributed several local deaths to fear of the French troops. Rathgeber, ed., *Colmar und Ludwig XIV*, 24.

66. AMC, BB 24, 8, fol. 1v–2r. On the problems of grain supply for the intendant, see Livet, *L'intendance*, 567–626.

67. AMC, BB 24, 8, fol. 2r. Cf. Burger, "Colmar entre Turenne et Brandebourg," 84–85; Rathgeber, ed., *Colmar und Ludwig XIV*, 26–27.

5

Economic Recovery and Social Change at Colmar, 1640–1679

The Peace of Westphalia ended warfare in most of the empire, but political instability and military campaigns continued in Alsace for several more years. The Thirty Years' War had taken its toll on the province, which may have lost 50% of its population to increased mortality and emigration.[1] The war's impact on individual localities varied widely. The villages in the open countryside suffered most severely, but many towns were also in ruins.[2] The small Imperial city of Turckheim counted only a handful of citizens at war's end.[3] Once proud Hagenau, the capital of the Decapolis and seat of the Imperial Bailiwick, bemoaned its impoverishment and its shrinkage from 1,300 householders in 1620 to 250 in 1654.[4] Even Strasbourg, which preserved its neutrality during the war, had fewer citizens in 1650 than at the beginning of the century.[5] The campaigning armies had not only destroyed the region's vineyards and farmlands, they had also robbed the Alsatians of the capital and human resources needed to rebuild quickly. All sectors of the economy suffered, and peace offered the only hope for recovery.

Although much of Upper Alsace had been devastated, Colmar emerged from the war with some economic reserves. The city quickly raised 7,756 florins to pay its share of the Swedish "satisfaction" as stipulated in the peace settlement. The neighboring Imperial city of Sélestat sought a loan at Colmar to cover the same obligation, but the regime pleaded that it had drained its reserves in extending credit to others.[6] Although the articles of the peace required the city to relinquish its control over the territories which the League of Heilbronn had bestowed on it, individual Colmarians retained the fields and vineyards that they had purchased in the city's hinterland during the war.[7] In 1650 Colmar was in a position to increase its economic influence in Upper Alsace, but the city faced its traditional competitors, Strasbourg and Basel, and a new potential opponent—France.

The French recognized the economic potential of the region's agricultural wealth. In 1664 the *subdélégué*, Domilliers, wrote of the "beautiful and fertile plain" in Upper Alsace but, unlike the earlier topographers, he also noted how the various streams powered Colmar's mills.[8] A decade later, a young French traveller described the Upper Alsatian countryside as "abundant in wheat and in all sorts of other grains; its slopes produce excellent wines, its pastures nourish so much livestock that the meat sells for a very low price."[9] He balanced this image of natural richness, however, with images of the devastation wrought by warring armies in the 1670s.[10] All around Colmar he passed through overgrown fields and deserted villages, whose abandoned houses sheltered packs of feral cats.[11] These contrasting images, fertility and devastation, formed the framework for the region's postwar recovery. Colmar's prosperity hinged on the productivity of the land around it, and peace alone could secure the agricultural potential of this "beautiful and fertile plain." Fortunately, for a few decades between 1650 and 1670, the Colmarians lived in peace, which allowed the city and the surrounding villages to repopulate themselves as a first step to rebuilding the economy.

I. CRISIS AND RECOVERY IN CIVIC POPULATION, 1640–1680

Confessional pressures, warfare, and famine had combined between 1627 and 1640 to reduce Colmar's population dramatically from around 8,000 prior to the war to just over 5,000 in 1640, when the city sheltered fewer residents than at any time since the end of the fifteenth century.[12] Over the next generation, the number of householders steadily expanded, gaining 15.4% between 1640 and 1650 and a further 16.5% in the following decade. In 1640 over one-fourth (199) of all households were headed by widows, which was 10% higher than in any other year sampled and reflected the extent of the demographic crisis. Between 1640 and 1650 the number of male householders rose over 30%, twice the rate for all householders, as many men married widows and joined civic guilds. By 1650 the number of female householders had fallen to 16.2% (142), and their percentage, though still high, was much closer to normal ratios of around 12%. In the 1660s, the overall growth of householders slowed to 1%, and by 1670 Colmar's population had nearly recovered its prewar peak. The military campaigns between 1673 and 1675, however, wiped away the previous generation's growth, and 1679 promised as much uncertainty for the city's inhabitants as 1649.

Colmar's post-Westphalian recovery combined long-term stability among the male householders with an influx of new men.[13] From 1640 to 1660 peace, better harvests, and the absence of epidemics extended life expectancies for the cohort of new householders who had settled in the city. In 1650 and 1660 more than two-thirds of the male householders had paid taxes ten years earlier, which far exceeded the fiscal longevity of their fathers and grandfathers. For a generation the presence of the same men in the tax rolls, church pews, and guild halls brought personal stability after the tumultuous war years. For example, in 1640 Colmar boasted six tanners, only three of whom had been working in the city ten years earlier. By 1660 four of them, all native Colmarians, were still active in the same workshops they had occupied during the war.[14] In 1640 forty-one men gathered in the *Trinkstube* of the peasants' guild, *Ackerleute*, and twenty years later, twenty-one of them could still reminisce with their younger colleagues about the hard times during the war. The absence of death registers hinders a full reconstitution of this generation, but evidence suggests that after 1640 a cohort of younger craftsmen and tenant farmers enjoyed long careers and imparted an aura of continuity to civic life.

For Colmar to survive, however, the city depended on a steady influx of new householders, whether native sons or immigrants. During the war, refugees had filled the city, and the civic leaders encouraged wealthy tenant farmers from the hinterland to purchase citizenship once the hostilities ended.[15] Recruiting in the 1640s was very successful, for in 1650, 344 householders (46.7%) had not paid taxes ten years earlier. After the war, however, the pattern changed, with the percentage of householders who had resided in the town less than a decade falling to 42.9% in 1660 and 35.5% in 1670. These figures were below those prior to the Thirty Years' War (46.5 in 1610 and 45.2 in 1620), and they suggest that the city offered fewer opportunities for new men after peace had returned to the province.

The decline in the city's population growth in the 1660s may have been a demographic echo of the high mortality of the 1630s, which possibly reduced the number of native-born Colmarians reaching maturity in the 1660s, while the aging householders who had repopulated the city in the 1640s pervaded the tax rolls. Colmar may also have reached its limit in terms of economic opportunities for new householders. Whatever the cause, in the 1660s Colmar's population appeared to be growing older and perhaps more wary of outsiders.

If the Colmarians had developed a more insular sense of community and were restricting new householders, then prospective immigrants should have faced barriers as they did in other German "home towns."[16] The Thirty Years' War had in fact drastically altered the geographic scope and volume of migration to Colmar for both men and women, as shown by table 5.1. Colmar's parish registers identify the place of origin of brides, grooms, and parents more systematically than during the fifty years before the war. From among those male householders who first appear on the *Gewerff* registers between 1640 and 1680, we can identify the origins of just over 78%, as opposed to 41% for the period before 1630. After 1631 around 72% of the new householders were native Colmarians. In the period prior to the war, only 55% were native born, but a significant number of the men whose origins were unknown were probably Colmarians, so that the increasing endogamy may be documentary rather than historical. Even among the known

TABLE 5.1
Origins of Men and Women, 1631–1680

	MALES (no.)	(%)	FEMALES (no.)	(%)
PLACE OF ORIGIN				
Colmar	918	71.6	1,266	82.4
Upper Alsace	137	10.7	193	12.6
Lower Alsace	56	4.4	14	0.9
Southwest Germany				
Breisgau	7		6	
Baden	22		2	
Württemberg	9	4.8	—	1.0
Swabia/Bodensee	14		6	
Bavaria	9		1	
Rhineland/Palatinate	13	1.0	—	
Central Germany				
Hesse	5		2	
Hohenlohe	4	2.1	—	0.2
Thuringia	5		1	
Franconia	13		—	
Northern Germany				
Brandenburg-Prussia	2		—	
Saxony	10	1.0	—	0.1
Anhalt	1		—	
Netherlands	—		1	
Eastern Regions				
Silesia, Moravia,				
Hungary, Poland,	7	0.5	2	0.1
Bohemia				
Switzerland	39	3.0	32	2.1
Italy	1	0.1	—	—
Western Francophone				
France/Lorraine	4		2	
Montbéliard	2	0.5	5	0.5
Region Unknown	4	0.3	4	0.3
Total Known	1,282		1,537*	
Total Cases	1,640	78.2		

*The figure for wives comes from data for first and second marriages in both confessional communities.

immigrants, however, the post-Westphalian city drew fewer men from distant regions. Alsace accounted for over 15% of the city's new householders, and most of those came from the city's immediate hinterland. In all, nearly 86% of the male householders were born in the city or the province, up from 71% before 1630, so that the Rhine had already become a border before the French conquest. Among the migrants from other regions of the empire, more than half came from the towns and villages of southwestern Germany, though the depopulation of the Breisgau, Bavaria, Swabia, and Württemberg had greatly curtailed migration from these traditional sources of new citizens. On the whole, the empire supplied only 8.9% of Colmar's householders.

Swiss immigrants, who played such a prominent role in repopulating other Alsatian communities, constituted only 3% of Colmar's new householders.[17] Georges Livet has noted a massive influx of Swiss *manants* into Colmar after 1650, and the parish registers of both churches record numerous Swiss brides and grooms, who do not show in the guild lists or tax rolls.[18] These men and women may have served as migrant laborers or as a permanent class of poor noncitizens, but they played little role in rebuilding the political and guild communities.

Finally, prior to 1680 the French political presence in Alsace had drawn only a handful of French-speaking migrants to Colmar, among them the future Catholic Stettmeister François Seraffond. Colmar's male householders, even its immigrants, had become more provincial.[19] In 1621 the erstwhile tinsmith and Calvinist, Augustin Güntzer, a native of Obernai, settled in Colmar after five years of travel which had taken him to Italy, the Tirol, Riga, Paris, and London. In 1671, when the bookbinder Ambrosius Müller, a native of Strasbourg, purchased citizenship in Colmar, he had just finished four years as a journeyman in Heilbronn, Strasbourg, Molsheim, Freiburg-im-Breisgau, and Soluthurn.[20] For the Colmarians of Müller's generation the world was a smaller place.

The Colmarians, nevertheless, did not discourage immigrants. Of the 344 householders who surface for the first time in the tax register of 1650, 76 (22%) were immigrants. In 1660 one in five new householders (78 out of 377) was nonnative, but the figure rose to 25% (82 out of 327) through the following decade, when growth had decelerated and fewer new householders settled in the city. Immigration may have become more provincial, but the city still depended on outsiders to maintain its demographic and economic health.

The one region from which the city drew more immigrants than before the war was Lower Alsace, and the bulk of these new men (forty-nine, or 87.5%) came from Strasbourg. Among the immigrants were several future regime members: Philip Albrecht Marbach, Johann Ulrich Heisch, Johann Michael Faber, Johann Michael Fridt, and Jeremias Trömer. All of the Strasbourgeois were Lutherans, except for Johannes Östermeyer, a Catholic, who arrived in 1680, when Colmar was already under French rule. Most of the Strasbourgeois joined Colmar's merchant and artisans guilds: nine *zur Treue*, ten *zum Adler*, and eight *zum Riesen*. The agricultural guilds welcomed only one immigrant from Strasbourg, and four others do not appear in the guild lists. The remainder joined Colmar's other craft guilds.

Among the women whose place of origin appears in the parish registers, the war had drastically reduced migration. Prior to 1631 over 82% were native to the city, and seven out of ten immigrants came from the surrounding villages. In the mid-seventeenth century, 95% of Colmar's female householders lived within a day's walk of their birthplace. The only region outside Alsace to supply the city with more than six female immigrants was Switzerland. Within the merchant and artisan communities, women were normally less mobile than men, and the war circumscribed their mobility further.

In the mid-seventeenth century, Colmar continued to depend on immigrants to maintain its population, but the city was smaller and there were fewer men and women who settled there from distant lands. In particular, Colmar drew fewer craftsmen and merchants from across the Rhine. Either the war or the Protestant community's affiliation with Strasbourg had severed ties with the network of Rhenish towns and culture which had informed Colmar's confessional swing to Calvinism in the early seventeenth century.[21] After 1648 nearly all Colmarian householders were native Alsatians.

Colmar's post-Westphalian Protestant church was closely aligned to Strasbourg, and these confessional ties clearly affected migration. Among the male householders attending Lutheran services, we can pinpoint the origin for around 86%, and over two-thirds were native Colmarians (see table 5.2). Through the 1650s, however, most "native" Lutherans had grown up in Reformed households, which underscores the constant confessional tension within the city's Protestant community. In time, though, without a local Reformed ministry, the distinctions in doctrine between the two Protestant confessions must have lost their meaning for all but a few citizens. For Catholic male householders, the Counter-Reformation had little long-term impact. The Lutherans outnumbered them by three to one, and, with over 80% native-born, the Catholics appeared to be just as closed and endogamous as they had been before 1630. In all, nine out of ten of Colmar's Catholic male householders were born in the city or its immediate hinterland, while the Protestant community drew less than 80% from the same region. As for the more distant sources of Catholic immigrants, only southwestern Germany and Switzerland provided more than two new householders. Given the demographic forces at work, the Catholics' inability to attract outsiders posed a direct threat to their place in the city's future.

The Lutheran parish, however, was also more provincial than its Reformed predecessor had been, as most of its immigrants came from the villages of the neighboring Alsatian Protestant powers and from Lower Alsace. The Lutheran community, nonetheless, also drew a significant number of Swiss

TABLE 5.2

Origins of Male Householders by Confession, 1631–1680

PLACE OF ORIGIN	PROTESTANT (no.)	(%)	CATHOLIC (no.)	(%)
Colmar	648	69.0	239	80.5
Upper Alsace	101	10.8	28	9.4
Lower Alsace	52	5.5	1	0.3
Southwest Germany				
Breisgau	2		5	
Baden	19		3	
Württemberg	8	4.6	1	5.4
Swabia/Bodensee	8		5	
Bavaria	6		2	
Rhineland/Palatinate	12	1.3	1	0.3
Central Germany				
Hesse	4		1	
Hohenlohe	4	2.6	—	0.7
Thuringia	5		—	
Franconia	11		1	
Northern Germany				
Brandenburg-Prussia	2		—	
Saxony	10	1.4	—	—
Anhalt	1		—	
Eastern Regions				
Silesia, Moravia,				
Hungary, Poland,	6	0.6	1	0.3
Bohemia				
Switzerland	34	3.6	5	1.7
Italy	—	—	1	0.3
Western Francophone				
France/Lorraine	2		2	
Montbéliard	2	0.4	—	0.7
Region Unknown	2	0.2	1	0.3
Total Known	939		297	
Total Cases	1,090	86.1	380	78.2

migrants, primarily from the villages around Bern (twenty-two out of thirty-four), and nearly all of Colmar's immigrants from across the Rhine. Colmar's Lutherans maintained some contact with the Imperial Lutheran estates and could still attract young men from Switzerland willing to change their religious practices to gain acceptance into the city's guilds.

Among civic women, the confessional contrast is much less dramatic (see table 5.3). Unlike their husbands, Catholic women (77.8%) were less likely to be native-born than Lutheran women (84.1%). The Catholic community drew nearly 17% of its female householders from the villages of Upper Alsace, but the vast majority of the brides of both confessions were born within a day's walk of the city (94.7% for the Catholics and 95.2% for the Lutherans). Only the mountainous regions of central Switzerland provided a reservoir for migrant women.

In the decades after the Thirty Years' War, Colmar's Protestants became more provincial, while the city's Catholics remained as parochial as they had become in the early seventeenth century. For Colmar's Protestants, the dissolution of the Reformed parish and the confessional swing to Lutheranism broke contact with the far-flung centers of Rhenish Calvinism in a manner that paralleled the severing of long-distance trade. The Protestants tightened their ties with Strasbourg and the Württemberg lordship of Horbourg-Riquewihr. Colmar's Catholics were extremely endogamous and more likely to attract female immigrants (75) than male (58). Colmar's Protestants dominated civic government, had more extensive and significant outside contacts, and were growing in proportion to their Catholic neighbors, who seemed to be closing in on themselves.

II. Citizens and Guildsmen

After 1633 the Protestants monopolized magisterial office and continued to dominate the regime as a whole. Furthermore, the guilds had lost their electoral role and many constituencies were underrepresented in the civic government. To purchase citizenship remained a personal decision which associated the householder more fully with the political establishment; and age, income, and Colmar's confessional and political climate affected that choice.

Graph 5.1 plots the overall trends for the purchase of citizenship and the confessional distribution of new citizens. Between 1640 and 1659, an average of eighty men purchased citizenship every five years, well below the sixteenth-century level of 116, and the number of men purchasing citizenship in the last decade of the Thirty Years' War, the same decade during which the city attracted so many new householders, was particularly low. The decline in inscriptions would have been more dramatic had not the magistrate ordered that all longtime non-citizen residents (*Seldner*) purchase citizenship in 1654 or face a fine.[22] Between 1649 and 1652 only twenty-two men had purchased citizenship, and in 1653 seventeen guildsmen inscribed. In 1654 sixty-two men responded to the magistrates' urging, and eighty-eight others

TABLE 5.3
Origins of Wives by Confession, 1631–1680

PLACE OF ORIGIN	PROTESTANT (no.)	(%)	CATHOLIC (no.)	(%)
Colmar	975	84.1	263	77.8
Upper Alsace	129	11.1	57	16.9
Lower Alsace	12	1.0	1	0.3
Southwest Germany				
Breisgau	2		4	
Baden	2		—	
Württemberg	—	0.6	—	2.1
Swabia/Bodensee	3		3	
Bavaria	1		—	
Central Germany				
Hesse	2		—	
Hohenlohe	—	0.3	—	—
Thuringia	1		—	
Franconia	—		—	
Northern Germany				
Netherlands	1	0.1	—	—
Eastern Regions				
Silesia, Moravia, Hungary, Poland, Bohemia	2	0.2	—	—
Switzerland	23	2.0	7	2.1
Western Francophone				
France/Lorraine	2		—	
Montbéliard	4	0.5	1	0.3
Region Unknown	—	—	2	0.6
Total Known*	1,159		338	
Total Cases	1,090		380	

*The figure for wives comes from data for first and second marriages in both confessional communities.

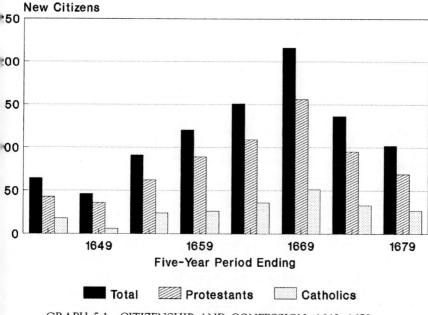

GRAPH 5.1 CITIZENSHIP AND CONFESSION, 1640–1679

followed suit over the next two years. After this flurry of oaths, the numbers fell again between 1657 and 1659 to fourteen per year. Apparently
prior to the regime's decision, the honor of being inscribed in the citizen
registers had lost some of its luster.

The number of inscriptions escalated sharply again in the 1660s, the same
decade in which civic population growth came to a halt. This rise in new
"citizens" resulted from a change in the registers, which after 1660 probably
recorded guild inscription rather than the distinct oath of citizenship.[23] Under
the new format, the number of inscriptions per five-year period doubled to
151. Within the guilds, at least, the 1660s marked a period of dynamic
growth which came to an end during the troubled years of the following
decade. This evidence challenges the impression of stagnation for the city's
population, but may be explained by a turnover of guildsmen caused by the
deaths of those men who settled in the city in the 1640s. In 1670 of the
four tanners who had practiced their trade continuously from 1640 to 1660,
only two paid taxes, and of the twenty-one members of *Ackerleute* who could
remember the bitter war years in 1660 only twelve remained.

As for the confessional balance within the citizenry, the Lutherans, with
over 70% of the new citizens for the entire period, outnumbered the Catholics,
though the overall ratio between the two confessions remained fairly stable,
except during the late 1640s, when only six Catholics inscribed. In 1654

the magistrate's threat of fines brought a disproportionate number of Catholics forward, which reflected their earlier political alienation.[24] The figures after 1660, drawn primarily from the inscription of new guildsmen, better reveal the proportional relation between the two confessional communities. On the whole, Colmar's Catholics comprised about one-fourth of the guildsmen, which was slightly less than earlier in the century. Furthermore, graph 5.2 below compares the confessional ratio of householders on the tax registers between 1640 and 1680. In 1640 there were 174 Catholic householders (31%), and, though the number of Catholics increased to 221 by 1670, this larger community only comprised 24% of all householders. The percentage of Catholic householders had fallen steadily since the Imperial Counter-Reformation.

Colmar's initial Protestant leadership had relied on the support of Colmar's guildsmen in establishing and defending bi-confessionalism. After 1648, confessional peace and civic order at Colmar rested not on community norms but on the guarantees of Imperial law, which now served as the safety valve in the conflict between the regime and the city's Catholic clergy. Both sides became more provocative as confessional relations continued to sour. The bishop of Basel bickered with the regime on several occasions over the public exercise of religious rituals and the administration of ecclesiastical properties, and the regime fought with the civic religious houses over un-

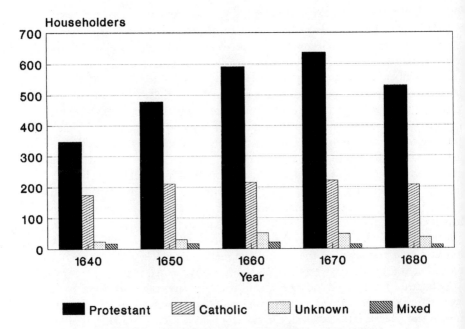

GRAPH 5.2 CONFESSIONAL DIVISION, 1640–1680

paid taxes.[25] These disputes were waged within the protocols of Imperial law, and the ecclesiastical houses rather than the Catholic guildsmen spearheaded these confessional conflicts.

Two factors prevented these confessional antagonisms from disrupting civic peace and fully dividing the commonweal. First, the Imperial constitutional basis of Colmar's bi-confessionalism limited the maneuverability of the confessional parties, and the guildsmen could gain little by provoking confessional confrontation. Secondly, both confessional communities possessed weak and divided leadership. Lutheranism had been imposed on Colmar's Protestants, and their ministers felt alienated from and often frustrated by a reluctant regime which, they feared, harbored "crypto-Calvinists." Even until 1660 a significant percentage of Colmar's Lutherans had first married in the Reformed church and a majority of them had attended Reformed services in their youth. The city's first Lutheran ministers had close ties to Strasbourg, and disputes between the ministers and the regime in the 1640s demonstrated the weak footing of the imposed church. Only by the late 1650s had Mogg's authority and the deepening economic and familial ties with Strasbourg strengthened the Lutheran leadership. A generation of catechetical instruction had also nurtured a new cohort of young Lutheran adults, some of whom were pursuing studies for the ministry in Strasbourg. Just as the Lutheran community was prepared to play a unified and more prominent role in civic life, the French began the drive to establish Louis XIV's sovereignty over the city. The king's agents favored Colmar's Catholics and once again they could claim a powerful protector, which forced the Lutheran leaders to move cautiously. The Crown had begun to influence confessional relations within Colmar at least a decade before the king forced his sovereignty on the city.

On the other hand, despite their new patron, Colmar's Catholics were also in no position to improve their political clout in the city. The diocese of Basel was in disarray following the Thirty Years' War, and by 1670 the bishops had hardly begun to implement the reforms proposed a century earlier at Trent. Prior to the French takeover Colmar had yet to experience a Catholic Reformation. The diocese of Basel would have no seminary until 1716, and neither the Jesuits nor the Capuchins had established houses in the city.[26] Colmar's other religious orders remained moribund and exerted limited religious influence, though they supported the city's Catholics by providing employment for stewards, goldsmiths, and tenant farmers. The Counter-Reformation of 1627–32 had been too brief to overturn the city's confessional structure; the more significant force of baroque Catholicism had yet to influence the city's Catholic clergy or laity. Confessional peace, therefore, reflected the temporary weakness of both parties.

Colmar's Lutheran leaders allowed Catholic representation on the regime as a practical way to handle the confessional disputes that did emerge and to avoid confrontation. As a result, the harsh letters exchanged between episcopal officials in Porrentruy and the municipal regime had minimal impact on civic peace and order. With control of the regime and the security of Imperial law, Colmar's Lutherans had little to fear from the complaints of the disgruntled Catholic clergy, so long as they were expressed in the political context of the old Reich. In 1658 the Lutherans reconsecrated the old Benedictine parish church of St. Peter's to meet the needs of the growing Protestant community. The city was becoming more and more a Lutheran town, as well as the most significant Protestant center in Upper Alsace.

III. PEASANTS, CRAFTSMEN, AND MERCHANTS

The Thirty Years' War had done much to disrupt the distribution of property and the relations of production in Upper Alsace. As the armies ransacked granaries and confiscated livestock, villagers fled into the walled cities, especially Colmar, for refuge. Isolated from their livelihood, the refugees became dependent on credit, and the wealthier Colmarians benefitted through the purchase of properties at bargain prices or through liens against peasant freeholds.[27]

In Colmar this growing power of the city over the land had a profound impact on the composition of the agricultural guilds. The growth of property investment within the merchant and craft guilds deprived Colmar's agricultural guildsmen of control of their work and its profits and neutralized the advantages of guild membership.[28] In 1642 a property survey in the neighboring estates identified 1,400 *Juchert* of recently purchased farmland and 1,700 *Acker* of vineyards owned by Colmarians. The city's ecclesiastical houses and noble families played an insignificant role in this land grab, for they held no farmland and only 100 *Acker* of vineyard. The enriched landowners came from all ten guilds, but few from the agricultural guilds. Members of *zum Riesen* held more fields than any other guild except the *Ackerleute*, while the merchants of *zur Treue* held more vineyards than any other guild and more than the members of *zum Haspel* and *Rebleute* combined.[29] After the war the commitment to agricultural and viticultural production benefitted Colmarians in all professions, which in turn undermined the agricultural guilds, but this was the final step in a long-term process, for Colmar's agricultural guilds had been in decline as political and economic institutions for more than a century.

In the early sixteenth century over one-half of Colmar's guildsmen had belonged to the agricultural guilds, but between 1580 and 1630 they accounted for only 32% of the city's guildsmen. Between 1631 and 1680 their share plummeted further to 24% of the new householders in a much smaller community. There had been at least 132 members of the peasants' guild, *Ackerleute*, in Colmar in 1620, and in 1640 the guild counted only forty-one members. Between 1640 and 1670 the city recovered its prewar population, but in 1670 *Ackerleute* only claimed sixty-four members, less than half its prewar total. The other two agricultural guilds fared somewhat better. *Zum*

Haspel had fallen from fifty-five members in 1620 to twenty-two in 1640, and by 1670 it had thirty-eight members. The number of vineyard workers in *Rebleute* fell from 177 in 1620 to 65 in 1640, but the wine industry flourished with the peace. By 1670 *Rebleute* comprised 113 members. It was not so much a particular guild as guild-based agricultural production that suffered. The Lutheran registers, which recorded occupations, show that between 1631 and 1680 at least 15% of the men in *Ackerleute* and 17% of those in *zum Haspel* were *Rebmannen*.[30] More and more, the basis of Colmar's agricultural economy was the production of wine.

Among the agricultural guildsmen, the war depressed the class of small landowners. In 1620 the members of *Ackerleute* possessed taxable assets valued at over 55,000 florins, and by 1640 their assessment had fallen to 30,000 florins. In 1650 their aggregate wealth rose to 35,000 florins, but it fell during the next two decades even as membership grew, so that in 1670 sixty-four members were assessed at 32,500 florin total. For the gardeners in *zum Haspel* the postwar recovery followed a similar course. Between 1620 and 1640, aggregate wealth fell from 37,770 to 31,190 florins. By 1650 the guild members had regained their prewar wealth, but over the next generation their assessments fell to 28,810 florins in 1670. The vineyard workers experienced a very different cycle of dearth and prosperity. From 42,790 florins in 1620 the guild members' assessed wealth fell by more than half to 20,440 in 1640. The economic recovery for the vineyard workers was steady and complete, and by 1670, their aggregate wealth had reached 44,910 florins for far fewer members than 1620. In the last decade of the war, the city's tenant farmers had done well, but the peace brought stagnation for the grain market.[31] On the other hand, the end of hostilities allowed for the replanting of vineyards, and by 1660 the development of new wine markets in Switzerland brought prosperity to the men who worked and controlled the local vineyards.

In the decades after the Thirty Years' War, the wealth within the agricultural guilds was unevenly distributed. In 1640 four rich tenant farmers, Matthaus Johner, Claus Dorss, and the elder and younger Hans Hüfflins, controlled more than one-third of the wealth assessed in *Ackerleute*. By 1670, however, none of these men remained, and no rich tenants had replaced them. Among the men in *Ackerleute*, Elias Lang was assessed at 3,600 florins, which was twice as much as the next highest assessment, but Lang was a professional architect, hired by the civic regime to supervise the maintenance of the fortifications. Johner and Dorss were the wealthiest tenant farmers, but both were assessed on smaller fortunes than they had claimed in 1640. Of the sixty-four members of *Ackerleute*, thirty-one were assessed at 300 florins or less.

During the same period, in *Rebleute* the distribution of wealth also favored a few men. In 1640 Andreas Sybert, a regime member, was assessed at twice the rate (2,350 florins) of the next highest assessment. He claimed eighteen times the wealth of twenty-three fellow guild members. Peace brought prosperity but only for some of the vineyard workers. By 1670 their aggregate wealth had more than doubled. Two men, the Catholic Georg Meyer and the Lutheran Elias Leiterer, were assessed at over 2,000 florins, and two others, Stephen Jundt and Matthis Haller, were assessed at 1,400 florins. No other vineyard worker could claim more than 1,000 florins of assessed wealth, and more than half the guild members paid taxes on estates assessed at or below 250 florins. The rural guilds had become divided into two classes: a small group of very wealthy tenant farmers; and a broad base of poorer peasants. Furthermore, only wealthier peasants could afford guild membership. The rural "journeymen" lacked the resources to join the guilds, and they became the laborers who worked the plots that were controlled by the wealthier tenants who now populated all of Colmar's guilds. Furthermore, the disputes over harvest taxes which the city faced with the officials from Turckheim, Riquewihr, and Ensisheim reflected an extension of this emerging class system into the villages surrounding Colmar. The division between those who owned the land and those who worked it had widened in Upper Alsace in the decades after the Peace of Westphalia.

The agricultural guilds were not the only ones undergoing significant changes in the wake of the Thirty Years' War. As in many towns in the post-Westphalian empire, Colmar's artisan guilds experienced the gradual erosion of their political responsibilities, though they continued to regulate production and trade.[32] Within the new system of paternal government, the civic regime actively defended its craftsmen in the disputes with the French officials over reciprocal market rights and customs waivers.[33] On the whole, Colmar's artisans prospered economically, which may have made the loss of their electoral role more palatable.

Among Colmar's artisans, those associated with wine production and the leather trades fared well in the city's mid-seventeenth-century economy and continued to do so until the century's end. When local officials assessed the city's economic potential in 1698, they emphasized the importance of the wine and tanning industries.[34] *Zum Riesen*, the principle guild for the wine industry, included coopers, vatmakers, tavern keepers, and wine merchants. In an era when the city's population had shrunk dramatically, its membership grew both in terms of absolute numbers and in percentage of all guildsmen. With the coming of peace, the planting of new vineyards provided employment and profit for all. In 1650 at least thirty-eight householders (7.8%) engaged in trades connected with wine production, and by 1670 their numbers had risen at least to fifty-three (8.6%). In 1620 the members of *zum Riesen* paid taxes on an aggregate assessment of 56,690 florins. In 1650 their collective estates totalled only 37,620 florins, but in that decade their wealth nearly doubled to 68,730 florins and by 1670 had risen further to over 70,000 florins. Ironically, the expansion of the wine industry occurred despite the closing of its long-distance markets. Local wine and brandy no longer appeared at the great fairs of the lower Rhine, for the city now sold the bulk of its vintages in Strasbourg and in the Swiss cities.[35] Peace had been very profitable for this regional wine industry.

Wine had always been a central component of Colmar's economy, but an expansion of tanning and the leather industry in post-Westphalian Colmar was a new phenomenon. From 1640 onward the leather trades grew steadily, chiefly in response to the demands of the French armies quartered in the region.[36] *Zum Wohlleben*, the guild which housed the tanners, shoemakers, and saddlers, expanded in relationship to the civic economy as a whole and out of proportion with its place in the city's prewar economy. In 1620 the guild had claimed sixty members, and by 1640 membership had fallen to thirty-five. By 1670, however, the guild counted seventy-eight members. In the same time span the number of tanners had risen from seven in 1620 to twenty-four in 1670 and their assessed wealth had risen from 3,300 to 15,400 florins. The industry demanded significant capital, and within *zum Wohlleben* the tanners formed an established middle-class trade, which suggests that they controlled not only the production but also the distribution of their goods.[37]

In the post-Westphalian city, among the other craft guilds, *zum Adler* also claimed a larger share of the city's guildsmen and a more prominent place in the city's economy. Colmar had no reputation for its cloth production and possessed few weavers. In 1650 there were only thirteen identifiable weavers in the city, but with the coming of peace in the province, Colmar's merchants and artisans attempted to expand local cloth production.[38] By 1670 the number of weavers had risen to twenty-four, but they could hardly supply a developing industry. To expand cloth production, Colmar depended heavily on immigrants. At least thirty-nine members, 35% of the men who joined the guild between 1631 and 1680, were immigrants, and some such as Michael Beneckin, a furrier from Schiffenburg in Prussia, had come a long way. Among Colmar's tanners only five out of forty-one (12%) were born outside of the city. Colmar's cloth workers thus formed a much more open community than most of Colmar's guilds. Finally, *zum Adler* welcomed the fewest Catholics of any guild, and among the immigrants only François Seraffond, a wool weaver from Burgandy and a future Stettmeister, attended mass at St. Martin's.

As the guild grew in size after 1640, it also grew in aggregate wealth. In 1620 the sixty-eight members of *zum Adler* paid taxes on wealth assessed at 18,490 florins. By 1640 their numbers had fallen to thirty-seven, and they held a combined taxable wealth of only 13,910 florins. By 1670, however, the guild claimed seventy members and their aggregate wealth had risen to 26,830 florins. Colmar's cloth industry, though small, played a much more significant role in the city's economy after 1648 than it ever had before. Furthermore, much of the wealth generated by cloth production ended in the hands of the *Tuchmannen*, who were primarily importers, and belonged to the merchants' guild, *zur Treue*.[39] Among the craftsmen within *zum Adler*, the distribution of income was relatively equitable. In 1640 six of the thirty-seven guild members had assessed wealth of between 1,000 and 1,400 florins, while fourteen paid on less than 200 florins. In 1670 six out of seventy members had assessed estates of between 1,000 and 1,300 florins, while twenty-eight paid at 200 florins or less. There were signs of a growing class of poor cloth workers, but no entrepreneurs had emerged to dominate production and distribution, as the Wörner family did in Nördlingen.[40]

The prosperity of Colmar's artisans and peasants depended on the economic expertise of the city's merchants. The *welsche Krämer*, whose investments had spearheaded Colmar's economic expansion prior to the Thirty Years' War, had abandoned the city during the Imperial Counter-Reformation, and few had returned with the restoration of Protestant worship. The post-Westphalian reconstruction of the city's economy required a new generation of merchants, nearly all of whom were native Colmarians or Alsatians. Of the fifty-six men identified as merchants (*Handelsmannen*) who lived in Colmar between 1640 and 1680, only four had originated from outside of Alsace. They included three Swiss merchants, Johann Burger and Johann Rudolph Döring from Basel and Daniel Hügene from Biel, and Caspar Kürtzel from Reichenbach in Baden. Of the eight Alsatians, four were originally from Strasbourg: Hans Georg Eisen, David Andres, Adam Schrick, and Hans Georg Gsell. The bulk of Colmar's post-Westphalian merchant community was native-born.

By 1670 Colmar was able to recover much of the wealth it had lost during the war, but the merchants' guild *zur Treue* did not recoup its prewar share. In 1620 the guild claimed 114 members whose aggregate wealth stood at 139,010 florins, which represented 28% of the city's aggregate wealth. In 1640 the guild claimed fifty-six members with an aggregate tax assessment of 64,560 florins, which was 21% of the city's total wealth. As the city's economic recovery progressed, however, the share claimed by the members of *zur Treue* fell. In 1670 the guild had 105 members whose total wealth equalled 82,790 florins, or less than 19% of the city's aggregate tax assessment. In that same year, only four of the twenty-five merchants had assessed estates over 2,000 florins, though two of them, David Andres and Martin Birr, claimed estates worth more than 4,400 florins. Colmar's post-Westphalian merchant elite was neither as large nor as wealthy as that of the early seventeenth century.

In all, the distribution of the wine and brandy to new, more proximate markets and the expansion of cloth and leather production on a relatively small scale brought Colmar's economy out of the devastation it had undergone during the Thirty Years' War. The limitations of the postwar recovery prevented Colmar's merchant class from expanding and accumulating the wealth it had claimed earlier in the century. Instead, a class of well-to-do cloth and leather producers and tenant farmers emerged and beneath them emerged a broader class of master artisans. These strata formed the backbone of the civic community, but it was a vulnerable backbone. So much of Colmar's economic prosperity depended on provincial political and economic security, and ultimately peace and prosperity in Alsace was in the hands of the French. The Lutheran-dominated city could not resist French pressure and survive economically. French rule, however, would favor Catholics, who had not benefitted much from the postwar recovery.

IV. CONFESSIONALISM AND CIVIC SOCIETY, 1640-1680

In the decades after 1640 Colmar's Catholics formed a distinct minority among the city's guildsmen and were unevenly distributed throughout the guilds, neighborhoods, and tax strata of the community. Prior to the Thirty Years' War, Colmar's Protestants accounted for over 65% of the city's guildsmen, while known Catholics formed a minority of 20%. Among the young men who first appear in the tax rolls after the Imperial Counter-Reformation, over 75% of those with identifiable guild affiliation and at least two-thirds of all householders were Lutherans (see graph 5.3). The Catholics represented just over 19% of the city's guildsmen and 23% of all male householders. Furthermore, the brief Counter-Reform interim had not stimulated much growth in the Catholic community; after 1633 Catholics formed a shrinking minority of the guildsmen. This trend combined with Catholic endogamy threatened the parish's future in the city.

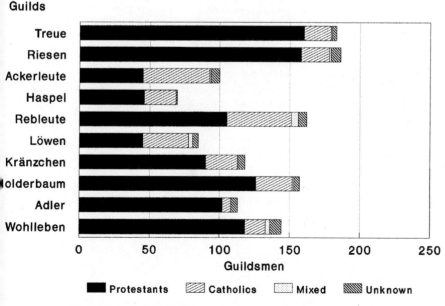

GRAPH 5.3 CONFESSION BY GUILD, 1631-1680

Not only were the Catholics less prevalent in the post-Westphalian guildhalls, but their distribution among the guilds had changed. Throughout the seventeenth century no guild was confessionally exclusive, and in the early seventeenth century the Catholics were most prominent in the agricultural guilds and among the city's victualers. Among the new guildsmen inscribed between 1631 and 1680, the Catholics could claim a majority in none of the guilds. The Catholic parish still included many vineyard workers, fishermen, butchers, and peasants. During these decades, the metal and building trades also accepted more Catholics (16%) than they had before the war, and the millers and bakers in *zum Kränzchen* maintained a small but stable Catholic minority. These sectors of the civic economy were closely connected to Colmar's immediate hinterland, where Catholic villages abounded.

On the other hand, many of the craft guilds had become almost exclusively Lutheran. Over 80% of the guildsmen among the merchants, wine retailers, leather workers, and weavers were Lutherans. These guilds housed the dynamic trades in Colmar's economy, and the Lutherans clearly controlled them. In 1670, for example, of thirty-nine coopers only three were Catholics, and among Colmar's twenty-five tanners and twenty-four weavers there was only one Catholic each. In that same year, Colmar's merchants were Protestant to a man. In all, the Lutherans formed a majority in every guild in Colmar except *Ackerleute*, and even there the Catholics had lost the predominance they possessed before 1627. Colmar's post-Westphalian economic recovery was, for the most part, a Protestant experience.

The first years after the French conquest saw a shift in the confessional distribution within the guilds (see graphs 5.4–5). In 1660 the Lutherans completely dominated the merchant and artisan guilds, where they comprised at least 84% of the members. Even in *zum Holderbaum* and *zum Kränzchen*, where Catholics had earlier held larger minorities, the Lutherans overshadowed their Catholic neighbors. Only in two of the agricultural guilds, *zum Haspel* and *Ackerleute*, were Catholics prevalent, and only in two others, *Rebleute* with 28% and in *zum Löwen* with 33%, were Catholics overrepresented. In 1660 the Lutheran parish serviced 76.9% of all guildsmen, and the Catholic church only 19%. By 1680 French rule began shifting the confessional distribution as Lutheran guildsmen fell to 72% and Catholics rose to nearly 26%. The number of Catholics not only increased in their traditional professional enclaves, they now formed at least 10% of the members in all the guilds except *zum Adler*. The Lutherans, at the same time, only claimed a majority greater than 85% in *zum Adler* and *zum Riesen*. In the late 1670s new Catholic guildsmen were establishing workshops in trades that had long known only Protestants.

Since the early seventeenth century, Colmar's neighborhoods, which often featured occupational clusters, had become confessionally segregated. Prior to the Thirty Years' War, Colmar's Protestants predominated in the city's

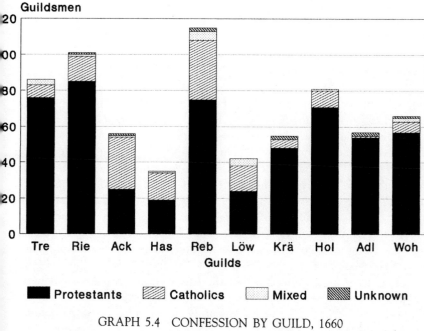

GRAPH 5.4   CONFESSION BY GUILD, 1660

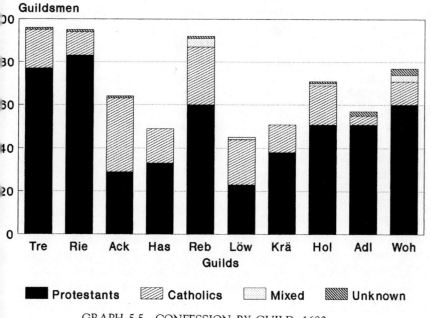

GRAPH 5.5   CONFESSION BY GUILD, 1680

central districts, while the Catholics favored the neighborhoods near the gates and in particular the streets and alleys in the north around the Dominican convents of Unterlinden and St. Catherine, which formed a distinct Catholic enclave. This pattern of confessional clustering was hardly disturbed by the rapid turnover of householders during the Imperial Counter-Reformation and the depopulation of the late 1630s.

Until 1670 the Protestant dominance of the city's core continued, with the Lutherans occupying over 80% of the households in all of the central neighborhoods (see maps 5.1–2). In 1670 the Lutherans claimed at least half of the male householders in every district except *zum roten Fahnen* (XIV). As for the Catholics, who comprised 24% of all householders, they had made some inroads in the northern neighborhoods of *Thunhof* (XX) and *Steinhaus* (XVIII). Nevertheless, the sign of the gradual decline of the Catholics' place in the city was that a growing number of Lutherans had settled in the traditional Catholic neighborhoods at the city's periphery. In 1670 people of both confessions were more likely to have neighbors who attended the other church than their parents had been, but this phenomenon reflected two distinct confessional experiences. The Lutherans held onto their traditional dominance of the city's center and were gradually assuming a growing presence in the outlying neighborhoods. On the other hand, the Catholics were a stable community closed in by a growing number of new Protestant neighbors.

As we have seen, in the early seventeenth century the city's economic growth had favored the small merchant elite which accumulated most of the growing wealth. The Imperial Counter-Reformation drove out most of the wealthy Protestant merchants and civic officials, and within a decade, famine and disease wiped out many households at all levels of civic society. In the ensuing decades, the community steadily grew, until it had nearly recovered its prewar size. In time it also recovered much of its prewar wealth (see tables 5.4–6). The city's aggregate taxable wealth had peaked at 487,000 florins in 1620 from a base of 327,000 florins in 1600. By 1650 a much smaller population of taxpayers paid on 342,000 florins of assessed wealth. By 1670 the Colmarian's assessed aggregate wealth rose to a mid-century peak of 440,750 florins, which marked a recovery of much of the wealth which had been lost during the Thirty Years' War. The military campaigns of the 1670s, however, destroyed some of the gains of the previous generation, though in 1680 the citizens were better off than they had been in 1650.

Colmar's demographic and economic recovery was spread unevenly throughout its tax strata. The demographic crisis had concentrated the city's wealth among the surviving householders in both confessional communities. In the 1640s, the number of taxpaying male householders grew by over 30%, but there were fewer householders assessed at over 1,000 florins in 1650 than in 1640. Most of the men who set up households in the 1640s started out much poorer than those who had benefitted from the consolidation of estates

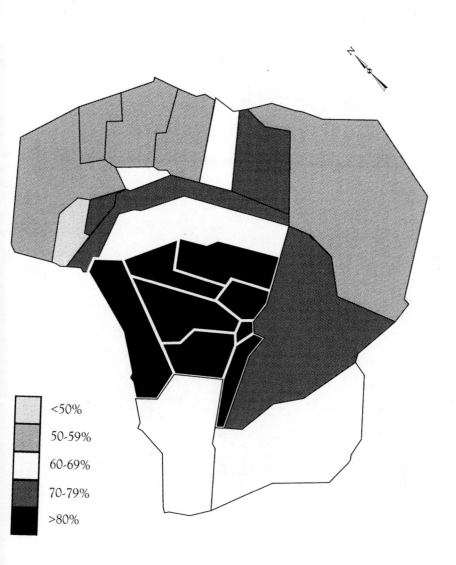

<50%

50-59%

60-69%

70-79%

>80%

100 meters

MAP 5.1   PROTESTANTS, 1670

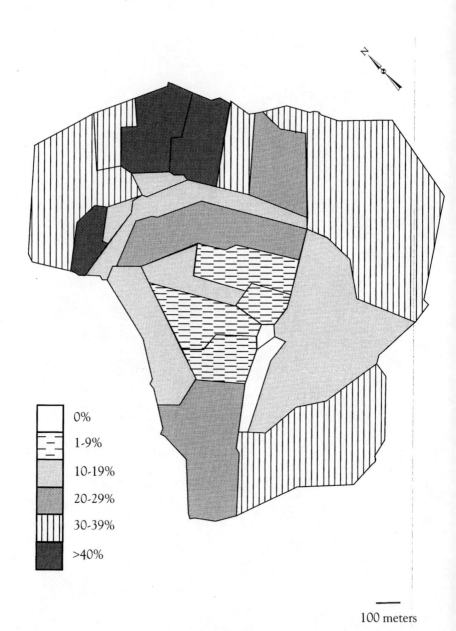

MAP 5.2   CATHOLICS, 1670

TABLE 5.4
Taxable Householders by Strata, 1640–1680

	1640 (no.)	(%)	1650 (no.)	(%)	1660 (no.)	(%)	1670 (no.)	(%)	1680 (no.)	(%)
>2,000 fl.	27	4.8	27	3.7	23	2.6	24	2.6	21	2.7
>1,000 fl.	70	12.5	65	8.8	85	9.7	88	9.6	53	6.8
230–990 fl.	194	34.5	282	38.3	436	49.7	455	49.5	400	51.1
80–200 fl.	248	44.1	329	44.7	297	33.9	325	35.3	287	36.6
Exempt	23	4.1	33	4.5	36	4.1	28	3.0	22	2.8
Total	562		736		877		920		783	

TABLE 5.5
Percentage of Overall Wealth by Strata, 1640–1680

	1640 (%)	1650 (%)	1660 (%)	1670 (%)	1680 (%)
>2,000 fl.	26.5	20.7	15.6	16.1	20.6
>1,000 fl.	30.1	24.0	26.2	25.1	18.9
230–990 fl.	30.5	39.5	44.9	44.9	45.7
80–200 fl.	12.9	15.8	13.4	13.8	14.8
Exempt	—	—	—	—	—
Total fl.	299,320	342,000	414,090	440,750	359,620

TABLE 5.6
Percentage of Change in Wealth by Strata, 1650–1680

	1650 (%)	1660 (%)	1670 (%)	1680 (%)
>2,000 fl.	−10.7	−6.3	+10.2	+4.2
>1,000 fl.	−8.6	+32.1	−27.4	+25.2
230–990 fl.	+48.0	+37.6	+6.5	−17.0
80–200 fl.	+39.9	+2.7	+9.9	−12.6
Exempt	—	—	—	—
Community	+14.3	+21.1	+6.4	−18.5

in the previous decade. From 1650 to 1670, the growth in the community seemed to be uniformly distributed throughout the economic strata, except for Colmar's wealthiest householders. Between 1650 and 1670, the number of householders assessed at 2,000 florins or more remained relatively unchanged, as did their aggregate wealth (70,820 florins in 1650 to 71,000 in 1670). The percentage of householders in the highest stratum, however, fell from 3.7% to 2.7% of the overall householders. This apparent stagnation among Colmar's wealthiest men occurred while the city's population grew 25% and its aggregate wealth rose 29%.

The spine of the community in terms of its recovery ran through a class of moderately wealthy tenant farmers and manufacturers and below them a large block of less wealthy master artisans. The consolidation of estates had established the capital base for many members of this class in 1640 when they formed 12.5% of the householders and held 30% of the city's wealth. Their numbers and wealth declined in the last years of the war, but they quickly recovered in the 1650s. Between 1660 and 1670 the number of householders assessed at between 1,000 and 2,000 florins rose slightly from eighty-five to eighty-eight, but their share of the city's aggregate wealth declined by 27%, while the troubled 1670s reduced their numbers but enriched the survivors. These dramatic scissors-like shifts suggest that this class was the most sensitive to changes in the civic economy.

Below this level of moderately wealthy householders was a broad lower middle class of craftsmen and small tenant farmers, who benefitted the most from the postwar prosperity. This class grew in size by 134% between 1640 and 1670, while their collective wealth also doubled from 91,292 florins to 197,896 florins. They had particularly prospered in the 1640s and 1650s, and they seemed to have suffered somewhat as the economic expansion slowed in the 1660s and the city experienced the deprivation brought on by renewed warfare in the 1670s.

At the bottom of Colmar's taxpaying community was a relatively stable class of poorer householders. Their numbers remained constant, and their apparent enrichment in the 1640s was due to the regime's decision to raise the lowest base assessment from 130 to 200 florins. Again these poorer men were taxpaying householders. Beneath them was a much larger class of journeymen and day laborers, who no longer had access to full guild membership, and more numerous still were the rural poor who inhabited the neighboring villages or the city itself.[41] Reduced to day labor on land controlled by the civic elite and middle classes, the large class of laboring poor, many of whom were Swiss migrants from the Bernese highlands, provided the workers needed to rebuild the economy, though they were excluded from guild membership and citizenship and did not share in the fruits of the postwar recovery. Furthermore, the new round of wars and royal sovereignty ushered in an era of sharpening social stratification, which would become the norm under French rule.

Between the Thirty Years' War and the French conquest, the Catholic community formed a minority which did not share in Colmar's demographic growth, but the distance in average assessed wealth between the two confessional communities was much less than before the war. The average Catholic was still poorer, and the gap between the confessions, which had narrowed between the Counter-Reformation and the Peace of Westphalia, widened again from six florins in 1650 (492 for the Lutherans to 486 for the Catholics) to twenty-four florins in 1670 (514 to 490 respectively). Much of the improved economic conditions for the Catholics had been achieved between 1630 and 1640. When the average Catholic paid taxes on 490 florins of assessed wealth, which represented an increase of 54% from 318 florins in 1620. The Catholics, however, made no further progress, with an average assessment of 490 florins in 1670; it was as if they had reached a ceiling they could not penetrate. Protestant wealth fell 24% from 620 florins in 1640 to 492 in 1650, then rose gradually between 1650 and 1670 to 514 florins. Oddly, the turmoil in the 1670s struck the Catholic community much harder than it struck the Lutheran community, for the Catholics were more heavily committed to agricultural production and, therefore, vulnerable to marauding armies. Between 1670 and 1680 the average wealth for the community as a whole fell 4%, for the Lutherans only 2%; while the Catholics were 10% poorer.

Since the Reformation, Protestantism had been the religious preference of Colmar's wealthiest householders. Prior to the Counter-Reformation, few Catholics were counted among Colmar's richest citizens, but the dissolution of the Reformed parish drove away many of the wealthiest Protestants and, for a time, secured a stronger place for the Catholics among the city's wealthy (see table 5.7). In 1640 and 1650 Catholics comprised a higher percentage of Colmar's wealthiest taxpayers than they did of the population as a whole. The core of this wealthy Catholic leadership were found among the tenant farmers, such as the Counter-Reform magistrate, Matthaus Johner, Claus Dorss, and the elder and younger Hüfflins. The deaths of Dorss and his co-religionists in the 1660s swept away most of the Catholic economic elite. Of the three wealthy Catholic householders identified in 1670, Matthaus Johner the younger, Georg Beyer, and Philip Brotbecker, none survived to 1680. The royal officials would have to build Colmar's Catholic leadership from new men who had not belonged to the mid-century elite either politically or economically.

Since 1600 the merchants in *zur Treue* had predominated within the elite, but after 1640 they formed a smaller and poorer cohort than the great merchants of the early seventeenth century, though, as was the case in civic government, most of Colmar's wealthiest men belonged to either *zur Treue* or *zum Riesen*. Except for some wealthy millers in *zum Kränzchen*, few members of the artisan guilds ever accumulated significant fortunes, and the expansion of cloth and leather production did not give rise to wealthy middlemen within those guilds. By 1660 the city's mercantile elite was Lutheran to the man, and it likely would have remained so if the French had not conquered the city.

TABLE 5.7
Colmar's Mid-Seventeenth-Century Elite, 1640–1680

Guild Membership for Householders Assessed over 2,000 fl.

GUILD	1640	1650	1660	1670	1680
Treue	9 (1)	11 (2)	7	10	8 (1)
Riesen	7 (1)	2	6	6	4
Ackerleute	4 (4)	6 (5)	5 (4)	1	2
Haspel	—	—	1	—	2 (2)
Rebleute	1	1	—	2 (1)	—
Löwen	—	—	—	—	2 (2)
Kränzchen	3 (1)	3	2	1	1
Adler	—	—	—	—	1 (1)
Holderbaum	1	—	—	—	—
Wohlleben	—	1	—	2 (1)	—
NA	2	3 (1)	2 (1)	2 (1)	1
Total	27 (7)	27 (8)	23 (5)	24 (3)	21 (6)

Key:
(n)   Number of Catholics
NA   Not inscribed in guild or citizen registers

Confession and Wealth

	1640		1650		1660		1670		1680	
CONFESSION	(no.)	(%)	(no.)	(%)	(no.)	(%)	(no.)	(%)	(no.)	(%)
Catholic	7	25.9	8	29.6	5	21.7	3	12.5	6	28.6
Ref/Luth	13	48.2	10	37.1	4	17.4	4	16.7	—	—
Lutheran	5	18.5	9	33.3	14	60.9	17	70.8	15	71.4
Unknown	—	—	—	—	—	—	—	—	—	—
Mixed	2*	7.4	—	—	—	—	—	—	—	—
Totals	27		27		23		24		21	

*Gall Gilg, who came from an important family in the Reformed parish, was married in the
Catholic church on 2 February 1629 and later became an important leader in Colmar's
Lutheran parish. Andreas Sybert, who had abjured the Reformed faith and served in the
Counter-Reformation regime, remained a Catholic after 1633.

Within the civic community as a whole, the Catholics experienced little growth in number of householders or in aggregate wealth between 1640 and 1670. Since the early seventeenth century, both parishes had rich and poor members, and the Thirty Years' War left the two confessions with very similar patterns for distribution of wealth (see tables 5.8–10). In mid-seventeenth-century Colmar, the Lutherans figure prominently among the tax exempt because they controlled the city's political institutions and patronage. As for the tax-paying householders, in 1650 the confessional communities possessed strikingly similar strata of assessed wealth. By 1670 the Lutherans predominated among the wealthiest householders, with over 87% compared to 69% for the city as a whole, while the Catholics were overrepresented among those Colmarians assessed between 1,000 and 1,950 florins. On the whole, the evidence suggests that there were no clear class barriers that separated the city's two confessional communities before the French takeover.

In fact the initial confessional impact of the difficult 1670s was the elimination of many householders in the upper-middle tax strata, whose numbers fell by nearly 40%. Among these men the Catholics, in particular, suffered disproportionally, with a decline of 69%. The wars in the 1670s left the Colmarians much poorer than they had been in prior decades, and ironically the first confessional community to suffer from the new political order was Catholic.

The overall impression for the decades after the Peace of Westphalia is one of social balance. The *Gewerff* registers depict a community with a substantial group of middling taxpayers. The conquest by Louis XIV and the wars that followed swept away the basis of their wealth by disrupting trade and the city's relations with its immediate hinterland. To be "open like a village" directly threatened Colmar's regulated central market and the city's economic place in the region. The even distribution of wealth had initially favored both confessional communities, but between 1650 and 1670 the Catholics gave every sign of having reached their limit. The number of Catholic householders remained the same, as did their aggregate wealth. The Catholics were slowly losing their place in the city's economy, and the French takeover seemed at first to complete the process. After 1680, however, royal sovereignty would dramatically alter the balance between the confessions through its effect on the wealth and tax structures and the economic life of the city. The conquest by Louis XIV ended the period of slow and steady growth and, after a brief lag, replaced it with an economic boom. This boom would not be shared equally by rich and poor nor by Catholic and Lutheran.

In many ways, the Thirty Years' War ended Colmar's "Golden Century." The war reduced civic population by nearly one-half. Political and confessional pressures exerted by the warring powers had driven many of the city's leading families into exile; disease and famine had ravaged the men, women, and children who struggled to survive through the devastating 1630s;

TABLE 5.8
Tax Rates by Confession, 1650

ESTATE	PROTESTANTS (no.)	(%)	CATHOLICS (no.)	(%)	UNKNOWN (no.)	(%)	MIXED (no.)	(%)	TOTAL (no.)
>2,000 fl.	19	70.4	8	29.6	—	—	—	—	27
>1,000 fl.	44	67.7	19	29.3	1	1.5	1	1.5	65
230–990 fl.	177	62.8	90	31.9	8	2.8	7	2.5	282
80–200 fl.	213	64.7	90	27.4	17	5.2	9	2.7	329
Exempt	26	78.8	3	9.1	4	12.1	—	—	33
Total	479	67.4	210	28.5	30	4.1	17	2.3	736

TABLE 5.9
Tax Rates by Confession, 1670

ESTATE	PROTESTANTS (no.)	(%)	CATHOLICS (no.)	(%)	UNKNOWN (no.)	(%)	MIXED (no.)	(%)	TOTAL (no.)
>2,000 fl.	21	87.5	3	12.5	—	—	—	—	24
>1,000 fl.	53	60.2	33	37.5	2	2.3	—	—	88
230–990 fl.	331	72.7	105	23.1	11	2.4	8	1.8	455
80–200 fl.	212	65.2	76	23.4	31	9.5	6	1.9	325
Exempt	20	71.4	4	14.3	4	14.3	—	—	28
Total	637	69.3	221	24.0	48	5.2	14	1.5	920

TABLE 5.10
Tax Rates by Confession, 1680

ESTATE	PROTESTANTS (no.)	(%)	CATHOLICS (no.)	(%)	UNKNOWN (no.)	(%)	MIXED (no.)	(%)	TOTAL (no.)
>2,000 fl.	15	71.4	6	28.6	—	—	—	—	21
>1,000 fl.	41	77.4	9	17.0	3	5.6	—	—	53
230–990 fl.	264	66.0	121	30.3	9	2.2	6	1.5	400
80–200 fl.	194	67.6	69	24.0	18	6.3	6	2.1	287
Exempt	15	68.2	1	4.5	6	27.3	—	—	22
Total	529	67.6	206	26.3	36	4.6	12	1.4	783

marauding armies stole livestock and drove the neighboring villagers into the city; and the abandoned farms and vineyards fell into ruin. The long-distance trade routes, which had plugged Colmar's market into the great Rhenish trading network and into Rhenish humanism and later Rhenish Protestantism, had become treacherous and unprofitable. The war closed off the city from its traditional commercial and cultural contacts.

After 1650 peace brought the opportunity for recovery. Although the commercial horizons of the civic economy shrank significantly, its productive capacity remained. Driven in on themselves and dependent on their own resources, the Colmarians tightened their control over their hinterland through the acquisition of properties and through favorable loans, which profited both the city's merchants and a coalescing class of master artisans and tenant farmers. In the generation after 1650, Colmar became a middle-class town whose economic recovery improved the conditions of many tax-paying householders. The picture is incomplete, for the tax registers do not record the Colmarians' extensive properties outside the civic territory, where investment allowed some merchants, guildsmen, and professionals to accumulate significant capital. In the mid-seventeenth century, a new Lutheran oligarchy emerged to replace the prewar Protestant elite. The post-Westphalian oligarchs secured full control over the civic regime and reinforced themselves with economic, marital, and educational ties with Strasbourg. Colmar's elite also pushed for commercial dominance in Upper Alsace, which made the Colmarians vulnerable to pressures from the French, who controlled much of the land surrounding the city. Thus the civic regime ultimately acquiesced to royal claims on property taxes and customs dues.

The Thirty Years' War provincialized Colmar's economy and prepared the city for the economic role it would serve under French rule. A stable indigenous population renewed itself with a small stream of immigrants drawn primarily from the neighboring villages and from Strasbourg. Entrance into the guilds had become more restrictive as marriage or substantial capital became the critical avenues for admission. The new restrictions fit into a general pattern of insiders and outsiders in the city. The regime gradually separated itself from the guilds, which turned the guildsmen into political outsiders. The guilds in turn restricted membership, which consolidated their control over production and distribution in the reduced market area dominated by the city. The outsiders in the work force were the journeymen, day laborers, and rural poor. Post-Westphalian Colmar had come to resemble what Mack Walker has called a "German home town."[42]

During the Thirty Years' War Colmar's economy lost touch with the Rhenish interurban trading network, and with the peace the Colmarians focused on exploiting the resources of Upper Alsace.[43] Symptomatic of the struggle for control were the city's feuds with Turckheim, Riquewihr, and the villages under French lordship over properties bought up by Colmarians during the war. Colmar had always served as a central marketplace for its hinterland,

and the civic regime had loaned money to several neighboring communities in the 1630s and 1640s.[44] With the peace the dependency of the Upper Alsatian economy on the city for products and capital investment increased. Colmar was not, however, a parasitical town simply extracting surplus value from its neighbors. The city's merchant community focused the region's productive resources and fostered its economic recovery. Three industries provided the necessary resources: wine, cloth, and leather. The presence of French garrisons in the former Austrian territories concentrated demand for cloth, leather, and foodstuffs. The city responded by successfully expanding leather production and attempting to develop its cloth manufacture. Ironically, the same troops that threatened civic independence profited local merchants and craftsmen. The mixture of internal and external forces framed an economic infrastructure in Colmar which prepared it for its later role as a royal administrative center. Colmar was already a financial center which relied on the royal army as a major consumer. All that was missing was an administrative elite.

Notes

1. Benecke, ed., *Germany in the Thirty Years' War*, xv; Roger Mols, *Introduction à la démographie historique des villes d'Europe du XVIe au XVIIIe siècle* (Louvain, 1954–56), 2: 470–73.
2. For conditions in the countryside, see Reuss, *L'Alsace*, 1: 109–12; Livet, *L'intendance*, 182–83. On the devastation of the Sundgau, see Paul Stinzi, "L'immigration suisse dans le Sundgau après la Guerre de Trente Ans," in *L'Alsace et la Suisse à traverse les siècles* (Strasbourg and Paris, 1952), 174. For the county of Hanau-Lichtenberg, see Walter Bodmer, *L'immigration suisse dans le comté Hanau-Lichtenberg au dix-septième siècle*, Collection d'études sur l'histoire du droit et des institutions de l'Alsace, 6 (Strasbourg, 1930), 10–12. For an analysis of the war's impact on rural life, see François J. Himly, "Les conséquences de la Guerre de Trente Ans dans les campagnes alsaciennes," in *Deux siècles d'Alsace française*, 15–60.
3. Scherlen, *Histoire de Turckheim*, 86; Billich, "Colmar et Turckheim," 96–97.
4. Burg, "Patrizier," 365.
5. Kintz, *La société strasbourgeoise*, 231–36.
6. Mossmann, "La France en Alsace," 30. The city also quickly resumed payment of its share of the *Pfundzoll* to the cathedral chapter at Costance. AMC, CC 45, 1.
7. On properties purchased in the Austrian domains, see AMC, AA 145, 46–59. On the extent of land purchased by the Colmarians, see AMC, DD 22, 7. Colmar also bickered with Turckheim over Colmarian properties in its territory. See Billich, "Colmar et Turckheim," 96–105.
8. AMC, JJ Divers, 4, fol. 499r.
9. L'Hermine, *Guerre et paix*, 192–93.
10. "Mais cet beau et malheureux pays se trouvant frontière de la France et de l'Empire, il se voit si souvent exposé au ravage et aux malheurs de la guerre que ses habitants vivent dans des alarmes continuelles, et ne peuvent jouir de l'abondance dont ils seraient comblés sans ce rude fléau." Ibid., 193.
11. Ibid., 48–49.

12. See above, graphs 2.1–2.
13. See above, graph 2.3.
14. Samuel and Hans Conrad Gsell shared the same shop in *zum roten Salmen* (district IX) from 1630 to at least 1660. Hans Jacob Graff was their neighbor from 1640 to 1660, while Johann Schloss maintained his shop a few blocks away in *Blaumseysens Ort* (district III).
15. Stein, *Protection Royale*, 498–99.
16. Walker, *German Home Towns*, 76–101. Cf. Christopher R. Friedrichs, "Immigration and Urban Society: Seventeenth-Century Nördlingen," in Etienne François, ed., *Immigration et société urbaine en Europe occidentale, XVIe–XXe siècle* (Paris, 1985), 65–77.
17. Swiss immigration was critical in repopulating many regions of Alsace. See Bodmer, *L'immigration*; André Marcel Burg, "Les Suisses et le repeuplement de Hagenau dans le seconde moitié du XVIIe siècle," in *L'Alsace et la Suisse*, 182–93; Stinzi, "L'immigration suisse," 173–82.
18. For example, the Lutheran registers identify three Swiss grooms in 1653 out of twenty-eight marriages, but only one Heinrich Müller later appears in the tax rolls. The Catholic community's marriage registers are not well kept in the 1650s and 1660s, but in 1667 they identify three Swiss grooms out of twenty total marriages. None ever appears in Colmar's tax rolls. Livet estimates that Colmar welcomed twenty to thirty Swiss *manants* per year from 1650 to the 1690s. Georges Livet, "La monarchie absolue et la bourgeoisie alsacienne: D'après les fonds notariaux et les registres des magistrates," in *La bourgeoisie alsacienne*, 133–52, here at 134–35.
19. The Swabian cloth towns faced a similar challenge, see Hermann Kellenbenz, "Die Wirtschaft der Swäbischen Reichsstädte zwischen 1648 und 1740," *Jahrbuch für Geschichte der Oberdeutschen Reichsstädte* 11 (1965): 128–66.
20. On Müller, see Julien Sée, ed., *Ambros. Müller's Stamm- & Zeitbuch: Hauschronik eines Bürgers von Colmar zur Zeit Ludwigs XIV. (1678–1705)* (Colmar, 1873), 5–11. On Güntzer, see Mieg, "Les tribulations d'Augustin Guntzer," 49–50.
21. Henri Strohl, *Le protestantisme en Alsace* (Strasbourg, 1950), 176–79.
22. The following figures demonstrate the impact of magisterial fiat (Catholics in parentheses): 1649, 10 admissions (0); 1650, 5 admissions (3); 1651, 5 admissions (1); 1652, 2 admissions (0); 1653, 17 admissions (6); 1654, 62 admissions (13); 1655, 34 admissions (11); 1656, 44 admissions (4); 1657, 11 admissions (1); 1658, 14 admissions (4); 1659, 17 admissions (6). Wertz, ed., *Membres du magistrat 1601–1700*, 89–108.
23. See the introduction by Jean-Marie Schmitt, in Bachschmidt, ed., *Le livre des bourgeois, 1660–1789*, v–ix.
24. Twenty-four of the ninety-six names (25%) inscribed in 1654 and 1655 were Catholics.
25. In 1655 the clergy of St. Martin's complained about restrictions against processions and bell ringing, and the Protestant regime's misuse of the church's fabric. AMC, GG 167, 14. On the dispute with the bishop, see AAEB, A 41, mappe 11. On the problems with the other houses, see AMC, GG 29c, 1–4. On confessional relations in the Imperial cities after 1648, see François, "De l'uniformité à la tolérance," 783–800, for Augsburg, 786–89. Cf. Lang, "Die katholische Minderheit," 89–90.
26. On the disputes between St. Martin's and the civic regime, see Goehlinger, *Histoire du Chapitre*, 116–18. On conditions in the diocese of Basel, see André Schaer, *Le clergé paroissial catholique en Haute Alsace sous l'ancien régime, 1648–1789*, Histoire et Sociologie de l'Eglise, 6 (Paris, 1966), 109–20.
27. On the extent of destruction in the rural properties controlled by the cathedral

chapter at Strasbourg, see Himly, "Les conséquences," 17–43, esp. 22–23. Cf. Fuchs, "Bourgeois de Strasbourg," 99–119. Not all villages suffered the same fate. Cf. Lucien Sittler, "Une siècle de vie paysanne, l'évolution d'une commune de la plaine d'Alsace: Fegersheim-Ohnheim avant et après la Guerre de Trente Ans," in .ibid., 81–98. For a list of Colmarians holding properties in the neighboring territories in 1642, see AMC, DD 22, 7.

28. Scherlen, Colmar, village et ville, 96–98; Sittler, La viticulture, 54–61; idem, "Landwirtschaft und Gartenbau," 73–93.

29. AMC, DD 22, 7.

30. In Ackerleute four Catholics and eleven Lutherans were identified as Rebmannen out of a hundred guild members. In zum Haspel three Catholics and twelve Lutherans out of eighty-four guildsmen.

31. See the discussion on postwar grain prices at Strasbourg in Kintz, La société strasbourgeoise, 254–58.

32. Black, Guilds and Civil Society, esp. 123–28.

33. The city engaged in similar disputes with other neighbors, such as Turckheim, Ammerschwihr, and Kaysersberg. AMC, CC 173, 7–8.

34. AMC, AA 166, 272, fols. 1r–3v.

35. Sittler, La viticulture, 75–77.

36. AMC, AA 166, 272, fols. 3v–4r. Cf. Scherlen, Colmar, village et ville, 108.

37. Based on the tax records for 1670 we can make the following comparisons between the tanners, their fellow guildsmen, and the city as a whole:

	TANNERS (no.)	(%)	ZUM WOHLLEBEN (no.)	(%)	CITY AS WHOLE (no.)	(%)
>2,000 fl.	1	4.2	2	2.6	25	2.7
>1,000–1,995 fl.	3	12.5	6	7.7	88	9.6
400–995 fl.	15	62.5	25	32.0	255	27.7
<400 fl.	5	20.8	44	56.4	525	57.0
0	—	—	1	1.3	28	3.0

38. AMC, AA 166, 272, fol. 3r.

39. Sittler, "Commerce et commerçants," 28–29.

40. See Friedrichs, Urban Society: Nördlingen, 239–87.

41. Livet, "La monarchie absolue," 133–53.

42. Walker, German Home Towns, see esp. 1–33. On conditions at Nördlingen, see Friedrichs, Urban Society: Nördlingen, 97–142.

43. Tom Scott has argued that by the end of the sixteenth century both sides of the upper Rhine valley were integrated into a cooperative economic region. Tom Scott, "Economic Conflict and Co-operation on the Upper Rhine, 1450–1600," in E. I. Kouri and Tom Scott, eds., Politics and Society in Reformation Europe: Essays for Sir Geoffrey Elton on His Sixty-Fifth Birthday (New York, 1987), 210–31.

44. Hagenau borrowed 7,500 florins in 1624. AMC, CC 9, 13. The counts von Rappolstein also borrowed money from the city and had authorized their officials in Guemar and Zellenberg to take out loans from the civic regime. AMC, CC 2, 8. Both the Austrian estates in Upper Alsace and the regency at Ensisheim owed debts to the civic regime. AMC, CC 32a, 8, fol. 5r.

Part III

An Imperial City under French Tutelage: Colmar and France, 1680–1730

6

Civic Politics under Royal Tutelage: Colmar's "Reunion" with France, 1680–1698

The Peace of Nijmegen in 1679 confirmed French authority over Colmar, and during the next two decades the royal government "reunited" Colmar to the Crown, restructuring the civic regime and redefining its functions.[1] The pressure of nearly continuous warfare was the principle reason for these changes. The lingering uncertainty generated by the disputed Spanish succession escalated every conflict into a major war waged primarily along France's fragmented borders. In the 1670s Alsace was an exposed outpost of French territory held by recent conquest and only loosely integrated into the kingdom. From 1673, when Louis XIV cemented his claims of sovereignty in Alsace, war or the threat of war dominated regional politics until the Peace of Paris in 1713. After 1673 a steady stream of regiments passed through Colmar, and the military campaigns disrupted trade and placed unbearable fiscal demands on the Colmarians. The first impact of Bourbon sovereignty was the disruption of Colmar's political life.

I. PRELUDE TO FRENCH RULE, 1673–1680

The Peace of Nijmegen reflected the Dutch War's complex origins and the emerging balance of power. Louis XIV was the central force in the negotiations, as he had been in the war. The French deflected attempts by the Imperial envoys to safeguard the liberties of the Alsatian Decapolis, but they failed to include clauses which would legitimize royal sovereignty in Alsace. In the end, the accord of 1679 merely reiterated the language of 1648, but Louis's agents were now willing and able to interpret that language more aggressively.[2] After Nijmegen the crown initiated the policy of "reunions," which called for the Alsatian estates' incorporation into the kingdom.[3]

The royal officials claimed that Louis XIV's descent from Charlemagne legitimized the king's conquest of the Alsatian estates, whose "reunion" to the Crown restored historic relations. In practice, "reunions" allowed the crown to break the hold of those estates which had stubbornly clung to the Imperial constitution since 1648.[4] Although the French had first raised the issue of "reunion" at Westphalia, until the 1670s the king's Imperial policy precluded a direct assault on Alsatian liberties. After 1679 the threat was finally realized.

As the "reunions" began in 1679, the royal agents assured the king's Alsatian "vassals" that they only sought recognition of royal sovereignty and not an outright despoliation of feudal rights.[5] Nevertheless, "reunion" cut off feudal rights from their Imperial source, leaving the estates to beseech the king to honor their liberties. Henceforth, "useful" privileges became free gifts of the king, subject to royal will. At Colmar the regime had long ruled in its own interest, based on privileges granted by the emperor and communal oaths exchanged with the citizenry. "Reunion" destroyed the Imperial foundation, but it also disfranchised the citizenry without overturning the regime.

Colmar's civic leaders learned their first lessons in the new political order even before 1680. In 1674 the intendant, La Grange, stepped in to secure the citizen's obedience to their regime. As the war progressed, La Grange's power in the province grew, and, like Croissy before him, he turned to the reconstituted *Conseil souverain*, now centered in Breisach, to execute his will.[6] La Grange and the *Conseil souverain* assumed legal authority over Colmar, and gradually incursions into civic legal authority would become the norm.[7]

Since 1673 the civic regime had proceeded cautiously through the rituals of *Schwörtag*. In 1674, 1676, and 1678, the regime had eschewed elections altogether and simply retained its officials in their previous posts. The magistrates had also carefully edited the various oaths, which now mentioned neither king nor emperor, hoping to offend no one.[8] The Court, however, was tired of Colmar's obfuscations and directed the new Grand Bailiff of Hagenau, the baron de Montclar, to force a public oath of obedience from all the cities of the Decapolis.[9] On 1 September 1679 Montclar arrived in Colmar to observe the oath. One by one, the magistrates and councilors stepped forward and respectfully refused on the grounds that to obey would violate their oaths to the emperor and the empire.[10] Montclar gathered together the city's royal agents and left in a rage, threatening military trials and executions or imprisonment to any Colmarian who held firm to this treason, then he proceeded to nearby Turckheim to let the regime stew. The magistrate convoked a hasty meeting with the "leading members" of the council. This unusual "rump" assembly decided to submit and dispatched an embassy of Catholic laymen and clergy to negotiate with the Grand Bailiff. On the next day, the regime finally gave its oath to the king as sovereign protector, and Montclar promised to maintain the city's traditional liberties.[11]

Whether the civic officials realized it or not, the oath to Montclar put them permanently under the king's authority. Their defiance before the Grand Bailiff had been their last public act of opposition to the king. The Colmarians protested the forced oath before the Imperial court at Speyer, but there was little the Imperial officials could do to dissuade the king from exercising his authority in Alsace.[12] A short time later, under royal pressure, the Decapolis recalled its embassy from the Diet at Regensburg.[13] In December 1679 the *Conseil souverain* registered the "reunion" decrees and a new phase of royal politics in Alsace had begun.

II. The Transformation of Civic Politics, 1680–1698

Between 1680 and 1698 the royal government altered the constitutional structure and the day-to-day procedures of Colmar's municipal regime. The changes occurred piecemeal and apparently without plan. Some institutions withered and disappeared; others survived with new agendas and new personnel. On balance, the civic regime lost most of its decision-making responsibilities to royal officials.

The royal government initially stepped in to dictate the recruitment of new regime members. In August 1680 La Grange ordered the regime to appoint a Catholic Stettmeister and four Catholic councilors to fill its vacant posts. When the regime refused, the intendant suspended it.[14] On 3 October, the *Conseil d'Etat* mandated confessional parity in all municipal offices, apparently in response to a petition from some of Colmar's Catholics.[15] The *Conseil* cited Imperial constitutional precedents, and by November Colmar's Lutheran leaders yielded. No incumbent lost his post, and the Catholics gradually filled the vacancies until the confessions achieved parity.[16]

The crown's desire for a confessional balance directly engaged provincial royal officials in civic politics and heightened confessional tensions within the community.[17] The demand for Catholic regime members disrupted the established patterns of co-optation. The guilds had long since lost their electoral role, so the confrontation occurred directly between the civic regime and the king's agents. Catholics had served in the regime between 1633 and 1679, but they had functioned as representatives of those guilds which had substantial Catholic membership. At Colmar the coming of confessional parity was nonetheless not as forced as it was at Lutheran Strasbourg, where the new Catholic councilmen were either converts or "carpetbaggers" from the kingdom's interior.[18] Whereas at Strasbourg the Catholic officials represented a direct rupture with Protestant political and confessional traditions, Colmar had been a bi-confessional town since 1575, and Catholics had served in the regime since at least the 1590s. After the Thirty Years' War, however, a narrow circle of Lutheran merchants and professional men had come to dominate civic political life, to the exclusion of the guilds.

Colmar's new Catholic officials, though appointed because of royal pressure, had deep roots in the community. They had all purchased citizenship before 1673, and in most respects they resembled the Lutheran incumbents. With his appointment in 1680, François Seraffond became Colmar's first Catholic Stettmeister since 1632. He was a Gascon who had married a local woman, and in 1654 they baptized their first-born daughter in St. Martin's church.[19] When Seraffond purchased citizenship in 1667 as a wool weaver in *zum Adler*, he owned a home next to the wealthy Lutheran physician, Zacharias Andres.[20] By 1680 he had moved to *Thunhof* (district XX) and had an assessed estate of 2,000 florins, which was twice as high as that of any other member of his guild but one. If Seraffond was involved in cloth production, he was a middleman rather than craftsman. The key point is that Seraffond, though French, was well established in Colmar before French rule.

The four new Catholic councilors came from the city's leading Catholic families. The fathers of Johann Johner and Wendlin Güntzer had served in Colmar's Counter-Reform magistrate. Güntzer was a wealthy apothecary who had purchased citizenship in *zur Treue* in 1663. In 1680 he lived in *zum roten Salmen* (district IX) and paid taxes on an assessed wealth of 2,400 florins. Although he purchased citizenship in 1661 in the traditionally Catholic peasants' guild, *Ackerleute*, Johann Johner was the lay administrator of the local properties of the Knights Hospitallers.[21] Johner's home was in *zum Schlüssel* (district XIII), and his tax assessment of 600 florins in 1680 seems low and may reflect a partial exemption. Michael Anton Barth was a merchant who had purchased citizenship in *zur Treue* in 1667, and Johann Haffner was a tanner who joined *zum Wohlleben*, also in 1667. Both could trace their ancestries back to the early seventeenth-century Catholic elite, although their tax assessments, Barth at 300 florins and Haffner at 450, placed them in Colmar's lower middle economic class.[22]

The new officials were apparently drawn from among Colmar's leading Catholic laymen, and the only distinction between this cohort and the traditional Catholic leadership was the new men's lack of ties to the rural work force. Except for Johner, these men were tradesmen. Royal interference in the regime's recruitment expanded representation by opening it to Catholics, but French pressure had not restored the guilds to civic political life. The intendant had bullied the Lutherans into sharing power with the Catholics, and Catholic power in the city depended on royal favor.

As they had in the 1620s, in 1680 Colmar's Catholics entered a regime which had undergone a major turnover in personnel since the battle of Turckheim in 1675. In 1680 nearly half (twelve of twenty-six) of the incumbent regime members had less than five years political experience, though this new generation sat in chambers with a cohort of elder statesmen. Ten members, including the four Lutheran magistrates, had served for more than eighteen years. The elder generation of councilors included men—such as Martin Burger, Daniel Barth, Jacob Buob, and Martin Birr—who fit the mold of merchants and professionals who had governed the city after 1648.[23]

In contrast to the previous decades, at this point all of the Lutherans who had joined the regime since 1675 were representatives for the guilds in which they purchased citizenship. In fact, with the inclusion of the new Catholics, twenty-two of twenty-six councilors represented their guilds of origin, and all ten guilds were represented. *Zur Treue* still accounted for six regime members; and of the others Daniel Schneider and Samuel Röttlin were professional officials without guild affiliation, so the new regime brought together some of Colmar's richest merchants along with guildsmen of more moderate means. Within the council the combined assessed estates of three Lutheran merchants, Martin Burger, Johann Georg Herr, and Hans Dürninger, and the jurist Martin Birr, totalled 19,600 florins and exceeded the combined estates of the twenty-two other councilors (including the Catholics) of 18,000 florins. In 1680 the Catholics joined a municipal regime in flux, its system of patronage in disarray and its solidarity shaken. The tensions within the Lutheran leadership can be seen in the unusual "rump" session convened by the magistrate in the face of Montclar's ultimatum. Furthermore, none of the Lutheran recruits of 1675–79 ever served in the magistrate or was welcomed into the society *zum Waagkeller*.

Forced parity did not return the guilds to the center of Colmar's political life, for the guilds had no electoral role. Under the new system, the intendant supervised the co-optation of Catholic recruits. In 1681 two new vacancies resulted in the appointment of two more Catholics to the council, Claus Hurst and Johann Jacob Meinweg.[24] Meinweg was an outsider who had served as a fiscal agent for the Grand Bailiff of Hagenau, and his appointment, secured by Montclar's patronage, must have pained the older members of the regime.[25] Hurst, on the other hand, came from one of the largest civic families, with collateral branches in both confessional communities.

In 1682 the vote for Obristmeister produced a deadlock between the Lutheran Ambrosius Riegger and the Catholic François Seraffond, despite a Lutheran majority among the electors. Following the advice of the Grand Bailiff's representative, the regime chose Seraffond with the understanding that henceforth the city's executive office would alternate between Lutherans and Catholics. The same election added two new Catholic councilors.[26] In the following year, a royal decree restricted the terms of civic magistracies in Alsace to three years.[27] The edict threatened the practice of life terms, long one of the foundations of civic oligarchy. The king's provincial agents did not enforce the decree, but its very existence troubled Colmar's magistrates.[28] In 1685 Montclar brandished the decree as a club to elect Colmar's second Catholic magistrate, Johann Johner, whose appointment and the simultaneous co-optation of three Catholic councilors raised the number of Catholic regime members to twelve.[29] The crown then ended the fiction of elections with a declaration that all future nominations would require the approval of the city's commandant or the intendant.[30]

The loss of their customary control over recruitment spread fear among the Lutheran regime members that the king would not respect the principle of parity, which, reversing their previous opposition, they now came to see as their chief safeguard. The first test came in 1688, when four vacancies led to a constitutional reorganization. The council of XIII ceased to exist, and the remaining councilors were consolidated into two committees of ten. The reform left one vacant post, which was awarded to a recent Catholic convert, Johann Klein.[31] This election established confessional parity, and henceforth, the royal government respected the balance, as both crown and civic regime came to regard the practice as an unwritten contract. The royal government's drive for parity between Protestants and Catholics in Colmar's regime had created two separate systems of confessional patronage. The Lutheran magistrates lost control of overall recruitment and faced continual reminders that their hold over their smaller power base rested on royal favor. Colmar's ambitious Catholics had gained access to the highest civic offices, but their careers were determined by cliental contacts with local royal officials. In different ways the status and authority of the political leaders in both parishes depended on their loyalty to the new political order.

Royal reforms in the 1680s also reduced the magistrate's influence in day-to-day politics, particularly through the creation of two new officials: the commandant and the *préteur royal*. When the crown authorized the construction of modest walls around Colmar in 1682 to defend the city's markets and customs' revenues, the intendant assigned a French commandant to supervise municipal defense. Early the following year, an iron-willed army officer, Lieutenant-Colonel d'Anastasy, assumed this post and with it control over police powers traditionally handled by the regime.[32] On 16 August 1686, a royal edict created the office of *préteur royal* in each of the major Alsatian cities. This official, who served as the king's representative in all municipal assemblies, resembled the medieval Imperial Schultheiss, whom the Colmarians had integrated into the magistrate in 1424. The *préteur royal* sat as chief justice in both civic courts, and he represented the king in all sessions of the magistrate and regime as a whole. A strong-willed man could dominate civic politics from this post, if he could play the role of broker between the intendant and the city's leading men, both Lutheran and Catholic.[33]

Colmar's first *préteur royal* was Jean Georges Duvaille. Since 1673 his father, an *avocat* of the *Conseil souverain*, had served as bailiff of Sainte-Croix-en-Plaine and in 1677 had been made a member of the society *zum Waagkeller*.[34] The younger Duvaille apparently had only a limited impact on the municipal regime, unlike Strasbourg's first *préteurs royals*.[35] After Duvaille's death in 1690, the regime argued with the intendant over the appointment of his successor. When La Grange's first choice, François Dietremann, declined the honor, the intendant ignored the city's nominee and selected François Sigismond Voegtlin. Voegtlin's appointment angered regime members, who had come to despise his high-handed and self-centered behavior as Colmar's court clerk. Voegtlin used his new office to extend his network of personal clients. As *préteur royal*, Voegtlin alienated municipal officials to the degree that the intendant recognized the problem.[36] Voegtlin's death again raised hopes among regime members that they might nominate a new appointee, but La Grange refused to relinquish his prerogatives, though he did select the regime's candidate, François Dietremann.[37]

Dietremann, who served as Colmar's *préteur royal* for more than thirty years, was born in Lorraine in 1656 and entered royal service as a *conseilleur* in the *Conseil souverain* in 1688. Six years earlier, he had married into an important family of the French administrative nobility (*noblesse de robe*), the Boisgartiers, whose patronage advanced his career. In 1693 he became bailiff of Sainte-Croix-en-Plaine, and in 1695 he accepted the post as *préteur royal* and held it until his death in 1729.[38] Once in office, Dietremann accumulated various titles and appointments as well as gifts from the king and the Colmarians. Besides his civic post, he continued to sit on the *Conseil souverain* and served as *subdélégué* for the intendant in Upper Alsace. He had contacts in both the judicial and administrative hierarchies and wielded tremendous patronage within the city and surrounding countryside. Dietremann became the political mediator between the city and the royal government and helped transform Colmar into the royal capital of Upper Alsace.[39]

Dietremann introduced the city's officials to the tastes and practices of the provincial robe nobility. He demonstrated the potential for personal profit and influence for those who participated in royal administration, while bit by bit he stripped away the last vestiges of local power. The *préteur royal* brought about the change in civic political mentality gradually, and his position and leadership were only one factor in the shift. The fiscal demands of Louis XIV's ramshackle war machine provided the incentive for a new political ethos in Colmar. Investment, both forced and voluntary, in the royal debt would gradually earn the loyalty of Colmar's elites.

III. The Changing Ethos of Colmar's Political Elite, 1680–1698

In 1694 Colmar's magistrate petitioned La Grange to restore the practice of life tenures, which had been abolished by an *arrêt* of the *Conseil d'Etat* in 1683. As with mandated confessional parity, this regulation only applied to newly appointed magistrates.[40] The first Colmar magistrates to face elections were Catholics, Johann Johner and Wendlin Güntzer. Both came up for re-election in 1691 under the immediate supervision of the meddlesome Voegtlin. The council of jurors, who served as electors, selected another Catholic, Johann Jacob Madamé, an outsider who was a client of Voegtlin's, to replace Güntzer.[41] The election prefaced a potential revolution within civic politics where, for more than two centuries, no magistrate had faced electoral recall. The magistrates feared both the alienated jurors and the ambitious Voegtlin.

Prior to 1691, Colmar's political leaders in the two parishes had begun to close ranks. In 1689 the Lutheran oligarchs invited the leading Catholics to join the society *zum Waagkeller*.[42] Solidarity within the elite, however, could not prevent the growing split between the regime and the citizenry. During the election, a group of citizens complained to the intendant about the accumulation of personal wealth and property by their magistrates at public expense. According to the citizens, "the magistrates and city clerk possess[ed] a quarter of the better properties in the city and daily [made] new acquisitions." They also objected to the magistrates' salaries and per-quisites, which stood in sharp contrast to conditions in nearby Turckheim.[43]

In their response the magistrates viewed the petition as the product of "malcontents animated against the magistrate to discredit it and to sow discord within the community."[44] As for their properties, the magistrates estimated that they possessed no more than a "fortieth" of the civic proper-ties. These holdings, for the most part vineyards, were so unprofitable that the magistrates had had to sell some to feed their families. When the defense shifted to a comparison with Turckheim, the imagery of impoverishment faded. The magistrates argued that a comparison with Turckheim was un-fair because that neighboring city was in ruins. Furthermore, Colmar's higher salaries were justified by magisterial responsibilities.[45] In their summary, Colmar's officials did not deny their wealth, but presented it as a virtue. Experience testified, in their view, that magisterial functions flowed "much more surely in the hands of the well-to-do" than in the hands of those forced to live on their salaries. Poor magistrates were subject to "corrup-tion" and could only live by "illicit means." Given these truths, from "time immemorial" the magistrate had always sought out the well-to-do to serve in the office honorably.[46] The defense touted the importance of magisterial *Obrigkeit* and oligarchy while discounting the traditions of contractual civic responsibility.

In 1694, with Voegtlin dead, no replacement in place, and new elections looming, the magistrates petitioned the intendant to restore their life ten-ures. They acknowledged that the *arrêt* was designed to suppress the abuse of power in office, but they argued that the excesses reflected the general problem of governing in wartime.[47] They also appealed to provincial cus-tom, for the Alsatian magistrates handled both judicial and police affairs, whereas these were separate functions in the interior of the kingdom.[48] The crown needed special men to govern in Alsace, due to multiple functions, the language demands, and legal complexities. Life terms, they concluded, would best serve the public good and the state.[49] The magistrates then turned to their specific objections to the elections. They expressed deep concern over the willingness of the citizens to conduct a proper election. The mag-istrates pointed out to La Grange that it would be cruel to leave the elec-tions "to a populace to whom the magistrates have made themselves odious because of frequent executions of his majesty's orders, which . . . in wartime cannot be carried out without extreme harshness." The magistrates believed that the citizens, if given the choice, would support "some rogue or some fool from among themselves" rather than the "more capable and more zealous magistrate." They felt that it would be unkind to expose them "to the judgment and hatred of an injudicious populace."[50] The injudicious populace, whom the magistrates feared, was not the entire citizenry but the council of jurors.

In their final defense, the magistrates defined themselves as venal *officiers*. An edict of 1692 had created a new tier of municipal offices throughout the kingdom. The city had purchased these offices for 117,000 *livres d'Alsace*, or twice the regime's annual revenues. The magistrates noted that they "had advanced considerable sums of money in order to finance the Reunion of Charges [Edict of 1692] and further had committed themselves and awaited payment on loans of more than 20,000 livres made in the king's service."[51] The purchase of these royal offices "had rendered nearly all the posts, which had been triennial or of lesser duration, perpetual and even hereditary."[52] In effect, the regime's financial commitment to the Reunion of Charges negated electoral politics and confirmed the right to bequeath the posts. The call for life terms reflected the magistrates' realization that their investments were only as secure as royal protection made them and that loyalty to their royal patrons had become the collateral for their status and office.

Between 1673 and 1698, therefore, Colmar's political leaders came to accept the destruction of the Imperial constitutional basis of their power. In "reuniting" the city with the kingdom, the royal government became the basis for the regime's authority. Power emanated from the court through a system of patronage which Colmar's political leaders, both Catholic and Lutheran, joined, making them less civic politicians and more royal administrative agents. The old political ethos, which had defined their behavior as leaders of a small but sovereign civic republic, gave way to a new value system of royal *officiers*. A part of the citizenry interpreted this change as a corrupt betrayal of traditions, and they petitioned the king, as they might the emperor, to restore the civic order and public peace. The royal government, however, had fostered the new political ethos and defended its local agents, as one form of *Obrigkeit* was replaced by another.

IV. PRIVILEGE, JUSTICE, AND TAXES, 1680–1698

Justice and tax collection were the two main tasks of seventeenth-century government, and in the years after 1680, provincial royal agents successfully grafted French practices onto Alsatian legal and fiscal institutions. Earlier, Colmar's regime had fought to preserve its judicial privileges, such as the right to judge all criminal cases without appeal, including cases of high justice, and the right to serve in civil affairs as the court of first instance, from which one might appeal to Imperial courts at Speyer and Vienna only in cases involving sums over fifty florins.[53] Between 1648 and 1673 the royal government had challenged Colmar's judicial privileges through the *Conseil souverain*, the courts of Imperial Bailiff of Hagenau, and the Parlement of Metz. The civic regime successfully resisted this first assault, but now, with its walls reduced to rubble and royal officials committed to subjugating the city, the regime had no prospects of withstanding the second push.

Beginning in 1675, the revived *Conseil souverain* at Breisach had inserted itself between Colmar's courts and the Imperial judicial hierarchy. Under the new policy of "reunion," the royal government constructed a new legal hierarchy on the base of the old system. The first step was the demand for the regime to produce a systematic justification of its rights.[54] In its response, the magistrate no longer claimed ties with Imperial courts and recognized the jurisdictional rights of the *Conseil souverain* at Breisach. The regime, however, complained that during the war the *Conseil souverain* had encouraged local plaintiffs to bypass the municipal courts and take their cases directly to it. The regime feared that such practices would undermine their authority by "destroying indubitably [the regime's] police powers" and "exposing the magistrate to the mockery of the inhabitants and fomenting disobedience among the miscreants and rebels," which would only make it more difficult to execute the king's commands and ultimately swamp the provincial courts with hundreds of petty complaints.[55]

The royal government delayed confirmation of the civic regime's legal privileges until 1685, which drove home to regime members their dependence on the king for legal authority. The Colmarians were relieved when the crown spelled out the new system, for the civic judicial structure remained. The regime retained its criminal courts, while parties could appeal civil judgments to the *Conseil souverain* for settlements in excess of 100 livres.[56] In practice, royal agents often interfered in the judicial process to protect their clients, and the magistrates learned the limits of their authority.[57]

The crown also preserved the structure of civic fiscal institutions, but profoundly altered their practices. During the 1660s the intendant, Colbert de Croissy, had reorganized the fiscal system in the former Austrian "territories of old dominion" and introduced tax farming for both direct and indirect taxes. Though common in the kingdom's interior, tax farming ran counter to Alsatian communal traditions.[58] In Colmar customary fiscal practices ritualized the relation between taxation and community membership; self-assessments, administered in the guildhalls under oath, provided the *Gewerff* rates which formed the basis of all other direct taxes. The procedure recalled the two foundations of civic participation: guild membership and public oaths. The introduction of tax farming into Colmar would destroy the civic ethos of taxpaying and create new social and political tensions within the community.

The *Umgeld*, a tax levied on the retail sales of wine in civic taverns, was the first municipal tax to be redefined.[59] Since 1428 a compact had divided the *Umgeld* receipts between the city and the Imperial Bailiff, but in

1677 the tax farmer of the now rechristened Grand Bailiff's revenues, Johann Jacob Meinweg, challenged the city's method of determining the shares.[60] He claimed to the duke de Mazarin that the regime sought to defraud him by distinguishing between the *Umgeld*, which was unquestionably subject to division, and the *Weingeld*, a separate tax levied on retail wine sales by individual merchants in the marketplace. The regime collected all *Weingeld* revenues because the tax did not appear in the original charter. Meinweg further complained that the city estimated the *Umgeld* shares only after paying the collectors. At first the regime responded within the Imperial context that these traditional customs had applied under all previous Imperial Bailiffs including Mazarin.[61]

Meinweg, however, ignored Imperial traditions and prohibited retail wine sales in the marketplace to increase the *Umgeld* receipts. With French troops in town, the regime had to follow the tax farmer's directive, but it immediately appealed to Mazarin on the grounds that Meinweg's motivation was profit rather than the pursuit of Mazarin's interests. The Grand Bailiff accepted the Colmarians' arguments and consented to "a reduction of part of his revenues."[62] Mazarin had not confirmed Colmar's rights or traditional practice; he had merely restored traditional practice as an act of grace.

Mazarin's patronage ended when the baron de Montclar replaced him as Grand Bailiff of Hagenau in 1679. Meinweg immediately reopened the case, and Montclar supported the tax farmer and declared that the regime was "quibbling." The new Grand Bailiff ordered the regime to take its case to the *Conseil souverain* at Breisach.[63] Montclar further brushed aside Colmar's chartered privileges and ordered the regime to divide the revenues of both the *Umgeld* and the *Weingeld* with Meinweg.[64] Montclar's decision was to be in force for three years and could only be changed by his orders.[65] For the first time, a royal official had dictated fiscal practices within Colmar's walls.

In 1681 Montclar offered to farm his share of the *Umgeld* for one year, and the civic regime purchased the farm for 1,200 *livres tournois* and promised to levy the tax according to Montclar's new guidelines.[66] The city farmed the tax until 1683 when the *receveur général* of Ammerschwihr, M. de Lamiguère, acquired the right to collect the tax for the next three years at 1,350 livres per year.[67] When the *Umgeld* came up for bidding in 1686, the municipal regime, which by then had seen its own revenues farmed to investors, abstained. Several leading citizens, realizing the potential for profit and political advantage in the system, participated in the lively bidding which eventually fell to M. La Vallée for over 2,000 livres.[68]

Tax farming ended the civic regime's traditional responsibility for the collection of revenue. When Montclar farmed his share of the *Umgeld*, he established a special commission to oversee assessment and collection with powers to prosecute transgressors.[69] The civic regime soon had to resolve conflicts between the new commission, private entrepreneurs who held the Grand Bailiff's rights, and the traditional privileged enclaves within the city. In 1687 several monks from the abbey of Munster in the nearby Vosges, which kept a small hostel in Colmar, sold wine without paying the *Umgeld*. At first the civic regime was unwilling to prosecute. The Grand Bailiff pressured the regime to assist his tax farmers, but the Colmarians replied that the intendant should settle the dispute. La Grange supported the tax farmers, but for several weeks the regime was unable or unwilling to force the monks to comply.[70] The abbey refused to recognize the civic regime's jurisdiction, and the Colmarians found themselves the unwilling policemen for the tax farmers and the Grand Bailiff. They informed Montclar:

> It is for the intendant to regulate differences of this nature, and it is not for us to judge the affairs of a monastery which does not recognize us competent to judge disputes; it is in the city's interest that we have not wanted to expose ourselves to the risk of being challenged as incompetent.[71]

Montclar and La Grange ultimately confirmed the regime's authority, which restored its administrative competence under their tutelage.[72]

The dispute over the *Umgeld* introduced the Colmarians to the French fiscal system. In March 1683 the intendant ordered the regime to farm all of the city's revenues to the highest bidder.[73] In 1686 a consortium of Colmarians, Johann Georg Barth, Johann Johner, Johann Jacob Madamé, Johann Thomas Staub, Friedrich von Turckheim, Paul Loffet, Christian Reichstetter, and Johann Mentzer, promised to advance the city 49,300 livres per year for the right to farm its revenues (see table 6.1).[74] Johner was a Catholic regime member, and Madamé, Loffet, and Reichstetter would later join him in office. Turckheim, Barth, and Loffet were Lutherans, while Johner and Madamé were prominent leaders within the Catholic community. For these men confession apparently was no barrier to an investment venture which mixed business and politics. The magistrate appointed Madamé as *receveur* of the city's revenues, which allowed him to combine public office with supervision of his personal investment. What is striking about the men who raised nearly 50,000 livres was their deflated *Gewerff* assessments

TABLE 6.1
Tax Farmers, 1686

NAME	GUILD	RELIGION	R1680	R1690
Johann Georg Barth	Treue	Luth	8.00	7.50
Johann Johner	Ackerleute	Cath	3.00	3.00
Johann Jacob Madamé	Adler	Cath	—	2.00
Johann Thomas Staub	Treue	Luth	—	2.00
Friedrich von Turckheim	Treue	Luth	—	2.50
Paul Loffet	Wohlleben	Luth	7.50	9.00
Christian Reichstetter	Riesen	Cath	6.25	7.00
Johannes Mentzer	Riesen	Cath	—	4.50

in 1690, which suggests that they benefitted from privilege before the fisc.[75]

In 1688 two Frenchmen, Calmet and St. George, purchased the munici-pal farm for 47,900 livres per year.[76] The new tax farmers came from the kingdom's interior. Calmet, who settled at Colmar for a career in govern-mental finance, was a shrewd businessman who served the royal adminis-tration well, though sometimes his tactics angered local officials.[77] In the 1690s local investors again purchased the city's tax farm, but this time they formed distinct confessional groups. In 1691 Georg Wilhelm Faber, a Lu-theran merchant and regime member, joined two other Lutherans, Friederich von Turckheim and Johann Thomas Staub, to purchase the farm.[78] In 1692 Stettmeister François Seraffond led a consortium of Catholic citizens who paid 61,000 livres for the farm.[79] In these ventures shared confessional identity apparently played a role in raising capital.

Tax farming was a relatively safe investment during the peaceful 1680s, but the renewed war between France and the empire in the 1690s made it more speculative. War strained the fiscal resources of both city and crown. Municipal revenues, which depended in part on the indirect taxes from trade, fluctuated wildly, and the bids on the tax farm rose and fell with the fortunes of war. In 1693 two brothers named Eydt, from Strasbourg, pur-chased the farm for 60,000 livres. At the end of the second year, they withdrew from their three-year contract because of losses. The farm con-tinued to fall in value: in 1695 to 45,480 livres; in 1696 to 44,500 livres; and in 1697 to 40,030 livres.[80] In 1698 La Grange canceled the auction and set the price at 47,000 livres, which the previous farmers agreed to pay.[81] The following year brought peace and an influx of immigrants into Colmar, and the municipal farm jumped to 60,200 livres.[82] With the new century the farm of municipal revenues continued to draw high bids, but henceforth most of the investors were from the kingdom's interior.

In 1673 tax farming was an alien practice to the Colmarians, though common in French cities. When the royal government farmed the civic revenues, the regime and the wealthy citizens accepted the change, and the city's first tax farmers emerged from the local elite, both old families and new, both Catholic and Protestant. Colmar's leaders gradually adapted to processes which blended public status and private investment, which sub-stituted administrative influence for sovereign rights, and which mixed the men of the old order and the new. The citizens perceived a growing gap between their tax assessments and communal goals, and they complained of the wealth of the regime members as early as 1691, and the fiscal crisis of the 1690s would only widen and deepen popular resentment.

V. THE FISCAL CRISIS OF THE 1690s

Until the 1690s, the levels of royal taxation in Alsace had been moderate. In 1679 the crown had extended the *subvention* system for direct taxation, which had existed in the "territories of old dominion" since 1661, to all of

Alsace. The royal government maintained the tax at a moderate level through-out the seventeenth century, for royal agents normally responded to the burdens of the king's wars by creating extraordinary taxes.[83] The pattern first emerged during the war years of 1673–79. After the war the fiscal pressure declined, and the municipal regimes struggled to quickly pay off their debts.[84]

French sovereignty had disrupted the political and legal structures which ensured the old relations between debtors and creditors. Colmar's regime had traditionally been both a borrower and lender, and before the Thirty Years' War it had been a net creditor. After 1650 the war and the city's ambiguous political status had cost the regime much revenue in interest.[85] The Dutch War turned Colmar into a net debtor, and the regime faced numerous creditors in the 1680s. Many debts dated from before the Thirty Years' War, but others had accumulated during the troubled 1670s, so that the regime faced new debts and unpaid interest on the older ones. Further-more, financiers had begun to work the speculative market in discounted notes of credit.[86] In 1688 the regime complained that since the Peace of Nijmegen:

> The city's creditors have begun to make war [on the magistrates] to ini-tiate processes against them for old debts, contracted by their predeces-sors long before the earlier troubles in Germany, whose interests have accumulated over several years combined with the considerable sums the [magistrates] have been obliged to borrow for the service of the king. . . . [The debts] have grown to excessive sums which the suppliants could never pay off without a moderation of the interest rate and a respite of several years.[87]

Strasbourg's regime had successfully petitioned for such a moratorium three years earlier, and the royal government granted Colmar a five-year morato-rium in 1688.[88]

The reduced pressure was short-lived. The outbreak of the War of the League of Augsburg soon forced the French to resort to a new round of extraordinary taxes, and Alsace shared the burden with the kingdom as a whole.[89] As a result, the tension between Colmar's regime and its citizens grew while the royal government's appetite for cash raised through the creation of new offices and forced loans entangled the civic elite in the financial and political structures of the Bourbon state.

In 1692 the Edict of Reunion of Charges created a new set of venal civic offices to supplant the existing regimes. Most city governments purchased the offices to secure their posts. Strasbourg's regime, for example, paid 300,000 livres, and Colmar's offered 117,000 livres for the new offices.[90] In 1694 the royal government again created new offices which the civic regimes could suppress by advancing funds to the crown.[91] The following year, the king established the *capitation*, a head tax assessed on all subjects without exception.[92] The Alsatians paid a variety of other levies over and above these taxes. They financed royal fortifications along the Rhine, and they carted tons of foodstuffs into the royal granaries for the army. In 1697 La Grange estimated that the Alsatians paid the crown nearly 3,280,000 livres of taxes in specie and kind.[93] Clearly, royal fiscal demands in the 1690s had made a deep impact on the provincial economy.

The Colmarians struggled to meet the crown's demands. In the 1680s the city had paid only nominal taxes to the royal fisc, but in the ensuing decade royal pressure drove the municipal regime deeply into debt. In 1692 it borrowed heavily to pay the 117,000 livres for the Reunion of Charges, and it had to borrow 20,000 livres each year between 1694 and 1698 to suppress a second set of offices. With surcharges and interests the payments totalled 114,287 livres by 1699.[94] The Reunion and Suppression of Charges forced the civic regime to raise 230,000 livres within a five-year span when the annual civic budget averaged only 60,000 livres.[95] The Colmarians also met the demands of the *capitation*, the Rhenish fortifications, and housed numerous royal regiments.[96] The outlay produced a credit crisis for the regime, and it turned to its wealthiest members for support.

The most significant challenge came from the Reunion of Charges in 1692, whose venal offices included in Colmar a *conseileur procureur de roi*, two *secretaires greffiers*, a *receveur des derniers d'octroi*, and three *notaires héréditaires*.[97] In late January 1693, La Grange informed the magistrate that the edict effectively disbanded the regime. The civic leaders moved quickly to prevent wealthy individuals from purchasing these offices but carefully enough to ensure that they had the money. The Colmarians offered "to pay his majesty for the reunion of all these offices, for the conservation of its privileges, for the free elections of all municipal charges, and for free administration of its revenues" the sum of 117,000 *livres d'Alsace*.[98] Unfortunately, their offer came too late to prevent the tax farmer, Calmet, from purchasing the office of *receveur des derniers d'octroi*.[99] The intendant, however, granted the regime all the offices including Calmet's.[100]

Deprived of his office, Calmet was not to be easily denied his profits. He pressed the city to pay his wages and other revenues, relenting only when shown a letter from the king.[101] Quieted for the moment, Calmet reemerged in April, as the city prepared to pay its first quarterly installment, to present the intendant with a bill for the expenses incurred in his "official capacities" and his unpaid wages. Calmet argued that the city owed him a return on his investment and that he should be allowed to hold the office and its privileges until the regime repaid him.[102] Finally, in May the magistrate agreed to pay Calmet his initial capital outlay of over 30,000 livres and his expenses, and he withdrew his suit.[103]

Calmet's claims were the prod that drove the regime to seek out ready capital and by April it had to raise emergency loans to meet its first installment to the *receveur général*.[104] In June, as the deadline for the second installment approached, the Colmarians begged for a delay for it had become "more difficult each day" to secure the loans, which they could only raise "with excessive interest" with both the civic revenues and their own capital as collateral. The citizens were unwilling to provide the money and the magistrates' only recourse would be forced loans among the city's wealthy.[105] There was no reprieve, and the regime met the final installment on 7 June 1693.[106]

The magistrates raised part of the payments from the municipal budget, but this only produced 48,000 livres.[107] In April and May 1693, the regime raised another 69,000 livres from voluntary and forced loans. They borrowed from 180 individuals, mostly citizens (see table 6.2).[108] Five major creditors (2.8%) forwarded more than two-thirds of the needed capital. Eight other creditors formed a second tier of major investors whose capital brought the regime to over 80% of its objective. The principal creditors included two Stettmeisters, Seraffond and Riegger, and the councilor, Meinweg. In all, nineteen of the twenty-six regime members advanced money to preserve their posts, but most offered only small amounts.[109]

The big investors attached stipulations to their loans, particularly in terms of collateral. The Catholic rentier Johann Jacob Meinweg received the annual revenues from the *Brückmühl*, a municipal grain mill, and eighteen *schatz* of vineyards as security for his investments.[110] Johann Andres, a Lutheran rentier, gained access to municipal pasture land and the promise of full repayment of his principal within six years.[111] Another consortium of four investors offered 4,000 livres for the right to hold the important office of *Weinsticher* for four consecutive years. The *Weinsticher* assessed the fair price for all wine sold in civic fairs, and the post brought with it both revenue and influence.[112] Christian Reichstetter and Johann Thomas Staub had previously collaborated in farming the city's revenues. All but Jundt showed up in the city's capitation rolls in 1694, and they were among the wealthiest burgers. By 1702 Christian Reichstetter had joined the regime. Under pressure, the regime had offered the use of communal properties and access to lucrative public offices to raise the money to protect its posts.

Two major loans, Johann Jacob Sandherr's and M. Le Comte's, caused the magistrates headaches for years. In April 1693, Johann Jacob Madamé and Andreas Sandherr travelled to Strasbourg with only 30,000 of the 50,000 livres needed to pay the first installment. The *receveur* for the intendant, de Courcelles, would not accept partial payment, and the worried magistrates turned to two Strasbourg financiers, a local merchant named Traeher and M. Le Comte, the chief surgeon at the *hôpital royal*, who each advanced 10,000 *livres tournois*, or 11,200 *livres d'Alsace*. The city's magistrates assured repayment of the loans within two years in their own names. When the two magistrates returned to Colmar, all the regime members cosigned the loan on these terms.[113] The regime apparently met the requirements because it was able to borrow from Le Comte again in 1697. The second loan proved more difficult, and Le Comte harried the Colmarians

TABLE 6.2
Loans for the Reunion of Charges, 1694

NAME	BACKGROUND	AMOUNT
Johann Jacob Sandherr	merchant	12,000
Traeher	merchant (Strasbourg)	11,200
Le Comte	surgeon (Strasbourg)	11,200
Johann Andres	rentier	6,000
Johann Jacob Meinweg	rentier (regime)	6,000
Subtotal		46,400
Elias Lang	rentier	2,000
Matthias Graff's widow	unknown	1,200
François Seraffond	official (regime)	1,000
Ambrosius Riegger	official (regime)	1,000
Christian Reichstetter	innkeeper	
Johann Georg Reichstetter	baker	
Joseph Jundt	vineyard owner	4,000
Johann Thomas Staub	iron merchant	
Subtotal		55,600
Daniel Pappelier	merchant	600
Daniel Hügene	merchant	500
Stephan Appfel	merchant	400
Johann Friedrich Dürninger	unknown	400
Madame Revillon	unknown	200
Johann Theobald Gerhardt	butcher	200
Subtotal		57,900

MINOR LOANS

NUMBER OF INVESTORS	AMOUNT	REGIME MEMBERS	TOTAL
16	150	2	2,400
1	110		110
20	100	4	2,000
1	90		90
3	60		180
55	50	9	2,750
64	30	1	1,980
1	28		28
Total			67,438

for the next several years to retrieve his investment.[114] The regime members offered their personal fortunes as collateral for both loans from Le Comte, though they ultimately managed to repay him from communal resources. Their personal commitment nevertheless gave them proprietary interest in their offices.

The most troublesome loan came from the Colmarian patrician, Johann Jacob Sandherr, a Lutheran. Sandherr, who was the nephew of the elderly Stettmeister Andreas Sandherr, paid a critical part of Colmar's first installment in 1693 with his loan of 12,000 livres.[115] He received no interest on his capital but acquired the lucrative post of *receveur des revenus* for the city for three years and a complete tax exemption during the term of his office. If the regime failed to repay him at the end of three years, his loan would then accrue the standard 5% interest.[116] Unlike Le Comte, Sandherr was not paid in time, and he approached the intendant in 1697 to pressure the civic regime for payment. He had expected to hold his post as *receveur* until his reimbursement, but the regime had appointed another in his place. Despite a series of letters from La Grange, the regime frustrated Sandherr with unfulfilled promises.[117] Finally in 1697 the regime borrowed money from Le Comte to meet obligations on its debts, including part of what it owed Sandherr. Even then civic officials did not repay Sandherr in full and denied his request for tax-exempt status.

The magistrates defended their actions by informing the intendant that Sandherr had been appointed to his office *after* his promise to serve without pay and to make the loan.[118] They noted that Sandherr's privileges included exemption from quartering troops, from ordinary taxes worth 106 livres per year, and from all extraordinary taxes for 1693. The magistrates argued that he should not hold exemptions from the numerous extraordinary taxes which the royal government had established since that year. In the end, they admitted that they owed Sandherr the money, but they maintained that because of his immense wealth he didn't need the money.[119] In 1698 the *Conseil souverain* arranged a settlement between Sandherr and the regime. The city had until 1 August 1699 to repay the remaining principal. Sandherr would renounce all claims to interest if the regime granted him tax-exempt status until the principal was repaid. When the regime ultimately failed to pay the principal, Sandherr and his descendants became privileged to exemption from civic taxes.[120]

The magistrates had petitioned for life-tenures in 1694 because of their personal commitment to the regime's debts. Some had loaned money, and all had offered their personal fortunes as collateral. Their motives mixed personal and civic pride with the desire to protect financial opportunities provided by regime membership. It is interesting that Andreas Sandherr, the last magistrate with roots in the pre-French civic regimes, would not lend money to protect his post. The city was spared rule by speculators such as Calmet, only to be ruled by speculators such as Meinweg, Madamé, and Johann Jacob Sandherr. Investment in royal debt offered potential profits and privilege before the fisc. It also marked a boundary of commitment to the new political order, and those who crossed it became insiders who often stood at odds with the old civic community. The growing alienation of the city's traditional political community focused on the triennial elections, and the magistrates begged for protection from accountability before the council of jurors. In 1700 the intendant finally granted life terms. A new political order was in place; and it would soon be reinforced by new institutions and privileged immigrants.

*   *   *

It was not with a brutal and abrupt hand that the French king brought about his transformations. He had a great deal of touch, and it is not in the French tradition to rely on force. The form of Colmar's government maintained itself with its organs, its magistrate, its council, and its elections; the ancient customs, dear to the Colmarians, remained, the respect for tradition was assured, and the inhabitants were not persecuted for their habits, their religion, or their language. . . . Little by little, and only in steps, the measures of French government were introduced, at first to exclude all that recalled the empire, then to assure the place of Catholicism in the magistrate and council, and finally to introduce and establish the domination of France.[121]

With these words, Lucien Sittler, Colmar's long-time municipal archivist, described the transformation of civic government under Louis XIV. Sittler's analysis depended on two concepts which have recently come under attack: nationalism and absolutism.

Louis XIV's initial act of subjugation, the destruction of the city's walls, certainly entailed abrupt force. When the Treaty of Nijmegen confirmed the king's authority over the city, the use of force did not end. Royal provincial agents threatened imprisonment and corporal punishment to force Catholic magistrates on the unwilling Lutherans. Both the blunt Montclar and the subtler La Grange used the dismantling of traditional civic politics to construct systems of clients within the regime. Under pressure, the old organs of government did not endure. The regime lost its power to appoint many of its officials, and the city's revenue collection fell into the hands of tax farmers, often private citizens. The regime had its judicial responsibilities circumscribed and its political role neutralized by the *préteur royal*, the commandant, and the *Conseil souverain*. These were royal creations and had little to do with civic political traditions. Colmar's officials ceased to function as elected representatives of the civic community held responsible by mutually sworn oaths, and instead became the administrative agents for the royal government at Colmar. The organs remained, but they functioned in a new body politic.

For a brief instant, the crown experimented with elections by the council of jurors, but the magistrates wanted no part of democracy. They could not be effective administrators if they were accountable to the citizenry. From 1680 onward, two distinct confessional systems of patronage emerged. For the Catholics, the royal provincial agents held the key to promotion within the civic regime and beyond. The Lutheran patronage network was soon limited to the city, which later would factionalize the Lutheran leadership as they squabbled over scant offices.

Royal agents had little respect for traditions they did not understand. They ignored political customs when it suited them. They openly perse-cuted and harassed Colmar's Lutherans and forced the French language and political culture on the community. All correspondence, official minutes, and court proceedings were to be conducted in French, and the civic elite had to quickly become bilingual in order to survive. The common Colmarians could preserve their language and civic culture, but they were effectively cut off from any understanding of the new official culture. As the civic leaders saw it, they served as the translators between the royal government and the king's subjects. The leaders belonged to the new official culture, the common folk to the king's subjects.

Colmar's political and economic elite also learned that access to wealth and influence in the swelling Bourbon state came through investment in public debt, venal offices, and tax farming. The French imported, for the first time in Colmar, a set of social values which supported *rentier* invest-ment and aristocratic manners. The pinnacle of the old civic social struc-ture lay just below the foundation of the new royal hierarchy. Within a generation, some Colmarians would cross the barrier and enter royal ser-vice, though many more who wished to could not.

The catalyst for these changes was not a program of political realignment and subjugation formulated in the drawing rooms of Versailles. Warfare, as an "organic need" of the early modern state, drove the royal government to employ brutal and abrupt policies to force revenues from reluctant subjects.[122] This fiscal appetite animated the "absolutist" policies of the French at Colmar, and the Colmarians adapted to the new system. They invested in govern-mental debt and learned that what the government could offer in return was patronage and privilege. In time, familial wealth, political authority, and social status depended on the continued success of the French in Alsace. This truth applied to both Catholics and Lutherans at Colmar. When in 1697 the Peace of Ryswick ended French authority in the Breisgau, hun-dreds of petty officials, financiers, and hangers-on of the royal regime there poured across the Rhine into Alsace. When the *Conseil souverain* moved into Colmar the following year, it brought many of these refugees with it. This great political immigration completed the process of Colmar's elite turning French, but the process was well under way before 1698. If Bour-bon power had been driven out of Alsace in the eighteenth century, a large and growing part of the civic elite would have had to retreat across the Vosges with it.

Notes

1. Sittler, "La transformation du gouvernement," 133–58.
2. Ragnhild Hatton, "Nijmegen and the European Powers," in *The Peace of Nijmegen 1676–1678/79* (Amsterdam, 1980), 1–16; Georges Livet, "Colbert de Croissy et la diplomatie française à Nimègue (1675–1679)," ibid., 181–223; René Pilloret, "La France et les états allemands au Congrès de Nimègue (1678–1679)," ibid., 225–36.
3. Reuss, *L'Alsace*, 1: 242. See also Robert Mandrou, *Louis XIV en son temps (1661–1715)* (Paris, 1973), 276–77. Pilloret calls this part of the treaty, Louis' *Diktat*. Pilloret, "La France," 231–33.
4. Livet, *L'intendance*, 384–87.
5. Ibid., 389–90.
6. The campaigns in Lower Alsace led to the dispersal of the administrative personnel of the Grand Bailiwick of Hagenau. The *Conseil souverain* filled the vacuum. On the role of the *Conseil souverain* during the war, see ibid., 390–91.
7. In 1675 the intendant served as an advocate on at least two occasions for individuals seeking redress from Colmar's regime. He helped a citizen of Sainte-Croix-en-Plaine recover a horse which the civic regime had confiscated. AMC, AA 168, 30. He later defended a woman from Jebsheim, who had had a quantity of salt seized when she tried to market it in the city in violation of Colmar's monopoly. AMC, AA 168, 31.
8. On the wartime elections and the oath, see Sittler, "La transformation du gouvernement," 139. In his index of civic officials, Roland Wertz includes results for 1676 and 1678, but not for 1674. *Membres du magistrat, 1601–1700*, 10, 15–32.
9. A copy of the oath appears in Livet, *L'intendance*, 392–93 n. 5. See also Zeller, *Comment s'est faite la réunion*, 136; Bardot, *La question*, 268.
10. Sittler, "La transformation du gouvernement," 140. When Montclar first proposed the oath, the Colmarians answered that "eine so schwer Sache nicht bey ihnen stünde, weil sie des dem Kayser und Reich geschwornen Eides nicht entlassen wären." Rathgeber, ed., *Colmar und Ludwig XIV*, 36.
11. The Kaufhaus chronicler noted: "Als der Magistrat den Ernst gesehen und bey dem schlechten Reichzustand keine Hülfe erwarten konnte, entschlossen sie mit etlichen des Raths sich zu unterwerfen. Die Catholische Clerisey und Bürger liefen nach Türckheim und erklärten sich für französisch." Rathgeber, ed., *Colmar und Ludwig XIV*, 36. Cf. Sittler, "La transformation," 140. According to Livet, these events marked a dramatic shift in civic political life: "cette periode qui équivaut pour Colmar à la plus grande révolution de son histoire, lourde de conséquences politiques, religieuses et économiques." Livet, *L'intendance*, 393–94, here at 394.
12. Bardot, *La question*, 269.
13. Livet, *L'intendance*, 474.
14. Sittler, "La transformation du gouvernement," 141.
15. AMC, BB 19, 1 & 2.
16. AMC, BB 19, 2, fol. 1v. On the royal campaign to place Catholic officials in all local posts, see Livet, *L'intendance*, 445ff. The Imperial constitution might support "parity cities," but Colmar had never honored parity.
17. Lucien Sittler and others have argued that before 1680 a "French party" existed in Colmar composed of Catholics and French immigrants. Sittler admits that the documents are mute on its activities. Sittler, "La transformation du

gouvernement," 136–37. See also Braeuner, "L'opinion publique," 46; Henri Strohl, "L'esprit républicain et démocratique dans l'Eglise protestante de Colmar de 1648 à 1848," in *Deux siècles d'Alsace française*, 430–33.
18. Ford, *Strasbourg in Transition*, 112–17; Greissler, *La classe politique*, 113–40; Streitberger, *Der königliche Prätor*, 96–109.
19. Sittler, "La transformation du gouvernement," 154, n. 11.
20. Wertz, ed., *Membres du magistrat 1601–1700*, 118, no. 864.
21. On the Güntzer family, see A. M. P. Ingold, *Miscellanea Alsatica* (Colmar and Paris, 1897), 3: 57–58. On Johner's family and career, see Julien Sée, ed., *Johann Joner's Notanda: Tägliche Notizen eines Stettmeisters von Colmar zur Zeit Ludwigs XIV.* (1687–1705) (Colmar, 1873), vi–ix. See also Sittler, "La transformation du gouvernement," 156 n. 59.
22. Wertz, ed., *Membres du magistrat 1601–1700*, 16, 23.
23. The older generation included the four Lutheran magistrates: Ambrosius Riegger (20 years); Jacob Oberlin (31); Daniel Schneider (20); and Andreas Sandherr (35). It also included six councilors: Daniel Barth (21); Hans Benedict Scholl (28); Michel Sitter (24); Jacob Buob (25); Martin Birr (18); and Georg Hoeffler (18). Four councilors had served between nine and fifteen years, including a Catholic XIIIer representing *Ackerleute*, Georg Hannser. Besides the five Catholics, twelve other regime members had entered politics since 1675. Wertz, ed., *Membres du magistrat, 1601–1700*, 15–31.
24. Sittler, "La transformation du gouvernement," 142.
25. Meinweg, as an agent for the Grand Bailiff, had succeeded in extending the bailiff's rights over the collection of the *Umgeld* at the expense of civic privileges. AMC, CC 56, 2–8.
26. On civic elections in the 1680s, see AMC, BB 18, 1.
27. AMC, BB 18, 5–8. See Sittler, "La transformation du gouvernement," 143.
28. AMC, BB 18, 10.
29. Sittler, "La transformation du gouvernement," 144; AMC, BB 24, 14.
30. Sittler, "La transformation du gouvernement," 144.
31. Ibid., 147. On Klein's conversion, see Sée, ed., *Johann Joner's Notanda*, 8.
32. Anastasy assumed the regime's traditional police powers. He ordered the city's streets cleaned and banned pigs from them. In 1685, following a civil disturbance, he closed the city's taverns and imposed a curfew. Sittler, "La transformation du gouvernement," 141–43.
33. Sittler, ibid., 146; Livet, *L'intendance*, 712–14.
34. The elder Duvaille was a baptized Jew. See Rathgeber, ed., *Colmar und Ludwig XIV*, 174. On his admission to the society *zum Waagkeller*, see AMC, HH 8, 24. On the younger Duvaille, see Sittler, "La transformation du gouvernement," 146–47.
35. There are no studies on the Colmar's *préteurs royals*, but those at Strasbourg have received extensive attention. See Ford, *Strasbourg in Transition*, 79–86. See also Streitberger, *Der königliche Prätor*, esp. 39–79.
36. On Voegtlin's character and tenure, see Sée, ed., *Ambros. Müller's Stamm- & Zeitbuch*, 41–42.
37. Sittler, "La transformation du gouvernement," 148–49.
38. On his tenure, see AMC, BB 13, 167, fol. 15. See also Sittler, "La transformation du gouvernement," 153–58.
39. On Dietremann's activities as the *subdélégué*, see Livet, *L'intendance*, 675, 909. His correspondence with the magistrate shows him actively defending civic interests before the intendant and the Court. For example, see AMC, AA 177, 131–33. I have discovered a few glimpses into his patronage network. In 1711, for instance, Dietremann apparently arranged for the appointment of a

M. Thirion as *Bürgermeister* of the Upper Alsatian town of Saint Hypolite even though "cela [the appointment] ne luy est point due de droit." AMC, FF 43, 64. He also secured the election of M. Preiss, the curé of Jebsheim, to the lucrative post of abbot of Murbach. AMC, FF 43, 84 & 86. Lucien Sittler presents Dietremann as the hero in Colmar's peaceful transition to a royal provincial center. Sittler, "La transformation du gouvernement," 152.

40. Two copies of this petition exist in Colmar's municipal archives. Neither is dated, but references within them suggest that they were drafted in 1694, following a disputed election. AMC, BB 18, 10 and FF 43, 3–5. For the wording of the *arrêt*, see AMC, BB 18, 5.

41. The magistrates attempted to direct the electoral process. In a joint meeting with the council, they proposed that "les anciens Stettmeisters dont les charges ne sont pas sujettes au changement porte par le dit arrest, doivent assister à la dite election et ÿ avoir voix conjunctement avec les habitans ... comme donc il suggest de l'explication d'un arrest du Conseil d'Estat et qu'il est necessaire que nous en soyons esclairis avant l'assemblée de l'habitans." AMC, BB 24, 19. The votes cast were as follows: J. Johner, 151; W. Güntzer, 78; J. J. Madamé, 89; J. Klein, 7; Claus Hurst, 2; J. (Klein)haus, 1. AMC, BB 24, 20.

42. The membership in the patrician society had declined steadily from thirty-three in 1664 to eight in early 1689. AMC, HH 8, 13–35. That year the society expanded to twenty-two members. Among the new initiates were Anastasy, Duvaille, the three Catholic Stettmeisters, Johner, Güntzer, and Serrafond, and at least one other Catholic, Johann Jacob Madamé. AMC, HH 8, 36.

43. I have not found the petition, only the magistrates' response, which addresses the citizens' complaints point-by-point. The magistrate discounted the complaint "qui a esté presentée au nom des bourgeois" as the product of "quelques mescontents animé contre le Magistrat pour le rendre odieux et semer de la division parmi la communauté." AMC, FF 43, 1–2.

44. AMC, FF 43, 1, fol. 1r.

45. Ibid., fol. 1v.

46. Ibid., fol. 2r.

47. There are two copies of this petition: one housed among the magisterial records (AMC, BB 10, 18); and the other among the evidence gathered during the Sonntag affair in 1711 (AMC, FF 43, 3–5). Oddly enough, the copy drawn up in 1711 seems to be closer to the original. It is more polemical and defensive in its language and thus, I would argue, older. Furthermore, it places strong emphasis on Colmar's rights and privileges, which would have been an anachronistic embellishment in 1711. The language differs, but the general argument in both copies is the same.

48. AMC, FF 43, 3, fol. 1 r–v.

49. After distinguishing between the various duties of the Alsatian magistrates "estoient cÿ devant villes libres et Immediatement sujettes à l'Empire," the Colmarians noted that "cette multiplicité d'affaires demande non seulement de l'application de zelle de la probité et la capacité mais aussy de la Science des langues et connaissance parfait des affaires de la communauté la quelle ne se pourant acquerir que par une longue experience et continuation d'exercise des charges de Magistrature il y va indubitablement du Service du Roy et de l'interest publique." AMC, FF 43, 3, fol. 2r.

50. The regime felt that good men, who were hard to find, should be maintained in their offices "sans qu'on en laisse l'election à la populace à qui les Magistrats se rendent odieux à cause des frequentes executions des ordres de Sa Majesté qui s'addressent au Magistrat et qui dans le temps de la guerre ne

peuvent s'executer sans la dernière riguer." AMC, FF 43, 3, fol. 2v–3r. The civic leaders felt that "le peuple commun" would choose "par la pluralité des voix quelque mutin, ou autre ignorant d'entre eux, au plus capable et plus zelé Magistrat pour le service du Roy. En effect il seroit bien Injuste, si après l'exercise triennal d'une charge si penible, on voulut exposer à la pluralité des voix et la haine d'un peuple indiscret les personnes du Magistrat." Ibid., fol. 3r.

51. AMC, FF 43, 3, fol. 3r–v.
52. For a copy of the original edict, see AMC, BB 33, 24. The edict disrupted communal regimes in other parts of the kingdom, see Pierre Deyon, *Amiens, capitale provinciale: Etude sur la société urbaine au XVIIe siècle* (Paris and The Hague, 1967), 467, 473–75; Pierre Goubert, *Beauvais et le Beauvaisis de 1600 à 1730: Contribution à l'histoire sociale de la France du XVIIe siècle* (Paris, 1960), 244; Benedict, "French Cities," 34. The Colmarians argued that "le Roy par ses edits a rendu quasi toutes les charges qui n'estoient que triennales ou de moins de durée, perpetualles, et mesmes héréditaires. L'Edit de Reunion des charges du mois de Fevrier qui permet aux villés d'Alsace moyennement les sommes considerables qu'elles en ont payé, les élections libres des charges de la ville et leurs anciens privileges, dont il leur accorde la mesme jouissance qu'elles avant auparavant semble avoir tacitement abrogée l'arrest du Conseil d'Etat." AMC, FF 43, 3, fol. 2r–v.
53. The magistrate outlined its privileges in AMC, AA 15, 3, paper 3, fol. 1r–v. On Colmar's judicial system, see Sittler, "Colmar au XVIe siècle," 17; Reuss, *L'Alsace*, 1: 470–71.
54. AMC, AA 15, 3. See also Livet, *L'intendance*, 475–77.
55. AMC, AA 15, 3, paper 4, fol. 2r–v.
56. The regime had pleaded with La Grange to expedite the confirmation. AMC, AA 168, 40–41. The *Conseil souverain* finally registered the privileges on 18 October 1685. AMC, AA 15, 4.
57. La Grange often stepped in to determine cases. AMC, AA 168, 32–33 and 37–39. Montclar on one occasion curtly ordered the arrest of the city's hunter, who had insulted one of the baron's retainers. Ibid., 36.
58. Roland Mousnier, *The Institutions of France under the Absolute Monarchy*, vol. 2: *The Organs of State and Society*, trans. by Arthur Goldhammer (Chicago, 1984), 423–45.
59. On the early history of the *Umgeld* in Colmar, see Sittler, *La viticulture*, 19, passim. On the signifance of the *Umgeld* for royal fiscal administration, see Georges Livet, "'Maspfennig et Umgeld,' Contribution à l'étude de la fiscalité du vin en Alsace sous l'ancien régime," *Annales de Société d'Ethnographie Française* 1 (1950): 83–94.
60. AMC, CC 56, 2–5. Meinweg later became a regime member from 1682 til his death in 1694.
61. For Meinweg's compliant, see AMC, CC 56, 7. For the regime's response, see ibid., 2.
62. On the regime's perception of Meinweg, see AMC, CC 56, 7. Mazarin's responded: "Comme les perts que vous avez soufferts par la guerre me font entrer entièrement dans les sentimens de compassion que je veux bien avoir pour vous en consentent la diminution d'une partie de mes droits." AMC, CC 56, 8.
63. AMC, CC 56, 16.
64. Montclar structured the new system on practices employed at Breisach. He ordered that "tous les cabarretiers, vivandiers et autres gens qui vendant du vin ou de la bière par pot ou par peinte payassant un florin par mesure, à

partager par moitié entre nous et la ville de Colmar." He also established a joint commission to police the tax's collection. AMC, CC 56, 18.

65. AMC, CC 56, 19.

66. AMC, CC 56, 27.

67. AMC, CC 56, 27, fol. 2v. For the fiscal year 1684–85, the *Umgeld* and the *Weingeld* provided the city with 4,000 livres of revenue, which profited the Grand Bailiff 647 livres. AMC, CC 13, 2.

68. The bidders included Valentin Reichstetter, M. Perdrix, Johann Jacob Guebel, Johann Wurching, the consortium farming the city's revenues, and M. La Vallée. M. La Vallée eventually acquired the farm for 2,090 livres. AMC, CC 56, 28–29. Guebel had been a citizen since 1668 when he inscribed in the guild *zum Haspel*. Wertz, ed., *Membres du magistrat, 1601–1700*, 120, no. 878. In the *capitation* of 1694, he was described as a *gros laboureur* and assessed 60 livres, which put him in the highest bracket. AMC, CC 155, 1694, p. 2. Valentin Reichstetter is listed in the same register as a *boulanger* and assessed the lordly sum for a baker of 30 livres. Ibid., p. 11.

69. The commission included two representatives each for the Grand Bailiff and the city. AMC, CC 56, 18.

70. On 24 July 1687, the regime petitioned La Grange for help. AMC, CC 56, 30. The intendant replied that the monks should pay. Ibid., 31. Yet Montclar complained to the civic authorities on 19 August that nothing had happened. Ibid., 32.

71. AMC, CC 56, 33.

72. AMC, CC 56, 34.

73. AMC, AA 165, 180.

74. Rathgeber, ed., *Colmar und Ludwig XIV*, 40.

75. Paul Loffet had died before 1694. Of the other seven, the magistrates, Madamé and Johner, and Reichstetter, an innkeeper and tenant farmer, all appear in the highest category, at 60 livres. Mentzer, a butcher, fell in the next category at 40 livres. Von Turckheim and Staub, who were iron merchants, and Barth, a retired merchant, paid 30 livres. AMC, CC 155, 1694.

76. Rathgeber, ed., *Colmar und Ludwig XIV*, 41.

77. Calmet was an important financier in the 1690s and early 1700s in Alsace. Livet, *L'intendance*, 804, n. 3. As civic tax farmer, he often quarreled with civic officials over assessments. AMC, CC 192, 5. He was quick to sense a profit. In 1697 as civic *receveur*, Calmet sold the remaining salt reserves at discount prices just before turning the warehouse over to the new farmers. AMC, CC 252, 2a. Earlier, in 1693, he had confronted the regime over the Reunion of Charges. AMC, BB 33, 20–33.

78. In 1694 Faber was listed as an merchant without a shop and assessed at 30 livres. AMC, CC 195, 1694, p. 6.

79. The consortium included Frantz Windholtz, Johann Heinrich Klein, Seraffond, Johann Michel Huget, and Joseph Danner, Rathgeber, ed., *Colmar und Ludwig XIV*, 42. Klein was a convert who joined Seraffond on the regime in 1688. Only Seraffond and Windholtz appear among Colmar's leading taxpayers in 1694, Seraffond as a magistrate, paying 60 livres, and Windholtz as a miller, 30 livres, AMC, CC 155, 1694, pp. 1 & 7.

80. Rathgeber, ed., *Colmar und Ludwig XIV*, 43–45.

81. Calmet purchased the tax farm in 1696 and 1697. AMC, CC 252, 2a. La Grange also set the bid for 1697. AMC, AA 165, 187.

82. In 1698 one of the Eydt brothers held the farm. In 1699 the bidders included two Colmarians, Johann Jacob Sandherr and Frantz Windholtz. Windholtz held the last candle. AMC, CC 252, 3a.

83. Livet compares the Alsatian figures with the much heavier burden in the Franche-Comté. Livet, *L'intendance*, 481–84.
84. Ibid., 426–28.
85. The Colmarians claimed to hold obligations from the Württemberg estates, Strasbourg, and numerous Alsatian noble dynasties "dont le principal se monte à la somme de 44,000 florins et dont ils [the Colmarians] n'ont touché aucune Interest depuis 1632... les quelles jointes aux autres rentes de la ville que les supplians ont esté obligés d'engager pour les debtes contractées dans la dernière guerre ont autrefois composés les fonds destinés au payement réciproque des debtes passives de la ville." AMC, CC 34, a2, fol. 2r. Many Imperial cities faced similar fiscal crises in the late seventeenth century, see Friedrichs, *Urban Society: Nördlingen*, 145–69; Bátori, *Augsburg*, 90–92.
86. "Ils se trouvant des particuliers dans la province qui taschent d'achepter des sommes capitales deubs de la communauté des villes à un prix modique dans l'intention de vexer les d. villes et d'en retirer puis après la somme principale entière avec tous les cens escheus." AMC, CC 34, a2, fol. 2v. Among the estates who owed Colmar money was the defunct archducal regime at Ensisheim, the town of Thann, the estates of the nobility of Upper Alsace, and the city of Hagenau. See ibid., fol. 3. On 8 January 1688, the crown in a "lettre de surcréance" granted Colmar a delay of "cinque années consecutive... pour l'aquit des debtes de la ville." AMC, CC 34, a3.
87. AMC, CC 34, a2, fol. 1r. Due to gaps in the sources, I can offer no statistics to back the regime's claim.
88. Rodolphe Reuss, *Histoire de Strasbourg depuis ses origines jusqu'à nos jours* (Paris, 1922), 284.
89. On the fiscal crisis of the 1690s, see Mandrou, *Louis XIV en son temps*, 309–21; Jean Meuvret, "Fiscalism and Public Opinion under Louis XIV," in Hatton, ed., *Louis XIV and Absolutism*, 213–22.
90. Reuss, *Histoire de Strasbourg*, 285; Livet, *L'intendance*, 485–86. On Colmar's offer, see AMC, AA 165, 27. Colmar's budget in 1693 was 34,184 livres, with an additional outlay of 41,000 paid towards the Reunion of Charges. AMC, CC 145, 1693.
91. Livet, *L'intendance*, 486.
92. In Colmar, the first capitation drew 10,807 livres from the city's inhabitants. AMC, CC 155, 1694.
93. Livet, *L'intendance*, 487.
94. AMC, AA 165, 15, fol. 2r.
95. According to reports filed with the intendant, Colmar's revenues during the critical years were as follows: 1693: 75,894 livres; 1694: 58,639 livres; 1695: 56,007 livres; 1696: 45,500 livres; 1697: 41,734 livres; 1698: 48,813 livres. AMC, CC 145, 1693–1698.
96. The *capitation* payments raised over 10,000 livres. AMC, CC 155, 1694. The demands for winter quarters varied from year to year: 1689: 10,168 livres; 1690: 14,930 livres; 1691–1693: 0; 1694: 11,520 livres; 1695: 5,172 livres; 1696: 7,500 livres. AMC, FF 43, 26–27.
97. AMC, BB 33, 21–23. See also AMC, AA 165, 15. For the impact at Strasbourg, see Hertner, *Stadtwirtschaft*, 354–68.
98. For La Grange's explanation, see AMC, BB 33, 24. For the regime's offer, see AMC, AA 165, 15, fol. 1r.
99. AMC, BB 33, 25–26.
100. AMC, BB 33, 37–38.
101. AMC, BB 33, 28a.
102. At the time Calmet held the post of *commissaire des guerres* in Sélestat. He

demanded to the intendant "ordonner à Messr. du Magistrat et communauté de la ville de Colmar de mettre le suppliant en possession de sa charge jusqu'au parfait et entièr remboursement et faire justice." AMC, BB 33, 29a, fol. 1r.

103. AMC, BB 33, 33.
104. AMC, AA 165, 30–32.
105. AMC, AA 165, 27, fols. 1v–2r.
106. AMC, AA 165, 19 & 20.
107. In 1693, the city paid 41,000 livres from its budget with 7,000 livres added in 1694. AMC, CC 145, 1693 & 1694.
108. A full list can be found in AMC, AA 165, 44–45.
109. Of the other magistrates, Johner and Güntzer advanced 150 and 100 livres respectively, while the elder statesman Andreas Sandherr does not appear among the creditors. AMC, AA 165, 45.
110. AMC, AA 165, 43, fol. 2r.
111. Andres was not a member of the society zum Waagkellar. AMC, HH 8, 131. In the city's capitation role of 1694, he is listed as "vivant de son bien" and assessed in the highest category at 60 livres. AMC, CC 155, 1694, p. 2. In 1699, just as his loan came due for repayment, Andres was coopted as a Lutheran regime member in the peasants' guild, Ackerleute. See Wertz, ed., Membres du magistrat, 1601–1700, 29. In the contract with the regime, Andres is listed as "Bürger und Handelsmann." The parties agreed "[a]lß namlich es gibt und leihet H. Johann Andres dem gemeinen wessen alhie zwey tausent Rthlr. oder Sechs tausant livres auf die sechs nechts nacheinander folgende jahr lang ohne Interest." The city for its part reserved from its farm "nach specificirt Matten, nemblich in Heyerley zwer tagen, in dem Eyerkuchen sieben tagen . . . als undt der gestalten dass er dieselbe Sechs Jahrs über gebrauchen undt an Statt der Interée nutzen und geniessen, dieselbe in guten standt, und damit sie nicht verändert werden gedächtnus erhalten, auch nach verfleissung der Sechs jahren gegen bezahl undt wider erstattung der vor gestreckte Sechs tausendt livres alhiesiger statt und gemeinen wesen widerumb abtretten undt einraumen solle." AMC, AA 165, 43.
112. On the Weinsticher and his duties, see Sittler, La viticulture, 66–67. On the contract with the creditors, see AMC, AA 165, 44, fol. 2.
113. For Le Comte, see AMC, AA 165, 77. I could not find a copy of Traeher's contract. On the difference between livres tournois and livres d'Alsace, see Livet, L'intendance, 503.
114. AMC, AA 165, 83–89.
115. Sittler, "Notice sur la famille Sandherr," 59–60. Sandherr, who was not a member of the society zum Waagkellar, was coopted into the civic regime in 1694 and became the receveur des revenus for the city. See AMC, HH 8, 131. Wertz, ed., Membres du magistrate, 1601–1700, 29. On his loan, see AMC, AA 165, 70.
116. AMC, AA 165, 69.
117. AMC, AA 165, 70, 72.
118. AMC, AA 165, 70–71.
119. AMC, AA 165, 71, fol. 2v.
120. AMC, AA 165, 74, 76.
121. Sittler, "La transformation du gouvernement," 152–53.
122. V. G. Kiernan, "State and Nation in Western Europe," Past and Present no. 31 (1967): 20–38, here at 31.

7

An Emerging Royal Administrative Center: Colmar and France, 1698–1730

Rodolphe Reuss's assessment of early eighteenth-century Colmar reflects the success of Bourbon subjugation of the city between 1673 and 1697:

> Colmar was ... the Alsatian city which most rapidly altered its physiognomy; from the first half of the eighteenth century, it became nearly French in customs and language thanks to the considerable influence of the *Conseil souverain*.[1]

Colmar's political elite responded to royal authority by embracing new attitudes toward their offices and duties. Colmar's regime had become an agent of royal power, its members integrated into the provincial system of patronage and faction. The men and women of the civic political families had to conform or be pushed aside by ambitious newcomers. The tensions between Catholics and Lutherans, between old families and new, between insiders and outsiders, fractured civic politics at the end of the seventeenth century.

In 1698 the Treaty of Ryswick confirmed French sovereignty in Alsace but ended it across the Rhine. Refugees poured from the Breisgau into Alsace, among them the *Conseil souverain*, which settled in Colmar as a privileged community of nobles. The new court planted French aristocratic culture at Colmar and fostered the gradual acculturation of the indigenous political elite.

In the early eighteenth century, Colmar's political elite faced two challenges: one from below and one from above. In 1711 a regime member, Johann Jacob Sonntag, led a protest movement against the magistrate, in which he appealed to the city's Imperial political traditions by calling on the crown, as a higher authority, to step in to adjudicate local political abuses.[2] Sonntag's protest failed, but he drew support from the lower-middle-class artisans, who formed the backbone of Colmar's traditional political community. His complaint reiterated the political frustrations that they had first voiced in the 1690s. In the wake of Sonntag's protest, the regime's leaders drew closer to the crown and further from their civic roots. After the death of Louis XIV in 1715, the regime weathered a second assault on its practices. Officials in the Regency challenged the close familial relations within Colmar's political elite, and under pressure, the Colmarians reformed recruiting practices and accepted some new men into office. Henceforth, however, pressures against the regime from royal authorities became more sporadic and less effective, while civic officials became more comfortable with their roles as royal agents.

I. THE *CONSEIL SOUVERAIN* AND CIVIC POLITICAL CULTURE, 1698–1715

The Treaty of Ryswick in 1697 ended the War of the League of Augsburg and forced France to restore extensive territories to Austria, including the Breisgau and the fortress at Breisach. The treaty also completed Colmar's separation from the empire and legitimized Bourbon sovereignty in Alsace.[3] The Upper Rhine now became the boundary between France and the Holy Roman Empire, and the royal government worked to strengthen its control over this critical frontier province. The surrender of Breisach necessitated the construction of Vauban's great fortress at Neuf-Brisach, along with an extensive network of supply canals, which employed Colmarian craftsmen for many years.[4] The French did not strengthen Colmar's own walls, though the city would serve the royal army as a supply depot and as a center for the treatment of sick and wounded soldiers. Many Colmarians profited from outfitting the royal army.[5]

In 1698 the crown transferred its administrative and judicial organs from Breisach to Colmar, which became the seat of royal government in Upper Alsace.[6] In the upper levels of the royal administration, officials came from Paris to serve briefly and move on to a new post, but much of the day-to-day operations fell to officials who settled permanently in the region. These officials either held noble status or aspired to it. In cities such as Colmar, royal agents, such as those assisting the *Conseil souverain*, formed the pinnacle of the social structure.[7]

The *Conseil souverain d'Alsace*, established in 1656 by Colbert de Croissy, had undergone several metamorphoses.[8] The intendant had first attempted to establish it at Colmar to extend royal jurisdiction over the Decapolis. That effort failed, and the court's authority remained circumscribed to the "territories of old dominion." Between 1663 and 1673, the much reduced *Conseil provincial* at Ensisheim answered to the Parlement in Metz. In 1673 the crown restored sovereign status to the Alsatian court, and La Grange used it as a tool in extending royal sovereignty. The *Conseil souverain* played a critical role in the "reunion" drive of the 1680s from its new center at Breisach. In 1681 the court moved again to the island fortress on the Rhine known as the "straw city." The *conseillers* found the environment unpleasant and the court met irregularly. Despite its less active role, in 1694 Louis XIV expanded the council to two chambers and offered its offices for sale with hereditary rights.[9]

The stipulations of the Peace of Ryswick called for the demolition of the "straw city," and the council again found itself homeless. At this juncture, the Parlement of Metz nearly succeeded in suppressing the chamber, but the Alsatian intendant, La Fond, convinced the king of the importance of the *Conseil souverain*. François Dietremann, a *conseiller* himself, arranged the move to Colmar, where the *Conseil souverain* set up offices in the city hall, which had also accommodated the society *zum Waagkeller*. Colmar was a pleasant environment for the court, and soon, with its procedures regularized and streamlined, it faced a rapidly expanding caseload. The *Conseil souverain* and the city grew together in importance, and Colmar became the provincial legal capital with jurisdiction even over mighty Strasbourg.[10] The *conseillers* overshadowed the municipal regime and restructured the social relations and attitudes of the civic elite. The court became a source of local pride and income. Many members of the elite, flushed with prosperity, eagerly adopted French customs and language, and some acquired the tastes and social consciousness of a provincial robe nobility.

The *conseillers*, all Catholics, transformed the community's confessional relations overnight. In the 1680s and 1690s the royal government had waged a campaign against the rights of Colmar's Lutherans. Jesuits and Capuchins arrived along with the *Conseil souverain* to revive civic Catholic culture, which softened overt pressure on Colmar's Lutherans.[11] Inspired or perhaps threatened by the new houses, the canons of St. Martin's also began a systematic reform.[12] French culture penetrated deeply into Colmar's Catholic social strata, while most Lutherans remained outsiders, though they did not emigrate to the extent that the Strasbourgeois did.[13] The city's new economic prosperity spilled across confessional lines and helped to persuade many Lutherans to stay.

The Peace of Ryswick brought only a brief respite in the prolonged struggle between Louis XIV and the Habsburgs over the disputed Spanish succession. When the sickly Charles II of Spain finally died in 1702, war returned. The royal government, already financially exhausted, resorted to credit schemes to keep its troops in the field. The arrival of the *Conseil souverain* had reinforced Colmar's growing role as a center of governmental finance and tax collection in Upper Alsace. After 1698 Colmar joined Strasbourg and Landau as the three centers for *receveurs particuliers* of royal taxes in the province.[14] The French officials who arrived with the *Conseil souverain* were deeply committed to the system of finance and annuities that attracted investments from the old regime's elite. More and more, Colmarians also assumed this lifestyle, as both Catholics and Lutherans alike abandoned commerce and became *rentiers*.[15] As the war dragged on, the crown's fiscal agents found it increasingly difficult to raise loans as interest rates and the values of the *rentes* fluctuated wildly. The Colmarians, far from the financial center, profited little from speculation but worried about the government's solvency.

Eighteenth-century Colmar sat on the kingdom's periphery. The central government's response to local problems could take a month, and day-by-day governing depended on local officials. Claude Le Pelletier de La Houssaye, intendant in Alsace from 1699 to 1716, was an ambitious bureaucrat with strong ties to Versailles. Often at Versailles or with the army, he relied on his assistants to handle most problems.[16] François Dietremann, who was simultaneously *subdélégué*, *préteur royal*, and a *conseiller* in the *Conseil souverain*, served as an important broker in provincial politics, and his accumulated personal influence accelerated Colmar's integration into the royal administration. Dietremann controlled a broad network of local patronage with numerous clients, but he was not the only official with clients and interests in civic politics. The Peace of Utrecht in 1713 ended war in Europe until 1740, and the death of Louis XIV in 1715 brought a softening of pressure from the central government. In the relaxed atmosphere after 1715, the city experienced firsthand the aristocratic infighting between the city's *commandant*, Chauvigny, and the *Conseil souverain*.[17] Most civic leaders aligned closely with the *Conseil*, which had handed out sufficient favors to generate the needed loyalty. The civic officials moved comfortably in this world of aristocratic privilege and factional self-interest. Some Colmarians who were not regime members sought entry into the system through their own means.

II. PRIVILEGE AND INVESTMENT: THE POSTMASTERS

Under French rule, more and more often, civic political disputes grew out of issues of personal privilege. When in 1693 the regime had sought loans to protect its offices, most major investors offered money in exchange for personal privileges. For his loan, Johann Andres had acquired the right to exploit the communal meadows, and Johann Jacob Sandherr assumed the office of *receveur général* for his. When the regime could not reimburse him, he and his descendants received perpetual exemption from taxes.[18] By the early eighteenth century, the distributing and safeguarding of personal privileges had become an important function for the civic regime.

The regime also worked to maintain its influence in directing the local economy, and in this capacity issues of privilege became intertwined with market rights. For example, in 1697 two Savoyard merchants attempted to set up shop in the city without joining the merchants' guild and paying traditional taxes. The civic regime successfully appealed to the intendant to force the outsiders to observe local customs and pay the required taxes.[19] In 1709 the municipal officials looked the other way while Johann Ulrich Goll, a wealthy Lutheran from an old patrician family, conducted private banking in direct opposition to a royal privilege granted to a M. Postan, an outsider.[20] In 1720 the civic leaders sought the authority to restrict the expansion of local vineyards in order to restore the quality and prices of

Colmar's wines.[21] Colmar's leaders understood that the royal government was the ultimate source of privilege and mercantilist policy, but they attempted to manage the policy for their own interests.

The linkage between local interest and the royal system sometimes broke down. In the 1720s the regime engaged in a long and bitter court struggle with Johann Jacob Schneider over his privileges as royal postmaster. Colmar had maintained a post house since the Middle Ages, and in 1682 Louvois incorporated Colmar's postal service into the royal system. From 1682 until 1686, Johann Andres, a local Lutheran, had served as royal postmaster. Andreas Sandherr, the son of the Lutheran Stettmeister, assumed the post in 1686. On Sandherr's death in 1706 Schneider, his son-in-law, succeeded him.[22] The postmaster's privileges were associated with his official activities, but he also operated a tavern and guest house which could accommodate nonofficial clients.

In 1661 the royal government exempted the kingdom's postmasters from the retail excise on wine, and twenty years later the crown waived property taxes for the postmasters' land used to provision the post horses. In 1701 the crown added exemption from quartering troops and from any taxes levied in lieu of housing soldiers.[23] These privileges represented substantial financial benefits to the postmaster. Furthermore, he received an annual salary of 600 livres, which equalled that of a magistrate. Unlike a magistrate, however, the postmaster by his very position possessed a source of personal income.[24]

The struggle between Schneider and the regime did not center on his right to royal grants, but rather on how Schneider had used his grants to increase his profits. In November 1718, the regime responded to a complaint from the city's tax farmers by fining Schneider 20 livres for butchering a heifer on his property the previous September without paying the municipal tax.[25] Schneider responded with a petition to the intendant seeking to protect his privileges.[26] The municipal regime retorted that they only sought to end Schneider's abuse of office. Schneider, they noted, owned one of the largest hostels in town, which was large enough to accommodate regional assemblies of craftsmen and all the cattle drovers who attended the city's quarterly fairs.[27] The civic regime argued that the royal privileges were to protect the postmaster, his family, and his official guests from local taxation. Schneider, however, had extended the privilege to cover all activities in his house.[28] The regime recognized the problems of sorting out official from unofficial activities, so they requested that the intendant set a ceiling on Schneider's exemption, which Andreas Sandherr had previously accepted. Schneider, they argued, should not use his privileges beyond the king's intention to facilitate postal services.[29] The regime concluded that Schneider's extensions came at the expense of his fellow citizens and communal revenues. After heated name-calling, the intendant set the limits.[30]

The municipal regime's dispute with Schneider demonstrates the complexity of privilege in eighteenth-century Colmar. In Imperial law, corporate privileges were contractual, and they formed part of the constitutional network supported by local and provincial custom. Under Bourbon rule, privilege was a gift of the king, and the system lost its contractual checks. Individuals claimed official privileges from royal grants, which in Colmar had filtered down through the royal patronage system under the protection of royal agents. The regime found itself in the position of policing abuses of privilege it did not control. Under fire, the civic leaders depended on contacts within the royal governments, and as time passed the regime members broadened and deepened those contacts.

III. The Changing Face of the Civic Regime

The migration of royal officials from the Breisgau following the Peace of Ryswick brought a cohort of talented and ambitious men into Colmar. Many of these men courted patrons to find employment in the *Conseil souverain* or the civic regime. By 1702 many of the regime members who were key players during the transition to Bourbon rule, were dead.[31] Only Samuel Röttlin, who was both city clerk and councilor, had political experience which antedated the French takeover in 1673.[32] Three other Lutheran councilors, Johann Georg Herr, Hans Jacob Fix, and Johann Heinrich Bössner, had entered city politics before the royal call for parity in 1680. Otherwise, the regime members had only known conditions under royal power and patronage, and they looked back on civic independence from afar.

Despite the presence of an enlarged and enriched Catholic elite, provincial officials continued to honor confessional parity, which now became the safeguard of Lutheran political rights. In 1698 the deaths of two Lutheran magistrates, Andreas Sandherr and Ambrosius Riegger, led to the appointment of the first new Lutheran magistrates since before 1680, and these men were selected by a caucus of Colmar's Lutheran leaders.[33] The new magistrates, Johann Buob, who was a lawyer, and Johann Benedict Schneider, a financier with a large estate of rural properties, were both descendants of important Lutheran families whose political roots extended back before the Thirty Years' War.[34] The royal officials would continue to support confessional parity until the end of the old regime, and as late as 1728 the intendant thwarted efforts by Dietremann and the Catholic magistrates to circumvent the practice.[35]

For the city's Catholic magistrates, the impact of the provincial administrators was more direct. The death of François Seraffond in 1700 led to the appointment of Niclaus Schepplin, a former *Bürgermeister* in French-controlled Breisach and an official in the *Conseil souverain*, who had sought refuge in Colmar in 1697. His appointment solidified the ties between the *Conseil souverain* and the Catholics in the civic regime.[36] In 1702 Madamé, Johner, and Röttlin were the senior members in the magistrate, but a few years later only Madamé remained. On Johner's death in April 1707, the civic regime selected his son, Johann Frantz, a lawyer, as his replacement with the intendant's approval.[37] When the Lutheran city clerk, Samuel Röttlin, died the following year, the intendant again acknowledged the regime's candidate, the city physician Georg Benjamin Gloxin, to replace him.[38] During the first decade of the eighteenth century, the regime continued to nominate its successors with the approval of the intendant.

Of the twenty-one councilors serving in 1702, ten had begun their careers before 1685, and to a man they were native Colmarians.[39] The others had joined the regime since the Reunion of Charges in 1692, and their backgrounds highlight the dramatic shift in the city's political environment.[40] Among the seven new Lutherans were two members each of the Andres and Sandherr families, both of which had committed heavily to financing the Reunion of Charges. All but one Lutheran, Georg Wilhelm Faber, were native Colmarians from established families. Faber was a merchant from Birckenfeld in the Palatinate, and he may have migrated into Alsace when the prince von Birckenfeld inherited the domains of the counts von Rappolstein. Among the four Catholics, Johann Tanner, a wheelwright, and Christian Reichstetter, an innkeeper, were from local families with guild roots. Georg Roman Baumhauer was a financier from Breisach, and Johann Peter Welsch was the administrator for the Dominican convent of Unterlinden and a native of Altkirch, an important ecclesiastical center in the former Austrian territories in Upper Alsace. The patterns suggest the increased insularity of the Lutheran elite and the tension between old families and new families among Catholics.

By 1702 the council of XIII had ceased to exist, though Wendlin Güntzer would hold the honorific title of XIIIer from his electoral defeat in 1691 until his death in 1703.[41] Under the system of parity each of the ten guilds was assigned a Lutheran and a Catholic councilor, who were not necessarily members of the guilds they represented. In 1702 only six of the twenty councilors represented their guilds of origin. Nevertheless all ten guilds had a least one member in the regime, though one-third (nine of twenty-five) were members of the merchants' guild (*zur Treue*). The butchers' (*zum Löwen*), the bakers' (*zum Kränzchen*), the leather workers' (*zum Wohlleben*), and the vineyard workers' (*Rebleute*) guilds had only one representative each. These men were true guildmasters, but all had joined the regime before 1682. The new systems of patronage would end direct connection between the guilds and the regime when these men died.

The intendant seldom interfered with local elections, particularly if the candidates were Lutherans. For example, in 1706, when two Lutheran council seats became vacant, the intendant only requested "two appropriate candidates." In 1712, however, the intendant recommended the appointment of Johann Rudolph Graff, who was the candidate of the prince von Birckenfeld, to the vacant Lutheran seat in the magistrate.[42] Graff's candidacy was an anomaly, apart from which a narrow circle of Lutheran oligarchs, such as the Andreses and Sandherrs, predominated among civic Lutherans.

In 1708 the intendant made one final structural adjustment to Colmar's regime when La Houssaye used the death of Samuel Röttlin, the city clerk, as an opportunity to confessionally balance the magistrate. The intendant wanted a Catholic in this critical post and appointed Johann Jacob Schepplin, the brother of the Stettmeister Niclaus, as city clerk. To placate the Lutherans a new Stettmeister position was created and granted to the city physician Georg Benjamin Gloxin. Previously, to assure parity, the crown had counted the Lutheran city clerk among the magistrates. To ensure parity in the future, royal officials treated the city clerk as a royal appointment which was limited to Catholics.[43] Schepplin's commission also marked the first time that two members of the same family worked together in magisterial chambers.

By 1710 most of the older political generation had passed away. Only four of the twenty-six regime members had begun their careers before the Reunion of Charges. The old guard, Johann Jacob Madamé, Claus Hurst, Martin Wöhrlin, and Johann Haffner, were all Catholics. In terms of political experience, the civic regime in 1710 was the youngest since the Counter-Reformation in 1628. For the Lutherans, all thirteen regime members were sons of citizens or civic officials. Family ties were tight, and three members of the Andres family sat in the council chambers. Six of the Lutherans were members of the merchants' guild. Among the others the financier, Johann Benedict Schneider (*zum Haspel*), and the court clerk, Adam Syffert (*Rebleute*), were not true guild representatives. Some new men, Johann Jacob Sonntag, Zacharius Klein, and Johannes Bentz, had joined the Protestant elite, but overall the Lutherans comprised a small circle of power. Ten of the thirteen Catholics were also at least second-generation Colmarians. Of the others, Schepplin, the former *Bürgermeister* from Breisach, and Pierre Milly were also officials in the *Conseil souverain*, while Johann Peter Welsch from Altkirch retained his post as administrator for the Unterlinden convent. Among the local Catholics, political dynasties had emerged, such as the Johners, the Seraffonds, and the Reichstetters. Guild membership carried less meaning for Catholics, and Johann Frantz Johner, Jean-François Seraffond, and Pierre Milly had not inscribed in a guild. Outside that inner circle, the remaining Catholic officials claimed membership in seven guilds, though this included the four old-timers. There was no effort to coordinate guild membership with guild representation, though once again six of twenty councilors represented their guild of origin and every guild had at least one representative.

In the last years of Louis XIV's reign, the magistrate sustained its place at the center of civic politics, and membership remained the prerogative of political insiders among the city's leading families. The magistrate had lost its political and military powers, but it conserved its rights to regulate communal police and judicial affairs. The Obristmeister had become a less exclusive office, and it rotated more freely among the magistrates, who, despite restrictions, still exercised fiscal powers, supervising tax assessments and distributing municipal revenues.[44] Nevertheless, the *préteur royal*, François

Dietremann, controlled day-to-day politics. Dietremann, who had held the post since 1695, had successfully accumulated titles, benefits, and influence. He was the king's man, but he also looked after the city's needs and defended them when necessary. Dietremann's power gave him control over an extensive patronage system. He arranged the appointment of local abbots and curés; he influenced the selection of village administrators; and his power over the civic regime must have been significant. He had to work with these men daily.[45] In all, the new politics had disenfranchised the leading guildsmen and isolated ambitious men without proper patrons.

Political patronage still emanated from the regime: its members possessed personal privileges and could dispense other exemptions and rights. Personal privileges were most obvious in regards to taxation, which made them coveted by ambitious men and despised by the nonprivileged. A growing part of the community held exemptions: the members of the *Conseil souverain*, the residents of religious houses, the Lutheran clergy, numerous royal officials, many of the regime's agents, and even some regime members. Both Catholics and Lutherans claimed privileges, and some men of modest means, such as gatekeepers or policemen, paid nominal taxes. More often, however, privilege belonged to the wealthiest and most educated part of the populace, with the result that a growing rift had emerged between Colmar's official community and the taxpaying citizenry.

The wars at the end of Louis XIV's reign brought economic dislocation and impoverishment. In Colmar many poor citizens found themselves overwhelmed by their tax obligations, and the tax farmers turned to the regime to recoup arrears. Municipal officials then surtaxed the people who lacked exemptions but who could pay. The fiscal weight carried by the middling groups of the city eventually fueled a tax revolt combined with a political reform movement. Its leader, Johann Jacob Sonntag, was a regime member; but its spirit emanated from the alienated master craftsmen—the former backbone of the city's political community—whose frustrations exploded in 1711.

IV. THE SONNTAG AFFAIR

On 1 October 1711 a contingent of the provincial police force (*maréchaussée*) came from Strasbourg to arrest Johann Jacob Sonntag. Sonntag, an apothecary, a Lutheran churchwarden, a regime member, and one of the richest men in the city, was also the self-proclaimed head of a civic reform movement. The lieutenant and his troop paraded Sonntag through the city's winding streets with deliberate slowness to broadcast his defeat before the entire community. They then escorted him to Strasbourg, where Sonntag received a tongue-lashing from the intendant, La Houssaye, and a six-month prison term. During the ensuing weeks, his supporters trickled into Strasbourg one-by-one to beg the intendant's forgiveness or to serve a brief prison sentence.[46]

Throughout the summer of 1711, Sonntag had orchestrated a very traditional civic protest movement against Colmar's magistrates. He brandished the royal decree of 1683, which had called for triennial elections of municipal officeholders throughout the kingdom and was not enforced at Colmar, as the tool to gain official sanction from the royal government for his protest. Sonntag expected the local royal officials to enforce the king's will. To further his cause, Sonntag drew up a list of grievances against the civic regime and examples of "misgovernment." La Houssaye sent a copy of Sonntag's grievances to Colmar's magistrate and demanded a point-by-point response. Sonntag's petition and the magistrate's response document two fully articulated and distinct political worldviews. Sonntag's call for justice founded on communal "rights and traditional practices" in the interest of the "public good" recalled the old civic community embedded in Imperial traditions.[47] The magistrate clearly perceived its place to be in royal provincial administration, where officeholding and clientage intermeshed. The intendant supported the magistrate, and Sonntag soon found himself in irons.

Sonntag's referendum drew on deep-seated anger among the citizenry. As we have seen, the triennial elections generated intense political debate between the magistrates and the jurors in the 1690s. Sonntag had brought the public opposition to Colmar's magistrate to the surface again, but the movement also drew on personal ambition. Sonntag's father had settled in Colmar after the Thirty Years' War. Although the magistrate claimed that Sonntag was a man of mediocre fortune, he was listed among the top 2% of the city's taxpayers in the first *capitation* roll in 1694. Despite his fortune Sonntag behaved like a political outsider. He had not, for example, advanced capital in 1693 to help protect the regime's offices.[48] In 1703 he married the widow of one of Colmar's wealthiest citizens, Elias Lang, and entered the local economic elite.[49] Like the founders of other civic dynasties, such as the Golls and the Andres, Sonntag might not expect political office, but he could anticipate that his sons and daughters would intermarry with the city's Lutheran oligarchs. Sonntag probably belonged with the other apothecaries to *zur Treue*, but he was never inscribed in the guild. Nevertheless, in 1704 he was selected to represent the city's gardeners in *zum Haspel* and served alternatively as guildmaster and councilor until 1710.[50] He made few friends among the elite. The magistrate claimed that Sonntag possessed

> a proud, restless, and rowdy spirit, [given to] grumbling much of the time when it is a question of contributing the least thing to the King's service, he who is one of the wealthiest in the city as regards to his estate . . . and who nevertheless only would have all the weight of the taxes fall on the middling folk (*les moyens*) and other poor citizens of this city.[51]

This wealthy and disgruntled apothecary wanted to be a magistrate, but he realized that he lacked the family connections and the commitment to the Lutheran patronage system to achieve his goal. So in the summer of 1711, he decided to take his case to the community and the crown.

In mid-July, Sonntag had begun to hold informal assemblies in Colmar in which the citizens vented their anger over taxes.[52] The news of the assemblies reached La Houssaye, who waited patiently at Strasbourg. In late July, he received an anonymous letter, which contained a direct attack on the *préteur royal*, Dietremann.[53] During the height of the troubles, the principle royal agents, La Houssaye, his secretary Rudolph Graff, and Dietremann, showed significant concern that the movement could damage their reputations at Court. Once La Houssaye had a copy of Sonntag's petition, he informed Dietremann that he could rest easy about "agitation of the unquiet spirits at Colmar," because the intendant had sent a letter to the Court which heaped ridicule on the movement.[54] Graff also quickly calmed Dietremann's concerns, for he had seen the petition and informed the *préteur royal* that it did not mention him by name.[55] La Houssaye pressed Sonntag on whether he had forwarded the petition to Paris. When Sonntag replied that he had not, the intendant sharply warned him not to do so.[56] Graff later marvelled to Dietremann over the astute handling of the affair by the intendant:

> I admire the wisdom of this lord to have acted mildly and given the rebel time to push his insolence up to the point that he pushed it, in order to have the means to chastise him [Sonntag] . . . and to cut his complaints by the roots.[57]

Having secured their personal interests, the royal agents paid little attention to the specific complaints. For them it was a question of preserving the appearance of order.

On 3 August Sonntag appeared at Strasbourg with Claus Hurst, a Catholic councilor from *Ackerleute*, to deliver a petition with eighty-three signatures to the intendant. The document called for uniform tax assessment and the public accounting of municipal revenues, plus the enforcement of the edict of 1683, which limited Alsatian magisterial terms to three years.[58] La Houssaye received the petitioners cordially and asked for time to examine the document. When they returned the following day, the intendant gave Sonntag and Hurst a tongue-lashing and sent the "self-proclaimed republicans" back to Colmar to await his decision.[59]

Graff and Dietremann anticipated that decision and immediately began to discuss possible replacements for Sonntag. The renewal of the regime and the citizen's oaths passed on 16 August without a "popular" referendum on the magistrate's policies, and for the moment Sonntag remained in office.[60] Meanwhile, the magistrate worked to discredit Sonntag by claiming that his petition, written in French, was incomprehensible to most of his supporters. The magistrates found at least one signer, Anton Reichart, who admitted that he was ignorant of French and had been duped by Sonntag into believing that the petition only challenged the regime's handling of inheritances.[61] Reichart then signed a document in opposition to Sonntag which was also written in French.

Sonntag responded by taking the traditional Imperial step of having his grievances and the edict, which had called for triennial elections, published at Basel in both French and German. This printed grievance sheet, drawn up when many began to suspect that he was in disgrace, broadened his public support at Colmar, where it garnered 220 signatures, which equalled roughly one-fifth of the taxpaying householders.[62] The second petition vindicated Sonntag with Colmar's political community but precipitated his arrest and his public humiliation at the hands of the royal government.[63] He was imprisoned without fixed term and released after six months. His leading followers received face-to-face reprimands from the intendant. The movement had been effectively broken without resolving the problems that had generated it.[64]

Georges Livet, in his analysis of Sonntag's movement, has emphasized the political ambitions of the leaders. One of Sonntag's associates, Jean-Baptiste Paillot, *sergent royal* and a carriage master, had hoped to become *procureur fiscal*; and Sonntag certainly had political aspirations.[65] Hurst had received eight votes for the magistrate in 1691, but it is unclear whether he sought higher office. Livet argues further that the movement was not an uprising of the poor, so that it lacked "social" impetus. Many of Sonntag's supporters were, according to Livet, among Colmar's rich, who were incensed over a new inheritance tax. The movement also lacked a confessional character because its leaders came from both parishes. Finally, Livet contends that the movement was not "factional," because the familial systems of patronage ensured political solidarity within the regime.[66]

Livet's assessment is incorrect, for Sonntag's movement did reflect factionalism in Colmar's political community. The two confessional elites had developed solid systems of patronage within the city's government since 1680 which excluded many ambitious men. Hurst, who had descended from an old Colmarian family of tenant farmers, lacked the education, language skills, and connections to move freely into the new Catholic elite dominated by men like Johann Frantz Johner, Jean-François Seraffond, and the Schepplin brothers. The circumscribed network of patronage available to the Lutherans restricted the careers of the recently rich and influential, such as Sonntag. Thwarted ambition motivated the ringleaders, but what of the signers?

Sonntag's strategy made sense in an Imperial context, where citizen leaders traditionally turned to outside powers to help keep the municipal regime in line.[67] The strategy appealed to those citizens who had been most displaced by the new system of power and privilege: the master artisan guildsmen, who had been the backbone of the old community-based political structure, in which they had played significant roles through the election of guildmasters and as jurors. Sonntag's strategy and his political vision appealed to the traditions of the Imperial city, but Colmar was no longer part of the empire. The petition lacked a clear political program, but it harbored a strong sense of traditional civic politics, for it attacked the new system of personal privilege and official patronage and sought to restore a proper order in civic political life.[68] That old order had become an anachronism, and the affair demonstrated the gulf between Colmar's traditional political values and the new ethos of the magistrate.

Sonntag's proposal assumed that the magistrate's unwillingness to hold elections was in defiance of royal will. As he saw it "the magistrates preferred their own interests to the will of the king and the public's welfare and utility, so they have so scorned the *arrêt* that they have only executed it once since its publication."[69] The six magistrates, according to the petitioners, circulated the offices among themselves and "had authority so strongly perpetuated and maintained in their offices that they only abandoned them on death."[70] Sonntag may have known that the intendant and *préteur royal* had suspended elections, but publicizing the *arrêt* stirred up popular animosity against magisterial conspiracy and provided leverage for negotiations because the *arrêt* was still in force.

The petitioners singled out the office of *procureur fiscal* as the center of abuse. This post, coveted by Paillot, had been in the hands of the Schultheiss "for more than twenty-six years." This official had fostered tax privileges which violated traditional community norms. The petitioners complained that the magistrates had come to assess taxes

in such a way that they are the sole masters of all, setting tax levies in money, kind, and foraging at such sums and quantities as seem good to them without ever informing anyone or rendering a public account, no more so than for the revenues of the city which are very considerable.[71]

The petitioners wanted to subject the office to public accounting and annual elections by the whole community.

The petition then turned directly to the question of the municipal taxes, and in particular the *Gewerff* registers. The tax farmer received the *Gewerff* register from the regime, and at the end of his farm he returned it to the municipal officials with a list of arrears or defaults. The regime then conducted a special levy among its more solvent citizens to pay the tax farmer. The middling men of the town found themselves caught. The general rise in the taxes had impoverished many Colmarians, and the special levy had grown yearly. Many householders had emigrated due to the burden and the nonprivileged wealthy found themselves shouldering the growing weight of taxes to accommodate the profits of the privileged tax farmers.[72]

The fiscal practices of the time had created an environment in which misery and privilege shared public space. But the petitioners felt that their misery was exacerbated by the magistrate, because

one never sees a fixed and just rate for the levying of the *taille*, commonly called the *Gewerff*, as it is done elsewhere in the province; the civic magistrates base it on an imaginary estimation suitable only to their interests for their family, and friends; [based on] this [rate] which sets the standard for all the ordinary and extraordinary taxes, they burden and crush those who meet with their caprice while they exempt and lessen others from it.[73]

The petitioners turned to the intendant to end the abuses and restore communal harmony. In this appeal to outside assistance, the petitioners called for something like an Imperial commission.[74]

The petitioners concluded by proposing a number of specific reforms. They called for the enforcement of the arrêt of 1683 and the election of new magistrates "by plurality of votes of citizens and inhabitants of Colmar" to end abuses. They envisioned a complete turnover of six posts every three years, with a general public accounting of magisterial management of the public trust. Guildmasters alone should assess the Gewerff without personal exemptions for the magistrates or the procureur fiscal. The city's tax farmers should not be reimbursed for uncollected revenues. The magistrates, with the exception of the Obristmeister, Schultheiss, and city clerk, should quarter troops in their homes. Finally, the community should elect quartermasters and punish them if they acted unfairly.[75] Sonntag's historical image of traditional civic politics was faulty, but his desire to bind the regime's authority once again to the citizenry reflected the old Imperial principles, the Grundwerte, if not actual traditional practice, for which he found widespread support within the community. Sonntag's reforms also looked forward in that his call for election by plurality of voices would have produced a "republican" community-based polity which was more modern than medieval.

Who were Sonntag's supporters? The signers of the first petition may be compared with the citizens as a whole through an analysis of the Gewerff lists of 1710 (see table 7.1). Sixty-two of the original seventy-four names appear in the tax registers, and many who do not were manants. Sonntag's supporters represent, as they claimed, the substantial taxpayers in the community, for they paid almost twice the assessment of the average taxpayer. Furthermore, they represented specific economic interests within the community. The three agricultural guilds accounted for 31% of the taxpayers in the city but only 13% of the petitioners, and the guild zum Löwen provided only one signer. Sonntag drew most of his strength from the middling merchants and craftsmen in zur Treue, the tanners and shoemakers in zum Wohlleben, and the smiths and builders in zum Holderbaum. The protest attracted many more Lutherans than Catholics. At least forty-seven (64.4%) of the petitioners attended Lutheran services, while only twenty (27.4%) are known to have been Catholics. Catholics probably figure strongly among the confessionally unidentifiable signers, who were primarily manants, for many of them carried French patronyms. Sonntag's ambition and political vision attracted the forgotten community leaders, as Colmar moved into a new social, cultural, and political system. His view of Colmar's traditional political order may have been myopic, but the alienation expressed in the petition was sharply focused.

TABLE 7.1
Sonntag Affair: Guild Background of Petitioners

GUILD	CITY AS WHOLE (no.)	(%)	PETITIONERS (no.)	(%)
Treue	155	15.3	17	27.4
Riesen	104	10.3	6	9.6
Ackerleute	111	11.0	3	4.8
Haspel	76	7.5	2	3.2
Rebleute	126	12.5	3	4.8
Kränzchen	73	7.2	6	9.6
Löwen	67	6.6	1	1.6
Holderbaum	99	9.8	9	14.5
Adler	69	6.8	4	6.4
Wohlleben	130	12.9	12	19.3
Total	1,010	100.0	62	100.0
AVERAGE YEAR OF GUILD INSCRIPTION	1693		1692	
AVERAGE ESTATE	364 fl.		724 fl.	

The magistrates' response to Sonntag's petition demonstrates clearly how deeply their new mentality as *officiers* had taken hold of them. They sought to denigrate their opponents by picturing them as outsiders and poor subjects. The petitioners were "unquiet spirits" led by Sonntag, whom the magistrates characterized as a constant troublemaker, and Hurst, "a very rich but entirely simple-minded man who lets himself be led about by anyone."[76] As for Sonntag's principal supporters, the regime passed off "these so-called notable citizens" as "foreigners, recently established in Colmar, men nearly always rebellious and like their leaders always grumbling when it comes to paying their taxes although their assessments are very modest."[77] Here the regime misrepresented their opponents, whose patronyms—Riegger, Goll, Bössner, Dürninger, Windholtz, and Baccara—were among the oldest in the community. The regime underestimated the communal power of this assembly, which later rallied one-fifth of the householders to sign Sonntag's second petition.

If they sought to misrepresent their opponents, the magistrates were very careful to clearly present their own dilemma, caught as they were between the royal government and the citizens. They flatly informed the intendant that

> there was nothing new in the formation of factions against the magistrates who are charged to collect the king's impositions; and since these troublemakers do not dare to complain against his Majesty they throw the blame on the magistrate.[78]

They further reminded the intendant that "not one of them had continued in office except by your express order." The magistrates recognized that the *arrêt* of 1683 was still in effect, but they felt that the intendant kept them because they were effective.[79] Moreover, they justified the suppression of elections, once again, because they had offered their personal fortunes several times as collateral for loans to the city so that it could meet its fiscal obligations. They simply could not trust the collection for repayment to someone else.[80] Their personal investments and their political offices were interconnected.

The civic leaders then addressed themselves to Sonntag's specific complaints. They agreed that the *procureur fiscal* alone controlled tax collection, but they countered that the system was just and inexpensive. The office alternated annually between a Lutheran and a Catholic magistrate, and the official received no wages but a simple tax exemption. They did not fear that La Houssaye might decide to end their magisterial appointments, because they had served him well. They pleaded with him, however, to prevent the free election of the *procureur fiscal*, first, because it would be expensive and a disservice to the community, and, secondly, because "change and novelties are always prejudicial and ought to be avoided at all cost."[81] Control of this office was obviously crucial to their power. All Colmarians were subject to the *Gewerff*, which formed the basis for all other levies, and its assessment was the one important function that the civic leaders still commanded.[82] The magistrates pointed out that the petitioners had misrepresented the tax collection system, for they followed the communal traditions and assembled the full regime each year to conduct the assessment. The guildmasters under oath levied the assessment for their respective guilds, and according to the magistrates, the system was impartial.

Finally, they defended their tax privileges as the natural prerogatives of office. As part of their wages, they were free of quartering troops and exempt from all extraordinary taxes, except the *capitation*. They added that this exemption was normal in the province and had been practiced in Colmar since 1682.[83] The magistrates then gave a long description of what parts of the civic fisc they still controlled. They administered the harvest of wood, wine, grain, and hay, which helped pay municipal wages or was sold for the profit of the city. The regime often leased communal properties to private investors at market rates. The revenues accrued from fiscal administration were critical to civic solvency, but the distribution of leaseholds and communal rights to private investors often generated jealousies. Thus, the magistrate discussed revenue management in a special and secret joint session. Despite their careful management, the regime was in debt, which, they claimed derived from the extraordinary tax demands levied on the city since 1693 and not from mismanagement. In the eyes of the magistrates, Louis XIV's wars had driven the regime to bankruptcy and alienated them from their citizens.[84]

Sonntag's movement did not expose unusual personal corruption but rather the nature of civic politics in the early eighteenth century. The magistrates' control of tax assessment, their personal exemptions, their access to communal properties, and their close association with the municipal tax farmers were normal features of Bourbon civic politics, though they seemed unfair to the common citizenry. The magistrates argued that the citizenry had become unruly subjects, who badgered the regime with complaints and who could not be trusted to handle political responsibilities. Colmar's magistrates and citizens perceived the civic world in two distinct and contradictory contexts. The magistrates may have spoken Alemannic at home, but their political discourse was distinctly French. The civic political system fit neatly into the network of patronage and largesse which governed French political behavior at the end of the reign of Louis XIV. The magistrate had adapted to French policy and built their defense on their conformity to the will of the intendant, their good service to the king, and their rights as *officiers*.

The petitioners were rich and poor, Catholics and Lutherans, recent immigrants and members of old established families. The movement was fueled by frustration, jealousies, and envy of people who had lived closely together through hard times. Its ideological vision was a myopic and anachronistic attachment to Imperial communal norms. The close working relationship that had emerged between provincial royal officials and Colmar's regime led to the movement's swift and total suppression. The Sonntag affair marked the last vestige of Imperial political life in Colmar. By Louis XIV's death, the regime, which had once clung so fiercely to its traditional rights and privileges, had learned a new political vocabulary of personal privilege and royal service.

V. Civic Factions and Patronage under the Regency

The death of the king in 1715 shook the entire fabric of the royal government. Struggles among the regents of the young Louis XV disrupted the workings of provincial administration throughout the kingdom. In Alsace the first years of the Regency saw the strengthening of some systems of patronage and brief skirmishes between conflicting factions.[85] In Colmar this produced infighting among the local French administrative *officiers*, as the *commandant*, Claude de Chauvigny, dueled for influence with François Dietremann.[86]

The dispute had been brewing since Sonntag's dismissal had opened a seat in the regime. Dietremann authorized the election of a local man, despite candidates proposed from Strasbourg.[87] The following year, Chauvigny proposed a candidate, Paul Loffet, for a vacant post, but Dietremann and the magistrate so vehemently opposed Loffet that La Houssaye called for "free elections."[88] It is unclear how these "free elections" were conducted, but the victorious candidate was Anton Bössner.[89] In 1716 the death of Niclaus Schepplin opened a magisterial post. Again, Chauvigny pushed for a candidate, Schepplin's nephew, also called Niclaus. The dispute required resolution from the Regency, which also called for "free elections." The intendant proclaimed his willingness to honor the Court's judgment by restraining his own influence. He expressed concern, however, that "not everyone was acting with the same disinterest," and requested a report on the behavior of the *commandant*.[90] In the end the elections favored the magistrate's candidate, Johann Tanner.

Chauvigny had made many enemies, and the magistrate responded to the intendant's request with a long catalogue of complaints. Chauvigny received his wages from municipal revenues, but unlike Dietremann, the *commandant* had used his office continually for personal profit. He had a privilege to fish in the Ill river without paying a tax, and his personal fishermen had used the exemption to catch fish to sell for market. Chauvigny had also presumed to augment his wages in kind through confiscation of hay and wood over the regime's objections. The magistrate complained that

> he treats us like men without spirit and without judgment, who act only by passion and self-interest.... He speaks to us only in terms of contempt and wants to regulate our functions, our lodgings, our farms and to dispose of the domains of the city as if they were his own.[91]

The civic leaders further noted that Chauvigny's main duty was to ensure public peace, but that instead,

> if he speaks of us to our citizens, it is to stir them up against us. Is it so surprising, Sir, to see a disobedient, rebellious, and undisciplined populace that one cannot control, and that one can only force to pay their royal taxes with threats of imprisonment?... How can magistrates, treated in the way that we are, do our duty and our functions troubled and persecuted at every moment in our offices, in our police duties, and in the domains of our city?[92]

The municipal regime could not force Chauvigny out of office, and he continued to harass them until 1720, when his opponents in the *Conseil souverain* engineered his dismissal.[93] The regime's struggle with the *commandant* resulted from tensions among provincial officials. Colmar's magistrates could not control Chauvigny without outside help. The key counterweight was no doubt Dietremann, whose contacts with the intendant and the *Conseil souverain* were critical. Why he couldn't remove his opponent until 1720 remains unanswered.

In 1717 the Regency decreed an *arrêt* which prohibited relatives within the fourth degree from simultaneously holding office within the kingdom's municipal regimes. In response to the decree, the *préteur royal* drafted a report on the entire regime, seasoned with character assessments.[94] Familial ties were strongest among the regime's Lutherans, as eleven of the thirteen

Lutheran officeholders were interrelated. This network allowed the *préteur royal* to suggest the deposition of specific Lutherans in order to comply with the *arrêt*. Dietremann targeted Georges Charlapour, who was a "mischievous troublemaker" related to several regime members through his wife, the daughter of Benjamin Gloxin. Dietremann also found the brothers Johann David and Johann Wilhelm Andres to be "poor subjects." Finally, in Dietremann's eyes, Anton Bössner and Johann Bentz had proven unfit, particularly Bössner, who had behaved with insolence on several occasions. Interestingly enough, the two men who formed the center of the familial networks, Johann Rudolph Dürninger and Johann Jacob Sandherr, were spared comment. Clearly Dietremann sought with this *arrêt* to root out opponents through its selected application.[95] Despite Dietremann's comments, no one initially resigned. In 1719, following the election of Johann Ulrich Goll, however, Dietremann evoked the decree to propose the deposition of either Dürninger or Goll, but Johann Jacob Sandherr stepped forward and resigned, which broke the relational chain and allowed Dürninger and Goll to remain.[96]

As for the thirteen Catholic regime members, although eight had family ties, the *préteur royal* expressed satisfaction with them all. Dietremann's assessment may have reflected confessional bias, but it is more likely that it reflected his secure control over the Catholic magisterial recruitment. They were his creatures, whereas the provincial administration allowed the Lutherans to select their replacements through "free election," conducted by the regime itself, through which the Lutherans in office co-opted relatives, friends, and clients. For a confessional community under siege, this right secured a tightly knit and unified oligarchy.

In 1720 the Regency began another full investigation into Colmar's municipal administration, ostensibly to reduce the cost of local governance. At the heart of the royal proposal was a call to reduce Colmar's council from twenty to ten members. The regime drew up a report which defended its size and its activities. The magistrates noted that

> one cannot dispense with the number of officials in a city which after Strasbourg is the largest in the province and the capital of Upper Alsace. It is just that those municipal officers whose functions prevent them from working at other affairs than those of the city be paid and salaried in such a manner that they live honestly so that they can devote themselves entirely to public affairs.[97]

Among these duties the regime members all served as judges in the first instance for all municipal cases. Under the grant of 1685, their verdicts were sustained without appeal in all civil cases up to 100 livres, while defendants in all criminal cases had the right to appeal to the *Conseil souverain*.[98] The magistrate handled civic police matters, such as regulating weights and measures and acting as building inspectors, as well as administering civic revenues. The magistrate occasionally consulted with the council on these matters, particularly in tax cases, and it selected all municipal officials. Councilors often served in these capacities, and they could hold an office permanently if they performed well. The *préteur royal* headed the government and when absent was informed of all of its decisions.[99]

After listing its functions, the regime defended its size. The civic leaders argued that they held a privilege from the crown to "freely elect" their successors and that the needs of confessional parity required twenty, with each guild best "represented" by one councilor from each confession.[100] The document then listed the council members by rank of seniority without any reference to guild or confessional affiliation. The Colmarians further reminded the regents that Alsatian municipal governments differed from comparable institutions in the kingdom's interior because the Alsatians handled both judicial and police matters.[101] In the end, the regime retained its structure.

At the same time the magistrates compiled a list of other municipal offices and evaluated the worth of each post. The patrons of the civic administration found only a few redundant posts or overpaid officials. Nearly all of the "excess" positions were held by Chauvigny's clients: the *commissaires aux revenus*, the city's gatekeepers, and the bell ringer. The city's gatekeepers were Chauvigny's personal servants, who received free lodging as part of their wages. The regime suggested that these houses be confiscated for the civic valets, who were overworked and underpaid. The valets were Dietremann's men. In all, the suppression of these posts would save the city roughly 1,000 livres in annual salaries.[102] The municipal officials also singled out the controller of the customs' house, the brother of the former intendant, La Grange, who had no duties, since the house was administered by the tax farmers, but who remained on the payroll out of "charity."[103] Finally, in an odd break with the assault on Chauvigny, the regime begrudged a raise recently granted Dietremann.[104] Perhaps this assault on everyone triggered enough opposition higher up to leave the matter unmolested. No reforms were undertaken.

The struggle between the separate clientage systems of Chauvigny and Dietremann reflected how deeply embedded in provincial politics the Colmar regime had become. It also reflected how effectively Colmar's elite had learned to function in the system. The regime moved into the mid-eighteenth century conscious of the limits of its power base but aware of its maneuverability within those limits. The new mentality of deference, privilege, profit, and patronage had been embraced by Colmar's civic leadership. Confessional, familial, and personal factions remained, but their struggles were carried out in French and within the etiquette of Bourbon politics.

In his classic study of the old regime, Alexis de Tocqueville aligned the collapse of municipal political autonomy with the development of Louis XIV's "paternal government," which he saw as the model for the modern Napoleonic state. He traced the survival of municipal regimes as "small democratic republics" into the late seventeenth century, dating the end of municipal autonomy to the Edict of 1692, which created a new layer of venal municipal offices. According to Tocqueville, Louis XIV's motivation was fiscal expediency, of which the end of the kingdom's civic republics was an unforeseen by-product. On no less than seven occasions over the next eighty years, the French communes would be asked to buy back the right to elect their own officials.[105] Each request precipitated local crises, as royal appetite for revenue stirred up deep tensions among communal factions.

The end of Colmar's political autonomy in the reign of Louis XIV was not the end of a "small democratic republic." In the decades before French subjugation, the oligarchy had eliminated guild elections as the last direct tie to popular political support. The end of the regime's autonomy, however, did not signify the end of civic political life. Royal absolutism ushered in a profound change in the political ethos of the men who served in municipal office. They continued to administer day-to-day civic affairs, but now as bureaucratic agents of the crown.

Two recent studies of urban revolts have delineated distinct French and Imperial models of early modern urban politics.[106] According to William Beik, in the French cities the crisis in the central government's authority during Louis XIV's minority turned traditional factional tensions into urban revolts. Louis XIV's absolutism restored a "central direction for a society built around inherited preeminence and private ownership of public office."[107] Thus, in the French context partisan civic politics had to function within the political hierarchy. Without patrons, Sonntag had no chance. According to Christopher Friedrichs, central direction was lacking in the Imperial context, which encouraged disputing civic parties to seek allies from among the conflicting parties beyond the city walls, were the interplay of internal and external partisan politics tended to prolong disputes rather than resolve them. In the Imperial environment, factionalism became the standard order of business, provided it did not threaten public peace.[108] Sonntag hoped to draw in outside support from the intendant to pressure the regime, and he sought open government in the name of public good. His movement had never threatened public peace, but the civic political traditions he called on were Imperial anachronisms in a city whose political culture was thoroughly French.

In his study of Toulouse, Robert Schneider has shown how the 1690s saw the reorientation of municipal officials away from civic culture toward the cosmopolitan values of the Court.[109] The 1690s had also been a turning point for Colmar's political elite, and by 1711 they recognized the guiding hand of royal government and their place in French political society. Prior to 1673 the Colmar regime had used the Imperial interplay of internal and external politics to delay the day of reckoning with Louis XIV. When Sonntag tried to employ these familiar tactics in 1711, he only hastened his own fall.

The decades following the Sonntag affair witnessed the citizenry's complete alienation from the regime. Colmar's municipal leaders governed without consent of the people; they used their patronage to secure favors for friends and relatives; and they invested in property in the region and began to attract immigrants from the elite of the neighboring villages and towns. Long before the French Revolution, Colmar had assumed the physiognomy of a departmental capital, an eighteenth-century bourgeois town dominated by *rentiers* and officeholders with extensive properties in the surrounding *pays*. Although it lacked a residing prince, in the Imperial context, Colmar's eighteenth-century society and culture more closely resembled a *Residenzstadt* than a *Reichsstadt*. Such a shift, however, reflected political, economic, and social gain, not loss.[110] By 1730 two generations of Bourbon rule had transformed the municipal regime from a medieval commune into a modern provincial city.

Notes

1. Reuss, *L'Alsace*, 1: 469–70.
2. On contemporary civic protests against the magistrates within the empire, see Walker, *German Home Towns*, 69; Soliday, *A Community in Conflict: Frankfurt*, 13–40. On Sonntag's movement, see Livet, "L'esprit d'opposition: L'affaire Sonntag," 69–84.
3. Livet, *L'intendance*, 637–38.
4. Ibid., 810–12.
5. In a report on civic commerce drawn up in 1720, the regime noted that tanning had been one industry which had benefitted from war and suffered from peace. AMC, AA 166, 272, fol. 3v. Cf. Hertner, *Stadtwirtschaft*, 360–68.
6. On the French administration in the Breisgau, see Hermann Kopf, "Unter der Krone Frankreichs, Freiburg-im-Breisgau 1677–1697," *Schau-ins-Land* 88 (1970): 23–124.
7. Cf. Schneider, *Toulouse*, 276–99; Sharon Kettering, *Judicial Politics and Urban Revolt in Seventeenth-Century France: The Parlement of Aix, 1629–1659* (Princeton, 1978), esp. 29–50.
8. Livet, "Colmar et l'établissement du Conseil souverain," 69–76.
9. Livet, *L'intendance*, 678–79.
10. Ibid., 680–81. See also Livet, "Colmar et l'établissement de Conseil souverain," 75–76.
11. On the Jesuits see Julian Sée, ed., *Memoires des RR. PP. Jesuites du Collège de Colmar (1698–1750)* (Geneva, 1873). On the Capuchins, see AMC, GG 138.
12. Goehlinger, *Histoire du Chapitre*, 120–21.
13. Kintz, "XVIIe siècle: Du Saint Empire au royaume," 95; Dreyer-Roos, *La population strasbourgeoise*, 88–89.
14. Livet, *L'intendance*, 691–93.
15. On the specific offers and the regime's commitment, see AMC, AA 164, 168–204. On the role of the Hôtel de Ville de Paris in the royal fiscal system, see Jean Bouvier and Henri Germain-Martin, *Finances et financiers de l'ancien régime* (Paris, 1964), 98–117. For the impact of these fiscal practices on the Alsatian bourgeoisie, see Livet, "La monarchie absolue," 133–52. As early as 1694, several leading Colmarians appear as *rentiers* in the *capitation* register: Johann Georg Herr, Elias Lang, Johann Andres, and Matthias Kyss. AMC, CC 155, 1694, pp. 1–3.

16. Livet, *L'intendance*, 657.
17. Ibid., 718–26; Sittler, "La transformation du gouvernement," 148–50. On struggles among royal agents in Colmar, see Georges Livet, "De quelques conflits entre la Plume et l'Epée: Contribution à l'histoire du Conseil souverain d'Alsace," *Annuaire de Colmar* (1966): 57–73.
18. On Andres see AMC, AA 165, 43 and 78. On Sandherr and his family, see AMC, AA 165, 74–76.
19. AMC, CC 252, 9a.
20. Lucien Sittler, "Change et banque dans le Vieux-Colmar," *Annuaire de Colmar* (1973): 64. On Johann Ulrich Goll's later career as a financier for industrial development, see Jean-Marie Schmitt, *Aux origines de la révolution industrielle en Alsace: Investissements et relations sociales dans la vallée de Saint-Amarin au XVIIIe siècle*, PSSARE, 18 (Strasbourg, 1980), 32 and passim.
21. AMC, AA 160, 270. See also Sittler, *La viticulture*, 33–37.
22. Lucien Sittler, "La poste à Colmar du Moyen-Age au début de XIXe siècle," *Annuaire de Colmar* (1967): 20–35.
23. Schneider catalogued and documented his privileges in his protest filed with the intendant, Angervillers, in November 1720. AMC, AA 165, 114–18.
24. Sittler "La poste," 31.
25. AMC, AA 165, 125.
26. AMC, AA 165, 124.
27. Schneider owned "un des plus fameux cabarets de la ville qui non seulement les marchands des bestiaux qui viennent icy aux marches et aux faires prennent leurs logement . . . [but also] plusieurs corps de métier y tiennent leurs assemblées générales." AMC, AA 165, 128, fols. 1v–2r.
28. AMC, AA 165, 128, fols. 2r–v.
29. AMC, AA 165, 110, fols. 1v.
30. AMC, AA 165, 121–22.
31. Due to a lacuna in the *Gewerff* registers between 1698 and 1701, I have chosen to analyze conditions in 1702. The generational change is noted in Sittler "La transformation du gouvernement," 151.
32. On Röttlin's career, see Metzenthin, "Les Roettlin," 62.
33. When Sandherr and Riegger died, La Fond recommended only that their replacements be Lutherans. AMC, BB 24, 22.
34. On Schneider see, Wolff, "La famille Schneider," 53–60. On Buob, see Wertz, ed., *Membres du magistrat, 1601–1700*, 18.
35. In 1728 the Catholic magistrates sought to establish a new post of *procureur fiscal* which would only be open to Catholics. The intendant opposed the plan and informed Dietremann that he saw no reason to change the practice of alternating the post between confessions. AMC, BB 19, 4.
36. Mossmann, *Recherches sur l'ancienne constitution*, 136.
37. AMC, BB 24, 25–27.
38. AMC, BB 24, 28–32.
39. The ten members of the older generation joined the regime in the following years: Samuel Röttlin, 1671; Johann Georg Herr, 1675; Hans Jacob Fix, 1677; Johann Heinrich Bössner, 1678; Wendlin Güntzer, 1680; Johannes Haffner, 1680; Claus Hurst, 1681; Philip Sybert, 1682; Martin Wöhrlin, 1682; Johann Jacob Saur, 1685.
40. The new generation included Johann Jacob Sandherr (1694), Johann Peter Welsch (1694), Andreas Sandherr (1696), Georg Roman Baumhauer (1697), Johann Andres (1698), Johann Wilhelm Faber (1698), Johann Georg Barth (1698), David Andres (1699), Johann Rudolph Dürninger (1701), Christian Reichstetter (1701), and Johanne Tanner (1702).

41. Sittler, "La transformation du gouvernement," 152; AMC, BB 13, 148–51.
42. On the election of 1706, see AMC, BB 24, 24. On Graff's candidacy, see AMC, BB 24, 37.
43. With Röttlin's death, the intendant began to fill the post with his personal secretaries. Schepplin held the position from 1708 to 1710, followed by Louis Olivier in 1710, Bernard Claude in 1712, and then his son-in-law Christian Sibour from 1713 until 1723, and finally François Anthon Chaffour from 1723 until 1750. See Scherlen, *Perles d'Alsace*, 3: 35. See also AMC, BB 24, 28–32.
44. Livet, "L'esprit d'opposition: L'affaire Sonntag," 69.
45. On Dietremann's patronage system, see AMC, FF 43, 64 and 84.
46. Livet, "L'esprit d'opposition: L'affaire Sonntag," 69–84; AMC, FF 43.
47. AMC, FF 43, 38, fol. 1r.
48. On Sonntag's family background, see Livet, "L'esprit d'opposition: L'affaire Sonntag," 72–73. For Sonntag's *capitation* assessment, see AMC, CC 155, 1694, pp. 5–6. For the list of Colmarians who did invest in the government's offices, see AMC, AA 165, 43 and 45.
49. Elias Lang was listed in the highest tax category in 1694. AMC, CC 155, 1694, p. 2. Lang owned the finest house in Colmar, which the intendant, La Houssaye, reserved as his residence whenever he visited the city. Livet, *L'intendance*, 664.
50. AMC, BB 13, 151–58.
51. AMC, FF 43, 41, fol. 1r.
52. AMC, FF 43, 38.
53. AMC, FF 43, 64.
54. On 3 August 1711, La Houssaye informed Dietremann: "ne vous inquietez point des demandes que l'on fait contre vous qui ne se tourneront qu'à vostre honneur." AMC, FF 43, 66.
55. On 5 August Graff boasted "si je suis escouté vous aurez certainement toute la satisfaction que vous pouvez desirer; quoi que dans tout ce qui a esté presenté il ne soit pas fait mention nommement de vous." AMC, FF 43, 65.
56. The event is recorded in a letter from Graff to Dietremann dated 7 August 1711. AMC, FF 43, 68.
57. On 30 September, Graff informed Dietremann of Sonntag's impending imprisonment and reflected on the affair: "J'admire la sagesse de ce Seigneur d'avoir temperé et donné tout le tems à ce mutin de pousser son insolence jusqu'au point où il l'a poussé pour avoir des moyens suffisans de le faire châtier par un ordre supérieur ... comme il aurait pu faire dans le veue de couper d'abord racine aux plaintes du d[it] Sonntag." AMC, FF 43, 83.
58. On Sonntag's arrival in Strasbourg, see AMC, FF 43, 65. The most complete copy of Sonntag's petition that I have found is AMC, FF 43, 30.
59. La Houssaye refers to the petitioners' pretensions in AMC, FF 43, 68. See also Livet, "L'esprit d'opposition: L'affaire Sonntag," 69–84.
60. AMC, FF 43, 69.
61. On 10 September, Anton Reichert signed a statement claiming that Sonntag had lied to him. AMC, FF 43, 73. His is the only public retraction that I have found.
62. Colmar's archives do not hold a copy of the second petition. Evidence suggests that it was published and distributed in early September. AMC, FF 43, 75 and 94.
63. AMC, FF 43, 75–83.
64. Sonntag was arrested on 2 October. AMC, FF 43, 37. His original term was to be one month, but the crown extended it to six months because of his second petition. AMC, FF 43, 88. Claus Hurst was not deposed from office,

nor did he face the intendant. The magistrate presented him as an old and muddled man. One wonders what patrons he had in the city to protect him. He remained in office until retiring in 1716. AMC, BB 13, 163. Sonntag's chief French supporter, Jean-Baptiste Paillot, was the only other conspirator consigned to prison. Paillot fled arrest in late September. AMC, FF 43, 33, fol. 4v. He turned himself in to the intendant in mid-October. AMC, FF 43, 90. La Houssaye publicly chastised Emmanuel Röttlin, Lorentz and Martin Windholtz, and Johann Waltz the younger. AMC, FF 43, 37, fol. 2r and fol. 5r.

65. Livet, "L'esprit d'opposition: L'affaire Sonntag," 80.
66. Ibid., 82.
67. For an analysis of citizen struggles with municipal regimes in the Holy Roman Empire in the years after 1648, see Friedrichs, "Urban Conflicts," S98–S123; idem, "German Town Revolts," 27–51.
68. Livet argues that Sonntag's proposal was vague and lacked a clear program. See Livet, "L'esprit d'opposition: L'affaire Sonntag," 82.
69. After referring to the Arret of 1683, the complaint states: "neantmoins ceux [the magistrates] de Colmar preferent leurs interests à la volonté du Roy: au bien et à l'utilité publique, ont tellement meprisé cet arrest, qu'ils ne l'ont executé qu'une fois lors de sa publication." AMC, FF 43, 30, fol. 1r.
70. AMC, FF 43, 30, fol. 1r.
71. AMC, FF 43, 30, fol. 1v.
72. AMC, FF 43, 30, fol. 1v.
73. AMC, FF 43, 30, fol. 1v–2r.
74. AMC, FF 43, 30, fol. 3v.
75. AMC, FF 43, 30, fol. 2v–3v.
76. AMC, FF 43, 41, fol. 1r–v.
77. AMC, FF 43, 41, fol. 1v.
78. AMC, FF 43, 41, fol. 2r.
79. "Il n'y a rien de nouveau de voir former de caballes contre des Magistrates, qui sont charges de faire le recouvrement des impositions du Roy et comme ces factieux n'oserient se plaindre contre sa majesté, ils tachent de rejeter tout le fardeau sur le Magistrat." AMC, FF 43, 22, fol. 2r. They reminded the intendant that "que pas un d'eux n'a été continué que par vos ordres." Ibid., fol. 3v.
80. "Il est necessaire souvent, que les Bourguemestres s'engagent en leurs propres noms pour emprunter des sommes dans les pressons besoins de la ville comme les suppliants ont esté obligés de faire plusieurs fois qu'il faut un tems considerables pour retirer les avances faite de cette manière et l'acquitter." AMC, FF 43, 41, fol. 4r.
81. AMC, FF 43, 41, fol. 5r–v.
82. AMC, FF 43, 41, fol. 5v–11r.
83. The magistrates admitted that "il est vray que les Bourguemestres sont exemptes des Impositions extraordinaires à la reserve de la Capitation, la quelle ils payent dans les rolles des exemptes, rolle que votre grandeur arreste tous les ans. Il est vray qu'ils sont exempts du logement des gens de guerre." But they argued that exemptions "conforme à l'usage de toute la province. Elle fait partie de leurs gages, qui ne sont pas plus forts qu'à Selestat et ailleurs." AMC, FF 43, 41, fol. 11v.
84. AMC, FF 43, 41, fol. 18r–v.
85. Anderson, *Lineages of the Absolutist State*, 106–7; Georges Livet, "Les intendants et leur oeuvre," 100–28.
86. Livet, "La Plume et l'Epée," 57–72.
87. La Houssaye's secretary, Rudolph Graff, who had worked closely with Dietremann

during the Sonntag crisis, proposed two candidates for the post, M. Du Comte and another Schuilqué. AMC, FF 43, 68. The proposal came early on in the crisis and for some reason these men were not appointed. AMC, BB 13, 159.
88. AMC, BB 26, 6.
89. AMC, BB 13, 160.
90. AMC, BB 24, 44–53.
91. Quoted in Livet, "La Plume et l'Epée," 64.
92. Ibid.
93. Ibid., 72.
94. AMC, BB 24, 66.
95. AMC, BB 24, 66.
96. AMC, BB 26, 10.
97. AMC, BB 21, 4, fol. 1r.
98. AMC, BB 21, 2 fol. 1r.
99. AMC, BB 21, 2, fol. 1r–2r.
100. AMC, BB 29, 9, fol. 1r–v.
101. AMC, BB 29, 9, fol. 2.
102. AMC, BB 21, 3.
103. AMC, BB 21, 3, fol. 2r.
104. AMC, BB 21, 4, fol. 3v.
105. Alexis de Tocqueville, *The Old Regime and the French Revolution*, trans. by Stuart Gilbert (New York, 1955), 41ff.
106. William H. Beik, "Urban Factions and the Social Order during the Minority of Louis XIV," *French Historical Studies* 15 (1987): 36–67; Friedrichs, "Urban Conflicts," S98–S123.
107. Beik, "Urban Factions," 62–67, here at 66.
108. Friedrichs, "Urban Conflicts," S123.
109. Schneider, *Toulouse*, 255–99.
110. François, "Des républiques marchandes," 587–603.

8

Society and Economy
in a Provincial
Administrative Center

French lordship rapidly altered Colmar's physiognomy after 1680. The city's political institutions changed, as did the values of the men who held civic office. Colmar experienced an economic boom, but the fruits of that boom were not shared by all Colmarians. Privilege before the fisc widened the distance between rich and poor. Anger over privilege fueled Sonntag's protest, and he drew his support primarily from the moderately wealthy master craftsmen, who had formed the backbone of civic order during the decades before the French takeover.

Privilege exempted many of Colmar's wealthiest residents from the need to join a guild or to pay taxes. Among the privileged were a few who crossed over into the robe nobility, but many more amassed fortunes through government finance, patronage, or industrial investment under the protective cloak of mercantilism.[1] The Colmarians who found their way into the provincial elite blocked access to other ambitious men, such as Sonntag, as privilege spread in concentric circles which circumscribed insiders and outsiders. Most Colmarians found themselves on the outside because of language, religion, or poverty.

French lordship stimulated demographic growth in the city and produced a second boom in the economy; however, the uneven distribution of prosperity increased tensions within the city between the confessions, between the trades, and between rich and poor. It would be this counterpoint of sustained growth and increasing disharmony which marred the face of civic culture in the early eighteenth century.

I. DEMOGRAPHIC GROWTH UNDER BOURBON RULE

The royal agents in the city conducted its first population surveys in the late seventeenth century, and their tabulations clearly depict the city's growth during the first half-century of Bourbon rule. In 1683 French officials counted

930 families in the city.[2] The city's population expanded over the next several years as the royal officials transformed the civic regime, and the number of households had increased to 1,078, containing 7,142 souls, by 1697, the year before the transfer of the *Conseil souverain* to Colmar.[3] The new courts combined with an influx of refugees from the Breisgau to rapidly push the city's population close to 10,000. The first decade of the eighteenth century was marked by numerous disputes between the civic regime and the *Conseil souverain* over access to housing, as local builders began the construction of numerous new homes in the French style.[4] A survey in July of 1709 counted 9,023 souls in the city.[5] The growth continued through the end of Louis XIV's reign and into the Regency, and in 1718 a new survey identified 1,225 citizen "hearths" and 516 noncitizen "hearths."[6] The civic political community, its citizenry, had increased, but nearly 30% of the households in Colmar were headed by individuals who were not citizens, nearly twice the figure of 16% for 1698. The census of 1718 also noted the presence in Colmar of numerous noble households: eighty headed by individuals directly associated with the *Conseil souverain* and thirty-six others belonging to royal provincial officials.[7] In all, the city, which sheltered 1,078 households in 1697, contained 1,877 households in 1718. Colmar in the early eighteenth century was an administrative boom town with a large number of householders, who either through privilege or poverty would not appear in the tax and guild registers. Following the multiplier employed in the census of 1697, each household accounted for 6.625 persons. Based upon this multiplier, the city's population rose from 6,161 in 1683 to around 12,435 by 1718.[8] Colmar's population grew and the city physically burst its walls in the early eighteenth century. It is quite possible that under French lordship Colmar's population doubled within two generations.

This demographic boom extended to Colmar's guildsmen (refer above to graphs 2.1–2). Following the Peace of Nijmegen in 1680, the tax collectors counted 783 male householders and 155 female householders, which suggests that Colmar's population was probably around 6,200. The war and disorder had reduced the city's population to the level of the 1650s. Between 1680 and 1690, Colmar's population grew around 20%, from 6,200 to 7,500, and the number of male householders rose 29%, from 783 to 1,011. The first decade of French rule produced a remarkable growth in the city's guilds.

In 1697 the Peace of Ryswick ended French lordship on the east bank of the Rhine and brought hundreds of refugees into Alsace; however, many of these householders were privileged and never appeared in the tax or guild registers. Two years earlier, in 1695, famine had cut into the city's population.[9] Between 1690 and 1702 Colmar's taxable population probably grew around 9%, but though the ensuing War of Spanish Succession did not spill into Alsace, the fiscal strain combined with the famine of 1709 reduced the number of Colmar's male householders from 1,106 in 1702 to 1,094 in 1710. The difficult years strikingly did not produce an upswing in the number of households headed by widows; their numbers remained the same (126) in 1710 as in 1702. The expansion of the 1680s and 1690s had stopped, though in fact the city sheltered more people in 1710, if we factor in the privileged and tax exempt, than it had during the economic boom prior to the Thirty Years' War.

By 1720 the city's population was certainly higher than it had ever been. Between 1710 and 1720, the number of male householders rose from 1,094 to 1,258 (15%) and the taxable population as a whole by 19% (from 7,837 to 9,321). Much of this growth occurred after Louis XIV's death in 1715, and the first years of the Regency must have brought a sense of relief after nearly forty years of war and high taxes. Through the 1720s demographic growth slowed again as the number of male householders rose from 1,260 to 1,330 (5.6%) and the estimated population from 9,335 to 9,963 (6.8%). The tax registers confirm the impression from the royal censuses that French lordship brought demographic growth among the city's merchants, artisans, and agricultural workers, as well as the addition of a block of privileged officials. The growth was not constant but, rather, was marked by dramatic spurts in the 1680s and 1710s and periods of stability or slight growth. Nevertheless, by 1730 the city was assuming its modern character as a populous administrative and market center.

Part of the growth can be explained by a high rate of retention among the city's householders, and part by an influx of newcomers (refer above to graph 2.3). Since 1640, more than 60% of the householders recorded in the tax rolls were still paying taxes ten years later. Following a break between 1670 and 1680, the rate of survivors never fell below 62.9%. Political stability must have played a significant role in this, for the famines in the 1690s and again in 1709 cost the city numerous householders. What allowed Colmar to maintain its numbers was that fewer householders emigrated in the early eighteenth century.

As for newcomers, the 1680s saw the highest percentage of new householders (480 householders, or 47.5% of those paying taxes in 1690) for the entire period studied. The new householders came from among the native families and from the surrounding region, and as with the generation of the 1640s, these men remained on the tax registers for several decades. The influx of new householders continued until the first decade of the eighteenth century, when 324 new men, or only 29.6%, appear in the registers.[10] The year 1709 had been a year of great famine, but it was among the new householders rather than the old that the famine had its greatest effect. In the decade between 1710 and 1720, a second boom of new householders occurred, though with the city's population already high the new householders accounted for only 42% of the householders assessed in 1720. Between 1720 and 1730 more householders survived (795) and more householders arrived (534) than in any decade since at least the sixteenth century, and given the size of the city before 1600, probably more than at any time in the city's past. Whether we consider the city's population as a whole or its core of taxed guildsmen, the period after 1715 marked a new era in Colmar's demographic history.

Prior to 1680 the city had drawn heavily from its own sons and daughters to sustain its population, but the unprecedented growth after 1680, depended on outside immigration to break the traditional demographic barrier. The data for this era are much more complete than those from previous decades, at least for the male householders, where we can identify the origins of over 87% (see table 8.1). Among these, 71.1% were native Colmarians, which continued a pattern in place at least since the end of the Thirty Years' War. Furthermore, most of the immigrants came from the same sources as had earlier immigrants. The villages and towns of Upper Alsace provided a significant number of new settlers, which highlighted the city's role as a regional market center. During these decades Colmar had also become an administrative hub, and the *Conseil souverain* served all of Alsace. Yet the percentage of Alsatian immigrants had declined, from 14.6% in the decades before 1680 to 12.8%. The number of Alsatians settling in Colmar had increased from the previous era (from 193 to 285), but a growth in immigrants from other regions led to the decline in the percentage. The numbers of immigrants from southwest Germany rose, triggered in part by a large influx from the Breisgau, which alone provided the city with fifty-six householders. The city also continued to attract occasional immigrants from the Rhineland, central Germany, and territories further north and east. Immigrants from the Swiss cantons had poured into Colmar in the decades following the Thirty Years' War, and some of them entered the city's guilds.[11] Swiss immigration continued in the first decades of French lordship, with the cantons contributing more immigrants than Lower Alsace.

Two new sources had emerged, however, which reflected the new political conditions. Between 1630 and 1680, six householders from French-speaking lands and one from Italy had settled in the city. Between 1680 and 1730, at least fifty-nine French and ten Italian householders came to the city, and this cohort did not include the privileged officials, soldiers, and servants who clogged the streets, taverns, and government offices of eighteenth-century Colmar. The orientation toward the west had begun; by 1730 native-born Colmarians such as Jean Bernard, a coppersmith, Christoph Michel, a tailor, and François Petit, a bookseller, came before their guilds to swear the oath of citizenship. By the early eighteenth century, French lordship had begun to affect Colmar's linguistic and cultural mix. Yet in the first fifty years of French rule, traditional patterns of recruitment survived while the French-speaking territories supplied a new but limited reservoir for demographic growth. Political practices changed in Colmar long before the dialects in the shops and streets did.

Among the women who married local householders and bore the new generation of Colmarians, nearly all (93.6%) were born within a day's walk

TABLE 8.1
Origins of Men and Women, 1681–1730

PLACE OF ORIGIN	MALES (no.)	(%)	FEMALES (no.)	(%)
Colmar	1,595	71.1	1,383	81.4
Upper Alsace	192	8.6	208	12.2
Lower Alsace	93	4.2	14	0.8
Southwest Germany				
Breisgau	56		10	
Baden	20		6	
Württemberg	18	5.8	1	1.1
Swabia/Bodensee	11		2	
Bavaria	25		—	
Rhineland/Palatinate	14	0.6	2	0.1
Central Germany				
Hesse	14		—	
Hohenlohe	3	1.2	—	—
Thuringia	5		—	
Franconia	6		—	
Northern Germany				
Brandenburg-Prussia	3		—	
Saxony	8	0.6	—	—
Netherlands	2		—	
Eastern Regions				
Silesia, Hungary,				
Poland, Bohemia	8	0.4	1	0.1
Switzerland	96	4.3	55	3.2
Italy	10	0.4	—	—
Western Francophone				
France/Lorraine	51		5	
Montbéliard	8	2.6	1	0.4
Region Unknown	4	0.2	11	0.6
Total Known	2,242		1,699*	
Total Cases	2,570	87.2		

*The figure for wives comes from data for first and second marriages in both confessional communities.

of the city. Little had changed since the decades before French rule when 95% of the female householders came from a similar radius. Few women from French-speaking towns and villages married Colmar's guildsmen, though some immigrants probably came to the city with a wife and perhaps a family. As in the past the only significant source for female householders beyond the immediate hinterland was Switzerland, and the number of women from the Swiss cantons was much higher (55) than it had been in decades before French rule (32).

From 1680 onward, royal officials ordered the Lutheran regime to recruit Catholics until it reached parity in 1688. Royal policy also encouraged Catholic immigration, and persuaded Protestants in Alsace to convert by offering tax incentives.[12] Confessionally mixed marriages were discouraged and finally prohibited, while excessive pressure was applied to catechize Protestant children.[13] The royal government also sought to prohibit immigration of Protestants into the kingdom.[14] In the years following 1690, an increasing proportion of the immigrants spoke French and professed Catholicism, and the pattern continued into the early eighteenth century.[15] Between 1703 and 1715, twenty to fifty Frenchmen arrived at Colmar each year, though they did not normally join the city's guilds. Some of these immigrants were servants and day laborers, some soldiers, and many officials. The French-speaking inhabitants had an advantage in their command of the official language, but that advantage isolated the newcomers from most Colmarians, as it did in contemporary Strasbourg.[16]

The new immigrants shifted Colmar's confessional complexion in favor of Catholicism. All of the royal *officiers* and many of the other newcomers were Catholics. Between 1671 and 1685, Colmar's Lutheran parish celebrated nearly twice as many marriages as St. Martin's (41.3 per year to 23.9). From 1685, when the royal Counter-Reform offensive began in Alsace, the differences in the number of marriages narrowed.[17] Between 1685 and 1698, marriages in the Lutheran community dropped to a rate of thirty-six per year. The decline was matched by a rise in Catholic weddings to 29.1 per year. During the entire era an average of sixty-five weddings per year were celebrated, but after 1685 the Catholics claimed a greater share. Prior to the arrival of the *Conseil souverain*, Catholics were still in the minority based on the data in the parish registers. From 1698 to 1724, both parishes grew, but the Catholic community's growth far outstripped the Lutherans. The number of Catholic marriages rose to 48.7 per year, while the Lutheran parish regained its mid-seventeenth-century levels at 41.7. The city as a whole was expanding, with ninety marriages per year, and the Catholic community claimed the lion's share of the growth.

Baptisms in the two parishes also depicted a shift in the early eighteenth century. In the Lutheran parish the number of annual baptisms dropped from 164.2 for the period 1671–85 to 154.1 between 1686 and 1698. Unlike marriages, however, the decline continued into the eighteenth century to

152.5 for 1698–1724. The decline in the number of Lutheran births in the early eighteenth century reflected complex conditions. The echo effect of fewer marriages in the 1690s combined with the remarriage of older individuals following the famine of 1709 may have produced the contrasting trends of more marriages and fewer baptisms. The baptismal rate for the Lutherans between 1699 and 1710 is only 141.3 per year with a low point in 1710 of 105. The rate for the period after 1710 rises to 162.2 and is connected to the second wave of overall population growth in the city between 1710 and 1720. Colmar's Lutheran community faced heavy pressure from French officials, which checked its growth for a time; but in the more relaxed atmosphere of the Regency, the Lutherans attracted more immigrants, at least from within the province, and encouraged the native sons to stay.

In the Catholic parish, the baptismal figures reflected the community's dynamic growth. Fewer than 100 infants per year (92.8) received baptism between 1671 and 1685. The number of baptisms per year increased to 137 between 1686 and 1698 and further to 191 in the first decades of the eighteenth century. Whether we consider marriages or baptisms, based on the data in the parish registers, Colmar's Catholic community doubled in size between 1685 and the early eighteenth century.[18]

The dramatic swings in the parish registers were not echoed in the tax rolls (see graph 8.1). Colmar's Protestant community formed a majority of

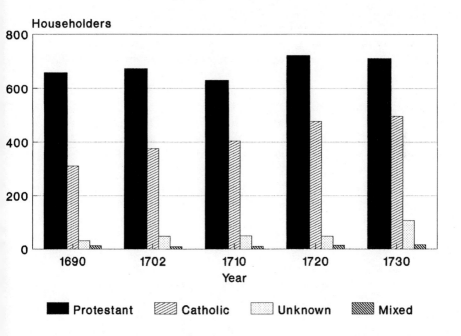

GRAPH 8.1   CONFESSIONAL DIVISION, 1690–1730

the taxpayers at least until 1730. The number of Lutheran householders steadily declined in terms of percentages from 65.1% in 1690 to 53.4% in 1730, but in terms of actual householders the Protestant community under Louis XV was larger than under Louis XIV. The Catholic taxpaying community, on the other hand, grew steadily from 30% of the population in 1690 to 37% in 1730, and in terms of absolute number of householders from 311 in 1690 to 496 in 1730. The more dramatic swings in the confessional balance in the parish registers reflected the transformation of the tax-exempt population. Yet even within the taxable core of the city's population, the Catholic community elicited dramatic growth, which was only possible through immigration.

Based on evidence from among the city's householders, during the first fifty years of French rule the Lutherans preserved their majority despite the rise in the number of Catholic marriages and baptisms (see table 8.2). Yet within the male taxpaying community, French lordship dramatically altered the patterns of immigration. For the Lutherans, the registers note the geographic origins for 1,208 (93%). Four out of five were native Colmarians, which contrasted with the figure of around 70% for the decades before 1680. From the 1680s royal policy prohibited immigration of Protestants from beyond the kingdom, and that policy failed in at least 109 cases.[19] Nevertheless, Colmar's Lutherans had become provincial, as Alsatian immigrants combined with native-born males to account for over 90% of the parish's householders.

For Catholic male householders the traditional insularity had ended. We can identify the origins for over 97% of the Catholic grooms, and less than two-thirds were native Colmarians. In the century before 1680, the Catholic community normally drew over 80% of its new householders from native families, and the bulk of Colmar's Catholic immigrants had normally come from the neighboring villages in the former Austrian domains. After 1680, nearly one in four of Colmar's Catholic householders had been born in more distant lands. Many immigrants came from southwestern Germany, especially refugees from the Breisgau, but the biggest shift came from the influx of French, Swiss, and Italian immigrants. Louis XIV's conquest weakened the city's Lutherans' ties with their traditional contacts across the Rhine and provincialized their community. There were also few Protestants from the interior of the kingdom who were willing to settle in the region. For the Catholics, the city's political reorientation to the west provided diverse new sources for immigrants, and patterns for the two confessional communities had completely reversed.

Among female householders, the contrast was much less dramatic, for, as had been the case through the seventeenth century, they only migrated to the city from short distances (see table 8.3). The vast majority in both parishes were native born. Like their husbands, Catholic women were less likely to be native born than Lutheran women (75.6% to 85.7%), and this

TABLE 8.2
Origins of Male Householders by Confession, 1681–1730

PLACE OF ORIGIN	PROTESTANT (no.)	(%)	CATHOLIC (no.)	(%)
Colmar	956	79.1	548	63.1
Upper Alsace	82	6.8	87	10.0
Lower Alsace	47	3.9	32	3.7
Southwest Germany				
Breisgau	8		39	
Baden	8		10	
Württemberg	13	3.5	5	8.4
Swabia/Bodensee	6		5	
Bavaria	7		14	
Rhineland/Palatinate	8	0.7	5	0.6
Central Germany				
Hesse	12		1	
Hohenlohe	2	1.9	—	0.4
Thuringia	5		—	
Franconia	4		2	
Northern Germany				
Brandenburg-Prussia	2		—	
Saxony	7	0.7	1	0.3
Netherlands	—		1	
Eastern Regions				
Silesia, Moravia,				
Hungary, Poland,	5	0.4	2	0.2
Bohemia				
Switzerland	30	2.5	58	6.7
Italy	—	—	8	0.9
Western Francophone				
France/Lorraine	—		46	
Montbéliard	4	0.3	3	5.6
Region Unknown	2	0.2	2	0.3
Total Known	1,208		869	
Total Cases	1,297	(93.1)	891	(97.5)

TABLE 8.3

Origins of Wives by Confession, 1681–1730

PLACE OF ORIGIN	PROTESTANT		CATHOLIC	
	(no.)	(%)	(no.)	(%)
Colmar	831	85.7	532	75.6
Upper Alsace	99	10.2	106	15.1
Lower Alsace	8	0.8	5	0.7
Southwest Germany				
Breisgau	1		9	
Baden	5		1	
Württemberg	1	0.7	—	1.7
Swabia/Bodensee	—		2	
Bavaria	—		—	
Rhineland	1	0.1	—	—
Eastern Regions				
Silesia, Moravia,				
Hungary, Poland,	—	—	1	0.1
Bohemia				
Switzerland	22	2.3	33	4.7
Western Francophone				
France/Lorraine	—		5	
Montbéliard	1	0.1	—	0.7
Region Unknown	1	0.1	10	1.4
Total Known*	970		704	
Total Cases	1,297	74.8	971	72.5

*The figure for wives comes from data for first and second marriages in both confessional communities.

fact had changed little since mid-century. For both confessional communities, the bulk of female immigrants came from either the neighboring villages of Upper Alsace or the impoverished cantons of Switzerland. Outside of these sources, all other regions combined accounted for only 4.6% of the Catholic wives and 1.8% of the Lutheran.

The changing political conditions had a more significant impact on men than women. Colmar's Catholic parish registers note a significant population of French-speaking women, but they lived in the townhouses of the *conseillers* or in the buildings assigned to the garrison. The Catholics, who remained a minority within the civic community, attracted numerous outsiders, but it is difficult to determine how closely the new French-speaking craftsmen interacted with Colmar's Alemannic-speaking peasants and vineyard workers. The Lutheran community was becoming more insular, but this probably solidified its leadership in resistance to outside interference and uppity insiders, such as Sonntag.

II. Citizens and Confession: Guildsmen under French Lordship

The decision to purchase citizenship reflected a commitment to the political community, and Colmar's subjugation took some of the lustre away from citizenship. Yet even before 1673, the guilds had lost their voice in civic elections. Into the eighteenth century, however, young men still needed to inscribe in a guild in order to practice their trade, and as the city grew the number of guildsmen increased.[20] Between 1680 and 1729, an average of 220 men joined one of Colmar's guilds every five years (see graph 8.2). These figures are well above the average of 115 for the entire period between 1555 and 1680, but the earlier figures reflected a narrower list of men purchasing citizenship rather than simple guild membership.[21] After 1680 applications to the city's guilds fluctuated in a pattern which mirrored the ebb and flow of Colmar's overall demographic growth. In the dynamic 1680s, 515 men inscribed into the city's guilds. For the remainder of Louis XIV's reign, the five-year totals are below 200, except for 1695–99, when the French sympathizers withdrew from the Breisgau and sought refuge in Alsace. Once again after 1715, new inscriptions rose above 250 per five-year period. The influx of new guildsmen stimulated at least part of the city's demographic growth.

French lordship had increased Catholic influence in municipal politics and brought a large community of Catholic officials and soldiers to Colmar. At least until 1730, however, these changes did not produce a Catholic majority among the city's guildsmen. For the entire period, Lutherans accounted for at least 53.7% of the new guildsmen, but beginning in 1700 the number of Lutherans seeking admission to the guilds began to dip below 50%. At no time did more known Catholics than Lutherans seek guild membership. In fact the Catholics only bettered 40% after 1715, although

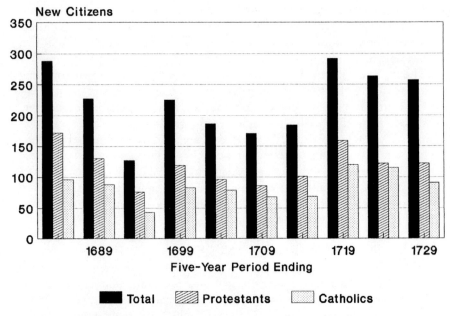

GRAPH 8.2   CITIZENSHIP AND CONFESSION, 1680–1729

for the first time since 1600 they consistently accounted for at least one-third of the new guildsmen. The confessional realignment within the guilds was a much slower process than it had been in the regime or the city's population as a whole.

The confessional offensive carried out by the royal agents against Colmar's Lutherans was in many ways a second Counter-Reformation with a much more significant impact because the pressure never relaxed. Politically, the Lutheran leadership chafed under the restrictions on their participation in governance, for the Protestants had dominated municipal politics for more than a century. Confessional parity in the regime ended the direct association between the Lutheran parish and civic government. Up to that time, the Protestant parish had been the civic church, directed by a consistory composed of a Stettmeister, four councilors, and the four pastors.[22] After 1680, the Lutheran pastors and schoolteachers continued to receive their salaries from the municipal budget, but parish politics ceased to mesh with civic politics.[23] Furthermore, the ministers, such as Andreas Lichtenberger, found themselves under the authority of the *préteur royal*, who ordered Lichtenberger out of the parsonage to make room for a royal official.[24] The Peace of Westphalia required the crown to observe Lutheran rights, but royal policies had already shown that the French would ignore their obligations when it suited them. Colmar's Lutherans thus publicly displayed their loyalty to the king as a gesture of self-defense. Yet despite the pressure, the parish appeared to undergo a revival in its religious life, as the Lutherans remodeled their church and adopted a newly revised catechism and church ordinance.[25]

Royal persecutions exacerbated the tensions between Protestants and Catholics in Colmar as it did elsewhere in Alsace.[26] Colmar's late seventeenth-century confessional disputes revolved around traditional rights grounded in the legal framework and practice of civic bi-confessionalism. The traditions had favored the city's Protestants under rights guaranteed by Imperial law. With Colmar's "reunion" to France, the opportunity for confessional disputes, particularly for Catholic harassment of Lutherans, ripened. Yet even during the Sonntag affair, Catholics and Lutherans were willing to join together in protest against and in defense of the civic regime. In part, confessional squabbling was limited because both the Lutheran ministers and the Catholic clergy were privileged groups isolated from the political community by special status. They were entitled to housing, wine, foodstuffs, firewood, and salaries. The rights disputed between the religious leaders held little meaning to the lay community, which felt its deepest concern over the education and religious upbringing of orphaned children.[27]

In March 1715 the Protestant community faced its severest crisis of the second Counter-Reformation, when Louis XIV ordered that the choir of the Protestant church, St. Matthew's, be turned over to the Catholics. The king's application of the *simultaneum* to Colmar's only Protestant church symbolized the reduction of Lutheran influence in the community.[28] The choir was reconsecrated as a chapel for the new *hôpital royal*. The Lutheran leaders vented their outrage in lengthy documentation of their rights and of confessional abuses, but they failed to prevent the Catholic takeover of the choir two years later.[29]

The French Counter-Reformation was not limited to an assault on Lutheran rights. The royal agents made a concerted effort to revive local Catholicism and to impart to it the spirit of seventeenth-century French Catholicism. In 1698 the crown invited Jesuits and Capuchins to establish houses at Colmar. Initially, the clergy were Germans, but royal officials actively recruited Jesuits from Champagne who knew German, in an effort to more closely ally the Catholic revival with royal aims. The French priests, whose orders were closely associated with the seventeenth-century Catholic revivals, brought new luster to civic Catholic culture. The Jesuits established themselves in St. Peter's priory, and they immediately opened a grammar school which the regime funded with 1,000 livres per year.[30] In 1709 Colmar sheltered 68 priests and 72 nuns. These figures can be compared with figures from Strasbourg, where by 1693 there were over 250 Catholic clergy and by 1709, 494.[31]

Despite the growing clerical community, Colmar's second Counter-Reformation produced few conversions among the city's Lutheran leaders.[32] The Catholic revival primarily affected the organization and discipline among the ecclesiastical elite. The establishment of diocesan seminaries, in Molsheim for Strasbourg and in Porrentruy for Basel, and the tightening of control of clerical appointments improved the quality of Catholic religious life in Alsace.[33] In the neighboring villages numerous rosary confraternities, the symbols of the expansion of Catholic baroque piety, sprang up in the late seventeenth and early eighteenth centuries, but in Colmar there were none.[34] Absenteeism among canons of St. Martin's and clerical arrogance had limited the impact of the chapter's clergy on Colmar's religious life prior to the city's annexation. From 1684 a new provost, Johann Christoph Haus, began to bring order to the chapter's religious and administrative life. In 1716, his brother, Johann Baptist, succeeded him and continued to lead the civic Catholic revival. The brothers were so effective that both were promoted to the role of suffragan bishops for the entire diocese.[35] Colmar's Catholic revival grew out of reforms within the diocese and the external impetus of the royal government, but the effects were only fully felt in the later eighteenth century. At least until 1730, the majority of Colmar's guildsmen continued to attend Lutheran services.

III. Merchants, Artisans, Peasants, and Privilege

The classic provincial town in eighteenth-century France was an administrative center clogged with judicial officials and tax farmers who regulated economic, political, and often religious life in its hinterland.[36] Such cities existed within the empire, and some served as capitals (*Residenzstädte*) for small territorial states.[37] Though they may have served as market centers, Imperial cities often lacked administrative influence over the surrounding villages.[38] The coming of French rule transformed Colmar from an Imperial city to a royal administrative center, which affected the mentality of the city's officials and the nature of town-country relations.

In French towns professional administrators either held noble status or aspired to it. Government service, particularly in the upper levels of the bureaucracy, was often peripatetic, and most *officiers* served in several provinces during their careers. Nevertheless, they depended on an army of local agents with deep roots in the province and limited horizons for promotion beyond the local administrative center, where they occupied the pinnacle of the social structure. When the *Conseil souverain* arrived at Colmar, most of its officials settled permanently in the city. As royal authority expanded in Alsace in the 1680s and 1690s, the role of the *Conseil souverain* in provincial administration had grown as it played a critical role in the "reunion" drive of the 1680s from its new seat at the island fortress on the Rhine not far from Breisach, known as the "straw city." Problems soon emerged, as the *conseillers* found the environment unpleasant and the court met irregularly. In 1694 Louis XIV expanded the council to two chambers and offered its offices for sale with hereditary rights.[39] The stipulations of the Peace of Ryswick called for the demolition of the "straw city," and the council found itself homeless and threatened with suppression by the Parlement of Metz. The intendant in Alsace, La Fond, successfully preserved the court, and François Dietremann arranged the move to Colmar. Within months the *Conseil souverain* underwent a procedural reform which regularized its sessions. Colmar was a pleasant environment for the court officials, and the reforms permitted a rapidly expanding caseload. The council and the city grew together in importance, and Colmar became the provincial legal capital with jurisdiction even over mighty Strasbourg.[40]

The arrival of the *Conseil souverain* reinforced Colmar's growing role as a center of governmental finance and tax collection in Upper Alsace. After 1698 Colmar joined Strasbourg and Landau as the three centers for *receveurs particuliers* of royal taxes in the province.[41] By the end of Louis XIV's reign, most royal officials mixed their legal duties with investment in governmental annuities and the pursuit of inheritable privilege. Ambitious Colmarians at the peak of the civic social hierarchy assumed this lifestyle, as Catholics and Lutherans alike abandoned commerce and became *rentiers*.[42] Colmar had long been a market center for Upper Alsace, and following the Thirty Years' War the city had acquired greater influence in the economic activity of the neighboring villages. These shifts had a profound impact on the distribution of productive activity among the Colmarians in the early eighteenth century.

Colmar's development as an administrative center apparently increased its role as a market center (see graph 8.3). The percentage of guildsmen inscribed in *zur Treue* rose to 16.7%. The growth of the merchants' guild was a long-term process, but the increase after 1680 is even more remarkable because the guild registers were more inclusive for the period than they had been previously.

A royal report, composed in 1697 following nearly a decade of war, identified the local merchants' continued dependence on wine and brandy sales, the region's fertility and potential abundance, and the value of the Ill river as a means of transport.[43] Conflicts with the empire had closed the critical market at Frankfurt am Main to the Colmarians, who in any case had little to sell due to the destruction of the vineyards. At the time the king's agents also believed that Colmar possessed the potential for industrial development (*fabrique*) because the city could feed a large work force, just as it had an army. Unfortunately, the cloth industry lacked readily accessible raw materials; and the leather industry, which had boomed in supplying the army, faced a serious crisis with demobilization.[44]

At this time, Colmar's merchants felt themselves overshadowed by the merchants of Basel and Strasbourg.[45] Colmar's aggressive *Brennenherren* of the early seventeenth century had given way to men who sought regulated shelters to protect them from free trade.[46] The city still served as a lively market for local wine, but outsiders came there to purchase the wine and ship it themselves.[47] After 1680 the city's wealthiest merchants redirected

Guilds

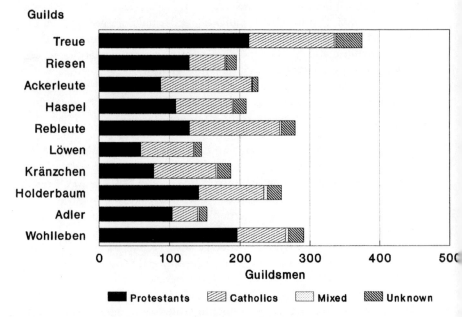

GRAPH 8.3   CONFESSION BY GUILD, 1681–1730

their entrepreneurial investments towards annuities and tax farms. With its leading merchant families abandoning local and regional trade, Colmar's market activities came into the hands of local retailers, who clung tightly to market privileges and favored regulations which confined trade to narrow limits.[48] Royal prohibition against Lutheran *officiers* channeled ambitions in the Lutheran elite to governmental finance or the accumulation of rural properties.[49] Whatever path they selected, among both Catholics and Lutherans, the wealthiest men were disappearing from the tax registers and trade activity.

The agricultural guilds also experienced significant growth, and the center of the recovery lay in Colmar's wine production. In 1698, Colmar's regime complained to the intendant of ruined vineyards, low prices, and poor markets.[50] Harvest failures had reduced the cultivators "to the last extremity," and the city's once flourishing brandy trade was disrupted because the war had "broken communication" and the cultivators faced "the sterility of the vines and the high price of wine." In 1698 the Colmarians felt that peace alone would restore the lost commerce.[51] By the 1730s expansion in wine production had outstripped demand, and the municipal regime sought to restrict new plantings and uproot some of the vines which were producing poor wine. Expanding production had deflated prices, and the civic leaders hoped to restore profits and the local wine's reputation through mercantilist regulations.[52]

The boom in the wine production led to the expansion of Colmar's agricultural guilds, which accounted for 30.8% of the new householders after 1680, up from 25% for the previous decades but still below the 32% for the era before the Thirty Years' War. After 1680 occupational distinctions among the agricultural guilds ceased, as vineyard workers regularly inscribed in *zum Haspel* and *Ackerleute*. In 1690, 135 householders (13.4%) identified themselves as *Rebmannen*; twenty-five were members of *Ackerleute* and twenty-four of *zum Haspel*. By 1730, 195 householders (14.6%) identified their chief occupation as vineyard workers; forty-two belonged to *Ackerleute* and forty-three to *zum Haspel*. Just the same, the agricultural guilds had never possessed the solidarity needed to regulate control of the vineyards or trade. In 1721 the regime had conducted a survey of vineyard ownership; and surprisingly, the two guilds most closely associated with wine production, *Rebleute* and *zum Riesen*, combined owned only 16% of the vineyards in the civic territory.[53] The magistrates, royal officials, and ecclesiastical institutions, all owned some plots; but most belonged to the city's guildsmen. Among the guilds, *zur Treue* and *zum Wohlleben* together held the most acreage, roughly 30%, which was double that of the agricultural guilds. Merchants, tailors, tanners, and shoemakers all found vineyards to be a good investment.[54] The distribution of properties among individuals was not recorded, but the regime's mercantilist concern for regulation in 1730 may have reflected a relatively broad social base of ownership and the desire to regulate this relatively free market.

When local officials assessed the city's economic potential in 1698, they emphasized the importance of the wine industry and tanning.[55] Ironically, at least for the wine trade, the expansion occurred despite the loss of its long-distance markets, and the apparent decline in membership in *zum Riesen*. Local wine and brandy no longer appeared at the great fairs of the lower Rhine, for the city now sold the bulk of its vintages in Strasbourg and the Swiss cantons.[56] Furthermore, despite the spread of ownership, control of processing had become concentrated in fewer hands, and many of these men were privileged and free from guild membership and regulation.[57] Of all of Colmar's guilds, *zum Riesen* experienced the sharpest decline in its share of the work force, from 14.1% before 1680 to 8.4% under French lordship.

Zum Adler was also shrinking in the early eighteenth century, from 8.5% of the work force to 6.6%, which perhaps reflected the growth of a rural cloth industry or more likely an absence of raw materials and tradition to support the industry's expansion.[58] The one artisan community that apparently continued to grow in this period was Colmar's leather workers. The guild welcomed 270 men between 1681 and 1730, and they represented 12.5% of Colmar's guildsmen. Prior to the Thirty Years' War, *zum Wohlleben* comprised only 7.2% of Colmar's guildsmen, and its share had increased to 11% in the decades after the war. In the early eighteenth century, Colmar's tanners and shoemakers continued to benefit from the ready market provided by the royal garrison and the massive fort at Neuf Brisach.

The royal government sought to stimulate manufacturing in the area but met with little success. Some firms which outfitted French troops had grown, but in the survey of local commerce in 1698, municipal officials complained of the overall lack of manufacturing.[59] Yet neither the royal government nor the civic regime followed policies which would have allowed for expansion in manufacturing. In 1720 the regime resisted efforts of magistrate Johann Ulrich Goll to expand his tannery on the Mühlbach. Goll sought tax exemptions from the regime and had requested open access to firewood, but his fellow magistrates sided with the city's smaller producers and refused to grant Goll his requests.[60] In the late seventeenth and early eighteenth centuries, industrial development in Alsace depended on privileges, protection, and monopoly. The initial outlay of capital forced the entrepreneur to seek the means to protect his investment. Colmar's officials were unwilling to provide the guarantees required by the local entrepreneurs, and as a result the regime sacrificed Colmar's potential role in the industrial development of Upper Alsace to Munster and Mulhouse.

Its elevation to a provincial administrative center confirmed Colmar's place as a regional market. Colmar had not been a proto-industrial town, and its complex economy mixed agricultural pursuits with victualing and craft production. Its chief commercial products continued to be wine and brandy, processed goods drawn from the land. The city preserved a commercial elite, who worked within royal trade regulations. As occurred on a larger scale at Strasbourg, Colmar's merchants exploited opportunities within the province; the most attractive investments came from profits drawn on the royal debt, and they sought to protect themselves with regulation and privilege.[61] Eighteenth-century Colmar lacked a resident duke or count, but its merchants and guildsmen possessed the economic mentality of inhabitants of a *Residenzstadt*.

IV. CONFESSIONAL CHANGES AMONG THE GUILDSMEN

The royal program of Counter-Reformation combined with the changing pressures in the city's economy to alter the traditional confessional relations within Colmar's guilds after 1680 (see above, graph 8.3). Despite royal efforts, Colmar's Lutheran community continued to embrace the majority (53.8%) of the city's guildsmen, though the Lutheran share was well below the more than three-fourths share they enjoyed between 1640 and 1680. Nevertheless, Colmar's Lutheran community had not shrunk; rather, the Catholics had increased and spread into all of Colmar's guilds. Nurtured by royal patronage and a rapidly improving clergy, Colmar's Catholic community expanded to represent nearly 38% of the city's guildsmen, and this overall shift produced significant changes within the guilds.

The polarization which had characterized guild life before 1680 ended, and the overall impression is one of balance. Within the traditional Protestant guilds, only *zum Wohlleben* (67.6%) and *zum Adler* (68.4%) could claim a two-thirds majority. Identifiable Catholics accounted for at least 20% in all guilds. The Lutherans continued to form a majority in the merchant and artisan guilds, but Catholics outnumbered Lutherans in *Ackerleute, Rebleute, zum Löwen,* and *zum Kränzchen.* These guilds had always had large groups of Catholics in them, but now they worshipped together with immigrant tinsmiths, tanners, tailors, and merchants. Colmar's Catholic community had been able to attract immigrants from a much broader geographic radius, and these new householders helped the Catholic community round out its productive activity. By the early eighteenth century, both confessional communities could function as independent economic entities. Confessional alienation and religious prejudice could develop more easily when the two parish communities were not economically interdependent.

The shift in balance within Colmar's guilds was not so much a product of a decline in Lutheran membership as the overall growth of the Catholic community (see graphs 8.4–5). There were more Lutheran guildsmen in 1720 (697) than in 1690 (637), but at the later date the Lutherans represented only 59.8% of the guildsmen as opposed to 67.7% a generation earlier. Catholic membership jumped from 280 guildsmen (29.8%) in 1690 to 427 (36.6%) in 1720. If the trend continued the confessions would reach parity by mid-century. In 1690 the Lutherans could still claim more than 70% of the members within the artisan guilds. In 1720 only *zum Adler* and *zum Wohlleben* held such Lutheran majorities. The Catholic community experienced steady growth in every guild, except *zum Haspel,* where the Lutheran majority rose from 58.3% to 69.1%. By 1720 Catholics had become participants in all aspects of Colmar's social and economic life.

As Catholics began to assume economic roles that they had not pursued in the past, they also began to settle into neighborhoods which had welcomed few Catholics prior to 1680 (see maps 8.1–2). The old Lutheran families, however, kept their homes, and in the inner neighborhoods Catholic integration took much longer than it would in the guilds. In 1720 Lutherans still comprised over 70% of the householders in *Lambs Ort* (IV), *zum Haupt* (VII), and *Hinter dem Cour* (VIII), but in district III (*Blaumeysens Ort*), which had long been a Lutheran enclave, they comprised a minority. As in the past, there were more Lutherans in the central neighborhoods than near the city gates. In 1720 the Catholics could only claim 50% of the households in tiny *Salzkasten* (XI) and in the northern neighborhoods surrounding the Dominican convents. There were more Catholics everywhere in 1720, but much of the city was still predominantly Lutheran.

Colmar's conquest by the French had produced sharp demographic growth, a shift in the balance of power between the two confessional communities, and the growth of a privileged elite. The growing presence of privilege exempted many of Colmar's wealthiest householders from annotation in the *Gewerff* registers, which lessens their value in assessing the city's overall

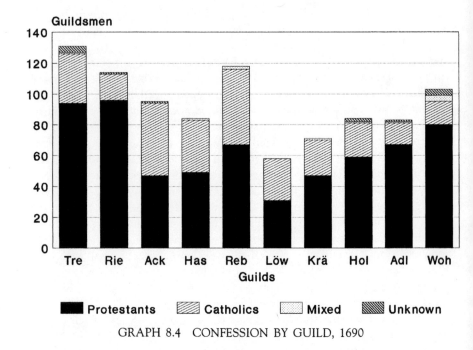

GRAPH 8.4   CONFESSION BY GUILD, 1690

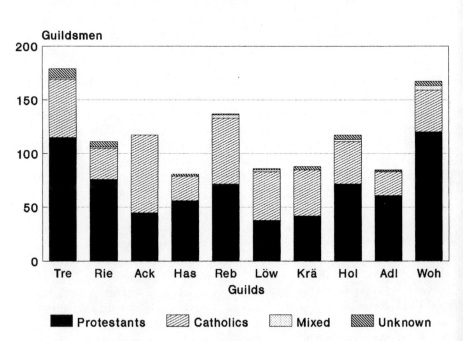

GRAPH 8.5   CONFESSION BY GUILD, 1720

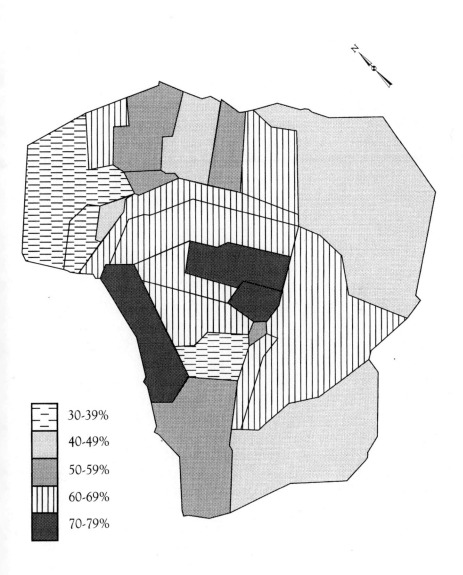

MAP 8.1 PROTESTANTS, 1720

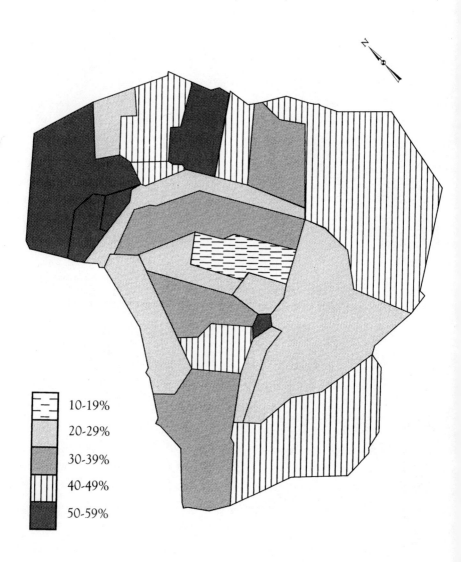

10-19%

20-29%

30-39%

40-49%

50-59%

100 meters

MAP 8.2   CATHOLICS, 1720

social and economic structure, but it is possible to draw some conclusions from the available data. Colmar became a much wealthier city under French rule, as even the aggregate wealth of the taxable householders grew steadily from 1690 to 1730 (see tables 8.4–6). The city's assessed aggregate wealth had peaked twice in the earlier decades, at 487,000 florins in 1620 and again at 440,000 in 1670. Assessed wealth did not regain these peaks until 1720, by which time the city had many more householders than in either 1670 or 1620. By 1730 the aggregate wealth was the highest for any year since before 1600. Nevertheless, many of the city's wealthiest men were tax exempt, and actual aggregate wealth had probably surpassed the peak of 1620 well before 1730.

The increasing civic wealth, however, was distributed less and less equally. Despite demographic growth, the number of taxpayers assessed on more than 2,000 florins of wealth had only risen from fifteen to sixteen between 1690 and 1730. Taxable households in the upper strata had fallen dramatically between 1690 and 1702, at the same time that the *Conseil souverain* moved into the city. Although the numbers of wealthy taxpayers rose again over the next decades, it remained below the figures for the decades before French rule. The 1690s also witnessed a fall of 15% in the number of householders assessed between 1,000 and 2,000 florins, while the population for the city as a whole grew over 9%. In the last decade of the seventeenth century, the burden of taxes swung from the wealthy to Colmar's poorer householders. At the same time, city taxes increased significantly to meet the growing appetite of the royal fisc and to service the debt for the Reunion of Charges.

After 1710 the number of men paying taxes on wealth assessed above 1,000 florins rose more quickly than the population as a whole, but their share of the assessed wealth only reached the level of 1690 in 1730. The elite taxpayers never accounted for more than 15.3% of the city's taxable wealth, well below the percentages for the decades after the Thirty Years' War, when they paid around 40% of the city's taxes. The general trend away from concentration of taxable wealth was broken only in the period between 1702 and 1710, that is, the years just before Sonntag's protest, and this renewed concentration must have triggered some of the resistance among men like Sonntag. The wealthiest taxable householders represented less than 1.5% of the overall householders in these decades, and less than 1% in 1702. Taxpayers in the upper middle strata dipped from 1690 to 1710, and regained their numbers by 1720, perhaps due to the influx of immigrants during the Regency. In both strata the percentages were well below the figures for the mid-century, when the rich represented over 2.5% of the householders and the upper middle strata anywhere from around 9% to 12.5% of the taxpayers. The core of the taxpaying community, both in terms of numbers and percentage of the city's taxable assets, were those assessed between 230 and 990 florins. They carried the burden of Colmar's fiscal obligations in the early eighteenth century.

TABLE 8.4
Taxable Householders by Strata, 1690–1730

	1690 (no.)	(%)	1702 (no.)	(%)	1710 (no.)	(%)	1720 (no.)	(%)	1730 (no.)	(%)
>2,000 fl.	15	1.5	8	0.7	14	1.3	20	1.6	16	1.2
>1,000 fl.	52	5.2	44	4.0	42	3.8	66	5.1	73	5.5
230–990 fl.	448	44.3	567	51.4	521	47.6	518	41.2	731	55.0
80–200 fl.	478	47.2	472	42.7	498	45.5	632	50.2	446	33.5
Exempt	18	1.8	13	1.2	19	1.8	24	1.9	64	4.8
Total	1,011		1,105		1,094		1,260		1,330	

TABLE 8.5
Percentage of Overall Wealth by Strata, 1690–1730

	1690 (%)	1702 (%)	1710 (%)	1720 (%)	1730 (%)
>2,000 fl.	11.2	5.4	13.5	15.3	10.6
>1,000 fl.	18.6	15.3	14.2	18.3	19.9
230–990 fl.	46.2	56.6	49.5	44.4	57.0
80–200 fl.	24.0	22.7	22.8	22.0	12.5
Exempt	—	—	—	—	—
Total fl.	372,050	377,110	390,260	443,660	485,950

TABLE 8.6
Percentage of Change in Wealth by Strata, 1690–1730

	1690 (%)	1702 (%)	1710 (%)	1720 (%)	1730 (%)
>2,000 fl.	−43.7	−51.4	+159.9	+29.5	−24.1
>1,000 fl.	+2.3	−16.8	−4.0	+46.6	+19.0
230–990 fl.	+4.6	+24.2	−9.4	+1.9	+40.6
80–200 fl.	+67.3	−3.8	+3.8	+9.5	−37.6
Exempt	—	—	—	—	—
Community	+3.5	+1.4	+3.5	+13.7	+9.5

Throughout this era the Catholic community remained a minority, but with royal patronage Colmar's Catholics had moved into civic offices, the traditional Protestant guilds, and Colmar's core neighborhoods. Catholic immigrants from distant lands expanded the horizons of this once insular community. During the decades before French rule, Catholics had been poorer than their Lutheran neighbors, but the differences were not great. Ironically, between 1690 and 1730, Colmar's Catholics became much poorer than their fellow guildsmen from the Lutheran parish. The average assessment in 1690 for the city's Catholics was 336 florins, and it fell gradually to 328 florins in 1720, then rose slightly to 331 florins over the next decade. For the Lutheran community average assessments shifted markedly from decade to decade, falling from 400 florins in 1690 to 353 florins in 1702, then rising again to 398 in 1710, then to 437 in 1730. Lutherans continued to predominate among Colmar's most highly taxed householders, though under the new fiscal system of privilege this reflected their inability to gain tax exemptions (see table 8.7). Among Colmar's richest taxpayers, the merchants in *zur Treue* continued to dominate, and these men were all Lutherans. Among the other guilds, none could claim consistent representation among the city's elite between 1690 and 1730, and Colmar's wealthy Catholics did not concentrate in any guild.

For the city as a whole, the two confessions maintained a balance throughout the era (see tables 8.8–9). The Lutherans were overrepresented among those assessed at over 1,000 florins in 1690, which were the strata which should have included the privileged Catholics. Both communities had their share of poor. In 1720 the two confessional communities were much more evenly distributed throughout the tax strata, though the city's highest taxpayers were more likely to be Lutherans. The one significant change was the number of Catholics identified among the exempt, and these men are not among the noble *conseilers* of the *Conseil souverain*.

Overall, for the period after 1680, the difference in wealth between the two confessional communities might have stimulated Catholic ambition and frustration if, in fact, the *Gewerff* registers recorded the whole picture. The tension that did exist lay between privilege and exemption, and here it was the Lutheran community which was frustrated by the inability to escape taxation. Part of the jealousy which fueled the anger against Johann Jacob Sandherr and the support for Johann Jacob Sonntag grew out of access to privilege. Beyond this, the overall balance in the confessional experience of unequal distribution of wealth in part prevented, as it had since the beginning of the seventeenth century, the volatile mixture of confessional bigotry and social envy. Sonntag was able to rally support from both parishes.

By 1730 the former Imperial city had become a center for French provincial administration, and in many ways Colmar resembled the *Residenzstädte* across the Rhine. Politically the regime had lost its autonomy, but the

TABLE 8.7
Colmar's Elite under French Rule, 1690–1730

GUILD MEMBERSHIP AND WEALTH

GUILD	1690		1702		1710		1720		1730	
Treue	5		4		9		9		9	
Riesen	1		—		1	(1)	1	(1)	2	
Ackerleute	2		—		1	(1)	—		—	
Haspel	2	(1)	2	(1)	1	(1)	2	(2)	—	
Rebleute	1		—		—		2	(1)	1	
Löwen	1		—		—		—		1	(1)
Kränzchen	2	(1)	1		1		—		—	
Adler	1	(1)	—		—		1	(1)	—	
Holderbaum	—		—		—		—		1	
Wohlleben	—		1		1	(1)	3	(1)	—	
NA	—		—		1	(1)	2	(1)	2	(1)
Total	15	(3)	8	(1)	15	(5)	20	(7)	16	(2)

Key:
(n)   Number of Catholics
NA   Not inscribed in citizen register

Confession and Wealth

CONFESSION	1690		1702		1710		1720		1730	
	(no.)	(%)	(no.)	(%)	(no.)	(%)	(no.)	(%)	(no.)	(%)
Catholic	3	20.0	1	12.5	5	33.3	7	35.0	2	12.5
Lutheran	12	80.0	7	87.5	10	66.7	13	65.0	13	81.25
Unknown	—	—	—	—	—	—	—	—	1	6.25
Mixed	—	—	—	—	—	—	—	—	—	—
Totals	15		8		15		20		16	

TABLE 8.8
Tax Rates by Confession, 1690

ESTATE	PROTESTANTS (no.)	(%)	CATHOLICS (no.)	(%)	UNKNOWN (no.)	(%)	MIXED (no.)	(%)	TOTAL (no.)
>2,000 fl.	12	80.0	3	20.0	—	—	—	—	15
1,000 fl.	41	78.9	10	19.2	1	1.9	—	—	52
230–990 fl.	292	65.2	145	32.3	7	1.6	4	0.9	448
80–200 fl.	303	63.4	148	31.0	19	4.0	8	1.6	478
Exempt	10	55.5	5	27.8	3	16.7	—	—	18
Total	658	65.1	311	30.8	30	3.0	12	1.2	1,011

TABLE 8.9
Tax Rates by Confession, 1720

ESTATE	PROTESTANTS (no.)	(%)	CATHOLICS (no.)	(%)	UNKNOWN (no.)	(%)	MIXED (no.)	(%)	TOTAL (no.)
>2,000 fl.	13	65.0	7	35.0	—	—	—	—	20
>1,000 fl.	44	67.8	21	31.8	1	1.4	—	—	66
230–990 fl.	310	51.7	187	36.2	15	2.9	6	1.2	518
80–200 fl.	348	55.1	245	38.7	31	4.9	8	1.3	632
Exempt	6	25.0	17	70.8	1	4.2	—	—	24
Total	721	57.2	477	37.9	48	3.8	14	1.1	1,260

officeholders, who should have felt the loss most deeply, were thoroughly ingrained into the new system. Confessionally, the citizens remained divided and alienated. If anything, the influx of French-speaking Catholics further fractured the religious communities. Finally, French sovereignty reinforced Colmar's economic domination over its hinterland by concentrating capital under the aegis of mercantilism. The city became an administrative center which drew the elites from the surrounding villages and towns to seek their fortunes. Property, finance, and tax farming concentrated the wealth and surplus of the region in what had become, in effect, the capital of Upper Alsace. The first two generations of French rule had molded the modern town. At Colmar, as elsewhere, political force, embodied in the state, ultimately defined national allegiance, though it could never fully absorb local loyalty. The resultant tensions presented the early modern Colmarians and their descendants with complex and often painful political, economic, confessional, and cultural choices.

Notes

1. Similar options allowed the elite in Strasbourg to accumulate privileges. See Greissler, *La classe politique*, 217–41. See also Dreyer-Roos, *La population strasbourgeoise*, 62–74. One Lutheran family that profited from these conditions in Colmar were the Golls. See Schmitt, *Aux origines de la révolution industrielle*, esp. 70–88.
2. AMC, AA 171, 1. The document also noted 1,020 houses, so that the city was apparently underpopulated.
3. AMC, AA 171, 2. This survey identified two parishes (one Catholic and one Lutheran), 1,078 "hearths," and 7,142 "souls" (of whom 3,109 were Catholic, 3,527 were Lutheran, 506 were "Huguenots," and none were Jews). A second document working with the same raw material divided the material differently. The adult male population of the 1,078 *feux* included 988 citizens and 192 "habitans qui n'ont possédes demeure fixe et l'a changement à leur volonté." The city also sheltered 103 "garçons non mariés au-dessus de dix-huit ans." The work force also included 43 *laboureurs*, 221 *vignerons*, and 14 *meuniers*. AMC, AA 171, 6. AMC, AA 171, 7 is a German draft of the same assessment.
4. "Kam das *Conseil souverain* von Breysach hieher, nahm seinen Sitz auf dem Wag Keller, worauf der Magistrat und Rath den grossen Saal auf der Schneiderzunft einnahm. Der Königl. hohe Rath plaidirte zum erstenmal den 22 May. Weil sie keine haüser hatten, wurden sie par *Billet* einlogiert und die Bürger musten ihnen französiche Zimmer (mit französischen Kaminen) zurechtmachen." Rathgeber, ed., *Colmar und Ludwig XIV*, 45. See also Livet, "La monarchie absolue," 140, 144–45.
5. The census listed 1,737 men, 1,945 women, 3,703 children of both genders, 6 secular priests, 62 male religious, 72 nuns, and 1,048 "valets et servantes," for a total of 9,023 persons. AMC, AA 171, 8.
6. AMC, AA 171, 9–10.
7. Strasbourg experienced a similar growth of noncitizen households. See Dreyer-Roos, *La population strasbourgeoise*, 45–51, 56–64.
8. These figures must be treated with caution. Henri Fleurent estimates 8,579

inhabitants in 1730 and then an extended period of growth until 1790, when there were 13,214 people. See Fleurent, "Essai sur la démographie," 9–10. The issue rests on the attitude of census takers to tax-exempt households and the floating population of poor.

9. On the volume of refugees from Freiburg-im-Breisgau, see Kopf, "Unter der Krone Frankreichs," 23–124, here at 119–22. On the impact of the refugees and the famine in Strasbourg, see Dreyer-Roos, *La population strasbourgeoise*, 109–38, 214–20.

10. These low figures can be explained in part from the fact that no registers exists for 1700 and the "decade" measured in this case lasted only eight years.

11. Livet, "La monarchie absolue," 135.

12. For a list of incentives to convert drawn up in 1683, see AMC, AA 166, 227.

13. AMC, GG 171, 19 & 36. See AMC, AA 166, 250.

14. On 29 August 1729, Johann Bichel was expelled from the city by order of the *Conseil souverain* because he was a Lutheran foreigner. The intendant ordered the regime to exercise better judgment in the future. AMC, GG 171, 37.

15. Georges Livet has analyzed the lists of *manants* who sought protection in Colmar in the late seventeenth and early eighteenth century. Prior to 1690, emigration from the Swiss Confederation had furnished Colmar, as well as many other parts of Alsace, with new residents of both confessions, but the Swiss immigration tapered off by 1690 while more and more newcomers came from France. French immigration remained low until 1690, then after an erratic decade, it became sustained and exceeded all other sources by two to one. Livet, "La monarchie absolue," 134. Livet's study does not consider local immigration from Alsatian communities, which represented nearly 57% of the newcomers in Strasbourg. Dreyer-Roos, *La population strasbourgeoise*, 118–19.

16. Livet, "La monarchie absolue," 137–38.

17. On the royal Counter-Reformation, see André Marcel Burg, *Histoire de l'église d'Alsace* (Colmar, 1945), 228–30.

18. See Hans Christoph Rublack, "Konfession als demographischer Faktor?" in Rabe, Molitor, and Rublack, eds., *Festgäbe für Ernst Walter Zeeden*, 62–96.

19. Henri Strohl first presented the image of an insular Protestant community under siege. See Strohl, "L'esprit républicaine," 431–32.

20. In 1697 the magistrate asked the intendant for the right to force two Savoyard merchants, Claude Conelluc and Etienne Messon, to join the guild *zur Treue* and pay taxes. They received their permission. See AMC, CC 252, 9a.

21. See the introduction by Jean-Marie Schmitt in Bachschmidt, ed., *Le livre des bourgeois, 1660–1789*, v–ix.

22. See Strohl, *Le protestantisme en Alsace*, 277–78.

23. Ibid., 278.

24. AMC, GG 171, 1.

25. See Strohl, "L'esprit républicain," 431–32.

26. Sittler, "La transformation du gouvernement," 152. Colmar's Lutherans had one of their pastors banished following a run in with the Jesuits after the takeover of the choir in 1715. AMC, GG 172, 19.

27. Regarding the dispute over confessional rights among the religious leaders, see BMC, Fonds Chauffour, Ms. 906. On disputes over the religious education of children, see AMC, AA 166, 250.

28. The decision triggered a stormy debate between the two communities. AMC, GG 172, 43, 48–49, 53–56.

29. AMC, GG 172, 2–3.

30. For an account of the early years of Jesuit activity in Colmar, see Sée, ed., *Memoire des Jesuites*, 1–31.

31. AMC, AA 171, 8. For Strasbourg, see Dreyer-Roos, *La population strasbourgeoise*, 64–65.
32. To my knowledge, only one local Lutheran converted and gained office: Nicolas Klein. See Sée, ed., *Johann Joner's Notanda*, 8. Strohl, *Le protestantisme en Alsace*, 279–81.
33. Burg, *L'église d'Alsace*, 231–40.
34. See Ingold, *Miscellanea Alsatica*, 1: 54–55.
35. Ingold, *Miscellanea Alsatica*, 1: 97. See also Goehlinger, *Histoire du chapitre*, 48–55.
36. Roger Chartier and Hughes Neveux, eds., *La ville classique de la renaissance aux revolutions*, vol. 3 of *Histoire de la France urbaine* (Paris: 1981), 23–29.
37. François, "Des républiques marchands."
38. Nuremberg, for example, controlled an extensive territory, while Augsburg's regime had no authority beyond the city walls. On Nuremberg, see Strauss, *Nuremberg*, 7–11. On Augsburg, see Bátori, *Augsburg*, 14. Mack Walker emphasizes the distinction between citizens and peasants through economic competition and legal identity. See Walker, *German Home Towns*, 112–19.
39. Livet, *L'intendance*, 678–79.
40. Ibid., 680–81. See also Livet, "Colmar et l'établissement du Conseil souverain," 75–76.
41. Livet, *L'intendance*, 691–93.
42. As early as 1694, several leading Colmarian Lutherans appear as *rentiers* in the *capitation* register: Johann Georg Herr, Elias Lang, Johann Andres, and Matthias Kyss. AMC, CC 155, 1694, pp. 1–3. On the spread of *rentiers* in the province, see Livet, "Royal Administration," 190–91.
43. AMC, AA 166, 272. The intendant, Jacques de La Grange, working from the Colmar report, summarized the general picture for the king: "This city was formerly one of the most illustrious in the province, as much for the fertility of its soil as for the wide pastures and quality of the vineyards which surround it. She has the facility to transport her commodities by the river Ill, which is very near." Raymond Oberlé, ed., *L'Alsace en 1700: Memoire sur la province d'Alsace de l'Intendant Jacques de La Grange* (Colmar, 1975), 156.
44. AMC, AA 166, 272, fol. 2r–v.
45. The regime was particularly frustrated because it viewed Strasbourg and Basel as entrepôts which denied local merchants profits. See AMC, AA 166, 272, fol. 4.
46. The struggle against outsiders had begun in the early seventeenth century as the market outlets for Colmar's goods began to dry up. See Sittler, "Commerce et commerçants," 29–32. For example, in 1697, Colmar's merchants pressured the regime into placing heavy tax burdens on two merchants, Claude Conelluc and Estienne Messon, who had settled from the interior of the kingdom. Letter to the intendant, dated 1 October 1697. AMC, CC 252, 9a.
47. Sittler, *La viticulture*, 46.
48. Similar patterns developed in Strasbourg. See Hertner, *Stadtwirtschaft*, 342–68. Mack Walker argues that commercial mobility was out of keeping with the insular economic mentality of the home townsmen. See Walker, *German Home Towns*, 120–25.
49. See Livet, *L'intendance*, 820–22.
50. AMC, AA 166, 171.
51. Ibid., fol. 1r–v.
52. AMC, AA 167, 158.
53. Out of 833 arpents under cultivation, the members of *Rebleute* owned only 68 (7%), while *zum Riesen* owned 81 (8%) see Sittler, *La viticulture*, 33.

54. *Zum Wohlleben*'s members held 114 arpents (13%), while the merchants and crafts in *zur Treue* held 157 arpents (18%). Sittler, *La viticulture*, 33.
55. AMC, AA 166, 272, fols. 1r–3v.
56. Sittler, *La viticulture*, 75–77.
57. Ibid., 34.
58. AMC, AA 166, 272, fol. 3r–v.
59. AMC, AA 166, 272, fol. 3r.
60. Lucien Sittler, "Notice sur les débuts de l'industrie à Colmar: Il y a deux cents ans," *Annuaire de Colmar* (1967): 52–55. See also AMC, AA 166, 90–109; and AMC, AA 167, 164–65. Johann Ulrich Goll was heavily involved in early industrialization in the region. See Schmitt, *Aux origines de la révolution industrielle*, 32.
61. On Strasbourg, see Hertner, *Stadtwirtschaft*, 342–54.

Conclusion

The political, economic, and confessional communities which inhabited early modern Colmar faced constant pressure from external forces and weathered several internal crises. The external pressure might have a political face, such as the expansion of French hegemony in Alsace, but its impact generated conflicts in the political, economic, and confessional arenas of civic life. A crisis between the city's confessional communities, such as the Counter-Reformation interim of 1627–33, also had political and economic ramifications. In this book, I have attempted to unravel these interwoven strands by separating early modern civic history into three eras which were highlighted by a particular type of external pressure and a particular internal crisis: first, the era of Reformation and Counter-Reformation; second, the decades of economic recovery and reorientation following the Thirty Years' War; and finally, a period of political transformation during the first decades of French rule.

Colmar's regime introduced Protestant worship in the city in 1575 based on the questionable claim to the *ius reformandi*, and civic officials assumed authority over the new church. The Reformation's shaky legal footing and the pressure from the nearby Austrian regime at Ensisheim forced civic Protestant officials to tolerate Catholic services. By 1600 Colmar's 7,000 inhabitants were divided into two religious communities, one Protestant and one Catholic. Most members of the oligarchy were clearly committed to Protestant worship, and, though they may have wanted to establish confessional conformity in the city, a small but stable Catholic community survived. From 1575 Colmar would remain a bi-confessional town, where religious differences posed a constant threat to political order.

Colmar's late Reformation triggered the first internal crisis brought on by the division of the city into two confessional communities. Kaspar von Greyerz has connected Colmar's experience with those encountered in Essen, Dortmund, Aachen, Aalen, and Hagenau. Their "late city Reformations" were primarily initiated "from above" as had been the case at Colmar, and each town faced particular external pressures brought on by the existing confessional divisions in the empire and the consolidation of coherent confessional parties. In particular, the dynamic impact of the Calvinist "second Reformation," which was illegal under the rubrics of the Religious Peace of Augsburg, politicized the Reformation process in these towns. All of them had to settle for bi-confessional resolutions to their internal confessional divisions, but the structure of their bi-confessionalism was different from the "parity" cities studied by Paul Warmbrunn. The Reformation came earlier in the parity cities, and the ultimate structure of their confessional politics emerged from the forced constitutional pressure of the Interim and the specific legal guarantees of the Peace of Augsburg. Those cities which established evangelical worship after 1555 appealed to the *ius reformandi*, though their right to claim it was questionable; and the Protestant leaders, who dominated the magistrates in every town except Dortmund, felt no compulsion to honor confessional parity in the regime or within the citizenry.

At Colmar, however, the Catholic minority was never excluded from political participation or guild membership, though by the 1590s Protestants monopolized the magistrate and basically controlled the council. By 1620 at least two-thirds of the citizens attended Protestant services, and the bulk of them belonged to Colmar's merchants' and artisans' guilds. Nevertheless, no guild was ever confessionally exclusive. Catholic worship claimed significant adherence among Colmar's peasants and vineyard workers as well as among the city's victualers. Most neighborhoods in the city were confessionally mixed, and each church had its rich and poor parishioners. Bi-confessionalism added a new division within the general community, but it did not reinforce existing divisions among Colmarians. This was not the case in many towns with religious minorities, and in the other bi-confessional Alsatian city, Hagenau, the Lutheran elite remained socially exclusive.

Colmar's confessional peace depended on the preservation of the Imperial peace, and when war broke out in 1618 Colmar's Protestants faced a reckoning for their confessional choice. In 1627 an Imperial commission, supported by a garrison, outlawed Colmar's Reformed church, deposed the regime, and drove the Protestant elite into exile. Though the Counter-Reform regime supported the gradual spread of Catholic influence, they would not force immediate conformity upon their Protestant neighbors; for they, like their Reformed predecessors, ruled from a shaky foundation dependent on the configuration of external forces. In the end, Catholic power in Colmar lasted only until 1632 when the Imperial garrison surrendered to the besieging Swedes, who restored bi-confessionalism with the Protestant community now served by a Lutheran ministry. The confessional realignment of Colmar's Protestant parish convinced many among the exiled political and economic elite to resettle permanently in Mulhouse and Basel. Colmar's Counter-Reformation resembled that of Hagenau, but there, when the elite abandoned the city, the Protestant community lost its social base. In Colmar the deep attachment to Protestantism within the craft guilds ensured eventual support for the Lutherans.

The Peace of Westphalia restored Colmar as a bi-confessional Imperial city, but the Protestants once again clearly dominated. A new cohort of Lutheran political leaders, who were Alsatian in origin and outlook and who had professional, familial, and mercantile ties to Strasbourg, assumed full control over the regime. Municipal officials also became increasingly professional in training and outlook, which paralleled similar changes in mid-sized Imperial cities such as Nördlingen. Colmar's Catholics retained a limited voice in civic politics from a power base in the agricultural guilds. Yet the position of the Catholics within civic life was deteriorating, for the Catholic parish barely maintained its size as the Lutheran community grew. By 1670 the Catholics had lost the share of civic wealth they had acquired during the Thirty Years' War and their majorities in the agricultural guilds. In the artisan guild halls and in the city's core neighborhoods, the presence of Catholics was becoming more and more rare. Furthermore, the dynamic religious innovations which animated the seventeenth-century reform movement within the Catholic church had not penetrated Colmar's clerical communities. Colmar's Catholics were rapidly becoming an insular enclave, most of whose members were born within sight of St. Martin's spire. The Lutherans, on the other hand, belonged to a dynamic community with political and religious contacts which spread throughout the empire and with particularly close ties to Strasbourg. The conquest by Louis XIV in 1673 ended this second phase of confessional history.

Once the royal agents had fully established their authority in the city, they began an offensive against Colmar's Lutherans. This second Counter-Reformation featured the demand for confessional parity in civic offices. The royal agents completely set aside constitutional practices to force Catholics into magisterial and council chambers. In time, however, parity became the one guarantee that the Lutheran leaders had to their offices. Similar tactics had polarized civic politics in Strasbourg, which had been a Lutheran town. At Colmar, however, many of the first generation of Catholic officials came from well-established civic families, which softened the blow.

Nevertheless, the Lutherans could not be hopeful for the future. The crown could not banish the Alsatian Lutherans as it had the Huguenots from the interior of the kingdom because the Edict of Nantes did not apply in Alsace. Nevertheless, pressure against mixed marriages and incentives for conversion gave the Alsatian Catholics all the advantages. At Colmar this Counter-Reform drive was reinforced when the Jesuits and Capuchins arrived in the city in 1698. The men in these orders sparked a Catholic revival which enlivened civic culture in the eighteenth century. Despite all these pressures, the majority of Colmar's guildsmen and taxpayers were Lutheran at least until 1730. French sovereignty enticed a steady stream of Catholic immigrants into the city, some from the kingdom's interior, but most from the Catholic villages in Alsace and Switzerland. The newcomers were primarily poor laborers, but in 1697 the *Conseil souverain* moved to Colmar and brought along a new Catholic elite with the tastes of the provincial robe nobility. By the early eighteenth century, education, office, finance, and faith stamped civic political culture with the cosmopolitan tastes of a provincial administrative center; but unlike such centers as Angers, Aix-en-Provence, and Toulouse, Colmar possessed a community alienated by language and religious culture. The isolation of Colmar's Lutherans prevailed well into the eighteenth century, but the striking feature of the first generation of French lordship was the resilience of the Lutheran community. In 1715 the crown called for the establishment of the *simultaneum* in the Protestant church. The sanctuary was walled off from the nave, and a Catholic chapel installed. Two centuries later, Colmar's Lutherans still gathered in their old church, while the former chapel lay in ruins. Nevertheless, French lordship soured relations between Colmar's Protestants and Catholics until the Revolution, and eighteenth-century Colmar resembled contemporary Augsburg, in which two confessional communities shared the same space but seldom interacted.

Tied to these religious changes was a complicated political history. Early seventeenth-century Colmar was an Imperial city, answerable to the authority of the emperor. Colmar's regime depended heavily on the legal guarantees provided it by the Imperial constitution, but civic leaders also recognized the constraints placed on it by its powerful neighbors, the Habsburg dukes of Austria, who controlled the Imperial Bailiwick of Hagenau and a large block of territory south of the city. Within Colmar's walls constitutional tradition grounded authority in the city's ten guilds, but actual power rested in the civic regime. Throughout the seventeenth century the regime distanced itself from the citizenry, though the annual *Schwörtag* symbolically allowed the guildsmen to confirm the contractual roots of municipal politics.

Colmar's Reformation strained the regime's constitutional relations within the empire, and the swing to Calvinism was an act without constitutional sanction. To achieve their confessional ends, Colmar's leaders sought the support of the guilds in order to sustain civic political order. When war broke out in 1618, however, this limited foundation could not hold. The Austrian Counter-Reformation in 1627 imposed Imperial sanctions in order to politically reintegrate the city into the empire. For the next two decades, the civic regime operated under the "protection" of external powers. First Imperial, then Swedish, and finally French officials oversaw Colmar's relations with its neighbors.

The Peace of Westphalia ended French protection, but it also replaced the Austrian power in the province with that of the French king. Conflict between Colmar and royal provincial officials soon followed, but disputes among the king's agents weakened their effective power and allowed Colmar's sovereignty to survive. Within the city, power became concentrated in the hands of one or two leaders, such as Johann Heinrich Mogg, who governed the city in their own right while preserving the constitutional appearance. The guilds lost their proportional representation in the council and probably their ability to elect their own members for conciliar office, a development which occurred in other Imperial cities, such as Nördlingen, Hamburg, and Frankfurt am Main. In some cases these shifts eventually triggered protracted constitutional struggles between the *Rat* and the *Bürgerschaft*, but Colmar's regime did not face a constitutional crisis with its citizenry because it was forced to submit to France. Civic oligarchs had alienated the citizenry, for when Louis XIV finally conquered the city in 1673, the regime could not rally popular support to resist.

In 1679 the Peace of Nijmegen confirmed French authority at Colmar, and over the next two decades, the royal government "reunited" Colmar to the crown. The process restructured the city's regime and redefined its functions. The city's political elite plugged into the patronage systems controlled by royal provincial officials and profited from tax farming and privileged office. Royal policy clearly favored Catholics, but both confessional groups found sufficient opportunities to cement their loyalty to the new system. The same developments occurred on a grander scale at Strasbourg. At Colmar the transformation of civic politics, however, isolated and frustrated the middling guild leadership. In the 1690s, citizens drafted complaints against the "self-serving" political ethos of municipal officials. In 1711 they rallied behind an ambitious council member, Johann Jacob Sonntag, who mounted a traditional Imperial protest movement of the *Bürgerschaft* against the *Rat*, but Imperial politics had become anachronistic in eighteenth-century Colmar. Sonntag and his supporters failed miserably. Citizens had become subjects, and the regime members had become royal agents who adopted a new political ethos, defined by official patronage and personal privilege, which would inform Colmar's political culture until 1789.

Early modern Colmar also served as a central marketplace for about two dozen neighboring villages and small towns. The city lacked political authority over this hinterland, but the Colmarians controlled regional market relations. Some local merchants exported wine and brandy to distant markets in the lower Rhine valley and imported products not available locally— especially cloth. In the early seventeenth century, Reformed merchants from Switzerland and Savoy assumed control of Colmar's long-distance trade. Their presence triggered a boom in the local economy, which benefitted everyone but concentrated great wealth and influence in their own hands. Early seventeenth-century Colmar was "turning Swiss" politically, confessionally, and economically.

The Thirty Years' War and the Counter-Reformation ended this economic boom. The murderous 1630s, in particular, brought famine, disease, and economic depression. Despite the general hardship, the survivors benefitted as the depression concentrated regional landholding and capital resources among those who remained in the walled city. By 1648 Colmar was in an ideal position to extend its economic dominance over the surrounding countryside. The war had severed the city's ties to the long-distance trading centers in the lower and middle Rhine. The city became provincial in its economic orientation even before the royal government had fashioned a province. Through finance and investment, Colmar's elite integrated the region's wine and brandy production into one market controlled in Colmar. They concentrated capital in the city, distributed patronage through employment, and secured a dominant place for civic craftsmen at the expense of neighboring villagers. For a time all Colmarians benefitted from the city's new economic role, but in the 1660s a new round of economic concentration, which exclusively favored the Lutheran merchants, increased both social and confessional tensions and further weakened the regime in its struggle with the French.

French lordship widened the gulf between rich and poor, between privileged and taxed. Part of the anger which had fueled Sonntag's political protest was a deep resentment of privilege before the fisc, which had enriched the upper crust of the civic elite. Some wealthy Colmarians crossed over into the robe nobility, and many more amassed fortunes through government finance, patronage, and industrial investment under the protective cloak of mercantilism. The Colmarians, who rose into the provincial elite, hindered other ambitious men, such as Sonntag, and circumscribed a clear border between insiders and outsiders. Most Colmarians found themselves on the outside because of language, religion, or poverty.

Between 1600 and 1730, the Colmarians contended with the gradual deterioration and eventual loss of their political autonomy, constant confessional pressure from both Catholic and Protestant powers, and the disruption of trade relations and local production due to chronic warfare. By 1730 the former Imperial city had become a center for French provincial administration, and in many ways Colmar resembled the *Residenzstädte* across the Rhine. Politically the regime had lost its autonomy, but the officeholders, who should have felt the loss most deeply, were thoroughly ingrained into the new system. Confessionally, the citizens remained divided and alienated. If anything, the influx of French-speaking Catholics further fractured the religious communities. Finally, French sovereignty reinforced Colmar's economic domination over its hinterland by concentrating capital under the aegis of mercantilism. The city became an administrative center which drew the elites from the surrounding villages and towns to seek their fortunes. Property, finance, and tax farming concentrated the wealth and surplus of the region in what had become, in effect, the capital of Upper Alsace. The first two generations of French rule had molded the modern town. In Colmar, as elsewhere, political force, embodied in the state, ultimately defined national allegiance, though it could never fully absorb local loyalty. The resultant tensions presented the early modern Colmarians and their descendants with complex and often painful political, economic, confessional, and cultural choices.

Bibliography

I. MANUSCRIPTS

Colmar, Archives Départementales du Haut-Rhin (ADHR).
4G: Documents Relating to the Cathedral Chapter of St. Martin.
Colmar, Archives Municipales (AMC).
AA 15: Privileges of the City of Colmar.
AA 19: Imperial Correspondance.
AA 142–145: Correspondance; Colmar and Swedish Government and Colmar under French Protection (1632–46).
AA 146–163: Letters Patent, Ordinances, Royal Proclamations; Letters from the Council of State and the *Conseil souverain d'Alsace.*
AA 164–171: Correspondance: Colmar and Bourbon Officials.
BB 11–17: Civic Government, Elections, and Lists of Members.
BB 18–27: Civic Constitution in the French Epoch.
BB 28–42: Officers and Municipal Functionaries.
BB 45 (1600–1730): *Rathsprotokol.*
CC 1–38: Civic Capital.
CC 39–105: Ordinary and Extraordinary Civic Obligations.
CC 142–151: General Civic Budget, Receipts, and Expenses.
CC 152–158: Direct Taxes.
CC 159–198: Indirect Taxes.
CC 199–252: Official Accounts.
FF 43: Correspondance Sonntag Affair.
GG 22–30: St. Martin and the Civic Regime.
GG 138: The Capuchins.
GG 162–167: The Counter-Reformation at Colmar.
GG 171–173: Religious Affairs under French Lordship.
GG 187–189: Parish Registers.
HH 8: The Society *zum Waagkellar.*
JJ Divers, 6: The Civic Law Code, 1593.
Colmar, Bibliothèque Municipale (BMC).
"Fonds Chauffour."
I CH 79: Lists and biographies of Colmar's Protestant Clergy.
Porrentruy, Archives de l'Ancien Evêché de Bâle (AAEB).
A 41, Colmariensis Ecclesia Collegiata.
Mappe 1: Statutes.
Mappe 4: Imperial Commission, 1627.
Mappe 5: Counter-Reform, 1627–1634.
Mappe 6: Correspondance French Era.
Mappe 10: Visitations.
Mappe 12: St. Trinité.
Strasbourg, Archives Municipales (AMS).
Archives du Chapitre de Saint-Thomas (AST).
41/I 98: *Deklarationsschrift,* 1590.
41/I 99: St. Trinité.

271

II. Published Primary Sources

[Anonymous.] *Apologia Civitatis Imperialis Colmariensis*. Colmar, 1645.

Bachschmidt, Jean, ed. *Le livre des bourgeois de Colmar: 1660–1789*. Colmar: AMC, 1985.

Finsterwalder, Paul Wilhelm, ed. *Colmarer Stadtrechte*. Vol. 1 (only extant volume). Oberrheinische Stadtrechte, Abteilung 3, vol. 3. Heidelberg: Carl Winter, 1938.

Ichtersheim, Franz Ruprecht von. *Gantz neue elsäßiche Topographia*. Regensburg, 1710.

Lebeau, Jean, and Jean-Marie Valentin, eds. *L'Alsace au siècle de la Réforme (1482–1621): Textes et documents*. Nancy: Presses Universitaires de Nancy, 1985.

L'Hermine, J. de. *Guerre et paix en Alsace au XVIIe siècle*. Toulouse: Privat, 1981.

Livet, Georges, ed. *Le Duc Mazarin: Gouverneur d'Alsace (1661–1713): Lettres et documents inédits*. Strasbourg and Paris: F.-X. Le Roux, 1954.

Memoires de deux voyages et sejours en Alsace 1674–76 & 1681. Mulhouse, 1886. Marseilles: Lafitte Reprints, 1979.

Merian, Matthaeus. *Topographia Alsatia*. Frankfurt a.M., 1663.

Münster, Sebastian. *Von dem Elsaß und seiner großen Fruchtbarkeit dem kein Lande am Rheinstrom mag verglichen werden*. Freiburg-im-Briesgau: Verlag Rombach, 1976 (1544).

Oberlé, Raymond, ed. *L'Alsace en 1700: Memoire sur la province d'Alsace de l'Intendant Jacques de La Grange*. Colmar: Editions Alsatia, 1975.

Rathgeber, Julien, ed. *Colmar und Ludwig XIV. (1648–1715): Ein Beitrag zur elsässischen Städtegeschichte im siebzehnten Jahrhundert*. Stuttgart: A Kröner, 1873.

Sée, Julian, ed. *Johann Joner's Notanda: Tägliche Notizen eines Stettmeisters von Colmar zur Zeit Ludwigs XIV. (1678–1705)*. Colmar: Jung, 1873.

———, ed. *Memoires des RR. PP. Jesuites du Collège de Colmar (1698–1750)*. Geneva: Flick, 1873.

———, ed. *Ambros. Müller's Stamm- & Zeitbuch: Hauschronik eines Bürgers von Colmar zur Zeit Ludwigs XIV. (1678–1705)*. Colmar: Jung, 1873.

Sittler, Lucien, ed. *Les listes d'admission à la bourgeoisie de Colmar: 1361–1494*. Publications des Archives de la Ville de Colmar, 1. Colmar: AMC, 1958.

———, comp. *Membres du magistrat, conseillers et maîtres des corporations de Colmar: Listes de 1408–1600*. Publications des Archives de la Ville de Colmar, 3. Colmar: AMC, 1964.

Symcox, Geoffrey, ed. *War, Diplomacy, and Imperialism, 1618–1763*. New York: St. Martin's Press, 1974.

Trouillat, Joseph, and Louis Vautrey, eds. *Monuments de l'histoire de l'ancien Evêché de Bâle*. 5 vols. Vols. 4 and 5. Porrentruy: Victor Michel, 1861–1867.

Waltz, Andreas (André), ed. *Sigmund Billings Kleine Chronik der Stadt Colmar*. Colmar: Jung, 1891.

———, ed. *Chronik der Colmarer Kaufhauses*. Colmar: Jung, 1897.

———, ed. *Chronik de Colmar de Félix-Henri-Joseph Chauffour dit le Syndic*. Colmar: Jung, 1903.

Wertz, Roland, ed. *Le livre des bourgeois de Colmar, 1512–1609*. Colmar: Publications des Archives de la Ville de Colmar, 2. Colmar: AMC, 1961.

———, ed. *Membres du magistrat, conseillers et maîtres des corporations de Colmar, 1601–1700: Livre des bourgeois de Colmar, 1610–1673*. Publications des Archives de la Ville de Colmar, 4. Colmar: AMC, 1967.

III. Literature on Colmar

Betz, Jacques. *L'Eglise protestante de Saint-Matthieu de Colmar et sa paroisse*. Strasbourg: Oberlin, 1971.

———. "Les imprimeurs Decker à Colmar." *Annuaire de Colmar* (1966): 82–101.

Billich, André. "Colmar et Turckheim au XVIIème et au XVIIIème siècles." *Annuaire de Colmar* (1954): 96–105.

Bischoff, Georges. "Colmar et la crise révolutionnaire de 1524–1525." *Annuaire de Colmar* (1975/76): 43–54.

Braeuner, Gabriel. "La préréforme à Colmar (1522–1575)." *Annuaire de Colmar* (1975/76): 55–72.

————. "L'opinion publique et le rattachement de Colmar à la France en 1673." *Annuaire de Colmar* (1973): 43–50.

Bücking, Jürgen. *Johann Rasser (ca. 1535–1594) und die Gegenreformation im Oberelsass.* RGST, 101. Münster: Aschendorff, 1970.

Burger, Pierre. "Il y a 300 ans . . . L'annexion de Colmar par Louis XIV en 1673." *Annuaire de Colmar* (1973): 7–41.

————. "Il y a 300 ans . . . Colmar entre le Maréchal-Vicomte de Turenne et Frédéric-Guillaume Prince-Electeur de Brandenbourg." *Annuaire de Colmar* (1974/75): 81–97.

"Colmar." Pierre Delattre, ed., *Les établissements de Jesuites en France depuis quatre siècles.* Wetteren: Imprimerie des Meister Frères, 1950, 1: cols. 1503–4.

Demandt, Dieter. "Konflikte um die geistlichen Standesprivilegien im spätmittelalterlichen Colmar." In *Städtische Gesellschaft und Reformation*, edited by Ingrid Bátori, 136–54.

Fleurent, Henri. "Essai sur la démographie et l'épidémiologie de la ville de Colmar." *Bulletin de la Société d'Histoire Naturelle de Colmar* 15 (1920/21): 45–111.

Goehlinger, François Auguste. *Histoire du Chapitre de l'Eglise collégiale Saint-Martin de Colmar.* Colmar: Alsatia, 1951.

Greyerz, Kaspar von. *The Late City Reformation in Germany: The Case of Colmar 1522–1628.* VIEGM, 98. Wiesbaden: Steiner, 1980.

————. "La préréforme à Colmar, 1535–1555: Continuité ou rupture?" *Bulletin de la Société de l'Histoire du Protestantisme Français* 122 (1976): 551–66.

Huot, Paul. *La Commanderie de St.-Jean à Colmar: Etude historique (1210–1870).* Colmar: Jung, 1870.

Kiener, Fritz. "Aperçu sur l'historiographie de Colmar." *Annuaire de Colmar* (1935): 11–38.

Livet, Georges. "Colmar et l'établissement du Conseil souverain d'Alsace (1658–1698)." *Annuaire de Colmar* (1958): 69–76.

————. "L'esprit d'opposition sous la monarchie absolue: L'affaire Sonntag à Colmar in 1711." *Annuaire de Colmar* (1953): 69–84.

————, ed. *Histoire de Colmar.* Toulouse: Privat, 1983.

————. "De quelques conflicts entre la Plume et l'Epée: Contribution à l'histoire du Conseil souverain d'Alsace." *Annuaire de Colmar* (1966): 57–73.

Metzenthin, Edouard. "Anciennes familles colmariennes: les Goll et leur origine." *Annuaire de Colmar* (1955): 56–67.

————. "Anciennes familles colmariennes: Les Kriegelstein et leur origine." *Annuaire de Colmar* (1954): 67–76.

————. "Anciennes familles colmariennes: Les Roettlin et leur origine." *Annuaire de Colmar* (1953): 58–68.

————. "La famille Hecker à Colmar." *Annuaire de Colmar* (1951/52): 33–44.

Mieg, Philippe. "Généalogie de la famille Goll de Colmar." *Annuaire de Colmar* (1955): 68–72.

————. "Notes biographiques et généalogiques sur les Güntzer de Colmar, de Sélestat et de Riquewihr." *Annuaire de Colmar* (1974/75): 159–79.

————. "Les réfugiés colmariens à Mulhouse au temps de la Contre-Réforme (1628–1632)." *Annuaire de Colmar* (1950): 45–56.

————. "Les tribulations d'Augustin Guntzer, bourgeois de Colmar, durant la Guerre de Trente Ans," *Annuaire de Colmar* (1958): 48–65.

Mossmann, X(avier). "La France en Alsace après la Paix de Westphalie." *Revue Historique* 101 (1893): 26–43, 225–49.

———. "Matériaux pour servir à l'histoire de la Guerre de Trente Ans tirés des archives de Colmar." *RA* (1876): 309–31, 554–77; (1877): 445–74; (1878): 226–38, 465–78; (1879): 249–65, 494–511; (1880): 336–58, 530–38; (1881): 112–22, 191–205, 362–74, 520–28; (1882): 256–63.

———. *Recherches sur l'ancienne constitution de la commune à Colmar.* 2nd, rev. ed. Colmar: Jung, 1878.

Pallasse, Maurice, and Charles Kuhlmann. "La 'garde bourgeoise' à Colmar sous l'ancien régime." In *La bourgeoisie alsacienne,* 119–32.

Scherlen, Auguste. *Colmar, village et ville.* Colmar: Alsatia, 1931.

———. *Perles d'Alsace.* 3 vols. Colmar: Alsatia, 1933.

———. *Topographie von Alt-Colmar.* Colmar: Alsatia, 1922.

Schmitt, Jean-Marie. "Les sepultures du XVIIIe siècle dans l'ancienne église des Dominicains de Colmar." *Annuaire de Colmar* (1990): 55–66.

Sittler, Lucien. "Les bourgeois de Colmar." In *La bourgeoisie alsacienne,* 21–34.

———. "Change et banque dans le Vieux-Colmar." *Annuaire de Colmar* (1973): 59–66.

———. "Colmar au XVIe siècle." *Annuaire de Colmar* (1975/76): 13–30; (1976/77): 39–48.

———. "Colmar et la Décapole: Une crise au sein de la ligne au XVIe siècle." *Annuaire de Colmar* (1954): 47–54.

———. "Commerce et commerçants dans le Vieux-Colmar." *Annuaire de Colmar* (1966): 14–48.

———. "Les corporations et l'organization du travail à Colmar jusqu'au début de XVIIe siècle." In *Artisans et ouvriers d'Alsace,* 47–78.

———. "Crimes et châtiments dans le Vieux-Colmar." *Annuaire de Colmar* (1962): 7–17.

———. "L'elevage à Colmar au Moyen Age et au début des temps modernes." *Annuaire de Colmar* (1968): 47–55.

———. "Etudes sur l'histoire économique du Vieux-Colmar: L'organization de la 'Douane' jusqu'à la Guerre de Trente Ans." *Annuaire de Colmar* (1956): 13–26.

———. "Etudes sur l'histoire économique de Vieux-Colmar: Le Ladhof et la navigation colmarienne." *Annuaire de Colmar* (1957): 13–23.

———. "Il y a six siècles: A Colmar en 1358." *Annuaire de Colmar* (1958): 18–27.

———. "Landwirtschaft und Gartenbau im alten Colmar." *Elsass-Lothringisches Jahrbuch* 20 (1942): 71–94.

———. "Les mouvements sociaux à Colmar du XIVe au XVIe siècle." *RA* 95 (1956): 129–45.

———. "Notice sur la famille Sandherr." *Annuaire de Colmar* (1950): 57–66.

———. "Notice sur les débuts de l'industrie à Colmar: Il y a deux cents ans." *Annuaire de Colmar* (1967): 52–62.

———. "La poste à Colmar du Moyen-Age au début du XIXe siècle." *Annuaire de Colmar* (1967): 20–35.

———. "La région de Colmar (jusqu'à 1800)." *Annuaire de Colmar* (Numéro spécial, 1970): 41–66.

———. "La transformation du gouvernement de Colmar par le roi France à la fin du XVIIe siècle." In *Deux siècles d'Alsace française,* 133–58.

———. "La vie économique de Colmar (jusqu'à 1800)." *Annuaire de Colmar* (Numéro spécial, 1970): 25–40.

———. *La viticulture et le vin de Colmar à travers les siècles.* Colmar: Alsatia, 1956.

Strohl, Henri. "L'esprit républicain et démocratique dans l'Eglise protestante de

Colmar de 1648 à 1848." In *Deux siècles d'Alsace française*, 429–74.

———. "Les expériences d'une église au cours de quatre siècles (Colmar)." In *Vom Wesen und Wandel der Kirche: Festschrift für Eberhard Vischer*, 116–61. Basel: Helbing & Lichtenhahn, 1935.

Vogler, Bernard. "Le corps pastorel de Colmar et des environs avant la Guerre de Trente Ans." *Annuaire de Colmar* (1975/76): 121–28.

Waldner, Eugène (Eugen). "La distillation et le commerce de l'eau-de-vie à Colmar au seizième et au dix-septième siècle." *Bulletin de Musée Historique de Mulhouse* (1891): 3–12.

———. *Kurzer Überblick über die Geschichte der Stadt Colmar*. Colmar: Lang and Rasch, 1914.

Wallace, Peter. "Finances publiques et richesse privée: La ferme des revenues patrimoniaux de Colmar à la fin du XVIIe siècle." *Annuaire de Colmar* (1980/81): 87–102.

Wehrlen, René Victor. "Il y a 300 ans: La Guerre des Tonnelets de Colmar en 1669." *Annuaire de Colmar* (1969/70): 49–58.

Weyrauch, Erdmann. "Die politische Führungsgruppe in Colmar in der Zeit der Reformation." In *Stadtbürgertum und Adel in der Reformation*, 215–34.

Wolff, Christian. "Les débuts de la famille Schneider à Colmar." *Annuaire de Colmar* (1957): 53–59.

IV. GENERAL LITERATURE

Abel, Wilhelm. *Agricultural Fluctuations in Europe: From the Thirteenth to the Twentieth Centuries*. Translated by Olive Ordish. New York: St. Martin's Press, 1980.

Abray, Lorna Jane. *The People's Reformation: Magistrates, Clergy, and Commons in Strasbourg, 1500–1598*. Ithaca, N.Y.: Cornell University Press, 1985.

Adam, Johann. *Evangelische Kirchengeschichte der elsässischen Territorien bis zur Französischen Revolution*. Strasbourg: Heitz, 1928.

L'Alsace et la Suisse à travers les siècles. PSSARE, 4. Strasbourg and Paris: F.-X. Le Roux, 1952.

Ammann, Hector. "La place de l'Alsace dans l'industrie textile du Moyen Age." In *La bourgeoisie alsacienne*, 71–102.

Anderson, Perry. *Lineages of the Absolutist State*. 2nd. ed. London: Verso, 1979.

d'Athenay, Jean-Benoist. *Le premier administrateur de l'Alsace française: Jacques de La Grange, intendant d'Alsace de 1673 à 1698*. Strasbourg: Istra, 1930.

Artisans et ouvriers d'Alsace. PSSARE, 9. Strasbourg: Istra, 1965.

Bardot, Georges. *La question des dix villes impériales d'Alsace: Depuis la Paix de Westphalie jusqu'aux arrêts de "réunions" du Conseil souverain de Brisach 1648–1680*. Paris: Picard, 1899.

Barth, Medard. *Handbuch der elsässischen Kirchen im Mittelalter*. Brussels: Editions Cultures et Civilisations, 1980.

———. *Der Rebbau des Elsass und die Absatzgebiete seiner Weine: Ein geschichtlicher Durchblick*. Strasbourg and Paris: F.-X. Le Roux, 1958.

Bátori, Ingrid. *Die Reichsstadt Augsburg im 18. Jahrhundert: Verfassung, Finanzen, und Reformversuche*. Veröffentlichungen des Max-Planck-Instituts für Geschichte, 22. Göttingen: Vandenhoeck & Ruprecht, 1969.

———, ed. *Städtische Gesellschaft und Reformation*. Spätmittelalter und Frühe Neuzeit. Tübinger Beiträge zur Geschichtsforschung, 12. Kleine Schriften, 2. Stuttgart: Klett-Cotta, 1980.

Bátori, Ingrid, and Erdmann Weyrauch. *Die bürgerliche Elite der Stadt Kitzingen: Studien zur Sozial- und Wirtschaftsgeschichte einer landesherrlichen Stadt im 16. Jahrhunderts*. Spätmittelalter und Frühe Neuzeit. Tübinger Beiträge zur Geschichtsforschung, 11. Stuttgart: Klett-Cotta, 1982.

Becker, Joseph. *Geschichte der Reichslandvogtei im Elsass: Von ihrer Einrichtung bis zu ihrem Übergang an Frankreich, 1293–1648.* Strasbourg: Heitz, 1905.

Beik, William H. *Absolutism and Society in Seventeenth-Century France: State Power and Provincial Aristocracy in Languedoc.* Cambridge: Cambridge University Press, 1985.

———. "Urban Factions and the Social Order during the Minority of Louis XIV." *French Historical Studies* 15 (1987): 36–67.

Benecke, Gerhard, ed. *Germany in the Thirty Years' War.* New York: St. Martin's Press, 1979.

———. *Society and Politics in Germany 1500–1750.* London: Routledge & Kegan Paul, 1974.

———. "The Westphalian Circle, the County of Lippe, and Imperial Currency Control." In *The Old Reich*, edited by James A. Vann and Steven W. Rowan, 129–47.

Benedict, Philip, ed. *Cities and Social Change in Early Modern France.* London: Unwin Hyman, 1989.

———. "French Cities from the Sixteenth Century to the Revolution: An Overview." In *Cities and Social Change in Early Modern France*, edited by Philip Benedict, 7–68.

———. *Rouen during the Wars of Religion.* Cambridge: Cambridge University Press, 1981.

Billich, André. *Histoire d'une ancienne ville impériale: Turckheim.* Colmar: Editions Alsatia, 1975.

Bircher, Martin, Walter Sparen, and Erdmann Weyrauch, eds. *Schweizerisch-deutsche Beziehungen im konfessionellen Zeitalter: Beiträge zur Kulturgeschichte 1580–1650,* Wolfenbütteler Arbeiten zur Barockforschung, 12. Wiesbaden: Otto Harrassowitz, 1984.

Bischoff, Georges. *Gouvernés et gouvernants en Haute-Alsace à l'époque autrichienne.* PSSARE, 20. Strasbourg: Istra, 1982.

Black, Antony. *Guilds and Civil Society in European Society and Thought from the Twelfth Century to the Present.* Ithaca, N.Y.: Cornell University Press, 1984.

Blendinger, Friedreich. "Versuch einer Bestimmung der Mittelschicht in der Reichsstadt Augsburg vom Ende des 14. bis zum Anfang des 18. Jahrhunderts." In *Städtische Mittelschichten*, edited by Erich Maschke and Jürgen Sydow, 32–78.

Bodmer, Walter. *L'immigration suisse dans le comté de Hanau-Lichtenberg au dix-septième siècle.* Collection d'études sur l'histoire du droit et des institutions de l'Alsace, vol. 6. Strasbourg: Heitz, 1930.

Bonney, Richard. *The King's Debts: Finance and Politics in France, 1589–1661.* Oxford: Clarendon Press, 1981.

———. *Political Change in France under Richelieu and Mazarin, 1624–1661.* Oxford: Oxford University Press, 1978.

Bopp, Marie-Joseph, comp. *Die evangelischen Geistlichen und Theologen in Elsass und Lothringen von der Reformation bis zur Gegenwart.* Genealogie und Landesgeschichte. Publikationen der Zentralstelle für Deutsche Personen- und Familiengeschichte, 1. Neustadt a. d. Aisch: Degener, 1959.

———, comp. *Die evangelischen Gemeinden und Hohen Schulen in Elsass und Lothringen von der Reformation bis zur Gegenwart.* Genealogie und Landesgeschichte. Publikationen der Zentralstelle für Deutsche Personen- und Familiengeschichte, 5. Neustadt a. d. Aisch: Degener, 1963.

Bornet, René. *La Réforme protestante du culte à Strasbourg au XVIe siècle (1523–1598): Approche sociologique et interprétation théologique.* SMRT, 28. Leiden: E. J. Brill, 1981.

Bosher, J. F., ed. *French Government and Society 1500–1850: Essays in Memory of Alfred Cobban.* London: Athelone, 1973.

Bourdieu, Pierre. *Outline of a Theory of Practice*. Translated by Richard Nice. Cambridge Studies in Social Anthropology, 16. Cambridge: Cambridge University Press, 1977.

La bourgeoisie alsacienne: Etudes d'histoire sociale. PSSARE, 5. Strasbourg: Istra, 1967.

Bouvier, Jean, and Henri Germain-Martin. *Finances et financiers de l'ancien régime*. Paris: Presses Universitaires de France, 1964.

Brady, Thomas A., Jr. "In Search of the Godly City: The Domestication of Religion in the German Urban Reformation." In *The German People and the Reformation*, edited by R. Po-chia Hsia, 14–31.

———. "Rites on Autonomy, Rites of Dependence: South German Civic Culture in the Age of Renaissance and Reformation." In *Religion and Culture in the Renaissance and Reformation*, edited by Steven Ozment, 9–24.

———. *Ruling Class, Regime, and Reformation at Strasbourg, 1520–1555*. SMRT, 22. Leiden: E. J. Brill, 1978.

———. *Turning Swiss: Cities and Empire, 1450–1550*. Cambridge: Cambridge University Press, 1985.

Brecht, Martin. *Kirchenordnung und Kirchenzucht in Württemberg vom 16. bis zum 18. Jahrhundert*. Quellen und Forschungen zur Württembergischen Kirchengeschichte, 1. Stuttgart: Calwer, 1967.

Briggs, Robin. *Early Modern France, 1560–1715*. Oxford: Oxford University Press, 1977.

Brunner, Otto. *Neue Wege Verfassungs- und Sozialgeschichte*, 3rd ed. Göttingen: Vandenhoeck & Ruprecht, 1980.

———. "Souveränitätsproblem und Sozialstruktur in den deutschen Reichsstädten der frühen Neuzeit." In Otto Brunner, *Neue Wege der Verfassungs- und Sozialgeschichte*, 3rd ed., 294–321.

Buchstab, Günter. *Reichsstädte, Städtekurie und Westfälischer Friedenskongress: Zusammenhänge von Sozialstruktur, Rechtsstatus und Wirtschaftskraft*. SVENGEV, 7. Münster: Aschendorff, 1976.

Burg, André Marcel. *Histoire de l'Église d'Alsace*. Colmar: Alsatia, 1946.

———. "Patrizier und andere städtische Führungsschichten in Hagenau." In *Deutsches Patriziat, 1430–1740*, edited by Hellmuth Rössler, 353–75.

———. "Les Suisses et le repeuplement de Hagenau dans le seconde moitié du XVIIe siècle." In *L'Alsace et la Suisse*, 182–93.

Chartier, Roger, and Hughes Neveux, eds. *La ville classique de la renaissance aux revolutions*. Vol. 3 of *Histoire de la France urbaine*. Paris: Presses Universitaires de France, 1981.

Chrisman, Miriam Usher, and Otto Gründler, eds. *Social Groups and Religious Ideas in the Sixteenth Century*. Kalamazoo, Mich.: The Medieval Institute, 1978.

Conrad, Franziska. *Reformation in der bäuerlichen Gesellschaft: Zur Rezeption reformatorischer Theologie im Elsass*. VIEGM, 116. Wiesbaden: Franz Steiner, 1984.

Czok, Karl. "Zur Stellung der Stadt in der deutschen Geschichte." *Jahrbuch für Regionalgeschichte* 3 (1968): 9–33.

Darnton, Robert. *The Great Cat Massacre and Other Episodes in French Cultural History*. New York: Basic Books, 1984.

Davis, Natalie Z. "The Sacred and the Body Social in Sixteenth-Century Lyons." *Past and Present* no. 90 (1981): 40–70.

Denecke, Dietrich. "Sozialtopographie und sozialräumliche Gliederung der spätmittelalterlichen Stadt: Problemstellungen, Methoden, und Betrachtungsweisen der historischen Wirtschafts- und Sozialgeographie." In *Über Bürger, Stadt, und städtische Literatur im Spätmittelalter: Bericht über Kolloquien der Komission zur Erforschung der Kultur des Spätmittelalters 1975–1977*, edited by Josef Fleckenstein and Karl Stackmann, 161–202.

Dent, Julian. *Crisis in Finance: Crown, Financiers, and Society in Seventeenth-Century France*. New York: St. Martin's Press, 1973.

Deux siècles d'Alsace française, 1648–1848. PSSARE, 2. Strasbourg and Paris: F.-X. Le Roux, 1948.

De Vries, Jan. *The Economy of Europe in the Age of Crisis*. Cambridge: Cambridge University Press, 1976.

———. *European Urbanization, 1500–1800*. Cambridge, Mass.: Harvard University Press, 1984.

Deyon, Pierre. *Amiens, capitale provinciale: Etude sur la société urbaine au XVIIe siècle*. Paris and The Hague: Mouton, 1967.

Dickens, A. G. *The German Nation and Martin Luther*. New York: Harper and Row, 1974.

Dickmann, Fritz. *Der Westfälische Frieden*. Münster: Aschendorff, 1959.

Diefendorf, Barbara B. *Paris City Councilors in the Sixteenth Century: The Politics of Patrimony*. Princeton: Princeton University Press, 1983.

Dollinger, Philippe. "Le Traité de Westphalie et l'Alsace." In *Deux siècles d'Alsace française*, 1–14.

Doubled, Henri. "La notion du ban en Alsace au Moyen Age." *Revue Historique de Droit Français et Etranger*, ser. 4, 39 (1961): 30–75.

Dreyer-Roos, Suzanne. *La population strasbourgeoise sous l'ancien régime*. PSSARE, Collection "Recherches et Documents," 6. Strasbourg: Istra, 1969.

Drouot, Marc. "Le commerce de sel lorrain en Haute-Alsace, Sundgau et Brisgau et la concurrence des sels tyrolien et bourguignon au début du XVIIIe siècle." In *Trois provinces de l'Est*, 119–27.

DuPlessis, Robert, and Martha C. Howell. "Reconsidering the Early Modern Urban Economy: The Cases of Leiden and Lille." *Past and Present* no. 94 (1982): 49–84.

Durand, Yves, ed. *Homage à Roland Mousnier: Clientèles et fidélités en Europe à l'époque moderne*. Paris: Presses Universitaires de France, 1981.

Ekberg, Carl J. *The Failure of Louis XIV's Dutch War*. Chapel Hill: University of North Carolina Press, 1979.

Ellerbach, J. B. *Der dreissigjährige Krieg im Elsass (1618–1648)*. 3 vols. Mulhouse: Union, 1912–28.

Elliot, J. H. "Revolution and Continuity in Early Modern Europe." *Past and Present* no. 42 (1969): 35–56.

Evans, R. J. W. *The Making of the Habsburg Monarchy, 1550–1700: An Interpretation*. Oxford: Clarendon Press, 1979.

Farr, James R. *Hands of Honor: Artisans and Their World in Dijon, 1550–1650*. Ithaca, N.Y.: Cornell University Press, 1988.

———. "Popular Religious Solidarity in Sixteenth-Century Dijon." *French Historical Studies* 14 (1985): 192–214.

Fleckenstein, Josef, and Karl Stackmann, eds. *Über Bürger, Stadt, und städtische Literatur im Spätmittelalter: Bericht über Kolloquien der Komission zur Erforschung der Kultur des Spätmittelalters 1975–1977*. Göttingen: Vandenhoeck & Ruprecht, 1979.

Flinn, Michael, W. *The European Demographic System, 1500–1820*. Baltimore: Johns Hopkins University Press, 1981.

Ford, Franklin. *Strasbourg in Transition 1648–1789*. Cambridge, Mass.: Harvard University Press, 1958.

François, Etienne, ed. *Immigration et société urbaine en Europe occidentale, XVIe–XXe siècle*. Paris: Editions Recherche sur les Civilisations, 1985.

———. *Koblenz im 18. Jahrhundert: Zur Sozial- und Bevölkerungsstruktur einer deutschen Residenzstadt*. Göttingen: Vandenhoeck & Ruprecht, 1982.

———. "Des républiques marchandes aux capitales politiques: Remarques sur la hiérarchie urbaine du Saint-Empire à l'époque moderne." *Revue d'Histoire Moderne et Contemporaine* 25 (1978): 587–603.

——. "De l'uniformité à la tolérance: Confession et société urbaine en Allemagne, 1650–1800." *Annales: ESC* 37 (1982): 783–800.

Friedrichs, Christopher R. "Citizens or Subjects? Urban Conflicts in Early Modern Germany." In *Social Groups and Religious Ideas in the Sixteenth Century*, edited by Miriam Usher Chrisman and Otto Gründler, 46–58.

——. "German Town Revolts and the Seventeenth-Century Crisis." *Renaissance and Modern Studies* 26 (1982): 27–51.

——. "Immigration and Urban Society: Seventeenth-Century Nördlingen." In *Immigration et société urbaine en Europe occidentale, XVIe–XXe siècle*, edited by Etienne François, 65–77.

——. "The Swiss and German City-States." In *The City-State in Five Cultures*, edited by Robert Griffith and Carol G. Thomas, 109–42.

——. "Urban Conflicts and the Imperial Constitution in Seventeenth-Century Germany." *JMH* 58, Supplement (1986): S98–S123.

——. "Urban Politics and Urban Social Structure in Seventeenth-Century Germany." *European History Quarterly* 22 (1992): 187–216.

——. *Urban Society in an Age of War: Nördlingen, 1580–1720*. Princeton: Princeton University Press, 1979.

Fuchs, François-Joseph. "Aspects du commerce de Strasbourg avec Montbéliard et la Franche-Comté au XVIIe siècle." In *Trois provinces de l'Est*, 109–17.

——. "Bourgeois de Strasbourg, propriétaires ruraux au XVIIe siècle." *Paysans d'Alsace*, 99–119.

——. "Les catholiques strasbourgeois de 1529 à 1681." *Archives de l'Eglise d'Alsace* 38 (1975): 141–69.

Gauss, Julia. "L'annexion de l'Alsace par la paix de Munster et ses conséquences politiques en Suisse." In *L'Alsace et la Suisse*, 161–72.

Goubert, Pierre. *Beauvais et le Beauvaisis de 1600 à 1730: Contribution à l'histoire sociale de la France du XVIIe siècle*. Paris: Editions de l'Ecole des Hautes Etudes en Sciences Sociales, 1960.

Greissler, Paul. *La classe politique dirigéante à Strasbourg, 1650–1750*. PSSARE, 33. Strasbourg: Le Quaie, 1987.

Gresset, Maurice. "Une fidèle de Louis XIV en Franche-Comté: Claude Boisot." In *Homage à Roland Mousnier: Clientèles et fidélités en Europe à l'époque moderne*, edited by Yves Durand, 169–82.

——. *Gens de Justice à Besançon de la conquête par Louis XIV à la Revolution française (1674–1789)*. 2 vols. Paris: Bibliothèque Nationale, 1978.

Greyerz, Kaspar von. "Basels kirchliche und konfessionelle Beziehungen zum Oberrhein im späten 16. und frühen 17. Jahrhundert." In *Schweizerisch-deutsche Beziehungen im konfessionellen Zeitalter: Beiträge zur Kulturgeschichte 1580–1650*, edited by Martin Bircher, Walter Sparen, and Erdmann Weyrauch, 227–52.

——, ed. *Religion and Society in Early Modern Europe, 1500–1800*. London: George Allen & Unwin, 1984.

——. "Stadt und Reformation: Stand und Aufgaben der Forschung." *ARG* 76 (1985): 6–63.

——, ed. *Religion, Politics, and Social Protest: Three Studies on Early Modern Germany*. London: Allen & Unwin, 1984.

Griffith, Robert, and Carol G. Thomas, eds. *The City-State in Five Cultures*. Santa Barbara, Calif.: ABC-CLIO, 1981.

Gross, Hans. "The Holy Roman Empire in Modern Times: Constitutional Reality and Legal Theory." In *The Old Reich*, edited by James A. Vann and Steven W. Rowan, 1–29.

Guggisberg, Hans R. *Basel in the Sixteenth Century: Aspects of the City Republic before, during, and after the Reformation.* St. Louis: Center for Reformation Research, 1982.

Gutmann, Myron P. *War and Rural Life in the Early Modern Low Countries.* Princeton: Princeton University Press, 1980.

Hanauer, A(uguste). *Etudes économiques sur l'Alsace ancienne et moderne.* 2 vols. Strasbourg and Paris: Fischbacher, 1876–78.

Harding, Robert R. *The Anatomy of a Power Elite: The Provincial Governors of Early Modern France.* New Haven: Yale University Press, 1978.

Hatton, Ragnhild, ed. *Louis XIV and Absolutism.* Columbus: Ohio State University Press, 1976.

———. "Nijmegen and the European Powers." In *The Peace of Nijmegen 1676–1678/79*, 1–16.

Heckel, Martin. "Reichsrecht und 'Zweite Reformation': Theologisch-juristische Probleme der reformierten Konfessionalisierung." In *Die reformierte Konfessionalisierung*, edited by Heinz Schilling, 11–43.

Hertner, Peter. *Stadtwirtschaft zwischen Reich und Frankreich: Wirtschaft und Gesellschaft Strassburgs 1650–1714.* Neue Wirtschaftsgeschichte, 8. Cologne and Vienna: Böhlau, 1973.

Himly, François J. *Atlas des villes medievales d'Alsace.* Publications de la Fédération des Sociétés d'Histoire et d'Archéologie d'Alsace, 6. Colmar: Alsatia, 1970.

———. "Les conséquences de la Guerre de Trente Ans dans les campagnes alsaciennes: Problèmes et orientations." In *Deux siècles d'Alsace française*, 15–60.

Histoire de l'Alsace rurale. Edited by Jean-Michel Boehler, Dominique Lerch, and Jean Vogt. Strasbourg and Paris: Istra, 1983.

Hochstadt, Steve. "Migration in Pre-Industrial Germany." *Central European History* 16 (September 1983): 195–221.

Hodges, Richard. *Primitive and Peasant Markets.* Oxford: Basil Blackwell, 1988.

Hohenberg, Paul M., and Lynn Hollen Lees. *The Making of Urban Europe, 1000–1950.* Cambridge, Mass.: Harvard University Press, 1985.

Holborn, Hajo. *A History of Modern Germany, 1648–1840.* New York: Knopf, 1964.

Hsia, R. Po-chia, ed. *The German People and the Reformation.* Ithaca, N.Y.: Cornell University Press, 1988.

———. "The Myth of the Commune: Recent Historiography on City and Reformation in Germany." *Central European History* 20 (September/December 1987): 203–15.

———. *Social Discipline in the Reformation: Central Europe 1550–1750.* London and New York: Routledge, 1989.

Ingold A(rmand) M. P. *Miscellanea Alsatica.* 3 vols. Colmar and Paris: Jung, 1894–97.

Kageneck, Alfred Graf von. "Das Patriziat im Elsass unter Berücksichtigung der Schweizer Verhältnisse." In *Deutsches Patriziat, 1430–1740*, edited by Hellmuth Rössler, 377–94.

Kamen, Henry. "The Economic and Social Consequences of the Thirty Years' War." *Past and Present* no. 39 (1968): 44–61.

———. *The Rise of Toleration.* New York: McGraw-Hill, 1967.

Kellenbenz, Hermann. *The Rise of the European Economy: An Economic History of Continental Europe from the Fifteenth to the Eighteenth Century.* Revised and edited by Gerhard Benecke. New York: Holmes & Meier, 1976.

———. "Die Wirtschaft der Schwäbischen Reichsstädte zwischen 1648 und 1740." *Jahrbuch für Geschichte der Oberdeutschen Reichsstädte* 11 (1965): 128–66.

Kettering, Sharon. *Judicial Politics and Urban Revolt in Seventeenth-Century France: The Parlement of Aix, 1629–1659.* Princeton: Princeton University Press, 1978.

———. *Patrons, Brokers, and Clients in Seventeenth-Century France.* New York: Oxford

University Press, 1986.

Kiernan, V. G. "Foreign Mercenaries and Absolute Monarchy." *Past and Present* no. 11 (1957): 66–86.

———. "State and Nation in Western Europe." *Past and Present* no. 31 (1967): 20–38.

Kintz, Jean-Pierre. "XVIIe siècle: Du Saint Empire au royaume de France." In *Strasbourg de la Guerre de Trente Ans à Napoleon 1618–1815*, 3–111.

———. "La mobilité humaine en Alsace: Essai de présentation statistique: XIVe–XVIIIe siècle." *Annales de Démographie Historique* (1970): 157–83.

———. *La société strasbourgeoise du mileau du XVIe siècle à la fin de la Guerre de Trente Ans, 1560–1650: Essai d'histoire démographique, economique et sociale.* Paris: Ophrys, 1982.

Konvitz, Josef W. *The Urban Millennium: The City Building Process from the Early Middle Ages to the Present.* Carbondale and Edwardsville: Southern Illinois University Press, 1985.

Kopf, Hermann. "Unter der Krone Frankreichs, Freiburg-im-Breisgau 1677–1697." *Schau-ins-Land* 88 (1970): 23–124.

Kouri, E. I., and Tom Scott, eds. *Politics and Society in Reformation Europe: Essays for Sir Geoffrey Elton on His Sixty-Fifth Birthday.* London: Macmillan Press, 1987.

Lang, Peter Thaddaeus. "Die katholische Minderheit in der protestantischen Reichsstadt Ulm." In *Bürgerschaft und Kirche*, edited by Jürgen Sydow, 89–96.

Langton, John, and Göran Hoppe. *Town and Country in the Development of Early Modern Western Europe.* Historical Geography Research Series, 11. Norwich, England: Geo, 1983.

Laufs, Adolph. *Die Verfassung und Verhaltung der Stadt Rottweil, 1650–1806.* Stuttgart: Kohlhammer, 1963.

Livet, Georges. "Colbert de Croissy et la diplomatie française à Nimègue (1675–1679)." In *The Peace of Nijmegen 1676–1678/79*, 181–223.

———. *L'intendance d'Alsace sous Louis XIV 1648–1715.* Publications de la Faculté des Lettres de l'Université de Strasbourg, fasc. 128. Paris: Les Belles Lettres, 1956.

———. "Les intendants d'Alsace et leur oeuvre, 1649–1789." In *Deux siècles d'Alsace française*, 79–131.

———. "'Maspfennig et Umgeld,' Contribution à l'étude de la fiscalité du vin en Alsace sous l'ancien régime." *Annales de la Société d'Ethnographie Française* 1 (1950): 83–94.

———. "La monarchie absolue et la bourgeoisie alsacienne: D'après les fonds notariaux et les registres des magistrates." In *La bourgeoisie alsacienne*, 133–52.

———. "Royal Administration in a Frontier Province: The Intendancy of Alsace under Louis XIV." In *Louis XIV and Absolutism*, edited by Ragnhild Hatton, 177–96.

Livet, Georges, and Francis Rapp, comps. *Strasbourg au coeur religieux du XVIe siècle: Hommage à Lucien Febvre.* PSSARE, 12. Strasbourg: Istra, 1977.

Livet, Georges, and Bernard Vogler, eds. *Pouvoir, ville et société en Europe 1650–1750: Colloque internationale du C.N.R.S., octobre 1981.* Paris: Presses Universitaires de France, 1983.

Maillard, Jacques. *Le pouvoir municipal à Angers de 1657 à 1789.* 2 vols. Angers: Presses de l'Université d'Angers, 1984.

Mandrou, Robert. *Louis XIV en son temps 1661–1715.* Paris: Presses Universitaires de France, 1973.

Maschke, Erich, and Jürgen Sydow, eds. *Städtische Mittelschichten.* Stuttgart: Kohlhammer, 1972.

Mattmüller, Markus, ed. *Die frühe Neuzeit, 1500–1700.* Vol. 1 of *Bevölkerungsgeschichte der Schweiz.* Basler Beiträge zur Geschichtswissenschaft, 154–154a. Basel and Frankfurt a.m.: Helbing & Lichtenhahn, 1987.

Mauersberg, Hans. *Wirtschafts- und Sozialgeschichte zentral-europäischer Städte in neuerer Zeit: Dargestellt an den Beispielen von Basel, Frankfurt a.M., Hamburg, Hannover, und München.* Göttingen: Vandenhoeck & Ruprecht, 1960.

Mettam, Roger. *Power and Faction in Louis XIV's France.* Oxford: Basil Blackwell, 1988.

Metz, Friedrich, ed. *Vorderösterreich: Eine geschichtliche Landeskunde.* Freiburg: Rombach, (1959) 1976.

Meuvret, Jean. "Fiscalism and Public Opinion under Louis XIV." In *Louis XIV and Absolutism,* edited by Ragnhild Hatton, 199–225.

Moeller, Bernd. *Imperial Cities and the Reformation: Three Essays.* Translated and edited by H. C. Erik Midelfort and Mark U. Edwards, Jr. Philadelphia: Fortress, 1972.

———. *Reichsstadt und Reformation.* Rev. ed. Berlin: Evangelische Verlagsanstalt, 1987.

Mols, Roger. *Introduction à la démographie historique des villes d'Europe du XIVe au XVIIIe siècles.* 3 vols. Louvain: J. Duchlet, 1954–56.

Mousnier, Roland E. *The Institutions of France under the Absolute Monarchy.* 2 vols. Chicago: University of Chicago Press, 1979–84.

Muir, Edward. "Virgin on the Street Corner: The Place of the Sacred in Italian Cities." In *Religion and Culture in the Renaissance and Reformation,* edited by Steven Ozment, 25–40.

Müller, F. W. *Die elsässischen Landstände: Ein Beitrag zur Geschichte des Elsasses.* Strasbourg: von Schlesien, 1907.

Murat, Inès. *Colbert.* Paris: Fayard, 1980.

Oberlé, Raymond. *L'Alsace entre la Paix de Westphalie et la Révolution française.* Paris: Les Editions Mars et Mercure, 1977.

———. *La république de Mulhouse pendant la Guerre de Trente Ans.* Collection de l'Institut des Hautes Etudes Alsaciennes, 20. Paris: Les Belles Lettres, 1965.

Oberman, Heiko. *Die Reformation: Von Wittenberg nach Genf.* Göttingen: Vandenhoeck & Ruprecht, 1986.

Overmann, Alfred. *Die Abretung des Elsass an Frankreich im Westfälischen Frieden.* Karlsrühe: G. Braunschen, 1905.

Ozment, Steven, ed. *Religion and Culture in the Renaissance and Reformation,* Sixteenth Century Essays & Studies, 11. Kirksville, Mo.: Sixteenth Century Journal Publishers, 1989.

Parker, David. *The Making of French Absolutism.* London: Edward Arnold, 1983.

Parker, Geoffrey. *The Thirty Years' War.* London: Routledge and Kegan Paul, (1984) 1987.

Paysans d'Alsace. PSSARE, 7. Strasbourg: F.-X. Le Roux, 1959.

The Peace of Nijmegen, 1676–1678/79. Amsterdam: Holland University Press, 1980.

Pfeiffer, Gerhard. "Der Augsburger Religionsfrieden und die Reichsstädte." *Zeitschrift des Historischen Vereins für Schwaben* 61 (1955): 213–321.

Pfister, Charles. "L'Alsace et l'Edit de Nantes." *Revue Historique* 160 (1929): 217–40.

Pilloret, René. "La France et les états allemands au Congrès de Nimègue (1678–1679)." In *The Peace of Nijmegen, 1676–1678/79,* 225–36.

Pirenne, Henri. *Medieval Cities: Their Origins and the Revival of Trade.* Translated by Frank D. Halsey. Princeton: Princeton University Press, 1925.

Polišenský, J. V. *The Thirty Years' War.* Translated from the Czech by Robert Evans. Berkeley: University of California Press, 1971.

Rabe, Horst, Hansgeorg Molitor, and Hans-Christoph Rublack, eds. *Festgabe für Ernst Walter Zeeden: Zum 60. Geburstag am 14. Mai 1976.* RGST, suppl. 2. Münster: Aschendorff, 1976.

Rapp, Francis. *Reformés et Reformation à Strasbourg: Eglise et société dans le diocèse de Strasbourg (1450–1525)*. Collection de l'Institut des Hautes Etudes Alsaciennes, 23. Paris: Ophrys, 1974.

Reinhard, Wolfgang. "Gegenreformation als Modernisierung? Prolegomena zu einer Theorie des konfessionellen Zeitalters." *ARG* 68 (1977): 226–51.

———. "Reformation, Counter-Reformation, and the Early Modern State: A Reassessment." *The Catholic Historical Review* 75 (1989): 383–404.

———. "Zwang zur Konfessionalisierung? Prolegomena zu einer Theorie des konfessionellen Zeitalters." *Zeitschrift für Historische Forschung* 10 (1983): 257–77.

Reuss, Rodolphe. *L'Alsace au dix-septième siècle: Tableau géographique, historique, politique, et économique.* 2 vols. Paris: 1897–98.

———. *Histoire de Strasbourg depuis ses origines jusqu'à nos jours.* Paris: Fischbacher, 1922.

Reynolds, Susan. *Kingdoms and Communities in Western Europe: 900–1300.* Oxford: Clarendon Press, 1984.

Rieber, Albrecht. "Das Patriziat von Ulm, Augsburg, Ravensburg, Memmingen, Biberach." In *Deutsches Patriziat*, edited by Hellmuth Rössler, 299–352.

Riedenauer, Erwin. "Kaiserliche Ständeserhebungen für reichsstädtische Bürger 1519–1740: Ein statistischer Vorbericht zum Thema 'Kaiser und Patriziat.'" In *Deutsches Patriziat*, edited by Hellmuth Rössler, 27–97.

Rocholl, Heinrich. *Zur Geschichte der Annexion des Elsass durch die Krone Frankreichs.* Gotha: Perthes, 1888.

———. *Der Grosse Kurfürst von Brandenburg im Elsass 1674–1675: Ein Geschichtsbild aus der Zeit, als das Elsass französisch werden müsste.* Strasbourg: Trubner, 1877.

Rohdewald, Wilhelm. *Die Abtretung des Elsass an Frankreich: Ein Beitrag zur Geschichte des Westfälischen Friedens.* Halle: Karras, 1893.

Rose, Carol M. "Empire and Territories at the End of the Old Reich." In *The Old Reich*, edited by James A. Vann and Steven W. Rowan, 59–76.

Rössler, Hellmuth, ed. *Deutsches Patriziat, 1430–1740.* Schriften zur Problematik der deutschen Führungsschichten in der Neuzeit, 3. Limburg/Lahn: C. A. Starke, 1968.

Rowan, Herbert H. *The King's State: Proprietary Dynasticism in Early Modern France.* New Brunswick, N.J.: Rutgers University Press, 1980.

Rowan, Steven. "The Common Penny (1495–1499) as a Source of German Demographic and Social History." *Central European History* 10 (1977): 148–64.

Rublack, Hans-Christoph. "Political and Social Norms in Urban Communities in the Holy Roman Empire." In *Religion, Politics, and Social Protest: Three Studies on Early Modern Germany*, edited by Kaspar von Greyerz, 24–60.

———. "Konfession als demographischer Faktor?" In *Festgabe für Ernst Walter Zeeden*, edited by Horst Rabe, Hansgeorg Molitor, and Hans-Christoph Rublack, 62–96.

Rule, John C., ed. *Louis XIV and the Craft of Kingship.* Columbus: Ohio State University Press, 1969.

———. "Louis XIV, Roi-Bureaucrate." In *Louis XIV and the Craft of Kingship*, edited by John C. Rule, 3–101.

Rykwert, Joseph. *The Idea of a Town: The Anthropology of Urban Form in Rome, Italy, and the Ancient World.* Princeton: Princeton University Press, 1976.

Safley, Thomas Max. "To Preserve the Marital State: The Basler Ehegericht, 1550–1592." *Journal of Family History* 7 (Summer 1982): 162–79.

Schaer, André. *Le clergé paroissial catholique en Haute Alsace sous l'ancien régime, 1648–1789.* Paris: Sirey, 1966.

Scherlen, Auguste. *Histoire de la ville de Turckheim.* Colmar: Alsatia, 1925.

Schilling, Heinz. "Between the Territorial State and Urban Liberty: Lutheranism and Calvinism in the County of Lippe." In *The German People and the Reformation*, edited by R. Po-chia Hsia, 263–83.

————. *Konfessionskonflikt und Staatsbildung: Eine Fallstudie über das Verhältnis von religiösem und sozialem Wandel in der Frühneuzeit am Beispeil der Grafschaft Lippe.* QFRG, 48. Gütersloh: Gerd Mohn, 1981.

————. "The Reformation in the Hanseatic Cities." *The Sixteenth Century Journal* 14 (1983): 443–56.

————, ed. *Die reformierte Konfessionalisierung in Deutschland—Das Problem der "Zweiten Reformation."* SVRG, 195. Gütersloh: Gerd Mohn, 1986.

————. "Die 'Zweite Reformation' als Kategorie der Geschichtswissenschaft." In *Die reformierte Konfessionalisierung,* edited by Heinz Schilling, 387–421.

Schmitt, Jean-Marie. *Aux origines de la révolution industrielle en Alsace: Investissements et relations sociales dans la vallée de Saint-Amarin au XVIIIe siècle.* PSSARE, 18. Strasbourg: Istra, 1980.

Schneider, Robert A. *Public Life in Toulouse, 1463–1789: From Municipal Republic to Cosmopolitan City.* Ithaca, N.Y.: Cornell University Press, 1989.

Scott, Tom. "Economic Conflict and Co-operation on the Upper Rhine, 1450–1600." In *Politics and Society in Reformation Europe: Essays for Sir Geoffrey Elton on His Sixty-Fifth Birthday,* edited by E. I. Kouri and Tom Scott, 210–31.

————. *Freiburg and the Breisgau: Town-Country Relations in the Age of Reformation and Peasants' War.* Oxford: Clarendon Press, 1986.

Scribner, R(obert) W. *The German Reformation.* Atlantic Highlands, N.J.: Humanities Press International, 1986.

————. "Ritual and Popular Religion in Catholic Germany at the Time of the Reformation." *Journal of Ecclesiastical History* 35 (1984): 47–77.

————. "Ritual and Reformation." In *The German People and the Reformation,* edited by R. Po-chia Hsia, 122–44.

Sittler, Lucien. *L'agriculture et la viticulture en Alsace à travers les siècles.* Colmar and Ingersheim: Editions S.A.E.P., 1974.

————. *La Décapole alsacienne, des origines à la fin du Moyen-Age.* Publications de la Institut des Hautes-Etudes Alsaciennes, 12. Strasbourg: Istra, 1955.

————. "Une siècle de vie paysanne, l'évolution d'une commune de la plaine d'Alsace: Fegersheim-Ohnheim avant et après la Guerre de Trente Ans." In *Paysans d'Alsace,* 81–98.

Soliday, Gerald Lyman. *A Community in Conflict: Frankfurt Society in the Seventeenth and Early Eighteenth Centuries.* Hanover, N.H.: The University Press of New England, 1974.

Stadtbürgertum und Adel in der Reformation: Studien zur Sozialgeschichte der Reformation in England und Deutschland. Edited by Wolfgang J. Mommsen with Peter Alter and Robert W. Scribner. Veröffentlichungen des Deutschen Historischen Instituts London, 5. Stuttgart: Klett-Cotta, 1979.

Stein, Wolfgang Hans. *"Protection Royale": Eine Untersuchung zu den Protektionsverhältnissen im Elsass zur Zeit Richelieus, 1622–1643.* SVENG, 9. Münster: Aschendorff, 1978.

Stinzi, Paul. "Die Habsburger im Elsaß." In *Vorderösterreich: Eine geschichtliche Landeskunde,* edited by Friedrich Metz, 505–64.

————. "L'immigration suisse dans le Sundgau après la Guerre de Trente Ans." In *L'Alsace et la Suisse,* 173–82.

Stone, Lawrence. "Prosopography." *Daedelus* 100 (Winter, 1971): 46–79.

Stoob, Heinz. "Frühneuzeitliche Städtetypen." In *Die Stadt: Gestalt und Wandel bis zum industriellen Zeitalter,* edited by Heinz Stoob, 164–84.

————. "The Role of the Civic Community in Central European Urban Development during the Twelfth to Fifteenth Centuries." *Transactions of the Ancient Monuments Society* 23 (1978–79): 67–91.

————, ed. *Die Stadt: Gestalt und Wandel bis zum industriellen Zeitalter.* Cologne and Vienna: Böhlau, 1979.

Strasbourg de la Guerre de Trente Ans à Napoleon 1618–1815. Vol. 3 of *Histoire de Strasbourg des origines à nos jours.* Strasbourg: Istra, 1980.

Strauss, Gerald. "The Holy Roman Empire Revisited." *Central European History* 11 (1978): 290–301.

————. *Nuremberg in the Sixteenth Century: City Politics and Life between the Middle Ages and Modern Times.* Bloomington: Indiana University Press, 1976.

Streitberger, Ingeborg. *Der königliche Prätor von Strassburg 1685–1789: Freie Stadt im absoluten Staat.* VIEGM, 23. Wiesbaden: Franz Steiner, 1961.

Strittmatter, Robert. *Die Stadt Basel während des Dreissigjährigen Krieges: Politik, Wirtschaft, Finanzen.* Europäische Hochschulschriften, Reihe III, 84. Bern: Peter Lang, 1977.

Strohl, Henri. *Le protestantisme en Alsace.* Strasbourg: Oberlin, 1950.

Sydow, Jürgen, ed. *Bürgerschaft und Kirche.* Veröffentlichungen des Südwestdeutschen Arbeitskreises für Stadtgeschichtsforschung, 7. Sigmaringen: Jan Thorbecke, 1980.

Temple, Nora. "Municipal Elections and Municipal Oligarchies in Eighteenth-Century France." In *French Government and Society 1500–1850: Essays in Memory of Alfred Cobban,* edited by J. F. Bosher, 70–91.

Tocqueville, Alexis de. *The Old Regime and the French Revolution.* Translated by Stuart Gilbert. New York: Vintage, 1955.

Trexler, Richard C. *Public Life in Renaissance Florence.* New York: Academic Press, 1980.

Trois provinces de l'Est: Lorraine, Alsace, Franche-Comté. PSSARE, 6. Strasbourg: F.-X. Le Roux, 1957.

Vann, James A. "New Directions for the Study of the Old Reich." *JMH* 58 Supplement (1986): S3–S22.

————. *The Swabian Kreis: Institutional Growth in the Holy Roman Empire, 1648–1715.* Studies presented to the International Commission for the History of Representative and Parliamentary Institutions, 53. Brussels: Les Editions de la Librairie Encyclopédique, 1975.

Vann, James A., and Steven W. Rowan, eds. *The Old Reich: Essays on German Political Institutions.* Studies presented to the International Commission for the History of Representative and Parliamentary Institutions, 47. Brussels: Les Editions de la Librairie Encyclopédique, 1974.

Vierhaus, Rudolf. *Germany in the Age of Absolutism.* Translated by Jonathan B. Knudsen. Cambridge: Cambridge University Press, 1988.

Vom Wesen und Wandel der Kirche: Festschrift für Eberhard Vischer. Basel: Helbing & Lichtenhahn, 1935.

Vovelle, Michel. *Piété baroque et déchristianization en Provence au XVIIIe siècle: Les attitudes devant le mort après les clauses des testaments.* Paris: Plon, 1973.

Walker, Mack. *German Home Towns: Community, State, and General Estate 1648–1871.* Ithaca, N.Y.: Cornell University Press, 1971.

Wallerstein, Immanuel. *The Modern World System: Capitalist Agriculture and the Origins of the European World Economy in the Sixteenth Century.* New York: Academic Press, 1976.

Warmbrunn, Paul. *Zwei Konfessionen in einer Stadt: Das Zusammenleben von Katholiken und Protestanten in den paritätischen Reichsstädten Augsburg, Biberach, Ravensburg, und Dinkelsbühl von 1548 bis 1648.* VIEGM, 111. Wiesbaden: Franz Steiner, 1983.

Weyrauch, Erdmann. *Konfessionelle Krise und sozial Stabilität: Das Interim in Strassburg (1548–1562).* Spätmittelalter und Frühe Neuzeit. Tübinger Beiträge zur Geschichtsforschung, 7. Stuttgart: Klett-Cotta, 1978.

————. "Über Soziale Sichtung." In *Städtische Gesellschaft und Reformation*, edited by Ingrid Bátori, 5–57.

————. "Zur Auswertung von Steuerbüchern mit quantifizierenden Methoden." In *Festgabe für Ernst Walter Zeeden*, edited by Horst Rabe, Hansgeorg Molitor, and Hans Christoph Rublack, 97–127.

Whaley, Joachim. *Religious Toleration and Social Change in Hamburg, 1529–1819*. Cambridge: Cambridge University Press, 1985.

Wiesner, Merry E. "Beyond Women and the Family: Towards a Gender Analysis of the Reformation." *The Sixteenth Century Journal* 18 (1987): 311–22.

Wolff, Christian. *Riquewihr, son vignoble et ses vins à travers les ages*. Ingersheim: Société Alsacienne d'Expansion Photographique, 1967.

Zeeden, Ernst W. *Die Enstehung der Konfessionen: Grundlagen und Formen der Konfessionsbildung im Zeitalter der Glaubenskämpfe*. Munich and Vienna: R. Oldenbourg, 1965.

Zeller, Gaston. *L'Alsace française de Louis XIV à nos jours*. Paris: Armand Colin, 1945.

————. *Comment s'est faite la réunion de l'Alsace à la France*. Paris: Les Belles Lettres, 1948.

————. "Manants d'Alsace, derniers manants de France." *Mélanges 1945*, 1. Publications de la Faculté des lettres de l'Université de Strasbourg, fascicule 104, 111–20.

Zschunke, Peter. *Konfession und Alltag in Oppenheim: Beiträge zur Geschichte von Bevölkerung und Gesellschaft einer gemischtkonfessionellen Kleinstadt in der frühen Neuzeit*. VIEGM, 115. Wiesbaden: Franz Steiner, 1984.

Index

Personal names in italics denote modern authors. Page references in italics denote tables, graphs, figures, or maps.